Embracing the Self

Finding Your Center and Learning to Live Authentically

DEAN SCHLECHT

ISBN: 150055779X
ISBN 13: 978-1500557799

For essays, meditations, and inner journeys guided by Dean Schlecht
go to www.deanschlecht.com.

CONTENTS

FOREWORD

It was late July, 1992. I had done everything I knew how to do. I'd read self-help books, gone to talk therapy, and attended workshops. I'd visualized, I'd affirmed, and I'd met with my minister. I can't say that I had talked to my friends, because I was only interested in talking to my friends about *their* problems, which helped to reassure me that I was actually fine.

I wasn't fine. In fact, I was terrified of the something that hurt so badly inside of me that I hadn't stopped sobbing for the past two years—not just crying, but something closer to full-out wailing on pretty much a daily basis. Yet I couldn't imagine that this problem wouldn't resolve itself eventually. I mean, generally, when you have a good cry, you're supposed to feel better, right? But new despair heaped upon the old as the realization awakened in me that I had a problem I couldn't solve.

In this period I'd met a new friend, who was a therapist. Over lunch one Monday, she told me about the work she did with her clients, which was based on the work she'd done with her own therapist, Dean Schlecht. She talked about her personal experiences with archetypal figures she referred to as the Great Mother, the Inner Wisdom, and the Divine Child. She talked about meeting and connecting with her own deeply wounded inner children, and about integrating those parts with the most powerful healing aspects of her consciousness.

As she talked about how her life had been transformed by this process, my head and heart exploded with the absolute certainty that *this* was my answer. I'd waited all my life to hear these words, and though I'd never heard them before, I recognized them instantly. The exhilaration pulses in me even now as I write this. I asked for Dean's phone number and called the moment I got home.

A very kind and steady voice answered the phone, and I was intensely relieved and excited. Dean said that his roster was full and that he probably wouldn't have room for another client for about six months, but he promised he would let me know the moment an opening became available. I hung up still high with excitement, because I knew it wouldn't be six months. He called that Friday.

August 7, 1992: I buzzed with enthusiasm and fear as I drove, for the first time, the ninety miles from Tulsa to Edmond, Oklahoma, where Dean practiced. As I sat doing my intake, Dean's gentle, centered energy let my soul know that I was safe. I'd waited a long time for that feeling, and I was infinitely relieved and grateful.

I had no idea how this "meeting with the archetypes of my consciousness and wounded parts" thing was going to happen, but at our second meeting, happen it did—so easily that, twenty-two years later, I still marvel at the process Dean calls "active imagination." He had me lie down and do some deep breathing exercises. Then he began a guided visualization and counted me down a set of mental stairs.

When I got to the bottom of the stairs, he told me there would be a meadow, and in the meadow there would be a tree. I saw the scene clearly. The tree was enormous, rising very high and stretching out in all directions. The trunk was huge. It felt strong and expansive, and I loved it.

Dean told me there would be someone there to meet me who wanted to talk to me. I found a little girl, about four or five, near the tree, playing with rocks by a shallow, rippling stream. She had on a purple dress with some sort of white overlay, white socks, and shiny white shoes. She was radiant and beautiful. Although she was relieved for me to hold her, I was beyond relieved, like a mother who'd found her lost child and discovered the child was unhurt and perfectly intact. The little girl's joy and wonder were palpable. She was still able to laugh freely from her belly, the way kids do, and her laughter bounced through her whole body.

I was overjoyed to have found what Dean called my Divine Child, realizing that I had grieved her loss without knowing it. I was scared and sad to leave her there at the end of that session. Dean assured me that we would find her again.

Over the next several years, I would enter that meadow and find that the line of children/people/creatures who wanted to talk to me extended from the tree so far into the distance that I couldn't see the end of it. This was profoundly discouraging because I could see that the job ahead of me was massive. It often felt endless. I would almost yell in frustration at Dean, "You said there would be an end to this!" With great love and patience, he would tell me again that there *would* be an end, as long as I was willing to do the work. He would say the same hard mantra over many years: "Tell your depth that you want the truth, no matter the cost. Tell your depth that you want the truth, no matter the cost."

As I worked my way through that line by the tree, I met the parts of me who'd been sobbing all those years. The parts that had driven behaviors I couldn't control or understand. They told me their stories, and although they were not stories I ever wanted to hear, with Dean's soft encouragement, I embraced their pain, anger, fear, and confusion.

Dean's role in these scenarios was as facilitator and guide. He never told me what to think or do, and only shared his own conclusions with me after asking my permission. As I'd enter the internal Active Imagination space (imagine going back into a dream you had last night), I'd report to him what was happening, and he would then suggest that I ask the person or "part" I was speaking with a question. He often encouraged me to hold that part's hands, or to try and merge with that energy. He constantly encouraged me to be open to what my inner world was trying to tell me, without superimposing even my own beliefs upon it.

To me, this is still the most mind-blowing part of this process: once the person would identify the problem, Dean would encourage me to invite the Great Mother (a divine feminine aspect) or my wisdom figure (a divine masculine aspect) to enter the scene and offer wisdom and guidance. These parts, along with countless others, literally guided me through my healing process, somehow knowing *exactly* what needed to happen for my deepest and truest healing. I type this aware that I'm using regular words to try and describe something so transformative and profound that I can't possibly convey the magic and the wonder of it.

May I say it again another way? A part of *my own consciousness* was wise enough to guide me from a life of crippling pain to an existence abundant with joy, and to an utter certainty that I am not alone in this universe and that my own personal connection to **all the love that exists** is real. All the help I have *ever* needed or wanted lives inside, around, and through me.

Occasionally, people have said to me, "How do you know you're not making all that up?" My response is multifold: First, did I make up the dreams I had last night? Part of my consciousness certainly did. Are my dreams "real"? Not by the standards of my conscious mind. Does that mean they never have meaning, messages, or value? In my experience, they've often had all three. So if the meaning, message, or value is real, is the dream real?

Further, is my conscious mind the only level upon which I exist? Certainly my internal experiences suggest that I exist at levels far more "real" than my gravity-concerned ego will admit.

Next, for the record, the stories that were told to me by these lost parts of myself were corroborated and confirmed by "real" people in the "real" world. I didn't know consciously much of what my inner children remembered, but I needed to know in order to heal and build a functional and happy life.

The last part of my answer to that question is this: Who cares if it's "real"? It saved me. It changed me. It allowed me to move forward into an honest and grateful life, a beautiful marriage, and transparent relationships, and it allowed me to acknowledge the pain I'd caused others and to make amends. It brought me to a level of living only my spirit still knew was possible.

Dean Schlecht is probably the most centered person I've ever known. His intuitive wisdom and brilliance are powerful, his instincts are driven by extraordinary integrity, and his compassion is inspiring. I have said many times that I have never known anyone with boundaries as solid as his, and I have learned from his example. He's always charged me only what I could pay (which was very little, in the beginning), and when I need him, he's always there and ready.

Dean and I are twenty-two years in now, and although we don't work nearly as often anymore, he and my Inner Wisdom still guide me to levels of awareness so transcendent that I still can't believe it's happening. I do not know who I'd be without this man and this work, and I am deeply thankful that I didn't have to find out. In the early days, "I want the truth, no matter the cost" seemed to come with an unbearable cost, in terms of facing my own pain. But the real truth is that the pain was bearable, survivable, and that the benefit on the other side far outweighs that cost. I pray that you find something you need in the words ahead. Something that changes, frees, awakens, and inspires you.

Deanna Walker
May 11, 2014

PREFACE

My fundamental understanding is that nobody is alone. We each have within our depths a lifelong partner who continually offers personal truth, healing guidance, and the unconditional love for which we have always hungered. It is known as the Self and it is an incredibly powerful, transformative presence. Connecting with this presence requires that we learn to let go of control and be in a receptive state. By accepting the gifts of the Self, most especially its unconditional love, we can become vessels for that same loving energy to flow freely within and through us. This healing, life-giving love and wisdom is our birthright, our deepest need, our constant support, and our fundamental purpose.

This insight is not a hope or a belief or a theory. It is a fact. For over three decades I have accompanied client after client as they learned to allow themselves to accept unconditional love and profound wisdom from a deep place within themselves that they never knew even existed. The reality, power, and ready availability of this incredible gift still leaves me awestruck whenever I stop and think about it. Our deepest heart's desire can and will be met if we are willing to reach inside in a spirit of openness to truth and love.

As you read this book, you will see case after case in which people's lives were touched and transformed by this extraordinary internal resource. My hope is that through reading these accounts you will be moved to give serious consideration to your own internal life and allow yourself to accept this gift as well.

Creating a life grounded in a vital relationship with this deep Self affects everything that matters. It will heal emotional wounds and resolve internal conflicts. It will transform our relationships, making them more genuine, less controlling, and much more loving. It will also help us align our professional lives with our deepest values and who we authentically are. I realize this sounds a bit like saying that it is good for what ails you, but that, in fact, is the case.

Before I was a psychotherapist, I was a Catholic priest. Although as a therapist I remained open to the importance of "spiritual" realities, what my clients and I experienced was very different from what I was taught in the seminary.

I've written this book to reflect as accurately as I can the true nature of consciousness (i.e. the inner life), and what its implications are for therapy, counseling, and spirituality. I've also included insights from contemporary neuroscience and the work of Carl Jung as a way of connecting my experience with broader research and scholarship.

In the last few decades there has been a shift in the Western worldview. Fundamentalist materialism still permeates psychology and especially neuroscience. The majority of the intellectual leaders in these two related fields are committed to the assumption that mind or consciousness is nothing more than an artifact of the brain. My position and that of a growing minority of scholars is that the brain does not produce mind or consciousness. The brain is simply an instrument for tuning into a preexisting field of consciousness, much like a radio can pick up electromagnetic energy and translate it into music. My own experience, very persuasive research in parapsychology, near-death experiences, and mystical phenomena offer a much more nuanced appreciation of consciousness as a phenomenon that is far more than its organic antecedents.

I hope that you will find this book to be both fascinating and life changing.

Enjoy!

INTRODUCTION

The goal of this book is to reveal to my readers the incredible potential for healing and awakening that lives within each of us. We all hunger for a fuller, happier, more meaningful life. Religion, philosophy, psychology, and the entire self-help industry all try to address this hunger.

What I have learned is that the most effective and reliable resource for becoming our own best selves, and having the fullest lives possible, is within each of us. Everyone has a profoundly wise, deeply loving intelligence within them, which C. G. Jung and mystics over the ages have called the Self. Truth and love are not "out there," outside of us, but lie at the core of our being. They are our foundation—a foundation most of us don't even know exists.

This book has three parts. The first part is meant to acquaint you with the reality of the Self, how it communicates with the ego, and what kind of impact this can have on one's quality of life. This part of the book will also provide many examples and specific, concrete guidelines for connecting with the Self so that the reader can initiate this process without having to depend on an external authority to facilitate this connection. An external support person can be very helpful and even necessary in some instances, but it is not necessary for most people.

What is necessary is a radical willingness to know one's own truth, even if it is painful, and a commitment to live a life open to love. Anyone who approaches the Self firmly dedicated to seeking personal truth and living out of love will be welcomed and shown the way. What the Self can offer to the ego may take a long time to unfold, as psychological and spiritual wounds are often deeply embedded. Moreover, distorted beliefs and misperceptions are so much a part of our culture that breaking free of them can be an arduous undertaking. The main impediment that must be overcome, however, is the ego's fear-driven need to defend its self-made identity and feel that it is in control. Eventually, as the process unfolds, the ego will become more and more transparent to the energy of the Self. It will come to realize that it is not a separate entity, but a living vessel through which the light and love of the Self are allowed to flow into the world.

This book and the process of becoming transparent to the Self that it encourages do not make a clear distinction between spiritual and psychological domains because no such distinction exists in the psyche. The Self is our fundamental resource for healing psychic wounds, knowing our hidden truths, and integrating denied aspects of ourselves. It is also the source of our most profound spiritual potential, the key to enlightenment, and the foundation of our relationship to God. The essence of enlightenment or awakening is the ego's clear, irrevocable realization that whatever is genuinely real or authentic within the psyche is contained within the Self, and that the ego is most alive when it is an open vessel for the expression of the Self. Recently a client asked her manifestation of the Self, "Are you me?" It responded, "I'm you and I'm so much more. I'm you and your connection with divine energy."

In my experience, counselors who wish to be most helpful to clients seeking their potential must see their primary task as helping the ego engage the Self. Secondarily, the counselor's role should be to support the ego as the Self unfolds the person's healing and eventual awakening. Such a counselor must be both spiritually aware and psychologically knowledgeable. When seen from this perspective, the only real difference between a spiritual director and a psychotherapist lies in their individual areas of expertise. Both should have a good awareness of the inner workings of the psyche.

The second section of this three-part book is directed toward both those who are seeking to live more authentic lives and toward counselors. Many who engage in the in-depth self-exploration that I am encouraging will want and sometimes need competent external support. This section will give them guidance on how to find it. It will also offer explicit guidelines to counselors on how to work in concert with the Self. Central to the work is a commitment to build a bonded, loving relationship with the client that reflects the Self's own caring for that person. This section will also include chapters on how to appreciate right-brain, metaphoric thinking, doing dream work, and guiding active imagination or internal work experiences. Additionally, there will be information on resolving traumatic history and coping with dissociative phenomena.

The third section of the book is more research oriented. It will present scholarship that supports the assertions in the first two sections. It will also further explore the spiritual implications of this work.

The basic assumptions of this book are:

- Everyone has two fundamental selves, the ego-self and the deep Self. The deep Self or Self is the source of who we authentically are. It embodies our wisdom and our capacity for love. The ego-self or ego embodies our drive to defend, control, analyze, and manifest ourselves in the external world.

- The ultimate purpose of the ego is to become the channel through which the Self is given the fullest expression possible in a person's life and relationships.

- For an ego that wishes to be open to the Self, the first step is to continually choose to know its own truth no matter the cost, and to choose to live in a way that is grounded in love to the best of its ability. Without these two choices, there will be very little room for dialogue with the Self, as there will be almost no common ground.

- The choice to live in truth and love must be supported by a willingness to live everyday life mindfully. In the words of Jon Kabat-Zinn, "Mindfulness means paying attention in a particular way: on purpose, in the present moment, and nonjudgmentally." (Segal 2002, 40).

- Mindfulness meditation is an invaluable resource for opening to the Self and practicing the skill of mindfulness. Mindfulness meditation allows the ego to become a compassionate, nonjudgmental observer to its own experience. This establishes a resonance with the Self, which allows the ego to become a clearer channel for the Self, as well as to become more open to guidance and insight from the Self.

- A second form of meditation, known as active imagination or internal work, facilitates direct contact with the Self in a highly metaphoric, experiential context that impacts the ego at multiple levels simultaneously. These experiences tend to have a profound and lasting impact, although the ego can resist and eventually ignore them.

- Even though the Self may present as a specific entity in dreams and internal work, this taking on of a specific form is done simply to make the Self more accessible to the ego. Ultimately the Self has no form and cannot be defined. It is more akin to a loving, intelligent energy.

- Rejected or dissociated aspects of the psyche (the Shadow) must be acknowledged, accepted and ultimately integrated before the ego can be fully open to the Self.

- Spiritual and emotional dysfunction are inevitable when the ego becomes invested in protecting its image or any specific form of identity, thereby distorting or blocking the emergence of the Self.

- The Self will readily support and guide the ego if it is willing to listen and is sincerely seeking healing and a truly authentic life.

- Communication with the Self can happen in both spontaneous and purposeful ways. Some dreams and intuitive awarenesses constitute spontaneous communication from the Self. The two principal paths for purposeful communication with the Self are mindfulness meditation and internal work.

- The Self will never force itself on the ego. The ego must choose to cooperate with every change the Self precipitates.

- Ideally, the encounter between the ego and the Self should be supported by an external guide and/or community that is committed to the same journey. If this is not available, the Self is more than capable of directing the process from within, but it may take longer than would have been the case if the ego had appropriate external support.

- The purpose of the Self is not to help the ego achieve any particular definable goal, but only to help it live the most authentic, loving life possible.

- If the ego is sufficiently open, this will eventually lead to awakening or enlightenment, the essence of which is the ego's clear realization that only the Self is real and that the ego is nothing more than a vessel that exists to serve this reality. Through this realization, meaning, genuine freedom, peace, and abiding happiness flow without effort.

SECTION ONE

The Inner World and the Way of the Self

CHAPTER ONE

The Essence of Jung

In the early 1980s I participated in a workshop by Morton Kelsey in which he discussed Carl Jung's thinking and how it related to liberal Christianity. At that time I had been working with two clients who were suffering from DID (then known as MPD). There was very little professional literature available on the subject, and what I could find did not fit my experience of these clients. As Kelsey outlined Jung's thinking, it became clear to me that the psychological realities Jung was describing were strikingly similar to internal experiences of my DID and other deeply wounded clients. Out of my desire to learn more, I began the Oklahoma City C. G. Jung Study Group. Of all the theorists I have read over the years, Jung is closer than any other I have known to describing what actually goes on in people's internal lives.

As in contemporary transpersonal psychology and Eastern philosophy, Jung did not make a distinction between psychological and spiritual issues. This merging of psychology and spirituality is one of his greatest gifts. Jung was deeply influenced by Eastern thought, as were most of the writers and philosophers of the German Romantic period with whom he was well acquainted. As a young man, he was particularly influenced by Schopenhauer and Goethe (Ellenberger 1970, 664).

According to J. J. Clarke, there are six core Jungian themes that are shared with philosophical or religious themes originating in China or India. He summarizes them as follows:

1) The emphasis in Jung's writings on the primacy of inner experience and on the reality of the psychic world.

2) His insistence that a certain kind of numinous experience, rather than creeds or faith, is the essence of religion.

3) The quest for an amplified notion of selfhood that goes beyond the narrow confines of the conscious ego.

4) The belief in the possibility of self-transformation by one's own efforts.

5) His endeavor to overcome the intransigent opposition of matter and mind, in particular with the concept of the psychoid archetype. As he put it, "Psyche and matter are two different aspects of one and the same thing."

6) Above all, the quest for wholeness is based upon creative interaction between complementary opposites within the psyche (Clarke 1994, 5–6).

Ancient Gnosticism was another significant influence for Jung. Stephan Hoeller states the following in his book *The Gnostic Jung:*

> Jung said in essence that human beings have a religious need, but this need is not for religious *belief* but rather for religious *experience*. Religious experience is a psychic event which tends toward the integration of the soul, and thus represents the functioning of the psyche as a whole. Religion is the acknowledgement of the higher realities that consciousness fails to recognize, and if carried to its full psychological fruition, it brings about the inner unity and wholeness of the human being. This objective—which Jung's spiritual forebears in the early Christian centuries called *Gnosis*—is never accomplished

by beliefs in ideas but only by realization in the form of experience (188).

Jung identified mental health with being "whole," by which he meant possessing a state of internal unity in which ego, complexes, and Self function as a harmonious oneness. He based this conclusion on his own personal and professional experience. This valuing of internal unity or wholeness is consistent with those of all the great mystics, who also sought inner unity and based their lives and teaching on the direct experience of inner reality rather than dogma or handed-down traditions.

My experience and that of my clients has been that what are usually considered to be spiritual experiences are simply integral parts of our inner lives and extremely valuable assets in overcoming psychological dysfunction. Time and again I have witnessed inner journeys in which clients experienced wisdom figures and other inner guides; powerful, transformative, internally generated metaphoric experiences; and mystical experiences in which boundaries dissolve and the fundamental oneness of things is experienced. All of these experiences potently facilitate the healing of psychic wounds and divisions.

The following eight fundamental Jungian themes provide a brief summary of many of Jung's central conclusions. They make dramatically clear the profound spiritual nature of Jung's perspective.

1. The central archetype of the Self

Sonu Shamdasani, the editor of Jung's record of his spiritual transformation, *The Red Book*, quoted Jung with regard to the Self:

> In 1921 Jung wrote concerning the self: But inasmuch as the *I* is only the center of my field of consciousness, it is not identical with the totality of my psyche, being merely one complex

among other complexes. I therefore distinguish between the *I* and the *self*, since the *I* is only the subject of my consciousness, while the self is the subject of my total psyche, which includes the unconscious. In 1928 Jung described the process of individuation as "self becoming" and "self realization." Jung defined the self as the archetype of order, and noted the representations of the self were indistinguishable from God images. In 1944 he noted that he chose the term because this concept was, on the one hand, definite enough to convey the sum of human wholeness, and on the other hand indefinite enough to express the indescribable and indeterminate nature of this wholeness (338).

Despite the fact that Jung considered the Self to be the "God image within," he chose not to capitalize "self" because he did not want to appear esoteric to his secular and scientifically oriented readers. I and other post-Jungians do not share his concern and believe that, given the profound spiritual significance of the Self, it should be capitalized.

That the Self should be so readily available to those who are open to it still astounds me. Jung initially encountered the Self in his own internal work in three different forms: "soul," Elijah, and ultimately Philemon. These encounters took place shortly after he broke with Freud, during a period of several years of intense introspection. Philemon, whom Jung considered to be an inner guru, instructed Jung on most of the major themes he would address throughout the rest of his professional life. For those who are willing, the Self will help the ego reconcile all of its polarities. Under its tutelage, according to Samuels, "the ego-ideal is abandoned in favor of self-acceptance and, more importantly, the super-ego, in its negative form of blind adherence to collective norms, is replaced as a moral arbiter by the self acting as an inner guide" (103). As Jung put it, "The self is located on a 'higher moral level' and a man must know something of God's nature if he is to understand himself" (CW II, paras 745–46). The Self is the image of God within, which man must know if he is ever to really know himself.

From Jung's perspective, a life that is whole, authentic, meaningful, and a genuinely positive influence for good, is a life that is firmly grounded in the Self. This is the core of his psychology, and a profoundly spiritual stance as well.

> As one can never distinguish empirically between a symbol of the self and a God-image, the two ideas, however much we may try to differentiate them, always appear blended together, so that the self appears synonymous with the inner Christ of the Johannine and Pauline writings…Psychologically speaking, the domain of "gods" begins where consciousness leaves off, for at that point man is already at the mercy of the natural order…To symbols of wholeness that come to him from there he attaches names which vary according to time and place (CW 11, para 231).

Put simply, healing and wholeness can only emerge through the embrace of the Self, which is the inner experience of God. All spiritual traditions teach that in order to live in communion with God, the ego must actively participate through the acceptance of various practices and perspectives. Jung's spiritual psychology does the same. Contrary to most traditions, however, Jung discouraged conformity to the assumptions of any tradition or group. He taught that in fact the opposite is necessary: embracing the Self, i.e., connecting with God, requires the relinquishment of all models and assumptions in favor of direct experience.

2. The complementarity between differentiation and individuation

Differentiation

In contrast to some strains of Eastern thought, Jung believed that it was not appropriate to stifle or quiet ego consciousness except for periods of respite. He believed that the ego has special gifts to bring to the journey toward wholeness, and that it must be actively involved in that journey. The ego's initial task is differentiation. Through the use of its ability to discriminate between me and "not me," the ego can become aware of the expectations and controls of family and culture and be willing to take a stance for or against them based on an internal sense of what is personally authentic.

> It is the individual's task to differentiate himself from all others and stand on his own feet. All collective identities…interfere with the fulfillment of this task. Such collective identities are crutches for the lame, shields for the timid, beds for the lazy, nurseries for the irresponsible (Jung 1961, MDR 342).

The ego must also differentiate itself from the contents of the unconscious, such as complexes (i.e., internal ego states) and other internal psychic energies, so that it can engage them in a healing dialogue rather than being controlled by them or merely reacting to them. This willingness to differentiate helps the ego overcome polarities and achieve the openness and balance needed for the Self and the ego to function in unison.

Before wholeness and balance can be achieved, opposites (i.e., polarities) must be reconciled—for example, the fearful, reclusive ego vs. an inner rage; or the deadened, hyper-responsible ego vs. the playful but immature Divine Child. All the many ways the ego is reacting to disowned psychic energies must be faced and worked through. Facing and owning all of oneself demands a strong, active ego that is willing to face the truth, gather threatening energies into itself, and risk the unfolding of unpredictable change. The emergence of an integrated or "whole" person is always dependent on a differentiated ego. While the ego can be clear as to what it is not, it must also be humble enough to know that its ultimate task is to become more and more open to the undistorted unfolding of what is most deeply real within the psyche, rather than to continue living as an imagined self.

Individuation

In a well-individuated person, the ego has become a master of allowing the unfolding of the inner, indefinable mystery that is our authentic Self, while at the same time the ego remains strong and vigilant against any forces internal or outer that would rigidify or define it. For Jung, individuation is never completed. It is not a concrete thing to be achieved, but a process or flow with which the ego ideally moves gracefully. Our deepest truth, what is most authentic within us, is a gift, but we must be its active recipient for the gift to be opened. Through dreams, visions, active imagination, and intuitions, the Self will actively guide any person willing to accept its authority toward individuation and wholeness. What is most heartening to me is how readily available the Self is to anyone who sincerely wants its help.

Jung views the psyche as a dynamic, growth-oriented entity poised between these two powerful and complementary drives of differentiation and individuation. Differentiation begins to free the ego from external and internal forces that would limit and rigidify consciousness. This differentiation process allows the ego to achieve the awareness, transparency, and flexibility necessary to be more fully open to the emergence of what is most authentic for the individual: individuation. Both sides of this process, differentiation and individuation, are supported and guided by the Self, which offers insight, wisdom, loving support, and unvarnished truth for the sake of achieving an integrated, transparent (i.e., without pretense or anything to hide) psyche in which the individual's full potential can be expressed in the world. The continual unfolding of this potential is the essence of the never-ending process of individuation.

The individuation process allows the emergence of the Divine Child. The archetype of the Divine Child is the embodiment of our personal potential, our unique, true nature in its nascent and undistorted form. Claiming and living out this potential is the ego's great task. Becoming whole, undivided, and grounded in the Self, and becoming real (i.e., becoming who you were born to be) are intimately related. Although it is possible for a person to awaken early in life to the realization that only the Self, the image of God within, is real, and that the ego is meant to be its vessel (which is the essence of enlightenment), the process of individuation is the task of a lifetime. The expression of our unique potential is a dynamic process that is ever unfolding; it defies definition and has no ultimate conclusion. An intimate connection with the Self is the ego's best resource for staying in tune with this unfolding and overcoming whatever internal or external influences might distort its expression.

Overcoming trauma, destructive patterns, and inner divisions is only the beginning of this process. For Jung, resolving inner conflicts merely opens the door to go deeper toward a life lived in intimate communion with the Self. Those who have worked through internal conflicts but choose not to seek an intimate bond with the Self may experience less psychic pain and even craft for themselves a more pleasant and socially acceptable ego, but at a more profound level, they have missed their opportunity to individuate.

3. The contents of the personal unconscious

The contents of the personal unconscious are generated by the ego's dissociation or rejection of aspects of the psyche: complexes, unintegrated traumatic life experiences, and introjects. What is rejected, stands in polarized opposition to the ego and constitutes what Jung called "the Shadow." Both the Shadow and the ego are equivalently out of balance or distorted. Each becomes more extreme and energized the more the other fights against it. The tension between the ego and the Shadow contents of the personal unconscious usually causes the ego to diminish sensitivity to all inner processes and become more rigid and external in its orientation. Consequently, it loses touch with the Self and its internal spiritual resources. Healing our wounds and overcoming inner divisions is a prerequisite for being able to live in a stable, flowing relationship with the Self, God within.

4. The collective unconscious

According to Jung, humanity possesses universal, shared, interconnected psychic elements that include drives such as instincts and archetypes as well as paranormal phenomena that transcend the ego's normal experience of space and time. These elements are all part of humanity's collective unconscious. The instincts are grounded in our shared physical nature. For instance, a person may have an innate talent or instinct for music that is brought to the ego's attention in the form of an internal archetypal figure, such as a muse, or through the spontaneous emergence of musical compositions. The archetypes organize and direct instinctual drives and present them to the ego in the form of images and other internal experiences that give rise to ideas, creative inspiration, and the motivation to make constructive change: "The archetypal image both represents and evokes the instinct" and will "signify the goal of the instinct" (Samuels 1985, 29).

Another example of this theme is the fact that everyone can sense childlike inclinations, needs, and feelings within themselves, such as the capacities for wonder and play, as well as the needs for nurturance and protection. These enduring, universal traits of childhood are part of our instinctual inheritance. The archetype of the Divine Child gives these instinctual traits a coherent focus or form whose purpose is to impact or motivate the ego, as when the image of a child who reflects our authentic self appears to us in a dream or active imagination. The ego can then choose to intentionally engage this archetypal image and constructively integrate its energy, or to misuse or reject it, in which case the energy will become distorted and drive the ego to a deeper degree of imbalance than before the archetype presented itself.

Jung said, "The Collective Unconscious is an image of the world that has taken aeons to form." It is the inborn cognitive structure that equips the individual to make sense of and order his or her experiences. The fundamental elements of this cognitive structure, which Jung called the archetypes, function as sorting mechanisms, making sense of the interplay between our instincts and sensory or psychological input, and simultaneously motivating us to react in a particular way. Archetypes help us clarify our experiences and guide us in our responses. They sort people, for instance, into friend, enemy, authority, etc., and then move us to respond. If a person appears as the dangerous enemy archetype, it might very well trigger my coward archetype, which over the eons has proven itself to have definite survival value. All human experience and behavior is under the influence of one or usually many related archetypes.

It is important to underscore that the archetypes themselves have no particular form or image. They are not symbols, but when activated they often take metaphoric forms and appear in active imagination or dreams designed to motivate the individual to respond in particular ways. When an archetype interacts with ego consciousness, the psyche will typically give it a symbolic form or image that best represents for that individual the nature of the archetype, mediating its energy and signifying its goal. Archetypal images are much more than simple signs that point to realities beyond themselves. They in fact have the power to transform the ego in accordance with the instinctual energy they reflect. For instance, connecting with a nurturing maternal archetype will move men to behave in a more gentle, caretaking fashion toward their families.

For Jung, the archetype of the Self is unique. It is the archetype "whose special function is to balance the pattern, not only of other archetypes, but all of a person's life in terms of purposes as yet unconsidered and unlived"

(Samuels, 92). In other words, the Self, or God within, is an integrating force that facilitates the smooth coherence of instincts and archetypes for the sake of the unfolding of the person's best potential. Jung concluded (and my own experience has demonstrated) that God, or the Self, has a purpose for us that is embedded in the unfathomable mystery of our own unique, authentic nature.

5. Unus Mundus: the fundamental oneness out of which all things arise

Toward the end of his life, Jung was asked if he believed in God. He said, "I do not believe, I know." He was referring not only to the God image within (i.e., the Self), but also to his personal experience of a deep, unifying, underlying ground out of which everything emerges, and which embraces everything. Evidence of its presence can be seen in synchronous phenomena with which Jung had considerable experience and in unitive mystical experiences with which Jung was also well acquainted.

About ten years before he died, Jung had a near-death experience that gave him further empirical evidence of this unifying, underlying ground. That the experience was a wondrous mystery, beyond words and rational explanation, did not make it any less real. Its impact upon him was profound. The three weeks of night visions he experienced as he recovered from his brush with death underscored the delight and freedom that near death gave as it freed him from the constricted, three dimensional world of normal consciousness. "It was as if I were in an ecstasy. I felt as though I were floating in space, as though I were safe in the womb of the universe – in a tremendous void, but filled with the highest possible feeling of happiness. 'This is eternal bliss,' I thought. 'This cannot be described; it is far too wonderful!'" (Jung 1961, 293). In fact, silencing the controlling, rational mind (i.e., ego consciousness) opens awareness to this same ground. Jill Bolte Taylor's book, *My Stroke of Insight*, describes powerfully the power of this unitive awareness when a stroke silenced her verbal, analytical left brain.

Some Eastern spiritual practices have a goal of silencing the ego so that this unitive ground might be directly experienced. Jung believed that introducing this idea that the ego should be silenced into the West would be a major mistake. He taught that a strong, fully functioning, individuated ego would lead to the same unitive awareness and at the same time present to the world a balanced, authentic expression of the individual's full potential. My experience with many clients has amply demonstrated the importance of a strong ego for dealing with inner conflicts and unresolved trauma. As they work through their issues and become more transparent to the Self, unitive experiences become more readily available.

The explicit description of a unitive experience by Allan Smith, MD, published in *The Journal of Consciousness Studies*, might be helpful here.

> My CC [Cosmic Consciousness] event occurred unexpectedly while I was alone one evening and was watching a particularly beautiful sunset. I was sitting in an easy chair placed next to floor-to-ceiling windows that faced northwest. The sun was above the horizon and was partially veiled by scattered clouds, so that it was not uncomfortably bright. I had not used any marijuana for about a week previously. On the previous evening I probably had wine with dinner; I do not remember the quantity, but two glasses would have been typical. Thus, we would not have expected any residual drug effects.

> The CC experience began with some mild tingling in the perineal area, the region between the genitals and anus. The feeling was unusual, but was neither particularly pleasant nor unpleasant. After the initial few minutes, I either ceased to notice the tingling or did not remember it. I then noticed that the level of light in the room as well as that of the sky outside seemed to be increasing slowly. The light seemed to be coming from everywhere, not only from the waning sun. In fact,

the sun itself did not give off a strong glare. The light gave the air a bright thickened quality that slightly obscured perception rather than sharpened it. It soon became extremely bright, but the light was not in the least unpleasant.

Along with the light came an alteration in mood. I began to feel very good, then still better, then elated. While this was happening, the passage of time seemed to become slower and slower. The brightness, mood-elevation, and time-slowing all progressed together. It is difficult to estimate the time period over which these changes occurred, since the sense of time was itself affected. However, there was a feeling of continuous change, rather than a discrete jump or jumps to a new state. Eventually, the sense of time passing stopped entirely. It is difficult to describe this feeling, but perhaps it would be better to say that there was no time, or no sense of time. Only the present moment existed. My elation proceeded to an ecstatic state, the intensity of which I had never even imagined could be possible. The white light around me merged with the reddish light of the sunset to become one all enveloping, intense undifferentiated light field. Perception of other things faded. Again, the changes seemed to be continuous.

At this point, I merged with the light and everything, including myself, became one unified whole. There was no separation between myself and the rest of the universe. In fact, to say that there was a universe, a self or any "thing" would be misleading—it would be an equally correct description to say that there was "nothing" as to say that there was "everything." To say that subject merged with object might be almost adequate as a description of the entrance into CC, but during CC there was neither "subject" nor "object." All words or discursive thinking had stopped and there was no sense of an "observer" to comment or to categorize what was "happening." In fact, there were no discrete events to "happen"—just a timeless, unitary state of being.

CC is impossible to describe, partly because describing involves words and the state is one in which there were no words. My attempts at description here originated from reflecting on CC soon after it had passed and while there was still some "taste" of the event remaining.

Perhaps the most significant element of CC was the absolute knowingness that it involves. This knowingness is a deep understanding that occurs without words. I was certain that the universe was one whole and that it was benign and loving at its ground. Bucke's experience was similar. He knew, "that the universe is so built and ordered that without any peradventure all things work together for the good of each and all, that the foundation principle of the world is what we call love and that the happiness of every one is in the long run absolutely certain" (Bucke 1961, 8).

The benign nature and ground of being, with which I was united, was God. However, there is little relation between my experience of God as ground of being and the anthropomorphic God of the Bible. That God is separate from the world and has many human characteristics. "He" demonstrates love, anger and vengeance, makes demands, gives rewards, punishes, forgives, etc. God as experienced in CC is the very ground or "beingness" of the universe and has no human characteristics in the usual sense of the word. The universe could no more be separate from God than my body could be separate from its cells. Moreover, the only emotion that I would associate with God is love, but it would be more accurate to say that God is love than God is loving. Again, even characterizing God as love and the ground of being is only a metaphor, but it is the best that I can do to describe an indescribable experience.

The knowingness of CC permanently convinced me about the true nature of the universe. However, it did not answer many of the questions that (quite rightly) seem so important to us in our usual state of consciousness. From the perspective of CC, questions like, "What is the purpose of life?" or "Is there an afterlife?" are not answered because they are not relevant. That is, during CC ontologic questions are fully answered by one's state of being and verbal questions are not to the point.

Eventually, the CC faded. The time-changes, light, and mood-elevation passed off. When I was able to think again, the sun had set and I estimate that the event must have lasted about twenty minutes. Immediately following return to usual consciousness, I cried uncontrollably for about a half hour. I cried both for joy and for sadness, because I knew that my life would never be the same (1998, 97–107).

6. The interrelationship of two fundamental polarities: ego/Self and feminine (anima/Eros) / masculine (animus/ Logos)

An appropriate ego-Self connection and the consequent accomplishment of individuation are dependent on a balanced, integrated blend of masculine and feminine cognitive styles. These two polarities, ego/Self and masculine/feminine, are the most fundamental "union of opposites" in the psyche. Ego and Self will never come into balance unless the ego accepts an appropriate relationship between masculine and feminine ways of knowing. The masculine, given its identification with Logos and thus with thinking, judging, and controlling, is life giving only when it functions to serve and protect the feminine, which is identified with Eros and thus with feeling, sensing, and merging. The feminine/Eros immerses us in our experience. The masculine/Logos stands apart. Essentially, this means that God can be truly known only when the feminine way is given precedence.

Ego consciousness has traditionally been identified with masculine energy, the sun, the hero, the sun-god, etc., whereas the unconscious has often been connected to the feminine, the moon, the deep, the dark, etc. Jung even identifies his feminine aspect, the anima, with the soul. According to Samuels, "Although Jung never designates consciousness as masculine per se, he does make a sharp and somewhat tenuous distinction between masculine and feminine consciousness. To feminine consciousness, Jung grants the realm of the 'infinite nuances of personal relationships which usually escape the man entirely.' But to the man he grants the wide fields of commerce, politics, technology, and science, the whole realm of the applied masculine mind" (1985, 219).

Arthur Deikman has developed an extensive analysis of these two different ways of approaching life. He calls the feminine/Eros style "receptive consciousness" and the masculine/Logos style "instrumental consciousness" (2000, 303).

A person who wishes to be open to the world of the unconscious must first embrace instrumental consciousness as his or her starting point by using this skill to differentiate oneself from external and internal expectations and pressures. Then he or she must embrace receptive consciousness with the intention to take in, be nourished, and grow in an expansive fashion. The fundamental intention of masculine, instrumental consciousness is to "act on" the other and focus on control. This masculine style, if given priority over the feminine, receptive way, will render the person incapable of accessing the Self and thus of knowing God. Even though *anima* means "soul" in Latin, feminine consciousness is not the same as the soul. But the feminine or receptive style of consciousness, which is the fundamental attribute of the anima, is clearly the gateway to the interior life.

Once the ego allows itself to be sufficiently receptive to relate to the Self, it can then utilize instrumental consciousness in service of the Self's transformative gifts. These gifts might include insights regarding internal healing and self-care, improvements in relationships, better alignment between one's deep values and everyday or professional life, creative expression, etc. Through receptive consciousness one can know and experience one's depth; through instrumental consciousness one can then present the gifts from the Self to the world. Before living out these gifts, however, instrumental consciousness must first test the gifts rationally. Then, if they make sense, one should actively claim them and live them out as effectively as possible in the outer world.

Before a person allows receptive consciousness or the anima to take its rightful place, however, there may have to be some significant groundwork done at two levels. First, the power of instrumental consciousness must be used to differentiate the ego from external and internal influences, as previously discussed, so that it can begin the dialogue with enough freedom and awareness to be a real partner in the process. Second, especially for males living in a control-oriented culture or anyone who has a problematic relationship with the feminine, there must be a willingness to reconsider cultural assumptions that discount the feminine.

Once the decision is made to embrace receptive consciousness and begin a serious dialogue with both the personal and collective unconscious, the individual must be prepared for a way of knowing that is vastly different from the rational/analytic style that is considered in the West as the only valid way to know truth. As described earlier in the book, the unconscious expresses itself through rich allegories and symbols that impact multiple senses and involve the ego experientially rather than merely at the level of language and ordinary understanding. Internal ego states (complexes) and symbols of the Self, such as Inner Wisdom, may talk to the ego and explain various things, but these conversations, if they happen at all, are almost always secondary to an imaginative, multisensory, and often numinous internal experience.

These experiences are called "numinous" because they are indefinable and transformative; they transcend a person's frames of reference and control. They are potent and may threaten to shatter old assumptions and stable patterns that had been a source of comfort and safety. These experiences not only invite change but have the power to actualize the changes they portray, if the individual embraces them—and sometimes even if he or she doesn't. The inner work or active imagination experiences described in the next chapters of this book clearly demonstrate this theme.

The spontaneous change that arises out of encounters with the Self and its various manifestations, such as Inner Wisdom, the Great Mother, or the Divine Child, is very different from the change that happens when the ego decides to be different and uses willpower and logic to get there. Ego-directed change may be necessary at times and to some degree helpful (e.g., giving up smoking or deciding to be a more attentive spouse or parent), but compared to the changes that arise out of an encounter with the unconscious, it is relatively shallow and frequently misses the mark—merely polishing up or adding another level of control to one's persona without him or her becoming truly different or living a more authentic life.

Even when you are committed to living a fully authentic life, but do not rely on the Self to guide the process, you are simply going to be making up another story about "who I am" that will invariably be wrong even though much effort and sacrifice may have been expended on the project. Attempting to make significant change without first embracing receptive consciousness and being willing to surrender to the Self is analogous to attempting to build one's house on the sand.

The ego's story about who or what it is is a construct, a myth, and as much an artifact as any part generated by somebody suffering from DID. As Jung pointed out, a defined ego is just another complex shaped by unknown or unacknowledged forces. The stability it may claim is merely a symptom of being frozen. A healthy, strong ego doesn't need an elaborate story to feel real. It feels no need to be a "this" or a "that." It readily acknowledges, "I don't know who I am, but I am discovering more of myself every day as my potential emerges and unfolds."

One's true nature can only be known as an evolving process that arises from the depth and is then owned and lived out in the world. It is a mystery beyond the ego's capacity to comprehend or control. It is a gift from a source that lies far beyond the realm of ego and beyond comprehension. It is a gift that only the feminine aspect of consciousness is able to open.

7. Wise Old Man, Great Mother, and Divine Child: three major facets of the Self

The Self per se has no form or defining limitations. In Jung's words, it is both "the center and the circumference" of the psyche. Ultimately, the psyche is nondual. All divisions are only surface impressions. The Self is the core of our consciousness, and consciousness is an indivisible reality. The products of consciousness may seem almost innumerable, but they are simply the multifaceted expressions of the one essence Jung called the Self. The waves on the ocean may appear to be unique and often dramatic entities, but they are all ultimately just the ocean. As Jesus said, "The Father and I are one." The elements of the psyche that have been discussed throughout this book, such as instincts, archetypes, and ego states or complexes, are all emanations of a singular consciousness embodied in the Self.

In order to help an individual overcome the illusion of separation or otherness, the Self will present in various archetypal forms through which the person is enabled to engage its potential. The three most common

21

archetypal expressions of the Self embody our universal quest for truth and understanding, our profound need to receive and give unconditional love, and the preservation of our authentic nature. When encountered internally in dreams or active imagination, these take the form of the Wise Old Man or Inner Wisdom, Great Mother, and the Divine Child.

The marriage of masculine and feminine styles of consciousness, as described in the previous section, make the Wise Old Man (Inner Wisdom or radical truth) and the Great Mother (unconditional love and nurturance) accessible to the ego. Truth and love are the fertile ground out of which wholeness can blossom. Without them, the ego is lost. With them, the fullness of life becomes possible.

Of particular significance is that the union of masculine and feminine consciousness allows the Divine Child to reawaken. It resides in "the Eternal Feminine where the divine child slumbers, patiently waiting his conscious realization." In a sense the Divine Child is the product of their marriage. Jung taught that the Divine Child is the precious essence of our nature, hidden in the Self, securely protected from all the distortions and pressures that would otherwise cause us to forever forget who we truly are:

> The child motif represents not only something that existed in the distant past but also something that exists *now;* that is to say, it is not just a vestige but a system functioning in the present whose purpose is to compensate or correct, in a meaningful manner, the inevitable one-sidedness and extravagances of the conscious mind (CW 9/1 para 276).

In another place he says, "A characteristic of childhood is that thanks to its naiveté and unconsciousness it sketches a more complete picture of the self, of the whole man in his pure individuality, than adulthood" (CW 16, 279).

Meanwhile Marie-Louise von Franz in *Puer Aeternus* speaks of the Divine Child as "something creative that is moving towards a future possibility of life. The child is always behind and ahead of us…If the child appears ahead of us it means renewal, the possibility of eternal youth, of spontaneity and of new possibilities—the life flow towards the creative future" (McGurn 1998, 69).

8. Individuation and enlightenment

Enlightenment and individuation are closely related concepts. Regarding individuation, Jung wrote the following:

> The goal of psychological, as of biological, development is self-realization or individuation. But since [we] know [our self] only as an ego, and the self, as a totality, is indescribable and indistinguishable from a God-image, self-realization…amounts to God's incarnation…And because individuation is an heroic and often tragic task, the most difficult of all, it involves suffering, a passion of the ego: the ordinary empirical [person] we once were is burdened with the fate of losing oneself in a greater dimension and being robbed of [our] fancied freedom of will. [We] suffer, so to speak, by the violence done to [us] by the self (CW 11, para. 233).

> Individuation appears, on the one hand, as the synthesis of a new unity that previously consisted of scattered particles, and on the other hand, as the revelation of something that existed before the ego and is in fact its father or creator and also its totality (CW 11, para. 400).

If enlightenment is understood as the ego's willing acceptance of the experience of union with the Self, which is the traditional understanding of most mystics, then Jung's description of individuation is clearly a description of enlightenment. Once a person is well aligned with the Self, he or she will experience the world as the Self does. The fundamental awareness from this perspective is of the unity of all things and the uncaused joy and love that spontaneously flows from this realization.

Jung also taught that this process is never complete, stating that individuation is a lifelong endeavor. Wholeness or the internal unity that is necessary for the ego to be truly resonant with the Self must be intentionally fostered by the ego on a daily basis. The ego's proclivity to define or name itself (even or especially if that self-definition accords with the notion that one is already enlightened) serves as an ongoing temptation to deny or ignore emergent aspects of our self that threaten this identity. This continual, internal unfolding can involve heretofore unrecognized personal potentials embodied in the Divine Child, or it can involve the surfacing of still unresolved internal conflicts and egocentric tendencies. Spiritual teachers have long recognized this possibility and have noted that the vast majority of those who experience enlightenment lose it after a period of time. Eventually, however, there are those who achieve a state of "abiding awakening" in which the experience of union between ego and Self never leaves, but remains as a constant background awareness. These individuals have achieved enlightenment, but the process of sensing and living out the ever unfolding potentials of their Divine Child continues on as the task of a lifetime. Both enlightenment and individuation describe the union of ego and Self, but individuation goes a step further in that it calls us to forever be attentive and faithful to the ever expanding expression of our own potential, whether that be before or after enlightenment.

One of the clearest descriptions of the experience of enlightenment I've seen is the following by Elaine Aron in *The Comfort Zone Newsletter*:

> What are these experiences? There are no hard and fast statements here. Generally it dawns suddenly, dramatically. But not always, and partial experiences leading up to the state may

last for years or come and go. By definition it is permanent once it is complete, although a Zen teacher (maybe more than one) is said to have had many such sudden shifts. There is usually a profound sense of expansion, of knowing one is not the same as one's body or ego, but something infinite, whether one is one with God or calls it something more abstract like Brahman or the Absolute. The needs, desires, suffering, and general importance of the personal self simply cease to matter. One is separate or detached from everything, but not in a dissociated way. Rather, one becomes a silent witness to everything. Or the state is more like a unity with The Everything. Or a sense of profound love.

This awareness remains all of the time, even during sleep. It is not something one thinks about, however. It remains in the background.

If one were wearing a coat, one would not always be thinking about it, yet one would be aware of it. As for the enlightened person's moods, which are always the ordinary person's undoing, they are said to be peaceful, secure, and blissful. Other emotions such as anger or fear may arise in response to the needs of the environment, but do not shake the deeper stillness. An analogy is that you are in a state a bit like the one a child enjoys when playing in the yard while aware that Mother is at home. The child does not think about the mother, yet her presence makes the child feel more secure, able to play wholeheartedly, and more likely to feel cheerful and see beauty in everything. Perhaps the most important feature is that the enlightened report losing all fear of death or suffering. Their body can suffer, but they do not. Often they report living only in the moment, in an eternal now, without any worries. For some, everything is exactly as it should be. For others, their deep love causes them to continue to act, but only for the sake of the world. They feel the suffering of others deeply, but there is nothing they themselves want or need. Miraculous abilities are often attributed to the enlightened, or miraculous things happen in their vicinity. But these are not done for self-aggrandizement, but to demonstrate the reality of what is possible, or else they simply occur naturally, without effort.

Perhaps, if there is a state of enlightenment, as so many have reported, one has to lower one's expectations about what kind of person it creates, and that is what I would tend to do. Perhaps it is possible for the nervous system to make a dramatic shift towards more security and peace. That in itself would be quite wonderful. Perhaps one cannot expect perfection from such a person, however, or even goodness always…The ultimate goal of consciousness is not to know or do anything, but simply to know itself (2004).

It is entirely possible for the ego to come to the clear realization that it is in no way distinct from the Self and thus universal consciousness or Unus Mundus, and yet still not have integrated all of one's own Shadow elements. Enlightenment can help the ego be freed from fear and no longer caught up in the story of "I." This gives it great flexibility as it continues the individuation process by integrating Shadow elements and allowing the continued unfolding of internal potential. Nevertheless, until this is well underway, enlightened persons can be off-balance and conflicted, as observed by Adyshanti, a contemporary spiritual teacher, in his book *The End of Your World* (2008, 130).

Jill Bolte Taylor describes with great clarity the work she had to do after her enlightenment to deal with residual patterns that were directly contrary to the newfound connectedness, openness, joy, and freedom that had become her fundamental way of being:

During the process of recovery, I found that the portion of my character that was stubborn, arrogant, sarcastic, and/or jealous resided within the ego center of that wounded left brain. This portion of my ego mind held the capacity for me to be a sore loser, hold a grudge, tell lies and even seek revenge. Reawakening these personality traits was very disturbing to the newly found innocence of my right mind. With lots of effort, I have consciously chosen to recover my left mind's ego center without giving renewed life to some of those old circuits (2006, 145).

Whether a person achieves enlightenment or not, the work of individuation is a lifelong task. The ego will do far better at this task after enlightenment than before, but it is still a task to be done. Conversely, embracing the process of individuation is the most effective practice I know for opening the ego to the possibility of enlightenment. The skills and strengths needed to positively integrate Shadow aspects and be open to the transformative power of the Self form exactly the frame of mind that will enable the ego to experience ultimate truth, or enlightenment.

Describing the individuated person, Jung said the following:

The individuated human being is just ordinary, therefore almost invisible…His feelings, thoughts, etc. are just anybody's feelings, thoughts, etc.—quite ordinary, as a matter of fact, and not interesting at all…He will have no need to be exaggerated, hypocritical, neurotic or any other nuisance. He will be "in modest harmony" with nature…No matter whether people think they are individuated or not, they are just what they are: in the one case a man plus an unconscious nuisance disturbing to himself—or, without it, unconscious of himself; or in the other case, conscious. The criterion is consciousness (Fadiman 1994, 82).

CHAPTER TWO

The Ultimate Gift

Jung's insights and my experience as a therapist can be boiled down to three fundamental lessons that we must all learn. The first and most important is that who we think we are at the level of ordinary awareness is not real. It is the ultimate delusion. The defined self we call by our first name, that we put so much energy into defending, that we worry about, judge, try to improve and make presentable to the world, or impose on others is a story we make up. It is a drama-infused fiction that is so compelling that nearly everyone gets lost in it and forgets who he or she truly is. This fiction is the story of "I." It is the delusional, egocentric ego.

A nondelusional ego has no form and refuses to cling to anything that would define or limit it. It does not allow itself to be "identified with the body, confined by feelings, or repressed by thoughts" (Sellers). It refuses to take seriously any imposed limits or self-defining assumptions such as judgments, titles, labels, hallmarks of status, etc. It knows that it is a process rather than an entity. Its purpose is to be the vehicle or channel through which that which is most profound and real within, the Self, can emerge and be manifested to the world.

The second lesson is that the real foundation of the psyche is the Self. It is simple, loving, intelligent awareness. It is the observer whose perception is clear and undistorted. It is a flowing, unfolding energy that manifests within everyone in a way that is unique to each individual. It is the essence of what is most authentic within us. It is our ground and our teacher, the ultimate guide to a life that is real, genuine, meaningful, and truly happy. It has many names: Spirit, Soul, Divine Spark, Inner Wisdom, and others. In this book I will follow the lead of Carl Jung and simply call it the Self. Although formless in itself, it will manifest itself through a variety of forms in dreams, spontaneous images, and active imagination experiences in order to facilitate a transformative connection with the ego. Typical examples of these manifestations in Western cultures are the presence of Inner Light, wisdom figures, and Great Mother or Divine Mother images, as well as representations of Jesus, angels, or the Divine Child. No matter the form, the goal is always the same: to guide and support the ego as it moves beyond the delusion of a separate, defined self into the freedom of an open, authentic life. This is a life in which our deepest spiritual instincts, potential, intellect, emotions, and imagination function as a harmonious, integrated whole.

The third basic lesson to be learned is that we have at our disposal two fundamentally different ways of thinking, one rooted in the left brain and the other in the right brain. Left-brain thinking emphasizes analysis, form, and distinction. Rather than connect directly with reality, it creates models and then uses its analytical skills to manipulate those models. It has a strong tendency to become so enamored of its models that it mistakes them for reality. Right-brain thinking has a more direct connection with both internal and external reality. It experiences things as they are without the filters imposed by preconceived models. Any meaningful encounter with the Self and thus any chance for a fulfilling, authentic life depends on the ego's willingness to give precedence to the receptive, experientially grounded consciousness of the right brain.

An ego dedicated to being fully alive will use the analytical and instrumental competencies of the left brain only in support of manifesting the truth and love emanating from the Self as known through the receptive consciousness of the right brain. These two forms of consciousness are grounded in contemporary neuroscience, but they were foreshadowed in the writings of Carl Jung, as described in the previous chapter, who identified left-brain consciousness as "Logos" and right-brain awareness as "Eros." In *The Red Book* he identifies the egocentric misuse of left-brain thinking as the "spirit of this time" and the approach to reality and the Self grounded in right-brain awareness as the "spirit of the depths."

This book is dedicated to exploring what it means to live a life in which these two polarities, ego-Self and Logos/Eros, are brought into the right balance.

At the beginning of my career as a therapist I had a surprising, life-changing experience when I participated in a workshop that featured guided imagery. In the imagery we were taken to a mountain cave where we were to meet a wise presence that would answer any sincere, personal question we might want to ask. I don't remember my question, but I do recall that many participants received profound and unexpected answers. Clearly, this exercise tapped into an intelligent awareness, a kind of inner wisdom that was not part of everyday consciousness. This demanded my attention. I couldn't help but wonder how available this intelligence might be to people in general and what impact it could have on my clients. Shortly thereafter I decided to try this with clients, using a similar guided imagery experience to help them meet and form a relationship with what I called their Inner Wisdom. Many were deeply touched, and the therapy process was transformed. Not only did my clients benefit from profound insights and guidance that far surpassed anything that I as a therapist or they themselves, at the ego level, could achieve, but they also realized that they contained within their own depths a compassionate presence or deep self that is our constant companion and reliable truth speaker.

At about the same time, around 1980, I began working with my first client diagnosed with multiple personality disorder (currently known as Dissociative Identity Disorder or DID). One aspect of her psyche claimed that it was not a part or ego state like the others. It said that it had been present within the client from birth and knew all that had happened to her. Although it could not protect her from the severe abuse she had endured, it had done all that it could internally to help her survive and preserve what was authentic and innocent within her. It had also helped her bury the memory of some of the worst abuse so that the outer self could function in everyday life without being overwhelmed by the pain of these traumas.

This presence knew all of the parts, how they related to one another, what their needs were, and how to help them. It knew the best order in which to deal with issues and was very effective in guiding parts through the resolution of internal conflicts and healing traumatic psychic wounds. It taught that all the parts, even those that seemed malevolent or self-destructive, had an ultimately beneficial purpose that needed to be appreciated and helped to flourish.

My relationship with this presence within the client evolved into a co-therapy process. In studying the literature on MPD, I later learned that other therapists working with MPD clients had encountered similar presences within their clients and were working with them in much the same way as I was. The presences were even given a technical name by these therapists: the Inner-Self helper, or ISH (see Chapter 20, "Dissociative Identity Disorder, an Overview").

As I worked with other MPD clients I encountered the same compassionate, wise dimension within them. It became obvious to me that the ISH and the Inner Wisdom I was helping my less dissociative clients connect with were the same energy, which I have come to call the Self.

I also realized in working with my less dissociative clients that the parts I encountered in my MPD clients were simply the extreme expression of a universal human reality. We all have a somewhat divided consciousness. How often have we heard declared, "That just wasn't me"? For some, the divisions are shallow and ephemeral. For others, they are deeply ingrained and long lasting. No matter where a person might be along the spectrum of dissociation, respectful engagement of the parts and helping them appreciate their true purpose following the guidance of the Self can radically transform a person's life.

There are several essential elements for anyone who wants to live out his or her fullest potential: connecting with the Self, healing traumatic psychic wounds, and helping parts learn their true nature and how to cooperate with one another and eventually integrate. All three are achievable with or without the help of a counselor.

Being allowed to share in the unfolding of these healing experiences as a therapist has been profoundly rewarding. In just one relatively typical day of counseling, I was privileged to share in several, powerful and wondrous internal journeys generated by the deep, wise, and caring intelligence of the Self. It manifested in a variety of ways unique to each client. For one it was Inner Wisdom. For others it was the Great Mother, Goddess, or Golden Child. As you read these experiences I hope you will be touched by their poignancy and be open to the possibility that you have within your depth the same profound wisdom, love, and capacity for beautiful metaphoric expression as did these clients.

Healing Visions

Typically, the therapy sessions I facilitate have three parts. The first part is a time for sharing the client's reflections and concerns about what has transpired internally and externally since the last session. In the second part of the session I help facilitate internal work which Carl Jung called active imagination. I do this by first guiding the client through a deep relaxation procedure after which I describe a beautiful, safe, imaginative, internal scene utilizing as many senses as possible. Usually this is a mountain meadow, unless the client prefers something different. Once the client feels focused in this internal, imagined space I suggest that he or she invite forward the Self in whatever form it takes for that person and then be open to whatever experience the Self generates. Sometimes I also suggest that the client invite forward into his or her inner space (i.e. the mountain meadow) particular aspects of the psyche that the client or I judge to be in need of special attention. The third part of the session is devoted to helping the client appreciate and integrate the internal work experience that just transpired.

The following is a description of the internal work experiences of several clients that happened on a single day. It happened to be my birthday. Every session that day felt like a generous gift. Without any exaggeration, I can say that the beauty and wonder of the unfolding inner life of my clients was in its own way much like an Alaskan cruise: dramatic, awe inspiring, and completely natural—the organic expression of upwelling primal energies that far exceeds any manmade artifact. Yet this day was not significantly different from most days at the office.

Jonathan

(Throughout this book all clients' names have been changed to protect confidentiality.)

Jonathan, brought me a birthday gift, a perfect sand dollar he had found on a recent trip. It now has a place of honor beside my office lamp. During that trip he had done some internal work on his own and continued a dialogue we had begun with a child part of himself. This part, Johnny, told him it was content with simple things.

Crying, Jonathan said he saw with clarity that his parents had just wanted a little boy they could cuddle and play with, but because of his ADHD he was much too agitated and erratic for them to be able to do so. This made bonding difficult. It is typical for clients in the process of active imagination to see themselves and their life experiences in ways that had not occurred to them before. In this instance, Jonathan was aware of a sense of disconnection with his parents, but couldn't understand why that would be so, since his parents were kind people who had tried to support him throughout his life. With this new insight he was able to be more accepting of his parents' love for him and more accepting of himself as well. Even though the source of the problem lay within himself, he could see that it was because of a neurobiological deficit, which was nothing to be ashamed of and didn't make him wrong or bad.

This realization came to him in an inner space he called the grove. One of the most salient features of the grove was that it was a place of peace and safety with a strong feeling of inclusion. By pairing the emotional realization of the cause of his disconnection from his parents with the powerful sense of inclusion and connection that emanated from the grove, his Self was strongly connecting the two awarenesses so that memories of the parents and feelings of inclusion within the grove would become bound to each other. If this connection became deeply rooted through repetition, it would significantly erode the embedded childhood feelings of alienation and rejection.

Another related issue also came to mind in this internal work experience. Jonathan said that one of the child's great burdens was his intense curiosity, which led to innumerable questions of which the adults quickly grew tired and soon ignored. Jonathan was assured that when he went to the grove (the place of his wisdom figures) he could ask questions about anything and be given answers. Again the grove was offered to him as a healing counterpoint to his lifelong feelings of rejection and aloneness.

Jonathan's Wisdom/Self then told him that it was his fear of being free of both fear and negative habits that held him back from moving more easily into his own best potential. Jonathan noted that every time he took a new step forward, he would fall back into his old patterns of self-destructive, compulsive behaviors, shame, and fear of reaching out. Although he was clearly aware of the pattern, he had not associated it with fearing the freedom that comes with positive change. After Wisdom pointed it out, it was obvious to him. This insight was quite meaningful to him. In itself, it did not lead to immediate changes in his behavior subsequent to this session.

It did, however, help focus our work on learning how to release his fear of change.

Jonathan went on to tell me that the inner child, Johnny, had been getting older and was seven or eight now. I affirmed that this was good news and, in my experience, a strong indication of continued healing. He said that the brief fusing he had experienced with Johnny, the wisdom figures, and himself during our last internal work session was very powerful. It had given him and Johnny insight into each other and their potential together that neither had experienced before.

Dealing with subpersonalities is an integral part of active imagination. The degree of autonomous existence these parts have varies from person to person. Some clearly preexist the therapy process and can even express themselves as voices the client hears. Others are artifacts of therapy, such as when I ask a client to use active imagination to invite forward a wounded child or some other aspect of the psyche, such as anger. Invariably the psyche will present an autonomous image in response to the request. If the client is willing to deal with it respectfully as well as to learn from it, the experience will be very fruitful. Such occurred with Jonathan and Johnny.

Jonathan disclosed having a real struggle making a connection with most people. Nevertheless, he was not getting depressed about it or indulging in the compulsive behaviors he was inclined toward because of it. Often persons who have experienced significant attachment deficits in the first years of life have impaired socialization skills. This handicap tends to persist even after there has been significant healing. With growing self-acceptance and a realization of the extraordinary beauty and love that lies at his core, a client will usually come to the conclusion that he is a precious gift that he is proud to offer to others, even if it comes wrapped in a rather awkward package.

Jonathan told me that in talking to a friend about his internal journey work, he realized that he was very happy, but something was still missing. He said he felt he was coming into an effulgent spirit (i.e., full of life and light). He said he felt the presence of God and a former dearly loved teacher, now deceased, named Grace, and that he was now eager to share this spirit.

Jonathan could feel the emergence of real power within himself and felt great gratitude. With this accepting of himself, he also became aware of a growing acceptance of other people.

Part of his remaining hesitation to open himself to others was that he didn't feel that he was being stern enough with himself and that he was therefore irresponsible. At times he would almost feel giddy, but then restrain himself from showing it to others, wondering if it was okay to feel this good and so full of love.

His inner world had become very accessible of late. As he put it, "All I need are a few quiet moments and we are there—with the gang inside."

He concluded the session by firmly stating, "This change is inevitable. The ego will embrace the light. It will be."

Lucy

Lucy, my next client, began the session by announcing that yesterday had been momentous. She had made a major decision and turned down a chance to become a full-time executive-level employee at her company to instead remain a part-time private contractor. Rejecting the offered position would cost her a considerable amount of money, job security, and benefits. This decision was a major fork in the road for her.

Several factors contributed to her decision. One of the most important was an outgrowth of our previous session. During the active imagination part of that session she had met an angry, obnoxious, gargoyle-like figure. After some dialogue with the figure and guidance from her Self / Inner Wisdom, she had realized the gargoyle represented her earthy, passionate, wild side, which she had submerged in her well-intended efforts to be good and responsible. This wild side would need time and energy in order to be properly expressed. She knew that it would be impossible to claim the wild side and hold down a full-time executive position in her company.

I strongly seconded her decision, especially for the way in which it affirmed the importance of the gargoyle over security and status. We then did an active imagination experience.

Upon entering the meadow she noticed it was covered with tiny flowers. They gave the landscape a texture like wool. It made the whole environment feel organic and very alive. Although briefly shown to her in daylight, the meadow soon settled into the purples of dusk. Fairies, almost like lightning bugs, gathered around her. They were curious about her, but their principal task seemed to be to lead her to another place.

She then noted a silver thread stretching from her solar plexus through the darkness into the forest ahead of her. As she moved toward the forest an ankh appeared in front of her. She knew that it was a symbol of healing and that much energy could be sent through it. At this point, she found herself at her destination. It felt like a temple—small, quiet, and dark. It was filled with the scent of lavender and many various herbs.

"This," she said, "is where a priestess should be found. It is my place. I am remembering I built this place. It is very beautiful, extremely intimate. A source of power for who I am." In a few moments she added, "I sense the presence of a woman here. Now I can see her face. She seems to be made of light and is quite hazy when I look directly at her. She is a night goddess.

"In front of me I see a very big silver bowl filled with water. The night goddess is in the bowl, beckoning me. As I look into it I realize my body cannot follow. It is anchored in the temple. My soul, however, does go with her. It is nighttime and we are flying. I love to fly. We soar over the trees and then float and watch. The air around me is very moist. Dew is about to fall. I feel myself becoming the dew as it covers the plants. The goddess is merging with me now. Something about mist comes to mind. It feels very quiet."

In her previous session Snow White was the immobilized "good self" who was a polarized counterpart to the earthy, lusty, often not very nice gargoyle. In this journey she said, "It's about the Snow White persona. Snow White is quiet right now. She might be unsure of herself. She feels weak and knows that she needs to reconnect with her source of strength. She is saying, 'If things are going to change, I don't know my role. Who is going to tell me?' Snow White is actually a very frightened little girl. The gargoyle sees her now and feels compassion for her." Lucy then laughed. "It's the other half of her. I feel a great love for both of them."

Lucy continued to describe the unfolding experience.

"They are embracing. Snow White is very happy and she feels greatly relieved. They were meant for each other, but split themselves a long time ago. The gargoyle is actually her prince. He has an amazing depth of compassion and understanding. Clearly they need each other. In their union I feel a tremendous sense of love. It is an ultimate compassion. When the prince accepts her, she feels very empowered. Without him she felt lost. She needed him to be there.

"Snow White is growing now like a tree. She is both woman and tree with an incredible trunk that spirals upward. There are big ridges in the bark and the limbs bear a golden fruit. This is the tree of knowledge, but there is nothing forbidden about the fruit. The prince/gargoyle climbs the tree and eats its fruit. He laughs a lot. He has become a kind of prankster or jokester."

As Lucy opened her eyes and refocused on my office, she added, "I love the symbolism. It is so funny. It was wonderful to experience the masculine and feminine energy being married. I was unaware of how beautiful the masculine can be. Without it I have felt weak."

As the therapist, I felt that anything I might add would only distract from a rich, powerful, abundantly eloquent experience. My only guidance to her before the session ended was that she be alert to the presence of this new strength within her and let it flow when she had the chance.

I am continually impressed by my clients' active imagination experiences. What unfolds is generated by a deep intelligence. These metaphoric stories are obviously carefully thought-through constructs created by an aspect of the psyche that operates beyond the ego's range of awareness. The purpose appears to be the healing of the psyche so that the person will become free to express the full potential of his or her deep Self. The counselor's role is to awaken the client to this extraordinary potential for inner healing, and to create a space for the ego in which wholeness can unfold and be claimed.

Gwen

Gwen, my final client for the day, began her session by telling me the results of a personal experiment she had conducted in the preceding weeks. Her primary spiritual practice had been chanting in a way taught by a particular Buddhist sect to which she belonged. The practice had begun to feel rigid and demanding. She found herself being motivated more by guilt than a willing embrace of the practice. She therefore quit the chanting and spent the time in a peaceful, quiet state. Upon doing this she noticed that something felt missing. Although peaceful, she was not experiencing the joy that had emanated from the chanting.

She then engaged in an active imagination experience at home. In it a Golden Child appeared who told Gwen that she needed more structure and routine than the simple quiet time gave her. Afterward Gwen returned to the chanting.

In another active imagination at home she met the Golden Child again. The child was very delicate, but not fragile. She was almost angelic. Gwen was angry. All of her life it seemed that others were able to abuse their bodies and not have any significant consequences. Whenever she neglected self-care, either through not getting enough sleep, drinking too much, or not paying attention to her physical needs, her body would react strongly and she would feel miserable. The child simply told her she must honor the sensitivity of her body, implying that it was a gift.

Gwen then noticed the child had no feet. Gwen gave her shoes so that she could walk with her on earth. The child, in turn, gave Gwen silver wings. In the exchange of gifts Gwen knew she was integrating body and spirit.

After brief additional conversation focusing on ways she was now exercising better physical self-care and clearer ownership of her spiritual values, we began the active imagination process. Her first comment was, "This is kind of funny." She then went on to describe a scene totally unlike any she had ever experienced in previous sessions.

"I am dressed in a transparent, gold gown thing with black, soft, suede boots. It's quite sexy. The steps in front of me are in rich black carpeting with gold tassels. They lead me to a beautiful gothic dining room. I see crystal and candles and tapestries on the wall. Wisdom is sitting at a long table. She tells me that all of this is mine. I have a crown on. At my side is a pet griffin, half lioness and half eagle. Her fur is like velvet also. Everything is velvety and silky.

"There is a bowl of beautiful fruit on the table. Beside me is a healer who knows all about herbs and proper care of the body. She has been taking care of me all my life. Although she works in mysterious ways, she is always right. She knows. She is telling me to stay close to the earth when I eat. It is very important for me to eat low on the food chain. My body is very delicate. I should emphasize grains, fruits, vegetables, nuts, and herbs. I don't need to worry about coffee, but I must drink no hard liquor. She recommends that I be in the water a lot."

Wisdom then drew Gwen's attention, telling her that she had things she wanted her to see today. Gwen continued, "The dining room is in the heart of the house. It's a big castle that has grand spaces for great gatherings of people. We are now going up into the tower and are on a circular platform. It is a gold and white space with no ceiling or walls. It is a launching pad from which I can fly. As I fly everything gets bigger. The house is beautiful and so is the land it is on."

She asked Wisdom what this place was for. Wisdom replied, "First, please stop worrying about everything. You will have enough in your life to take care of you."

Gwen acknowledged that a big part of her consciousness was occupied with worrying whether her needs could be met.

Wisdom added, "Share your wealth and be generous. Don't stop the flow. You aren't actually giving and receiving; you are just rearranging energy."

An example of how this had worked in her life previously and how it felt, came to mind. Gwen remembered a piece of art she had purchased to help support an artist suffering from AIDS. She had paid a lot for it, but found great delight in its beauty. It also spurred her to do creative things with some crystals she had had for some time but had done nothing with.

Wisdom told her, "In your body you have the gift of very free movement. Energy can move through you so very easily."

Gwen answered, "I will take care of my body so that I can serve the energy in a better way."

Wisdom took everything and folded it into a black velvet box. She handed it to Gwen.

Proper care for the body is a theme that often arises in active imagination. When we live mostly out of mind control or ego we tend to feel disconnected from our bodies as well as nature, other people, emotions, etc. The Self that is revealed in active imagination sees internal and external reality both in their physical and nonphysical aspects as an interrelated, connected whole. Even though we may be living out of the mechanistic, disconnected style that permeates our culture, when we are shown the other path through internal work we know intuitively it is by far the better way.

This Self, encountered within, obviously knows the person intimately, cares about him or her, and is eager to offer the guidance necessary for living the most meaningful, authentic life possible. I have spent my life seeking to understand the nature of this inner presence and explore its implications for psychological healing and spiritual development. *Embracing the Self* is a summary of what I have learned, and I am excited to share it with you.

CHAPTER THREE

A Partner for Life

As I have emphasized previously, everyone has at least two selves, a deep Self and a surface self or ego. (Many have more than one ego, usually thought of as parts, some of which may be highly developed and autonomous while others are fragmentary and limited in focus.) The purpose of the surface self or ego is to interact with the outer world in such a way that the person's life is as safe and meaningful as possible. Negotiating relationships, protecting oneself from threats, and taking care of basic physical, mental, and emotional needs are central to its agenda. To accomplish this, its principal tools are the capacity for analytical thinking, the ability to draw lessons from past experience, and the ability to make mental models of future possibilities as a way of creating virtual realities to test out possible, planned actions.

The ego's ultimate gift is the capacity for choice in determining the course of a person's destiny. Given the ego's gifts and tasks, it is not surprising that the ego would be inclined to approach reality from a disconnected, control-oriented mentality. The ego's need to manage life inclines it to stand apart from experience. Its proclivity to establish boundaries can lead to a sense of disconnection. This is both necessary and its Achilles's heel, since egos almost inevitably fail to realize that the gifts of the ego are meant to serve a reality greater than itself—i.e., the Self. Largely driven by anxiety and ignorant of the presence of the Self within, the ego generally comes to see itself as a distinct entity separate from all others, the captain of the ship. In this false view, fear becomes a central motivating force and reigns throughout our days.

Ideally, the ego and the Self work together as a tightly knit team. The Self perceives the world in its interconnected wholeness and is focused on the direct experience of the present moment both internally and externally. This current moment is the only place where reality can be encountered. It is here that true vitality is possible. Only in this moment can love be actually experienced and expressed. The Self is willing to help the ego learn from the past or heal historical wounds. It will also assist in creating and supporting life-giving dreams for the future. But this is done so that the ego might rest more easily in the experience of the moment.

Likewise the Self will use language, imagery, and models when communicating with a person, but always with the intention of encouraging the ego to let go of overdependence on the security of its mental models and evasion of the present experience.

When a person is in right balance, she appreciates the importance of staying grounded in the perspective of the Self. She understands that her ability to learn from the past and anticipate the future as well as to analyze and manipulate her environment must always be in the service of the Self. This means that she chooses to live as fully and openly as possible in the direct experience of life, motivated only by the desire to love in the same way as she has experienced love from the Self. A balanced ego understands that his labels, self-descriptions, titles, or culturally assigned roles are just words and not reality. The ego's foundation and purpose is to bring the unfolding and intangible mystery of the Self to life into the world at large. How one is welcomed and gently treated by the Self internally is now the model for accepting and loving all others in one's life.

In a session with a client this afternoon, her Self told her the following: "Your job is to see the Soul Self. Focus on it. Enjoy your oneness with it. Let go of all the fear-based thoughts ideas, beliefs, and habits that are not formed and founded in love."

Many strains of contemporary and ancient thought have helped me appreciate the significance and implications of living a life grounded in an ongoing communion with this deep presence. Among them is Carl Jung, who revealed posthumously in *The Red Book* the depth and breadth of his own inner guidance. Jung called the source of this guidance the Self. Its principal manifestation to him was a figure he named Philemon, whom he met in a dream and who later became a major figure in his internal work (which he called Active Imagination). Jung said that everything he wrote after he had met Philemon was simply an elaboration on what Philemon had taught him.

The Self as I have encountered it in myself and hundreds of clients over thousands of sessions is remarkably consistent from person to person: void of any judgment and always offering deep listening, wise guidance, and unconditional love to those who deign to open themselves to it.

If such an incredible gift actually exists, why do so few people know about it? Even among those who do know, why do so many, including myself, resist fully embracing it? In my own case, my early life experience convinced me at a profound, preverbal level that I was deeply flawed and did not deserve love. A constant fear of rejection caused me to put up walls and do whatever I could to control my internal and external environments. I eventually learned to rely almost totally on my intellect and to disconnect from my needs, feelings, sensations, and body awareness. Shame, fear, and a detached, insular lifestyle made me almost impervious to the gentle, healing love that was always at my core. Slowly, through becoming a father and through witnessing and sharing in my clients' transformations as they allowed healing to flow from their Self, I cautiously and slowly allowed my own Self to become the central force in my life. It took decades, but I am grateful beyond words for having gotten as far as I have. Recently this energy has taken on a very specific image.

My Self now presents as a beautiful, kind, and earthy woman. She first came to me in a dream almost a year ago. In the dream I was living in a new place that was reminiscent of a home I had designed and built many years ago. I knew that numerous kind people had helped me to build my house. One woman in particular had gone out of her way to help in any way she could. During the dream, she was mowing the front yard. I wondered why she was so helpful. I was given to understand that she loved me and delighted in helping me. I offered to get her something to eat. She said that there was only one thing that she wanted. It was a kind of energy drink called Amour, which, of course, is French for *love*.

Last week I had a conversation with this dream figure (whom I now call Dear Lady) when I was doing internal work. She told me, "Love from within is eager, tender, playful, passionate, absolutely honest, and contains no judgment. I am always available. I know who you are and why you do what you do better than you do. I want to be known, welcomed, and embraced. I want to see you flourish and can help in so many ways. I love you. Let yourself fall in love with me."

I responded, "You are what I have always longed for. It feels too good to be true."

She answered, "You don't feel like you deserve me and you have no precedent except for your partner, Karen."

I then remembered a dream from two nights before in which I had been told of a beautiful young woman who was coming to live with me. Her masculine companion in that dream was the part of me that loves gadgets and technology. This stirred a realization that I shared with Dear Lady. I told her, "The beautiful woman who is coming to live within me is like your daughter. Our union will give birth to her."

Dear Lady responded, "Think of me often with love. Let yourself joyfully, eagerly connect with me. I have so much to give. Open your heart and take it."

The principal gift the Self wants to grant us is to help us become an authentic, whole person, our own true self. A common contemporary assumption is that there may not be any such thing as a core "true self." In this point of view whatever we are is a construct created by the interaction between the ego, neurological predispositions, and the environment. If this created self isn't to our liking, then our best option is to choose another way of being and then do all we can to manifest it by changing our environment, altering our neurology if possible, and enacting a different way of being. By trying hard, through grit and determination, we become our own creator, a self-made person, the product of our choice and ego rather than the expression of a deeper, preexisting reality that we are allowing to emerge.

The consistent message, in the inner work guided by the Self of client after client, is that we are all an unfolding mystery born with a unique set of gifts and proclivities that will emerge and blossom appropriately only when they are rooted in the Self. The messages of our culture and our life experiences, especially those of a painful childhood, distort or conceal our gifts and create a barrier between the ego and Self that stunts our potential and diminishes our awareness as we seek to adapt to the demands of family and culture. The self-made self we are left with at the conscious, ego level is a pale reflection of who we are at the deepest level.

Attempts to change ourselves so that we might become more functional, successful, or resilient, are merely a more sophisticated reiteration of the childhood need to adapt. Attempting to fit in is what caused us to lose ourselves in the first place. The good news is that we can give up this misguided effort at self re-creation or improvement. Instead we are invited to allow ourselves to relax into the embrace of pure, unconditional, non-judgmental love. We are encouraged to rediscover ourselves through the loving eyes of the Self who sees who we truly are right down to the core, where eventually we discover that we are the Self that has been calling and guiding us all these years. All who accept this invitation soon discover that not only does love uncover their truth (both the good and the ugly), but that their deepest truth as expressed through the Self is that they *are* love itself and one with the Self.

The Self is a cornucopia of all the gifts that matter the most: love, truth, freedom, joy, connection, and meaning, all grounded in direct experience, which far transcends anything that can be put into words. The Self's only desire is to bring us to the place where we can appreciate and receive these gifts. Even for a willing ego that understands the value of these gifts, this takes time. The ravages of painful life experience and the pervasive impact of culture, which aggrandizes and hardens the ego, must be peeled away and released in a process that does not happen quickly. The Self exquisitely knows how to release the ego, as demonstrated in the internal work of the clients described above.

Letting go into the loving embrace of the Self changes everything. In the release that comes from surrendering to the all-encompassing embrace of the Self, the energy used to maintain the ego's boundaries, roles, and sense of self is freed, with an accompanying surge in vitality. As ego and Self merge, the values and perspective of the Self become the ego's new foundation. This is experienced as a radical liberation.

From the vantage point of the Self, I can clearly see that this ego-self I have been protecting, shoring up, or struggling with all my life, although useful for a time, is just a phantom, a story I tell myself, a made-up, imaginary thing. It not only limited and twisted my personal reality, but clouded my perception of everything by forcing me to look through a distorting lens of words and assumptions. This story of "I" and my efforts to defend it blinded me to the profound, uncaused joy of simply being immersed in what is. I lost the sense of awe and wonder the young child feels as he takes in the world around him without defenses, interpretation, or labels. When we see through the eyes of the Self, we experience curiosity, wonder, and gratitude in the unfolding present, rather than seeing the present as an obstacle on our path to the future. Guilt, worry, grasping, and regret fall away as the Self steadies my focus on the now.

A few days ago a client I will call Julie had a long talk with her Self, who took the form of Christ. He told her she was at a turning point in which it was no longer necessary to live a life driven by fear and the need for self-protection. Instead, she could let herself embrace the emergence of a life in which she allows herself to give free reign to her deepest hopes and dreams.

Christ told her, "I want you to express your hopes and dreams. So much of your life has been survival and trying to please or protect yourself from other people. [At this point Julie was crying.] It is not your fault. Up to now you really haven't allowed yourself to dream. You have not had the luxury of being present and future based."

Julie commented, "This touches me deeply. It makes me cry because he knows me better than I know me. I have never even thought these things."

Christ went on to say, "Basically, your main goals have been to stay alive and not screw up. You tried to stay close to me and not hurt anyone just by being yourself. The effort to survive and the need you felt for self-protection, as well as the need to protect others from yourself, has taken a great deal of your energy."

Julie responded, "I don't want it to be the truth. It's too dramatic, sad, hard, and dark."

Christ then said, "The grieving heart you brought me today was not about what happened [her history of abuse]. It is the acknowledgement of what can be no more. For years you have said that you don't want to be here [alive on earth] anymore. I want you to be here, but not with survival and protection as your only purpose and goal. This change frightens you. You are reluctant to step away from the survival mode of the past into the stillness and quiet of the present or future world where there is space for dreams and visions—for prayers that are full of hope for those you love, as opposed to your lifelong preoccupation with worries and a need for protection from a world that you know can be dark and dangerous."

"It's ironic that *hope* is your favorite word. It's the thing you try to give to everyone else, but you dare not offer it to yourself or allow yourself to feel it. I want you to do something most would enjoy, but I know you will find daunting: try to dream more!"

I (Dean) then offered the comment, "Imagine yourself in a world that is safe and beautiful. See it as the unfolding of God all around you, a world that welcomes your own unfolding as you blossom into the full potential of your birth."

Christ affirmed my comment, "Remember this many times a day. Embrace this grateful awareness."

Julie responded, "I can only remain in it for short periods of time before I return to survival and not screwing up."

Christ said, "I am giving you permission to lay down your sword. Enter into the fullness of my protection. Your main goal for the moment is to explore the tenets that Dean spoke of. Allow me to embed these truths in your heart, mind, and soul. Allow them to become the foundation of your hopes and dreams. Allow my vision of you to become your own.

"You consider me good and the source of goodness. Let me remind you of your favorite scripture quote which you have often used to give hope to others, Jeremiah 29:11: 'For I know the plans I have for you, says the Lord, plans for welfare and not for evil, to give you a future and a hope.'

There is so much else I want to give you beyond helping you through tragedies and supporting you in your desire to be good and stay alive. There is so much more than that. I know these words surprise you. They are not a chastisement. It's an invitation. It's an opportunity. It's like a reward, like a badge of completion.

"Congratulations! You have survived. Now I want you to thrive. This is when you are really able to bear fruit. Plants and trees that are just surviving, as in a drought, don't blossom or bear fruit. Lots of people only survive, but it is not what I want for them.

"I know you want to walk away from this. It challenges your psyche. Be open to the possibility of dreams."

Julie responded, "I'm sorry I'm not excited about being here."

Christ emphasized, "I understand. You are afraid of being disappointed. I am going to do all the work. Just allow me to embed it. I will wipe that part of your limbic drive clean. Can you imagine what it would be like if you got to enjoy every day versus just survive each day, if you knew that absolutely nothing was going to come to you and overwhelm you or destroy you or harm you? That's my job. That's always been my job. I'm sorry that the circumstances of your life have made it so hard for you to know that. This isn't about you messing up or being too dull minded to get to this point. It's about deep and cavernous wounds that allowed nothing but survival and an indestructible hope for a future. Now that future is present, and a new future needs to be defined, but not based on survival and recovery.

Think of it like moving to a new country. It will take some time to learn the language and culture and get your bearings."

Christ continued, "This is a different kind of healing, beyond trauma and triage. It's a new beginning. I know you don't like new things, because they are not dependable. Accept my invitation. You will never regret it. I am here and will always be here. I have hopes and dreams for you and with you. You don't have to generate them. Just be in the stillness, let them unfold and live them."

Julie then realized, "I don't have to suddenly develop a new skill that I've never been good at."

This ended the internal work for that session. Afterward, Julie said that she felt weak and weird, but not bad. She noted that she was surprised by the direction the process had taken, since she'd had a very different agenda in mind when we began the session.

Julie's experience with Christ is far from unique. Another client I will call Ellen had two sessions of internal work in the last two weeks that reiterated the same fundamental theme as expressed in Julie's work; it is, "Give up trying to be what you think you ought to be or believe you are. Instead, give yourself the freedom to actually be the gift you truly are."

Ellen's Self presents as a Great Mother figure. In her first session of internal work Ellen found herself going down long, wide steps that wound into a beautiful garden. There were small, young, new palm trees all around. The trees went along a path that opened to an ocean beach.

Ellen remarked with pleasure, "This is exciting, and it is gorgeous."

The Great Mother replied, "There is so much more that you can't see from this place. Notice the benches from which you can take in the beauty wherever it is. The path itself will lead you. You will have direction because the path is there."

Then the Great Mother continued, "You are accustomed to change much more than you realize. Don't fear the big changes that have been and are continuing to come. You will ride big waves as an explorer and then as a guide. At twelve you knew you would go to the depths of pain and sorrow and also to the heights of joy. Want that! Don't want to miss any part of truly living. Read the signs as you go. You will be guided every step of the way, as you always have been.

"Focus on me and on Spirit and on the vastness. Look at the sky at night and follow your heart. Don't be afraid to ask for all you want. Let go of guilt, unworthiness, and every obstacle to loving deeply and joyously, and being loved in that same way. You are worthy of great love because you are that love."

Ellen responded, "I will be a source of blessing to everyone in my life, instead of feeling like I am a burden, which has been my inclination all my life."

Great Mother added, "You have been so afraid you wouldn't complete your mission on earth. These days are the culmination of your mission. Also remember that you do not owe me anything. Let go of the feeling of indebtedness that weighs so heavily on you."

In her next session on the following week, the Great Mother met Ellen on the first step as she descended into her internal world. Once again the steps were big, broad, and winding with a very mild descent, not at all steep. She was taken by how pretty it was with the flowers all around. At the bottom was level ground. Three paths led away from the bottom step. They went straight, then left, and then right. It was a mystery to her as to where each led. The Great Mother asked her which path called to her. As she held the Great Mother's hand, she said that it was the one to the right. With the decision made she could feel her shoulders relax, and she sighed deeply.

The Great Mother told her, "No matter what you choose, I will be with you. If you stay close to me, I will never let you go too far in any one direction. I will show you where to turn or come back, but you must choose and I will be with you."

Ellen reported, "She is eager to help me. More divine help is available than I could ever imagine."

The Great Mother continued, "We have only just begun. Because you can accept more, we can show you more."

Great Mother then reminded Ellen of the internal work from two sessions ago, in which she had let go of her old fundamental attitude of focusing on not wanting to have been born into all the pain and tragedy that awaited her, and on the idea that madness was her destiny.

Ellen made a new decision, which was, "I will embrace being born. I will be a blessing to people and they will be a blessing to me. I will be sane. I am going sane."

Great Mother added, "You have tasted the fullness of life before, but you haven't fully accepted who your soul self is. Retire from trying to be what you have always been."

Ellen concluded the internal work with the observation, "This is a time of flowering in my life."

The Self seems to never tell people specifically who or what they are, or to define with clarity a specific direction they should take, with one exception: the Self will give firm direction toward the resolution of a significant trauma. As in Ellen's case, multiple options are typically offered, and assurance is given that support and guidance will be available no matter what choice is made. Security that might be gained from having a defined sense of self or clarity regarding one's destiny is not going to be found from the Self. Although it may seem counterintuitive, the wisest and most loving gift that can be given is to encourage the acceptance of not knowing who I am or what I am called to be. We must learn to be in acceptance of our essential mystery. Whatever is truest about ourselves transcends words and intentions.

Our true nature is a moment-by-moment, gradual, self-revealing, unpredictable life force, which continually beckons us to venture beyond our expectations, conditioning, and presumed limitations. It is like dancing with a beautiful but mysterious partner who continually reveals new dimensions of herself even as we fall deeper and deeper in love. It is a life-giving insecurity in which the only thing we can be sure of is that passion, meaning, and joy will continue to grow even as we see our possibilities expand without any end in sight. John O'Donohue's poem "Fluent" in his book *Conamara Blues* captures this theme beautifully:

> I would love to live
>   like a river flows.
>   Carried by the surprise
>   of its own unfolding.

Reflecting this theme, my partner Karen wrote the following after a moving encounter with her Self:

Irrepressible Ripples 2/05/2014

"What the world needs now is love sweet love.

It's the only thing there's just too little of.
No, not just for some but for everyone."
1965 song by Burt Bacharach and David Hall

* * *

Who is that faultfinding critical gremlin speaking to me from my mirror?
What does *she* know?
I innocently inquire her opinion.

I'm startled as she has a boatload of judgments, evaluations, comparisons which
She seems too eager to share with me:
"For starters, Do something about your hair, your face, your body,
Never mind. It's all too late."

From somewhere inside I hear: "Look again, listen to the one speaking *behind* your face.

I see her lips move but the voice is inaudible beneath the roaring, harsh din careening off the Cliff walls of my mind: "*You* can never make it. You are too timid, never enough, too stupid, too Old, too much. . . . and *way* too late. . . ."
Still, I effort to hear the other, *hushed* voice.

"Say again. Please say again".

I sense my determination to hear her, emboldens her. The critical clatter is muffled.

Barely audible, she starts with a whisper, "*May I offer you a second opinion?*"
"Behold your beauty, your magnificence.
Treasure the one life given. Hold it lightly, reverently in your hands.
Caress its delicate mystery.
Hold tenderly this day, given only once and never again.
Bow low in gratitude for the miracle of birth, death, laughter, breath and the life you are.

Look deep into the pool *behind* the mirror. Behold, your wondrous being.

See how deeply you are loved, how absurd to fear anything at all.

Ah sweetheart, how strong, how resilient, how rich you are, reflecting facets of the Divine.

Do not hide your exquisite light under a lie, a false face.

Come out. Shine. It's time.

Dance the dance only *you can.*

Dance to the singing and clapping of the Universe.

Yes, you are deeply loved, yes cherished, celebrated.

There is *nothing* wrong with you.

Pay no mind to the critic. That's just her day job.

I am your Wise Advocate. I've been with you from the beginning. Waiting. Come. Let's talk.

This love letter is your truth. Trust it. Take and run with it.

Put it beside your pillow at night. Dance with it.

Like a pebble thrown in a pond, let this love grow wavelets of radical self acceptance,

Extending out into an ever widening arc. . . until. . . . .

These irrepressible ripples join and connect everyone you touch in a circle of love."

The mirror twinkles and winks in the sacred stillness.

The secret is *out. K. Wickham*

CHAPTER FOUR

The Divine Child

The Self will not define us. It will, however, give us a glimpse of who we truly are inside and who we were meant to be before the pain of life and the impact of culture and family caused us to harden ourselves into the defended fortress that we now mistake for ourselves. This glimpse of our original face is what Carl Jung called the Divine Child. What remains, after stories of "I" and mandates from caregivers and culture are peeled away, is a unique, beautiful, innocent, wide-eyed child still longing to blossom and play.

No matter what life may have done to us, no matter what we may have done to ourselves, no matter how profound our psychological wounds might be, ultimately we remain inviolate and unbroken. Aside from organically based brain dysfunction, underneath all the scars, open wounds, and distortions that mar the psyche, when one breaks through to the kernel, the core of one's being, it remains whole. In the depth of our center, we remain vitally alive and real—nothing lost, nothing ruined. The core remains undamaged, life embracing, and life giving.

In *The Archetypes and the Collective Unconscious*, Jung offers a rich description of the Divine Child. He says,

> The child-motif represents not only something that existed in the distant past but also something that exists now; that is to say, it is not just a vestige but a system functioning in the present whose purpose is to compensate and correct, in a meaningful manner the inevitable one-sidedness and extravagances of the conscious mind.

...the "child" paves the way for a future change of personality. In the individuation process, it anticipates the figure that comes from the synthesis of conscious and unconscious elements in the personality. It is therefore a symbol which unites the opposites; a mediator, bringer of healing, that is, one who makes whole (Jung 1980, 162–164).

Later, in the section "The Special Phenomenology of the Child Archetype," (170), Jung says,

It [the child motif] is a personification of vital forces quite outside the limited range of our conscious mind; of ways and possibilities of which our one sided conscious mind knows nothing; a wholeness which embraces the very depths of nature. It represents the strongest, most ineluctable urge in every being, namely the urge to realize itself.

Coming into the fullness of my human potential (the only worthy goal of anyone's life), requires the eager welcome of the child I left behind long ago. She or he is my true voice, the deep source of my vitality. She or he is my joy and the template for measuring what is and is not truly authentic. The learning and coping skills I have gained over the years are not an end in themselves. Nor are they merely meant to serve as aids for survival. Their highest purpose is to give the Divine Child the protection, permission, and opportunities it needs to fully express itself. A life in balance is a life rooted in its source.

When I encountered my Divine Child in internal work, he was three or four years old. He was by a pool of water, curious about the things that lived in and near it. He then began to dig a little ditch in order to observe how the water would flow and build up behind the dams he created. This bit of engineering absorbed and delighted him. He was very content to be by himself experimenting and learning. He welcomed my adult presence, but didn't pay much attention to me. This glimpse into his world helped me appreciate and respect several things about myself. Curiosity and figuring things out is clearly a core aspect of who I am. My hunger to understand the world is part of my original blessing and to be treasured. The experience also made clear that I have always needed less socialization than most people, but that it is completely okay to be the way I am. Later in life, my inclination to isolate had become magnified by emotional wounding. However, a preference for my own company is not pathology. It is my nature.

Encountering the Divine Child is an important moment in anyone's process of self-discovery. The following is a brief verbatim transcript of a client's spontaneous encounter with her Divine Child. In previous sessions she had done considerable internal work with the Hurt Child.

In this session of internal work I had asked her to go to the child most in need of her. When she found the child, she reported, "This is the first child I ever met in our internal work. This is the child without a face."

I suggested that she ask the child who she is. The child responded, "I don't have a face, because people make fun of me. I quit having a face so people wouldn't make fun of me."

The client then commented, "The child says that she just crawls inside when people make fun of her. She said she quit coming out because it hurt too bad. She stays in her world all the time. She gets what she needs there."

As the session continued, it became clear that this child was the original self, the Divine Child. The child had been brought into a family that did not respect her and would not attend to her emotional needs. This Divine Child found it necessary to go within, to hide in the internal world. Once she hid within, a different child emerged. This child, who took all of the very early pain, was herself replaced by several other Hurt Children who reflected emotional wounding later on in life. Now that all of these Hurt Children had been reclaimed and healed of their wounds, through several sessions of Internal Work, the original Divine Child reemerged—still hiding somewhat, but nevertheless revealing herself to the ego.

At the end of the session, the client reported, "We're being real quiet and soft. We've been playing ring-around-the-rosy. Kurt seems to feel this is it." (Kurt is a positive masculine presence in the internal world of this woman and a source of great gentleness, strength, and wisdom.) The final comment before the woman returned from her internal work was, "She is taking me back through bad times. We're dismantling the fear there."

This was, for the woman, the most profound turning point in her entire therapeutic process. She owned her Divine Child, but it could not have happened if she had not first dealt with the pain of all the hurt little ones inside.

In another client the Divine Child existed simultaneously with the Hurt Child. Sometimes the agenda for internal work involved the needs of the Hurt Child. In this case, the client would invite the Hurt Child to direct the journey and take the client back into unresolved traumas or repressed feelings.

On other occasions, the Divine Child would take the lead in the internal work, taking the client into an experience bursting with light, beauty, colors, music, and play, inviting her to taste her true beauty, giving her hope and the courage to face her childhood wounds waiting to be encountered in future sessions.

The Divine Child is simple and unsophisticated. It would fit very nicely into a hunter-gatherer tribal context. Unfortunately, the Divine Child does not fit so well into contemporary Western culture. In fact, in many families in this culture, it does not fit at all. By the time a person is between five and seven years old, and frequently long before then, the child comes to realize that the ways of the Divine Child are no longer welcome in the external world. In order to protect it from the destructive demands of the external world, the Divine Child is hidden in an internal space in which it continues to live—vibrant, joyful, powerful, but hidden—as a gift once glimpsed, but now enclosed in a secret part of the psyche, of which the ego is unaware and can no longer readily access. This withdrawal of the Divine Child has been described as the moment when the light goes out in the child's eyes.

The Divine Child is not a fantasy or wishful thinking. It is certainly not a form of irresponsible, regressive self-delusion. The Divine Child is an individual's highest potential manifested in the form of a child. It is an authentic part of the psyche, revealing who the person truly is to the degree that the ego is willing to accept. Bennett Braun, a leading theorist in the study of dissociative identity disorder (DID) during the 1980s, said in reference to the "original personality" or Divine Child in *Treatment of Multiple Personality Disorder*, "The original personality is often difficult to locate and work with, but this needs to be done to achieve a stable and lasting integration" (xiv). By "integration" Braun is referring to a person in whom all of the facets of the psyche function in a harmonious unity that is an adult reflection of the original self.

The Divine Child can be thought of as potential, insofar as the external world is concerned, because it is so rarely expressed. In the internal world, the Divine Child is intact and powerfully real. In fact, it is the ego that is a largely fabricated entity. In right order, the ego should be a constantly receptive potential that is enlivened and formed by the ground or truth that lives in the Divine Child.

Given a genuine opportunity and appropriate safety, the Divine Child will gladly come forward, graciously accepting the invitation to return to the external world. The Divine Child is eager to live not just in the internal world but in the midst of nature and relationships, drinking deeply of the beauty and goodness of life. Those who choose to venture into the hidden depths of the psyche and reclaim the Divine Child are in for an extraordinary treat.

Every human being is very unique. The Divine Child within is even more distinctive than the differences between individuals that can be seen at the level of ego and body. For this reason it is somewhat difficult to describe the Divine Child in general with any precision. It is, by definition, a subjective reality that is never expressed in the same way twice. However, there are some common patterns.

Commonalties I have found in the Divine Child of those who have shared their internal work with me are qualities that are easily observable in healthy young children. These qualities include a strong inclination to live in the present moment, innocence, affection, compassion, playfulness, spontaneity, willing trust, curiosity, and especially joy. The principal hallmark of the Divine Child is a joyful exuberance. Notice how often young children laugh and giggle. They seem to be delighted in life for no obvious reason other than just being alive.

The right brain in young children is much more fully developed than the left brain. Jill Bolte Taylor's experience of consciousness when her left brain was silenced by a stroke is relevant here. Forced by the stroke to live predominantly out of right-brain awareness, she was able to reclaim the perspective of a very young child, before the defenses and disconnection inherent in left-brain thinking had a chance to dominate awareness. In her book, *My Stroke of Insight*, she says,

> If I had to choose one word to describe the feeling I feel at the core of my right mind, I would have to say *joy*. My right mind is thrilled to be alive…If you have lost your ability to experience joy, rest assured the circuitry is still there. It is simply being inhibited by more anxious and/or fearful circuitry (171).

The Divine Child is sensual. It lives in its senses, and it finds life to be a playful adventure to be fully experienced. The Divine Child knows no shame, feels no guilt, and is constantly ready to embrace whatever new experiences might present as gifts.

The Divine Child is spontaneous. It expresses how it feels with a straightforward honesty that has no room for pretense. If it is displeased or angry, this is immediately evident, and passes quickly. What the Divine Child wants, it reaches for. The Divine Child does not establish clear boundaries, enabling it to embrace both the joy and the pain of the other. It is inclined to be naturally affectionate and kind.

The Divine Child emanates a deep goodness. It is also drawn to the good and the beautiful, which it tends to see everywhere. I remember watching my daughters when they were very young. A grasshopper, a blade of grass, or a leaf would captivate them. Sometimes in nature they were very still, just taking it all in, experiencing the day flowing by. Unfortunately these qualities of stillness are often lost by the time children are four or five, replaced by words and naming things. Many people can still capture these early childhood moments when life felt fresh and they were steeped in wonder.

This original Divine Child is never jaded nor bored by life. It has the capacity to sense things as always fresh. It is eagerly open to the changes in life that are constantly occurring. The Divine Child sees the flow of life as a constant unfolding of new gifts. Bored children, who are jaded even though they live in the midst of a plethora of stimulations, are children who have been hurt by the disconnected, detached nature of our culture, what Jung called the Spirit of this Time. They are children who had to shut down and withdraw from a world that had no place for them and that in many instances had become dangerous. Wisely, their original child went underground. The Divine Child knows nothing of their boredom. It is alert, open, and deeply engaged, seeing in the most minute of things a very special beauty that beckons for exploration.

The uninjured Divine Child, trusts naturally in life. With only minimal exposure to the vicious side of existence, the Divine Child feels a deep connection to life. The Divine Child has a sense that life cares about it and invites it into an ecstatic mutual participation. The Divine Child is open to letting life flow through it. There is no need to control, because life is good. The Divine Child does not have to defend against life or channel it into particular goals. Life is that which embraces the Divine Child gently, and therefore the Divine Child feels only a minor need to protect itself.

The undifferentiated oneness that the infant knows with all of its environment, and most especially the mother, is never really broken in the Divine Child. The Divine Child does grow into a fuller sense of its uniqueness, and is capable of perceiving itself as different from the other. However, undergirding that is the knowledge that it has never finally been separated from that which it loves and which loves it.

Unfortunately, in most instances the Divine Child has had to separate itself from the ego and the external world for the sake of its survival. It then rests very deep within because it could not withstand the intrusion of the external world. What the world usually meets instead of the Divine Child is a broken, Hurt Child. The Hurt Child lives according to the dictates of the external world, either fearfully seeking to please or reacting in anger. Moreover, because it hurts to feel, the Hurt Child quickly learns to experience the world through the filter of thinking.

The Divine Child feels no need for pretense. It is simply who it is, transparent to whoever looks upon it. To live in pretense is to live a barricaded life in which a mask stands between the individual and the world. The Divine Child has little use for masks. It feels that it is perfectly fine as it is, and expects others to see that, too. This may seem arrogant, but actually it is an expression of profound self-acceptance. I remember when Karen and I took the train to visit my eldest daughter and her family. Her three-year-old daughter was with her when they picked us up at the station. Shortly after we got in the car, she blurted, "I'll bet you are really glad to get to come see me."

Nearly everyone is longing to reclaim this self-assurance and simplicity, but few of us know how to get back there. How wonderful it would be to live once again as a sensual, compassionate, joyful, and transparent person without any need or desire for pretension. Most people know someone who has never lost touch with the Divine Child and still lives out its qualities in an adult fashion. Most of us, however, have been banished from our core by life, and we don't know how to get back home because we have forgotten the Divine Child who is the way. One of our most fundamental life tasks is to embrace this child and through him or her live in harmony with the Self. As Jung said, "The child…is a mediator, bringer of healing, that is, one who makes whole" (CW 9/1, 164).

The Hurt Child can be considered an expression of what Christianity has called original sin—the brokenness children suffer at the hands of those who should protect them and against which they have no defense, but for which they must pay with their lives. The Divine Child can be considered an expression of original innocence—the living internal expression of the fact that we are born whole, beautiful, and good. Everyone is best served when each has an opportunity to live out that original innocence. If it is lost due to the impact of a destructive external world, salvation is found not by appeasing an angry god, trying to be good, or detaching from the earthly realm, but by reclaiming the very earthy innocence embodied in the Divine Child. No matter what a person may have done with her life, or what may have been done to her throughout her life, she can reclaim her innocence. She can, once more, become genuine—become who she was meant to be. The reason she can reclaim it is that she has never fully lost it. It remains alive within her.

Jesus admonished his followers that if they wished to enter the kingdom of heaven they would have to become as little children. In Zen, *Kensho*, or "seeing into one's true nature," requires that "you show me your original face." Reclaiming the Divine Child is another way of talking about the process of becoming whole. Wholeness is a matter of claiming one's natural inheritance. It is a divine right of human beings to be whom they were born to be. Wholeness simply describes a person in the full and balanced possession of her potential. That potential is not just an abstraction that might or might not be attained. It is an active, present, dynamic reality embodied in the Divine Child. As Carl Jung put it, "The privilege of a life time is to become who you truly are." This will come to pass, not because of new learnings, but through remembering your original truth and relinquishing the false, rigid, controlling assumptions that dominate contemporary life and are mistaken for maturity. A truly mature person is one who uses the left-brain gifts of adult consciousness to protect and encourage the full emergence of the Divine Child.

The Divine Child can be seen as a gold standard to compare one's life against. In general, the Divine Child is very similar from individual to individual: its innocence, its interest in living life in an experiential, sensual fashion, its capacity to live in trust, and its joyfulness and spontaneity are all part of our inborn, natural human endowment. Although those who suffer from profound biogenetic disorders such as autism or schizophrenia may find access more difficult than most, everyone has the potential to approach life with the innocence, simplicity and spontaneity of the Divine Child. Nevertheless, each of us has a very unique way of expressing that potential. This unique style of self-expression can be seen with great clarity in the internal experience of the Divine Child. The Self and its expression in the Divine Child is everyone's private, personal foundation and only worthy life goal.

The Self has one goal - to live fully, grounded internally in ultimate reality on the one hand, and to connect without restriction to the world on the other. The ego is its necessary partner in the embrace of outer reality. Always respecting the ego's autonomy, the Self will guide and nurture the ego as much as the ego will allow, so that everything false is stripped away. What then emerges is the authentic expression of the Self in the world. Although universal in its fundamental aspects, such as compassion, equanimity, sensitivity to beauty, vitality, and intuitive awareness, the expression of the Self will be colored by the unique combination of gifts and limitations in each individual. The Divine Child is the principal way the Self reminds us of this ultimate destiny that both awaits us and already exists within us, patiently beckoning the ego's willing embrace. Whatever form the Self takes—Inner Wisdom, loving Great Mother, or innocent Divine Child—they all serve this one purpose.

Recently, a client had a powerful internal journey that clearly embodies what I have been describing.

The experience began quite slowly. The woman, whom I will call Denise, could feel a deep, persistent resistance. With much support from the Self, helping her more fully access a sense of peace and resolve, she was finally able to open her heart and mind. The Self, which Denise experiences as the presence of God within, told her, "You've been very receptive to me for others. Will you now look inside your mind and allow yourself to know what's going on in there?"

Denise said that it looked like a bunch of dark corridors, as in an abandoned building. There was the sense of a secret. She saw a little girl holding a Chatty Cathy doll in an empty, gray room with no color. It had a window, and there was light in the room. Denise told the little girl that she wasn't supposed to be there and then asked her somewhat gruffly what she wanted. Denise felt angry and a little afraid of what the child might say.

The Self told Denise, "This little girl represents the heart and mind connection. It will be clearer after this is completed." Denise's chest felt heavy. She took the child's hand. The Self said, "I'm sorry your head and heart are exploding right now."

The child said that her name was Denise. Denise said that she wasn't happy to hear it, but figured that was the case. The child explained, "I'm here for one reason. I care about you. A long time ago there was a you not like the you of today. I'm like the original template of how you were created before things were dark and trusts were betrayed." This made Denise cry. The little girl continued, "You've done a pretty good job dealing with everything [Denise's childhood abuse and its ramifications in her life]. There wasn't a lot I could do about it."

At this point Denise became quite distressed and told God (i.e., the Self), "You made me defective!" She then began to cry on his shoulder.

God replied, "You are just angry about all that transpired. And your weight gain is just another way to destroy who you really are. You are being eaten up inside by all the lies." Denise then said that she was tired and decided to lie down.

The child began to take care of her. She put a warm cloth on her forehead and covered her with a blanket. Then the child started to explain who she was. "I've witnessed everything. I've experienced it with you. I'm just not affected by it. It all gets processed through you."

Denise asked her, "Why were you in that gray room with that doll?"

She said, "You would have been threatened if I had presented as a grown version of you. I am how you have seen yourself be with other people, but haven't allowed yourself to acknowledge for a long time."

Denise commented, "When I talk about things like this I get scared and embarrassed. I do not want to take any more chances. This seems like a lie compared to how I feel in the outside world. All I can really hope for is to try to be good and not injure other people. I must keep everything under control and not screw any more things up."

God responded, "What you are saying is self-hatred, self-loathing."

Denise replied, "This part said she could come inside me. She said she could meet me where I look all gray. I don't deserve her."

God answered, "Nobody does. Can you believe that you were created in the image of God, that this is your original template?"

Denise asked, "How will this change things?"

God said, "It just will."

The part that originally presented as the child then said, "I am all your strength, your goodness, and your purity. I am your compassion, your gratitude, your joy, your humor, and your generosity. I am your spark, your energy. I am your wisdom and your intelligence. I am your patience and your acceptance. I am your willingness, your openness, and your stillness. I am your connection with God. I am your soul, and you are meeting me for the first time. Your heart and mind have to be of one accord to allow for my emergence.

"Think about it. Think of all the years you have tried to access your soul and how you have written about this. I am your soul. Every soul is a template, an unmarred image of the God who created us in his image. Through me you can live in your truth, accessing all the energies of heart, mind, and body. You can be authentic and open. God can flow through you unfiltered.

God said, "That little girl sitting in the room by herself with just her dolly was the only thing that would allow you to access me.

"At your deepest self you are loving, and you cannot stand for people to feel isolated, excluded, or abandoned."

Denise said, "This feels peaceful. It feels right. If you come inside me, I feel like I would love you. It took me so long to find you today. I'm excited, although I don't know what to do with it."

God told Denise, "You have been praying for wisdom for a long time. You have knowledge about me. You know that you were created in my image and that you have a soul. You want to be good and loving. For a long time you have been asking how to put the puzzle together."

Denise then asked, "What is the benefit of this healing for others?"

God replied, "It is not just to be free. The point of all this is to grow in wisdom. Your soul is your source of wisdom. It is where you and I meet. Wisdom is not the same as knowledge. It is the deepest level of intimacy, reciprocity, and exchange. It is the seat of understanding. Today is about you believing in your ability to love and that your soul is where God resides and emanates through you.

"This is an unfathomable truth: I make my home in you. Eternal life, which is being eternally with me, does exist, here on earth, in the deep intimacy of your own soul. Any wounding or harm cannot taint it. I will not be harmed. You will not be penetrated at the level of your soul. You will push out your egocentricities at a level that is inconceivable to you. Your soul has no need for them. This is the state of 'being' I promised many weeks ago."

Denise responded, "This is an offer I cannot refuse. Like Mary in the Bible, my answer is, 'Be it done to me according to your will.' It is not that my soul must step into me. I must discard the gray form that held my body, mind, and heart and take them to the place where I was created. I must leave behind the shell. I must not put new wine into an old-wine skin. My soul is color and vitality. As I walk toward God, all of that goes under the skin. It looks like me. I thank God for leading me here, and I hug him."

Denise then asked God, "Why did today's session take so long?"

God told her, "You had to know the truth about your ego. It is driven by the need for self-protection. It wants to kill your hopes and dreams. You couldn't leave it behind, but it couldn't exist in the land of never-been. It was constructed by you for protection, not by me. Your soul has been with you all this time, but it was overpowered by ego and self-protection.

"The soul will power your human gifts. It is the generator that fuels your system and allows these gifts to explode in creativity and potential. Morning, midday, and evening, acknowledge, reconnect, and keep the channels open.

"I reside in every soul, ready to respond and guide, always protecting. I love you. I anoint you. I anoint your hands, mind, and heart and send you into the world. Go in peace."

Denise knelt briefly and said, "Thank you."

She walked back to the tree and noticed that it was full of energy that shone with a white outline. She realized that the whole tree was God's presence. She also realized that "the land of never-been" was her soul. It was the place she had never known about, but which had always been there. She said, "Wisdom and understanding are the greatest gifts. With wisdom we can offer love."

After returning from the internal work, Denise said, "Today I am making a conscious decision. Ego is not an option. Surrender is the only authentic form of life. Everything else is construct, pretense, defense, and justification. It's not about being good. This is beyond good. It's about being honest about who we are. I was given a good template, and I am capable of responding in this way."

The first step in reclaiming the Divine Child is a matter of honestly appraising your life as you live it now so that you might make an effective comparison between your present life and the nature of the Divine Child. Wherever there is discrepancy, it will point to the need for personal work.

The second step in embracing the Divine Child is a willingness to become more like the Divine Child in everyday behavior. Becoming real means relinquishing socially approved goals and external supports that the individual, and perhaps everyone she knows, holds in very high regard. The Divine Child may delight in the simple joys of nature much more than in the adult kind of pleasure that comes from owning a fancy car or maintaining a particular social status. The Divine Child may find it very burdensome to fulfill the requirements necessary to make a large income. It may prefer living simply and having sufficient time to play. Moreover, it will be inclined to be very nonjudgmental. If the individual is willing to align herself with the Divine Child, she may find herself also in alliance with people whom everyone else finds easy to reject. She may also be rejected herself.

Owning the Divine Child, one's basic inheritance, may cost a great deal. If the ego is unwilling to accept the potential cost, there is no point in even meeting the Divine Child. Such an encounter would only set up a painful kind of discrepancy that would not go anywhere. Ego willingness is essential. However, even if the ego is willing, that may not be enough. A person may have honestly looked at her life and the ways it is discrepant from her Divine Child. She may be very willing to live out of the Divine Child, even if it costs her externally. But when she attempts to do so, she repeatedly fails. She may prize the openness and innocence, yet not be able to drop her defenses. She may want to trust, but cannot—absolutely cannot—and when encountering anything the least bit different or strange, may hide in panic. She may be very angry or profoundly sad, and be unable to do anything about it. In these instances, willingness and honesty are simply insufficient. They are prerequisites for finding the Divine Child, but by themselves they cannot overcome the wounds that life has inflicted.

CHAPTER FIVE

The Hurt Child

Many people have been hurt in a profound fashion by life. All the honesty and willingness they can muster will not be sufficient to overcome their scars. In such cases, much effort and energy must be put into healing the Hurt Child so that the ego has the capacity to become open to the presence of the Divine Child. Aside from the Self and the ego, the most significant aspect of the psyche with regard to psychological healing is the Hurt Child.

The Hurt Child is, in many ways, the only path to the capacity for living as the Divine Child. Paradoxically, to embrace joy, spontaneity, innocence, and true freedom, the ego must first embrace pain, fear, deep hurt, and the many dissociated experiences that have had the power to hide the Divine Child and crush one's spirit. Hurts must be owned, felt, and responded to before the ego can accept the natural gift embodied in the Divine Child. For some the accumulated impact of continual childhood stress and even terror will so disorder the brain's natural mechanisms for modulating fear that even after intensive, effective therapy, the person will need the help of antianxiety medications and a nonstressful lifestyle in order to maintain balance. Within those constraints, however, the person can still live out of the Divine Child's energy.

Most who engage in internal work will encounter various versions of the Hurt Child, usually at different ages. Fear and shame tend to be the predominant emotions of the child, although for some anger may be the principal affect. Clients typically have a wide range of reactions to the Hurt Child. There will usually be some compassion, but more often than not it will be mixed with revulsion, judgment, and fear. Once a person

74

encounters the Hurt Child through internal work, it quickly becomes clear that this aspect of the psyche has been driving many of the dysfunctional emotions, behaviors, and attitudes that have often been a heavy burden throughout the person's life.

Many people's initial reaction to the Hurt Child is an understandable desire just to get rid of this crippling aspect of the psyche. The Self, however, will never permit this. The Hurt Child or children must be accepted, understood, and allowed to be themselves and tell their story. The stories may be very painful to hear and at least in part will probably be unknown to the ego. Through this process of loving acceptance and with the guidance of the Self, the Hurt Child can be relieved of its burden and reintegrated as a positive force in the life of the psyche. Once brought to light and integrated, the patterns of self-destructive thoughts, feelings, and behaviors that had formerly controlled the ego will fade in intensity and become areas open to choices grounded in a more mature sense of appropriate self-care.

The following client experiences of the Hurt Child help show how the Self guides and supports the ego in being a central resource for healing the Hurt Child.

Eve

Eve had a long history of abuse, both at home, primarily from her mother, and at school from other children. The profound insecurity that she felt because of the distorted relationship with her mother caused her to be a very anxious child, and therefore a ready target for the more aggressive or angry children at school.

Recently in her therapy, she was told by her Self to once more review in detail the suffering that she had undergone in school. She was told she needed to reclaim these memories because she had previously dissociated them, and in doing so had lost touch with many of her important feelings. So Eve carefully reviewed each of the major forms of abuse or rejection that she had experienced within the school context.

Having brought that back to mind, and feeling once more the pain of it, she was then left with the dilemma of what to do with the material. I suggested that we go through my regular procedure in which the ego is the central agent of healing. Eve was adamant that she was not up to the task of supporting her hurt child. For the ego to go back and support the child, it is assumed that the ego has matured beyond the pain of the child and can offer a certain amount of balance and perspective, as well as the strength needed to protect the child.

In the case of this client, that simply was not so. At twenty-six, she was still caught up in fear and panic, almost as much as when she was a little girl. To go back to the school as the ego accompanying the child through the abuse would simply mean that they would both be terrorized. This would make things worse rather than better.

I accepted her hesitation, and we let the matter sit for a little while. Eve then had an intuition that proved to be the key for unlocking the healing process. Over the last year or two, she had nurtured a relationship with the divine in which the divine presented itself to her as the Goddess. The Goddess was perceived by Eve as her true mother, in contradistinction to the client's biological mother, who differed from the Goddess at almost every point.

The intuition she had was that she needed to reenter the school with her twenty-six-year-old consciousness, but with a totally different self-perception. Rather than going into the school as the daughter of her biological mother, she decided to return to the school environment as the daughter of the Goddess. This she did. The following are her own words describing an active imagination experience in which she began the process of healing her childhood wounds within the school environment.

"I was at the edge of the schoolyard with the Goddess, going to kindergarten. She led me into the classroom and left me there, but I could feel her watching everything. I was four, but with most of the intelligence of my twenty-six-year-old ego. I was really nervous about being there, but not having a full anxiety attack. It kept going through my head, 'Just remember who you are.' I knew that no one else there knew of my 'bloodline,' but I knew.

"Then the boy was there, pinching me. This made me even more nervous. I didn't know what to do. I knew he was after attention. To tell the teacher would give him attention and he would continue to do it. To ignore him would only make him see me as a challenge, and he would still continue. I considered punching him out, but that would get me in trouble, too. I wanted him to stop. But how? Then I sort of froze the action and considered, 'What is the appropriate response?' And then it came to me: 'I am her daughter. As her daughter, I have available very special abilities.' So I created a small force field around me, sort of like an electric fence. Anyone who tried to pinch me would get mildly zapped. And I pretended to be totally oblivious to what was happening to him.

"This created for my social personality a mysterious but innocent aura. Not dangerous as such, or labeled evil—just, 'Who are you, really?' That sort of thing. Someone not to mess with, as far as being mean to, because it will mysteriously backfire.

"Then I sat in class, coloring and such. I could hear this voice, almost like some sort of tutor, explaining to me that I should be proud of my bloodline. Therefore, I should not walk around with my head down, as though inferior. I should hold my head high. Not superior, either. Just proud of who I am— the daughter of the Goddess herself. And I could feel her physical beauty in me, in my eyes, and in the softness of my face. And I sat there working, feeling strong, and basically secure, feeling pretty, divinely pretty.

"I didn't feel strong and secure in the sense that 'I'm the daughter of the Goddess, and if you hurt me she will defend me.' There was a sense of being able to defend and take care of myself, because of who I was.

"I felt like I had the energy and the ability to really hurt people, like I had special powers. But being her daughter had taught me to do things gently and not to act in aggression. What I did do only hurt, and only mildly hurt, those who were aggressive toward me.

"Now I have a foundation from which to work my way through the rest of the years in school. A foundation of strength and self-esteem and beauty, and the ability to defend myself against my attackers."

Eve did this active imagination or internal work on her own, with the help of the Goddess and without any intervention or support on my part. The two following case studies are examples of internal work in which I played an active role. They represent fairly typical therapeutic work with the Hurt Child.

Fred

Fred was twenty-six years old when he entered therapy. He had had three and a half years of business experience as an insurance salesman, and had spent four years in the army prior to that. During Fred's military service, he had completed about two years of college.

Fred's reason for entering therapy was anxiety. He experienced panic while making sales calls, and the panic seemed to be escalating.

Working in sales had never been easy, Fred stated. But "few things in life were." Over the last year, Fred had met a young woman he really cared for, and was thinking of getting married. This caused him to take a new look at his career and earning potential. With the prospect of supporting a family, Fred, more than ever, felt it incumbent to succeed.

He had tried very hard to talk himself out of the anxiety and panic he felt before making a sales call. He had also worked with several self-help books, tapes, and deep breathing exercises. He had even been through biofeedback training. None of it had seemed to work, however, so Fred had concluded he should seek out a professional counselor.

Fred was very interested in and responsive to the idea of internal work and the Self. The concept of a whole world waiting inside strongly appealed to Fred, and reminded him of an interest he had had earlier in his life regarding fantasy and science fiction. Fred approached the process of internal work with anticipation.

Soon Fred discovered that his internal world was not interested in helping him become a more effective salesman. The internal world had its own agenda and direction. This increased Fred's panic attacks. He was at a crossroads. He either had to delve more deeply into the truth offered from within, stop counseling altogether, or seek a form of therapy more supportive of the goals he had chosen at the ego level. Fred decided to commit to the course of therapy before him.

When he first encountered the Inner Child, the child was sitting in a park, listening to the birds, and reading a science fiction book. The child experienced the adult Fred as something of an intrusion. Once the child learned the adult Fred also liked science fiction, a rapport was established, and the child was willing to lead him back into the past. Fred discovered great differences between who he was as a child and how he was functioning as an adult.

Fred's Inner Child displayed a love for music. As a child he was delighted when his mother offered lessons on the piano, as well as on grandmother's violin. Other kids in the neighborhood seemed to gripe about music practice time, but for Fred as a child, those moments were pure pleasure. Playing music offered him a sense of elation. Joy flowed through Fred as he touched the piano keys or ran his bow across the violin strings.

Fred's father was not so pleased at his son's musical interests. Fred's father was currently in upper-level management at the insurance company where Fred worked. He had been an insurance salesman while Fred was growing up. His father wanted his son to display more "masculine" interests, such as football, soccer, arm wrestling, and Scouts.

Fred was not muscular and large like his father. He had a slender frame, similar to his mother. Fred's father, according to the child, seemed to feel Fred simply needed encouragement or, more correctly, harassment, in order to get going and be a "real boy."

The adult Fred had come to accept that he couldn't ever be what his father wanted. Fred learned through the Hurt Child his true nature was almost in direct opposition to what his father wanted. Fred's talents and gifts did not lie in the area of sports. As a child, he had displayed strong verbal skills and been a good reader, imaginative, and very adept at playing musical instruments.

Fred saw incident after incident from his childhood internally as his Child tried to model what the father demanded. The Child joined the father in a Scouting program, but hated all the trips and noisy sessions with other little boys. The Hurt Child showed Fred times when his father would bring other salesmen to the house and laughingly call Fred into the room in order to force the boy to arm wrestle with one of the adult men. The salesmen and his father would jeer, laugh, and cajole the boy. They presented this sport as a form of play for him, but the child felt shame and ridicule. As an adult, Fred could see how callous this behavior was.

Fred's Child felt convinced that if he'd just try harder, he'd finally make it. He'd finally get it right. When Fred went out for football in high school, he spent more time sitting on the bench than he did out on the field. His fine motor coordination on the piano and the violin was outstanding; his motor coordination on the football or soccer field seemed abominable. The

Hurt Child, as a teenager, died a thousand deaths every time the coach chewed him out for his clumsiness or his teammates made fun of him.

Fred's mother had been supportive of his love of music, but she did not encourage his interest in science fiction and fantasy. His mother, being a very religious woman, felt Fred's time would be better spent reading the Bible or other spiritual books.

As it reviewed family history, what the child showed Fred was that, to his father, Fred would never be man enough to measure up; to his mother, he would never be religious enough or good enough to measure up. He explained to Fred that he had bought so completely into the father's interpretation of what a man should be that it was why they decided to join the army upon completion of high school. Following four years in the service, Fred decided to enter sales in his father's firm. The Child would have rather played the piano or the violin, or worked in a bookstore or library.

Fred recalled that when he completed his last year of high school, he talked to his father briefly, timidly, about the possibility of a career in music or library science. The suggestion was met with resounding laughter and derision on his father's part. "Why would you want to do something like that, when you could enter sales and earn big money?" the father demanded.

Fred admitted there was logic to what his father was saying. He wanted his father's approval and he did want to succeed. He hoped that with maturity and experience he could finally measure up to his father's standards.

The Child told Fred very bluntly, "Get out of sales! Move to a different state from where your father lives!" The Child wanted Fred to spend four hours a day playing music, and at least a couple hours a day reading books or perusing bookstores. The adult Fred felt deeply frightened. His father's message about who he should be seemed absolute. It was the only thing he'd ever truly believed in. Could he now, after hearing the child's story, completely turn his life around? Could he allow himself to become internally directed for the first time in twenty-six years? Could he make a stand against his father and embrace the truth of his Hurt Child?

Fred is still struggling with freeing himself of these messages from his father's and mother's introjections. He quit his job in sales and now works in a small bookstore. The young woman he became so serious about is still an active part of his life, and they plan to get married.

Alice

Alice came into therapy complaining of massive bouts of depression. She described herself as introverted and shy. Her periods of depression seemed to be increasing both in time and scope.

Alice had never been to a counselor before. She felt people should handle problems by themselves, or with the help of friends or family. Alice now found friends and family weren't enough to pull her through. There were days when she could barely get out of bed or take her children to school or get herself to work. She would find herself during lunch hours falling into tears over the computer. Occasionally, during the late afternoon, she would need to leave her desk, go to the bathroom, and cry.

Alice said she had a very good marriage. Her husband was stable and responsible. She had two children, who were above-average achievers, and two pets. Alice believed she had an ideal family. Why should she be depressed, she wondered?

Soon after the crying spells began, Alice went to see the family doctor. He told her these emotions might be due to early menopause and a hormonal imbalance. She took test after test and tried numerous medications. The doctor and Alice both concluded the problem was not going to respond to standard medical treatment. Alice's physician suggested she seek the help of a psychotherapist.

Alice didn't know where to begin to find a psychotherapist. She timidly asked one of the secretaries in the building if she knew of someone who could help with depression. From this conversation, Alice had received a referral, as well as sympathy.

Alice spent her first few therapy sessions trying to explain why she shouldn't or didn't need to be in therapy: her family life was comfortable, her children were well behaved, her husband was a better person than the husbands of many other women she was acquainted with, and so forth. Why, then, couldn't she shake this sadness?

It was not until the third session that Alice was willing to do internal work. At first her contact with the Self was tenuous. She thought she saw a light, maybe, or maybe she didn't. As soon as she tried to make a connection with the light, it faded. Alice's communication with the Self did increase as she continued to do internal work.

Her first journey to meet the Hurt Child was powerful. It was temporarily devastating to her. The story that she had told herself, and her therapist, was that she had had a very happy childhood and loving parents. Money had not always been plentiful, but she had not really wanted for anything. Alice's Hurt Child, however, painted a different picture. The Child was discovered balled up in a knot, crying under a tree. It was two sessions before the child was even willing to talk to Alice.

While Alice had not been the victim of an alcoholic home or physical or sexual abuse, she nevertheless had been molded and distorted to fit the family's values and needs.

Alice had a sister, Betty, who was four years older than her, and a brother, Tom, who was one and a half years older. When Alice had been a very little girl, she and Tom had been great playmates.

The Child showed Alice how she and Tom had both enjoyed the outdoors and other pastimes, such as riding bicycles, roller skating, going to the creek, building forts, and playing cowboys and Indians. Alice fit in very well with Tom's friends. They did not really think that it was strange for a girl to be playing with them, even one who was younger. If Tom's friends were hesitant in the beginning, after they saw that Alice could run, wrestle, and ride her bike as well as they could, they quickly forgot their reservations.

The Hurt Child emphasized that Alice and her brother were quite different from their sister, Betty. Betty was always very neat, fastidious in her dress, and extroverted. Betty was highly popular with children in school. Alice's Child reminded her of the shyness she experienced in the school setting. This was quite different from playing with the boys. Alice always looked at her older sister with wonder. The Child did not like the shyness she felt at school, and hoped one day it would go away. The Child hoped that with age she might become more like Betty.

She was frequently told by both her mother and her father of Betty's successes, Betty's prettiness, and what a wonderful man Betty would finally meet and marry. This caused the Internal Child pain and tremendous self-doubt. The Child showed Alice that by the age of seven she had decided that what it meant to be a girl, in the ideal sense, was to look and act like Betty. She did not feel like Betty, however. Being tidy was a bore and a bother. The Child complained to the adult Alice, how could she be tidy and build a fort? How could she be tidy and make wooden boats, or wade in the creek?

The Child showed Alice another important interest she had: animals. Alice could always help other children teach their pets tricks. Whenever one of the pets was hurt, Alice seemed to know what to do to make it feel better.

When Alice was eight years old, her mother spent increasing periods of time in bed, complaining of headaches and low energy. The Child told Alice she did not like this, and it scared her. Beginning at this time, Alice's mother started to complain that she needed help doing housework and preparing meals. Even though Alice was young, it was clear she had great energy and was quick at learning things. Alice's mother said that it would therefore be easier for her to step in and lend a hand, rather than Betty, who was so busy in after-school activities. The Child expressed to adult Alice how angry she was about this, and how unfair she felt it was.

Soon Alice had to tell Tom and his friends she did not have time for play. Her mother needed her. When Alice came home from school, there was usually a list of chores awaiting her attention. The child Alice retreated into fantasy, where she was queen and had lots of servants to wait on her. She felt too guilty about being angry at her mother to express it much. As the adult Alice learned, most of this anger was denied and repressed. When Alice was not doing chores, her mother wanted company while she watched soap operas.

Alice was told repeatedly that her mother really was sick. Her father reinforced this message daily. The Inner Child told adult Alice she had wished desperately to be Betty. Not only was Betty pretty, tidy, and popular, but she did not have to work. These thoughts made the child Alice feel guilty and ashamed.

The periods when her mother had migraine headaches came and went throughout Alice's growing up, but the pattern of Alice coming home from school, preparing dinner, doing laundry, and in general taking care of the family persisted. She only got relieved of her duties when she went to live in a college dorm.

When Alice was a sophomore in college, she met a nice young man who seemed to care for her very much. He was completing his junior year and said that if she would be willing to drop out of school and go to work, they could get an apartment and be married right away. He said he would help her finish her degree later, of course. Alice did not really have a career goal after graduation, so this seemed like a good idea.

Although she and her husband talked about her returning to finish her education, she never did. She started having babies instead. Alice's husband became a reasonably successful accountant, and Alice began a ten-year career as a secretary. When Alice encountered her young adult self during internal work, she told her that she felt resentment and anger toward her husband for pursuing his life goals, and for seemingly crushing her in the process. She felt like the childhood theme had been played out all over again. Her husband, like Betty, got to do what he pleased, while she got to take care of the family and chores. She showed Alice what a deep level of resentment she had always felt about the whole process.

Alice's Inner Child began to teach her that the depression she was experiencing as an adult was directly linked to the child's despair. Alice's natural gifts suited her well to be a veterinarian or botanist, but her interest in and love of the outdoors had been squelched during growing up. Now this interest only found expression on occasional family camping trips. At the age of thirty-five, Alice felt totally dead inside. Most of her potential, revealed in her Divine Child, was overwhelmingly rejected by first her family and then her husband. Repeating the early pattern, Alice had chosen a man who, like her mother, expected her to live her life to meet his needs.

Alice's healing is taking place through a slow process of recovering her latent gifts. She has decided to return to college and then attend veterinarian school. Alice has applied for a grant to help with finances and has told her husband she will only work part-time at her secretarial job. His response, at first, was resentment, but now he is trying to be supportive. Alice's children are eight and nine years old, and fairly self-sufficient. The marriage is on shaky ground, but Alice is determined to continue with her plans. She is committed to the process of allowing her authentic nature to live within the external world at last.

CHAPTER SIX

The Way of the Self

Despite the Self's ready availability and the fact that its gifts fulfill our heart's deepest desires for love and an authentic life, it is largely unknown and unwelcome in contemporary culture. Its existence and its message are a radical challenge to Western society and to most people's sense of who they are. Accepting the gift of the Self's guidance leads to healing and the most meaningful, joyful life possible. It comes, however, at the cost of facing unknown, threatening truths about ourselves, relinquishing our personal stories and self-definitions, and learning to live an open-hearted, flexible, ever forgiving life in which the fear-driven grip of tight control is released. For many this is too much to ask, and they persist, as I did, in clinging to an egocentric, fear-based life of emptiness and suffering. Being freed from this can feel like a kind of dying—a loss of all one has known and one's way of being in the world.

The way of the Self is also a threat to Western culture in general. Core assumptions that define the West are that wealth is the hallmark of success, being in control is a highly esteemed competency, analytical thought is the only reliable source of knowledge, and the ego is the central organizing force of the psyche. The existence of the Self and the reality it reveals undermines all of these. It is no wonder, then, that even though the great treasure and our heart's desire is within us and all around us, we are repeatedly told not to see. We are also afraid of what we accurately intuit would be the disruptive impact of seeing and accepting this wise, loving, and healing internal presence.

In my experience of myself and with clients, the Self is characterized by five qualities.

1. It is always carefully observing you, and it knows you at every level, from the inside out. The range of its awareness is far greater than the ego's and not compromised by any of the ego's defense mechanisms. It can be relied on to know your truth and to share it with you if you are able and willing to hear it.

2. Despite all that it knows about you, there is never any sense of judgment or shame. Whatever you may have done or thought about doing, it welcomes you with compassion and understanding. It knows what has driven your choices better than you do and only wants you to have the fullest life possible. This may require making amends, offering restitution, etc., but even in this it will stand by you as a kind, supportive friend.

3. However distorted, broken, or disfigured you may be at the ego level, the Self knows who you really are beyond that. It sees and has actively preserved the wondrous beauty of your original, authentic self. Even though you may have forgotten who you are, it has never been lost. The Self has a profound appreciation for who you are at the most fundamental level and wants nothing more than to help what is most authentic within you emerge and flourish.

4. I have seen the love the Self feels for the person shown in many ways. Sometimes it will embrace the person in a healing light or golden warmth, as happened just today with a client. Other times it will communicate with a quality of tenderness and respect that will melt away fear and shatter the ego's defenses. Frequently it will present in the guise of a Divine Mother who wants nothing more than to embrace and encompass you with love and wipe away your tears.

5. The Self never aims to control you. You are always free to refuse its gifts or guidance. When you decline its guidance or support and suffer the inevitable consequence of your choice, it is there to encourage you and renew its guidance if you are willing to listen. If the truth it is seeking to share with you is important and you are unable or unwilling to hear it, it may take extraordinary steps to get your attention, such as causing powerful dreams or intuitive flashes that cannot be ignored. Nevertheless, it is always your choice, and you will never need to fear judgment. Instead it will be there to help you pick up the pieces and learn from the outcome of your poor decisions.

The Self's qualities are precisely those that an infant needs from the mother in order to thrive. They are the foundation of what John Bowlby, Mary Ainsworth, and more recently, Allan Schore describe as secure attachment, which both enables the emergence of the child's authentic self and is necessary for optimal neurological development.

David Richo in his book *How to be an Adult in Love* identifies the fundamental qualities of secure attachment as the essence of unconditional love, summarizing them as the five As: 1) Attention given to the infant as opposed to the mother's being preoccupied with her own needs and interests, 2) Acceptance as opposed to criticism or judgment, 3) Appreciation as opposed to indifference, 4) Affection as opposed to disconnection, and 5) Allowing as opposed to controlling.

The need for these qualities is as important as the need for food or shelter. Without them we will not thrive as infants, and may not even survive. As adults, without these elements of secure attachment life feels empty and meaningless; it is as though there is a hole in our soul that we desperately try to fill or ignore by all manner of addictions and distractions.

As young children, we need a loving caregiver to offer these qualities. If this is not present, most will feel driven throughout their lives to seek an external other that can give them what the mother or original caregiver could not. Since this is highly unlikely between adults over the long term, relationships driven by this need usually end up in quiet disappointment or worse. So it is almost unbelievably good news that this unconditional love is and has always been a constant presence in our depth and is so readily available. Even if our caregivers in infancy or early childhood were not able to give us the love we needed, it can still be accessed from within. The hole can be filled. The need can be met even if it has never been satisfied before.

In his essay "Rediscovering Fire," Bill Miller, the founder of Motivational Interviewing (commonly considered to be the most effective counseling methodology currently available), states clearly that agape or unconditional love is the most powerful catalyst for change that exists. When a counselor is able to be with a client in a way that expresses the five qualities of unconditional love (attention, acceptance, appreciation, affection, and allowing), constructive change and healing become real options. Reflecting the counselor's stance, clients may begin to respond to themselves in a similar fashion. Even more importantly, having experienced what this love is like, they may become receptive to the experience of it from their own depth, the Self.

I know that the phenomenon of the Self is real, as I have described it, because I have witnessed it unfold in the lives of hundreds of clients over the past thirty-five years, as well as in my own life. With the possible exception of Richard Schwartz, PhD (the founder of internal family systems therapy), I do not know of any therapists who engage the Self as extensively as I do in the therapeutic process. Nevertheless, there are many with the best of credentials who acknowledge its reality and importance.

Carl Jung's life was transformed by his encounters with what he called the Self over several years through the use of active imagination. He spent significant amounts of time being instructed by Philemon, who was a personification of the Self. He initially encountered Philemon in a dream and then in his active imagination experiences. He later said that everything he taught subsequent to that time was merely an elaboration of what he had been taught by that figure. The Italian psychiatrist Roberto Assagioli, who was a contemporary of Jung, was also aware of the Self and how important it could be. He called it the Higher Self.

Many modern therapists and scholars also embrace this reality and encourage clients to be open to its healing presence. These include many who work with DID (Dissociative Identity Disorder) clients, who often exhibit a unique internal presence (the ISH or Inner Self Helper that I referred to at the beginning of chapter one) that is not an alternate personality, but is deeply aware of all the parts, their needs and proclivities, and what steps need to be taken for healing and fusion to occur. John and Helen Watkins developed a psychotherapeutic method for clients in general they call "Ego States Therapy," which was derived from their experience with MPD clients and which acknowledges and utilizes the Higher Self. Jeffrey Schwartz, MD, who is widely recognized for having developed the most effective treatment methodology available for OCD (Obsessive Compulsive Disorder), writes explicitly in his book *You Are Not Your Brain* about the importance of maintaining an active relationship with the Wise Self as a central ingredient in the healing process. Ian McGilchrist, MD, one of the world's most widely respected psychiatric scholars, describes right-brain consciousness and intelligence in ways that strongly echo the perspective and values of the Deep Self. Allan Schore, MD, one of America's premier psychiatric researchers, strongly seconds McGilchrist's insights in his book *The Science of the Art of Psychotherapy*.

In his book written in 1980, *LSD Psychotherapy*, Stanislav Grof, MD, observed that when ego controls are removed through psychedelic medication, a deep intelligence guides clients through powerful, carefully structured internal experiences designed to expand awareness, foster healing, and enhance the emergence of a mystical spirituality. New research into the use of psychedelics is demonstrating eeven more conclusively than ever that when the ego releases control and is willing to listen, another intelligence takes over that is capable and willing to help the person find healing, wholeness, and a life-altering spiritual consciousness.

I recently took ayahuasca (a psychedelic developed by indigenous South American tribes) on two occasions when I participated in religious services offered by a local branch of the Church of Santo Daime. My hope was that this would help me have the same kind of ecstatic, mystical experience that so many others who have taken ayahuasca describe. This did not happen. Instead, I was given a flow of awareness that I did not expect and would never have predicted. Even though what I was given was not what I expected, it was definitely what I needed. There is no way my experience could be explained as some sort of wish fulfillment or any kind of ego-controlled phenomenon. It is obvious to me that something very wise and caring was eager to help me once I released ego control.

The first experience began with feeling intoxicated, as if I had had a couple glasses of wine. I was feeling cheerful and enjoying the music. Then the insights began to flow. These are my notes following the experience:

> I have never forgiven my mother, who apparently suffered from postpartum depression, for the abandonment I felt as an infant. The angry, abandoned infant and my left-brain ego-self are allied forces. Each fuels the other. The child is enraged, sad, lonely, needy, necessarily self-sufficient, fearful, and suspicious. It is isolated and disconnected. This infant must be cared for. Since this child is connected to the ego, I can take him to the Deep Self who presents herself in my psyche as a loving woman. At the same time I need to take a protective, caring stance toward him at the ego level. If I do not actively help this child, his pain will forever cast a shadow over my life.

After all of this was made clear to me, I was given a mantra to help me focus on healing this child: "Dear lady, I give you this precious child." Subsequently, it has made a significant difference in my life. Although I am reminded of the pain of the child from time to time, when triggered by some external event, I try to remember what I was shown and once again focus on giving the child to the Self.

The second experience was quite different, but also very important and insightful. These are the themes that developed while I was under the influence of Daime (also known as ayahuasca) for several hours:

> Self-judgment is not appropriate. Internal conversations in which I identify myself as wrong, bad, displeasing to God, etc., are harmful ways to evaluate my choices. They make the journey a burden and increase shame, which makes me averse to engaging in my own growth. The only useful questions are: "Does this choice really help me? Does it advance or retard my journey?" After I ask the question, I must do what I choose and accept the consequences. No one is judging me, and I will get home eventually.

> I am reminded of the many times in which I either ignore the growth I have been given or discount the goodness within me. I must claim every bit of the good that I have with enthusiasm. This will lead to gratitude and make me more receptive. It will also shield me from the inclination to make false claims to compensate for shame.

> My sexuality, hedonism, social reservation, memory deficits, physical limitations, and delight in junk food are natural, integral parts of who I am and need to be respected. With the Deep Self's guidance, they can all be celebrated and turned into assets.

I was told that it is one thing to use my analytical abilities to defend myself. It is very important that I do so. It is another thing to play out aggressive scenarios in my mind. This does not help and intensifies the wounding of my ego.

I was also given a mantra. "Dear lady, please help me to know, love, and serve God as you do." Let go into the simple, sincere desire to be in love with God. False sophistication does no good. Most importantly, be content with never being sure about anything.

I cannot know for certain where these insights come from. I cannot know for certain if the assumptions I base my life on are grounded in reality. The few things I can know for certain are not relevant to having a meaningful life. I must go with the best insight I have and make an act of faith toward the idea that the universe is conscious and loving and embraces me.

Pride, shame (along with guilt and self-judgment), and fear are the three major stumbling blocks. When I get lost in them, I slow down my journey home. I and everyone else will eventually get home. The only question is sooner, or later?

I had been hoping that the ayahuasca might open me to the kind of mystical experience that many others had reported in the literature. It did not happen. Instead I was told that right now I was not ready to meet God face-to-face, and that it was unlikely that any psychedelic would make it happen. The desire I have for numinous experience is grounded in curiosity, the fun of a "wow" experience, and bragging rights. This is not the frame of mind that will truly open my heart to God. I need to accentuate the deeper, simpler longing to love God and receive God's embrace in return. Besides, I already have a direct, experiential connection with God that I have not fully appreciated. It was clarified in what I call my Trinity insight. Embracing this is my present task.

The divine has a threefold reality:

- Father – The all-inclusive nothingness of pure love

- Logos – The drive of the nothing to manifest in process, form, and structure

- Spirit – The divine essence (love) that permeates everything

Father

The foundation of everything is nothing. Whatever can be named or described is not it. Everyone who has ever surrendered to the experience of this emptiness reports that they were filled with knowledge and love and were never the same afterward. Beyond that, I have no words for it.

Logos

When I am using my analytic and verbal skills to enhance and clarify structures and processes, I am merging with Logos. My search for truth, meaning, and beauty is just another way of opening to God. My Logos and divine Logos are one. When I engage Logos with a sincere desire to seek truth and serve the common good, I am having a direct experience of this aspect of God. I need to recognize this, celebrate it, and be grateful. Although I have been glad for my analytic mind, I have never appreciated it as a way of experiencing God.

Spirit

Because I am so focused on being aware of my inclination to disconnect, I have not truly appreciated how much Spirit does move through me. Because of this I am ignoring and taking for granted another powerful way in which the experience of God is right in my face. Spirit, divine love, and connection are at work in many ways in my life:

- My way of manifesting a healing environment for my clients

- My generosity and tenderheartedness

- My humor and playfulness

- My hedonism and strong passions

- My feeling of revulsion at the thought of being disrespectful or hurting someone else's feelings

  All of these are God as Holy Spirit flowing within me. As with Logos, this is another way of directly experiencing God. If I embrace it, it will grow exponentially. There is no need to doubt any longer the depth and sincerity of my commitment to God. My task is to acknowledge and vigorously embrace it.

  I do know God, I do love God, and I am seeking to serve God. **OWN IT!**

These awarenesses touched me deeply at the time and still do as I go over them again today. They ring true, and I am changed for having accepted them.

Opening to the Self blurs the line between psychology and religion, and consequently between psychotherapy and spiritual direction. From the perspective of the Self, our internal life is a singular reality with multiple aspects each of which is intimately bound to the other. The Self is also a universal quality that manifests itself in the same way in everyone. Ultimately, it seems itself to be a single reality that has a unique relationship with each individual. Mystical writers will sometimes compare God to an ocean and their deepest interior self to a wave in that ocean. This seems to me to be an apt way to describe the Self.

Everything religion purports to offer, such as grace, healing, forgiveness, transformation, and union with God, the Self embodies. It is unconditional love and the internal guide who will show us the way to unitive consciousness or communion with ultimate reality. All of the wounds, distortions, and illusions that warp our psyches are known to the Self, as is their healing. In Hindu spirituality the Self is called Atman. Buddhists call it Buddha nature. Christians refer to it as the indwelling of the Spirit or having a personal relationship with Jesus. Whatever it is called, it is all the same reality, and absolutely nothing is more important than building the closest possible relationship with it.

The principal tools I have used for developing this relationship are internal work or active imagination, mindfulness meditation, and doing everything possible to develop a habit of ongoing communion with the Self. Any who are willing to do the work necessary to know their own truth and commit to a loving life will not be disappointed.

The thought of taking seriously that there might be a nonphysical entity who knows what we are thinking and feeling and wants to communicate with us may seem more than a little odd to the typical Westerner. Even most religious people who believe that there are such things as saints and angels and profess a personal relationship with Jesus don't really anticipate the kind of explicit dramatic visions and interchanges that I have described previously in this book.

This disconnection from internal resources and psychic phenomena over which you have no control is a very recent aberration. In all of recorded human history and in every culture, dreams, visions, and voices (whether spontaneous or induced by psychedelics or meditative practices) were considered vitally important realities that needed to be attended to and learned from. In contemporary culture, because some instances of visions and internal voices are associated with mental illness, most experts in the field of mental health, imbued as they are with the tenants of scientific rationalism, have made the generalized assumption that all visions and voices are indicators of pathology and that they should be stifled or at least ignored. Very few treat them with respect and fewer still would encourage nurturing these processes. Because of this prejudice, Western culture has lost touch with its spiritual roots and its most powerful resource for growth and healing.

Also, as dissociative phenomena are becoming better understood, the possibility of a plurality of ego states (often expressed as voices) within a single person is now generally accepted. Ego itself is now being understood as just another construct. Moreover, attachment studies are demonstrating conclusively that love is essential for human growth and development. And although most psychological researchers still discount mystical states of unitive consciousness as nothing more than the artifact of a temporal lobe dysfunction, a growing number of scientists see them as a potent, life-altering resource that opens a person to love at a deeper level than ever before and leads to enhanced mental health and social awareness. This new perspective will be explored in depth in the third section of the book. The point I want to make at this time is that although the experiences and practices outlined in this book reflect an ancient perspective, they are consistent with serious contemporary research and with what is very likely to become a new consensus in the coming decades.

CHAPTER SEVEN

Embracing the Gift

The ultimate gift of the Self is profound spiritual transformation, often described as enlightenment or awakening. The essence of this transformation is the unconditional realization that one's ego identity is just a convenient story, and that the self one has constructed so carefully and defended so fiercely is a fictional narrative, even though it feels like the realest thing in the world. Any who wholeheartedly accept the guidance of the Self will ultimately be freed from the illusion that they are their egos and will realize beyond any doubt that everything that is real or authentic within them is an expression of the Self. This realization is full of paradox. The final answer to the question, "Who am I?" is "Nothing that can be named or fully described."

Unlike the typical ego, with its boundaries, attachments, elaborate self-descriptions, drama, and concerns about reputation and titles, the Self is a flowing process that has no firm boundaries, no form, no name, no future-oriented goals, and no need to control or cling to anything. It lives fully in the moment, embracing whatever goodness, truth, or beauty is available in immediate experience, motivated only by love. It is quiet, clear sighted, patient, wise, and free. Its gift is itself. It is both our foundation and the guide who will show us the way.

This is the gift that everybody longs for, but few realize it. We all want peace of mind, security, freedom, and a meaningful life, and we assume that somehow these can be manifested through better boundaries, more control over ourselves and others, a better belief system, or a more sophisticated philosophy. The partial consolations that these ego-level competencies offer generally persuade people that depending upon the ego is an effective path. The sense that something fundamental is missing is seen as a sign that one just needs to try harder. Instead of trying harder, some persuade themselves that what they have is good enough and settle for whatever level of comfort is available, shoring it up with diminished awareness so as not to disturb what peace of mind they have managed to achieve.

The path of the Self disrupts all of the ego's typical efforts to create meaning. It contradicts the common sense of contemporary secular man. It teaches us that truth transcends formulas and analysis; that freedom is not a matter of being able to choose anything you please, but of becoming fully yourself, freed from illusion and clinging; and that taking an identity seriously is an unnecessary and constrictive burden. It's no wonder that in our egocentric culture the invitation of the Self is mostly unheard and unwelcome.

Yet there are those who are seeking the Self, and their number is growing. More and more contemporary Westerners are awakening. Many are well known and widely read. Among them are Eckhart Tolle, Jan Frazier, Adyshanti, and Gangaji. We seem to be at a turning point. As more people align themselves with the Self, the power of their presence touches many others, some of whom will also be moved to seek a similar connection.

Besides being motivated by observing the freedom, authenticity, and joy of those whose lives are grounded in the Self, there is also another reason many people are motivated to engage it: the emotional pain in their lives is beyond their ability to control, and they are open to accepting the Self's guidance because they have exhausted their own ego-level resources. This is the case for most of my clients. Their initial work with the Self is for the sake of alleviating emotional suffering, which the Self is more than willing to do. Generally, it is only after significant healing is achieved that the person will have sufficient flexibility to begin to transcend ego and merge with the Self.

Our suffering can be both a curse and a blessing. It drives ego rigidity and defensive barriers, but it also makes us face the limits and powerlessness of the ego at the same time. This hard-won humility can create a space for the Self to make its presence known and offer its gifts. The cracks in our psyches allow the light to shine through. If the suffering is intense enough, it can shatter our world, calling into question our beliefs and assumptions, forcing us to ask the questions that only the Self can answer. For most people, suffering is the primary catalyst for the ego's transformation.

Emotional suffering is a complex reality. It can be divided into three categories, usually interrelated. First is the ordinary suffering of everyday life. As embodied creatures embedded in a social milieu, we are subject to sickness and death, loss, rejection, betrayal, unrequited love, and the inevitable cruelties visited upon us by those who are disconnected from their own moral center. Everyone knows this kind of suffering. If it isn't too severe and the individual is relatively resilient, usually the hurt will pass, especially if loving support is available and there is an opportunity to grieve the losses involved. It is, however, possible to get stuck in this pain when the natural, self-righting mechanisms of the psyche are thrown off-balance by fear, lack of flexibility, or the ego's need to control. In this instance the presence of a loving other is essential in order for the wounded ego to experience the support and protection it needs to become sufficiently vulnerable to face and resolve the pain.

The second category of suffering is that which is what we bring upon ourselves by the way we think about who we are, what our lives should be, or how we choose to behave. Cognitive Behavioral Therapy (CBT) has helped many overcome emotional pain by learning to practice new behaviors and by having clients reconsider their assumptions about themselves or how life should be and then offering them a more realistic and flexible way to think about whatever may be causing their distress.

Another way we cause more suffering for ourselves than necessary is by struggling with our pain. Sometimes changing behaviors or thought patterns will not resolve our emotional pain. Our natural instinct then is to fight the pain. We may rage against it or try to deaden or ignore it with the help of drugs, alcohol, food, sex, etc., or we may act as if it weren't there, or, alternately, give into it and allow it to dominate our lives, feeling victimized by it. All of these strategies tend to make matters worse. A contemporary therapeutic methodology called Acceptance and Commitment Therapy (ACT) can be very helpful when this happens. Through it clients learn mindfulness skills that can enable them to take a more peaceful and balanced approach to their pain. They are also helped to clarify how they can enrich their lives by acting on their deepest values.

Both CBT and ACT are effective and very helpful, but require a trained, external therapist. The Self offers the same basic gifts in a more powerful way than any external therapist ever could. Its perspective is broader and more profound. It knows the person from the inside out. It knows one's thoughts, values, hidden agendas, and unspoken fears and how to most effectively confront them. By connecting with the Self, the ego will receive the gift of its guidance, often embedded in potent internal experiences and metaphors.

Through spending time with the Self, the ego is also given a model of how to be receptive to emotional pain in a way that ends the inclination to fight it and opens up multiple creative options for approaching life. Since the ego's approach to life is based on mental models, it has a hard time seeing options or possibilities that are not extensions of those models.

The Self's approach to reality is direct and experiential. It is not constrained by preconceived notions about the way things should be. Following the example of the Self, the ego can learn to be with the pain as a compassionate, curious observer. This stance immediately lowers the impact of the pain, but, as importantly, it also expands the ego's awareness so that options and choices that would have never occurred to the ego in its or-dinary, control-oriented frame of mind become clear and available. As fresh and more viable alternatives present themselves, the ego will usually gladly accept them with a sense of relief and gratitude. The ego's old path of struggle and control created more suffering; the new path of embrac-ing the way of the Self now offers a more expansive consciousness and a feeling of liberation and new possibilities that develop spontaneously and effortlessly, without having to rely upon an external counselor to drive the process.

Some of the most severe emotional pain, however, will persist no matter how the ego responds to it. This is the third category of emotional pain. Taking the stance of a curious, compassionate observer can help insofar as it stops the ego from making matters worse, but it will not in itself lead to resolution within any reasonable time frame. This kind of pain is driven by neurological deficits or by destructive life experiences that have had such a strong impact on the psyche that they caused persistent changes in the personality of the individual and continually trigger strong, negative emotional reactions (principally fear, anger, and shame) to what for most people would be the ordinary demands of life.

There are four principal causes for this persistent, deeply embedded kind of pain.

1. Impaired Attachment: This happens when the bond between moth-er and infant is significantly disrupted. Typically, this causes a person to "know" at a deep, preverbal level that she is worthless or unlov-able. This usually leads to a lifetime of feeling empty and searching for the kind of love the mother could not give, or doing whatever is necessary to push the hurt and longing out of awareness. The discon-nection and aloneness inevitably triggers fear, since the primordial experience of life is not one of welcome or safety. The sense of de-privation that accompanies disrupted attachment also gives rise to

significant anger or even rage. Given the primitive, preverbal origins of these feelings, they are not amenable to language-based therapies or ego control.

2. PTSD: The second cause of seemingly intractable, severe emotional pain is abuse or significant trauma—technically called Posttraumatic Stress Disorder, or PTSD. Some destructive life experiences are so powerful that they overwhelm normal coping mechanisms and cannot be integrated into a functioning sense of self by the ego. Since they cannot be fit into a larger, more balanced, and inclusive perspective, they act as an autonomous process that feels alien to the ego but impacts and limits it in multiple ways, principally by generating fear, but also anger and shame. Frequently these experiences are either partially or wholly blocked from ego awareness, although their impact continues unabated. Sometimes they will even generate internal ego states that threaten and demean the ego, creating even more confusion and pain.

3. Moral Injury: Related to trauma-based pain is a recently identified phenomenon called moral injury. In the past it was called the pathological secret. Moral injury occurs when a person becomes involved in an experience or set of experiences that trigger sorrow, remorse, shame, guilt, regret, or alienation. It is related to PTSD in that the trigger often involves a significant trauma, and many of the symptoms are the same as those for PTSD: anger, depression, anxiety, insomnia, nightmares, and self-medication with alcohol or drugs. Whenever a person has a life experience that seriously challenges his or her sense of being a good or moral person, it can have a long-term destabilizing impact. These may be experiences that violate the person's ethical standards, or choices in which the person may have had no other alternative, such as killing in war. Even when a person is a helpless victim, there can be a deep sense of degradation, of feeling dirty or shamed by what happened.

Losing self-respect and the sense of being a good person is devastating. Connection with self and others is badly impaired. Frequently the capacity for trust is also impaired. Hopelessness and self-loathing are commonplace. Spiritual foundations are undermined. None of this is easily resolved, since resolution demands open acknowledgement of what was done without being judged by others. Feeling such judgment would only intensify the pathology. Because of their own self-judgment, few are willing to risk the judgment of others as well. This leaves those carrying this burden trapped with a secret that can poison their lives. Some military counselors say that the majority of soldiers and marines returning from Iraq and Afghanistan suffer from moral injury, and that it may well be the principal cause of homelessness and suicidality among veterans.

More than any other group, those suffering from moral injury need the direct experience of unconditional love from the Self. Unlike the support given by an external counselor or confidant, there is no doubt, ambiguity, or potential for judgment in the love offered by the Self. Moreover, there are no secrets hidden from the Self. The entire dilemma as to whether to share the experiences that gave rise to the moral injury is moot. The Self also knows better than any external counselor ever could what kind of restorative experiences would be most helpful in undoing the damage of the moral injury. As in all instances of psychic pain, the ideal would be for the Self and an external support person to work closely together, but in the absence of such a person, deep and lasting healing can be found through connection with the Self alone.

4. Neurological Deficits: The fourth and final category of intractable emotional pain is that which is driven principally by neurological

deficits. The first thing to be aware of in considering this possibility is that many mental health professionals are much too quick to ascribe psychological symptoms to unbalanced neurochemistry. Just because medication or other neurological interventions can ameliorate depression, anxiety, or other psychological problems does not mean that altered brain chemistry is the basic or even the most significant cause of the problem. Psychotropic medications are often offered even when the prescriber suspects that counseling would be a better alternative but the needed counseling is unavailable, or the patient is unwilling. There are instances, however, when the primary source of the pathology is principally neurological. Obsessive-compulsive disorder, bipolar disorder, some instances of personality disorders, schizophrenia, major depression, and some phobias and anxiety disorders have more to do with brain structure and function than with destructive life experiences, although the relationship between the two is complex and often cannot be disentangled.

Even when emotional pain and psychological dysfunction have a strong neurological basis, the quality of an individual's response to them can radically affect a person's prognosis. Many major psychiatric disorders, such as schizophrenia, bipolar disorder, and affective disorders, are triggered by too much change or interpersonal stress. Clear self-awareness regarding the limits of what one can tolerate, and a willingness to accept these limits is an important part of stabilization.

An very important part of self-care is gentle, loving self-acceptance, in which a person is able to tell himself, "I acknowledge that I fit this diagnosis and that it limits my life in certain ways. Although I would prefer it weren't so, it is part of who I am. Even though I am somewhat disabled by it, I am nonetheless a loving, good person and have much to offer life." Obviously, a reaction of shame and self-rejection leads to greater stress and isolation and more intense symptoms.

A kind, sensitive counselor can help encourage the self-awareness and self-acceptance described above. The Self, however, can do so with far greater impact. When it comes to challenging the destructive assumptions or judgments of either the ego or the broader culture, the authority of the Self carries great weight for most clients. The purity and immediacy of the Self's love provides an effective template for the client to learn how to treat himself or herself. Relying on the Self will not necessarily resolve these neurologically based psychiatric disorders, but it can show the way to the best life possible while accepting their reality.

Some major psychiatric disorders, though thought to be largely incurable except through the use of psychotropic medications, are in fact resolvable with the help of the Self. A prime example is the case of those who hear voices. This is generally considered evidence of psychosis that should be treated with strong medications. For some people medications do deaden the voices, but they also reduce the person's overall quality of life. The Self takes an entirely different approach to voices. It sees them as an expression of ego states that must be treated with the same respect and deference as the ego itself. If the ego follows the guidance of the Self, the origins and needs of the voices will become clearer, rapport will develop, and ultimately there will be integration. Later in this chapter I will offer more detailed guidelines for working with parts. Whether or not they express as "voices," they are a very important part of the psyche and major drivers of psychopathology, as well as keys to unlocking important hidden potentials.

The standard response of a well-intentioned ego, when life is not going as one thinks it should, is to try harder. We all tend to believe that if what we have been doing isn't working, we must not have been putting enough effort into it. The common assumption tends to be that by giving the project more energy and exercising more control, we should be able to get the outcomes that we want. This is usually a bad idea.

What I want or think I need at the ego level may not be in my best interest when seen from a deeper perspective. Even if what I am wanting is the cessation of emotional pain, the pain may point to matters of great importance that I have been unaware of. The ego goals that I am putting so much energy into achieving could therefore be a huge mistake. Such goals could leave me empty and spiritually dead if I ever achieve them. The importance of working hard at life, as if it were a major task to be achieved through diligent effort, is a bedrock assumption of our culture. If you achieve your goal, you are a success, even if it leaves you dead inside. If you don't achieve your goal, you will either have to reconsider what success really amounts to, or you will have to accept that you are a failure.

When you are in close alignment with the Self you have an entirely different attitude toward trying hard and working at life. First, whatever goals you have are held lightly. You may want to get beyond some particular emotional pain, but you understand that the pain is likely to contain a truth that you must first embrace. Rather than trying harder to get on with life and ignore the pain, you sit with the Self in a meditative state of mind and allows yourself to be present to the pain and its context. Through the clarity and realization that emerges from this introspection, you will inevitably be given a broader perspective and a wider range of choices, some of which will be much more in keeping with your fundamental values. By opening rather than trying harder, you have become more authentic and more in tune with the Self.

Opening to internal experience and accepting the guidance of the Self can lead to profound changes that emerge as gifts requiring little more than a ready welcome to become part of a person's life. Some of these changes can be subtle shifts in perspective that accumulate over time. Others can be momentous, such as the abrupt ending of an addiction. These changes come as a gift. The ego knows it did not make these things happen and is grateful for the help.

Nevertheless, it is sometimes necessary for the ego to put significant time and energy into achieving important internal goals. A good example of this is the treatment methodology developed by Jeffrey Schwartz, MD, for persons suffering from obsessive-compulsive disorder. OCD is clearly a brain-based psychiatric dysfunction. Until Dr. Schwartz's work, the best available interventions for it were cognitive behavioral therapy and medication. Although helpful, they left much to be desired. Dr. Schwartz's method, which is now the recognized standard of care for OCD, is based on the assumption that the destructive impulses of OCD are the result of deceptive brain messages that have become hardwired in the brain and taken on a life of their own. This, however, is not the end of the story.

The relationship between the brain and the mind goes two ways. Just as the brain can overwhelm the mind with the irresistible impulses of OCD, the mind can counter these brain messages and over a period of ten to twelve weeks of systematic hard work rewire the brain so that its false messages lose their potency. A central part of the healing process is the development of a close relationship between the ego and the Self, which Dr. Schwartz calls the Wise Advocate. As he puts it in *You Are Not Your Brain*, "To help you along the way, we provided you with two allies who believe in and support your true self: your mind, which enables you and gives you the power to choose what to focus your attention on, and your Wise Advocate, which empowers you to see yourself from a loving, caring perspective and helps guide your true self in making choices about how to focus your attention" (336).

What Dr. Schwartz calls "your mind" is what is usually identified as the ego in terms of its capacity for awareness, analysis, and choice. In dealing with disturbed brain function, as in the case of OCD, the ego can override the distorted or false messages the brain is sending and through intentional practice actually change the brain's structure and function due to a phenomenon known as neuroplasticity. Three things are required for this to happen. The ego must listen to the Self (Wise Advocate) regarding the actual nature of the person's authentic self, be willing to systematically choose ways of thinking and behaving that are consistent with this authentic self, and be willing to seek out and be receptive to the kind of loving support described by David Richo and discussed in this chapter. Although possible, significant restructuring of the brain is a difficult, time-consuming endeavor that is unlikely to succeed without strong, loving support.

I have not used Jeffrey Schwartz's methodology with OCD clients. However, I have followed its basic principles in working successfully with persons diagnosed with bipolar disorder, PTSD, dissociative disorders, borderline personality disorder, and schizophrenia. Regarding schizophrenia, I doubt the validity of most of my clients' schizophrenia diagnoses, as they were often based on clients' complaining of voices and hallucinations that were actually the result of dissociation rather than a brain disorder.

A commitment to truth, love, and openness to the Self is the key to overcoming unnecessary emotional pain, even if it is the result of brain dysfunction. An ego or mind that is committed to this path will flourish and ultimately awaken to its full reality and a rich, meaningful life grounded in the Self.

In my experience, a close working relationship with the Self requires three things of the ego. First the ego must accept that such a connection with the Self is both possible and desirable, and then it must be willing to invest the time and energy to make it happen. Secondly, the ego must be unconditionally committed to truth. Although frequently painful and costly (at least from the ego's perspective), this commitment to truth, especially internal truth, is absolutely necessary for genuine freedom and the sense of an authentic life. Without this commitment to reality the Self is blocked from helping the person achieve the self-knowledge required to make the liberating decisions necessary to actualize one's potential and achieve emotional and spiritual balance. Thirdly, the commitment to truth must be combined with an equally strong commitment to love. The fundamental energy of the Self is love. A person who is not being as transparent to this energy as possible cannot be in tune with the Self.

The profound importance of truth and the questioning that uncovers it was central to one client's internal work experience.

Bonnie began the session by reflecting on her father who had just undergone a surprise quintuple heart bypass surgery. She had sat with him for five hours, but only a few words had passed between them. The distance she had felt since childhood was still there. Yet Bonnie was no longer angry. She had worked through her hurt and disappointment and could say without hesitance, "I really want to be there for my parents. There's an honoring that is called for here. I appreciate what they have done and feel respect for them at the core. Just as I get to the place in my life where I can appreciate and respect them, they are getting old. I have a great sense of gratitude for having gotten here."

She added, "My father only saw the model of power. He wanted something else, but didn't know what it was."

That "something else" for Bonnie was the inner journey. She quoted a priest whose class on contemplative spirituality has been important to her: "The hunger for truth will move us to the vertical path."

In the active imagination part of the session her Inner Wisdom picked up on this theme. "I am being reminded," she said, "that even the questions I am asking are part of what needs to occur. They are essential to the process of evolving." She continued, "I feel a sensation of everything moving in close together. Everything is becoming a part of everything else. There is a cave in front of me composed of question marks. I see it going down and in."

Her Inner Wisdom commented, "You ask questions because they take you deeper."

Bonnie went on, "Internal work helps me move out of the physical world a little bit. I see more and I see it differently. It stirs questions I didn't have before, deeper questions. My questions are what I've had for a long time. I wonder if they will help me learn something I need or produce an unexpected good."

As she returned her attention to my office, I shared with her how I was impacted by her experience: "As I see it, the journey isn't from point A to point B as outlined by any one authority. Awakening happens when I learn to simply be with what is without intellectual rigidities or insisting things be a certain way or agree with my assumptions. Persistent questioning is an opening through which truth can meet us."

CHAPTER EIGHT

Truth and Love

Love and truth are intimately intertwined. Love is a prerequisite for truth to emerge and vice versa.

As mentioned previously, according to David Richo's model of love, which is based in part on maternal attachment studies, love is composed of five interrelated elements: attention, acceptance, appreciation, affection, and allowing. These are precisely what are required to truly know both internal and external reality.

Attention

First, it is necessary to pay attention to your actual life experiences. If you aren't looking carefully, you will never know what reality is. Most of the time people operate on the basis of assumptions and models so that they don't have to attend fully to the events of their lives. This is a useful tactic in that it saves time and energy. The cost of the ego's preconceived models, however, is a distorted perception of actual reality. This skewed view leads to a disconnected and stagnant sense of a vital, ever changing world that is far richer than models and assumptions can allow. The more rigid the models and opinions a person has, the less coherence there is between the ego's perception and the actual thing perceived. This is true both for internal and external experience. For example, when you approach another person with your mind made up about what kind of person he or she may be; you will inevitably be wrong about the nuances or even the substance of that person. To the degree that perception is in error, connection is diminished.

Although language and the models it builds can help deepen our understanding, understanding is not the same as actually experiencing something. In a relationship you may have some understanding of the needs or motives of your partner, but this is nothing like being present to your partner in an empathic, compassionate moment of intimacy. Paying this kind of attention, which goes beyond preconceptions, models, and language, opens the window to what truly is. Commitment to the truth demands an aversion to deception, especially self-deception, but it goes far beyond that. More fundamentally, it entails a commitment to know reality in the most undistorted way possible. Fundamental truth can only be known through direct experience. Everything else is a form of virtual reality that only approximates actual direct experience.

This distinction between direct experience and thinking about experience is especially relevant in the development of accurate self-awareness. The first reaction of nearly everyone when faced with painful or threatening emotions, memories, or images is to escape the experience by ignoring, analyzing, or trying to change it. We are inclined to treat challenging internal experiences with the same kind of immediate withdrawal as someone touching a hot stove.

Nevertheless, a willingness to stay with what is uncomfortable is a prerequisite for actually knowing the reality that the experience contains. Truth and the healing that comes from being aligned with the Self demands that we embrace our pain and allow it to reveal to us whatever darkness, conflict, or unfinished business is at work within us. The typical Western response of avoidance or trying to fix internal pain through various forms of self-control or thought control hardens the ego's shell. It is like the chrysalis that restrains the butterfly. Avoidance and control only make the shell stronger and delay the emergence of the beautiful, free potential that is longing for expression.

The Self invites us first to pay attention to what is presenting and get to know it experientially in all of its complexity. A loving parent does not ignore a distressed child, nor will he or she seek to soothe the child with-out first giving full attention to the child's distress in order to determine its root causes. Our pain, especially our shame over the mistakes we have made, is a rich repository of truth and insight if we are willing to stay with it. If we pay attention, the Self will stand by us and help us open successively deeper levels of appreciation of who we are and what we can become. The ego does not have to figure out how to make life better. At the level of the Self our lives are already far better than we can imagine or hope for. By paying attention to who we really are, including those things that are pain-ful, ugly, or hurtful to others, we open ourselves to the possibility of com-ing to know our fullest, deepest truth. Everything in us, including our fear, shame, hurt, and meanness, ultimately arises from a profound goodness that we will never be able to know unless we embrace the very things that we believe make us unworthy or unlovable. Facing these things will always be difficult, but when we do so in the company of the Self, its power and loving kindness give us the assurance we need to know that we are safe. We need not fear being overwhelmed, as above all we are not alone as we probe our own darkness in search of the light.

Some things demand our attention. Great beauty can enrapture a person. It rivets one's attention and for a period of time frees one from the con-straints of analytical mind and ego boundaries. The impact of the beauti-ful breaks down the artificial boundary between self and other that feeds the ego's illusion of being a distinct, separate entity. This is why art, music, and natural beauty of all kinds can feel so liberating and even at times ecstatic.

Pain, whether physical or emotional, also commands our attention. Like beauty, it has the power to focus our awareness on itself. This is an im-portant source of motivation for taking care of ourselves. Often, however, rather than accepting the implicit invitation to understand and respond to whatever is driving the pain through paying deeper attention to its roots, people simply opt to seek relief through medication, addiction, dissociation, or other defense mechanisms. Of course, intractable physical pain whose root causes are irresolvable or cannot be found serves no good purpose and ought to be blocked if possible. The same can be true for emotional pain whose primary or only cause is faulty neurochemistry. Unfortunately, much emotional pain is too readily written off as an organic problem and medicated. In my experience, most of our emotional pain points to an out-of-balance internal process that needs to be explored and resolved. Instead of following our impulse to turn our attention away from the pain by ignoring it or trying to control it, we would be better served by giving it more and deeper attention. This needs to be done carefully, following the guidelines I will be offering later in this book. Otherwise, there is a real danger that if the emotional pain is severe enough it could be overwhelming and drive the ego into greater rigidity and isolation, in a mirror opposite to how beauty impacts the ego. Nonetheless, not facing emotional pain is also a choice to not know one's own truth and thus to continue living a distorted life stuck in a defended ego with diminished connection to the Self.

People can understand that self-identity at the ego level is just a story, not to be taken seriously. They can do everything possible to let go of a fear-driven or control-oriented lifestyle. Yet unresolved and often unconscious internal conflicts will still spontaneously drive an egocentric, distorted perception of self and other, clouding the search for both truth and love. The hallmark of these conflicts is emotional pain. When we force our attention on the pain itself, it invites us to take the next step to ultimate freedom and even shows us the path to take.

Acceptance

The second element of love in Richo's model is acceptance. Having paid attention and attended to what is presenting in the first step, you can now either accept or reject the object of your attention. If you accept it, you are letting whatever it is be without judgment. On the other hand, imposing right/wrong or good/bad categories on an experience or external other is a way of filtering experience. By using ego-constructed categories you deem some things acceptable only because they fit within your idea of how things or people ought to be, and you reject others because they do not. In doing so, you never get to know in any depth either one.

In this state I naturally put up barriers to what I deem unacceptable and am inclined to see only those aspects of it that reinforce my preconceptions. A similar although less divisive risk exists for those objects or experiences I categorize as "good." If I am strongly attached to that categorization, I will be disinclined to experience the other in all of its complexity. As many romantic partners have complained, "I do not want to be put on a pedestal. I want to be known and loved for who I really am." Love and truth require that we approach our life experiences with eyes wide open, embracing the full complexity of what lies before us and trusting that the ultimate foundation of everything is love itself.

Emotional pain typically triggers judgment either of the pain or of ourselves. We can see the pain itself as a burden or a curse and spend great amounts of energy fighting it. The typical outcome of this is that the struggle keeps us entangled in the pain, and simultaneously we never allow ourselves the perspective to get to the roots of it. More often than not, those suffering from emotional pain also judge themselves, considering themselves crazy, weak, or even stupid because they are unable to control their own emotional lives. In response to this self-judgment, they become more shut down and closed in, which isolates them from the Self as well as from the support and love of others.

Acceptance in the face of emotional pain means that you quit struggling with it and instead learn to observe it gently and with an open mind. Although it seems unpleasant, you remain open to the possibility that this pain may be a gift that points to a treasure for which you have heretofore been unaware. Acceptance is an act of trust that, with the help of the Self, may help you find and claim the treasure of your authentic self. Instead of berating yourself for having the pain, acceptance means that you set aside the inclination to judge or categorize yourself. Your energy is now put into practicing being kind to yourself and engaging the pain in a spirit of curiosity. Let your only identification be "one who seeks truth and love," and act accordingly.

Appreciation

Acceptance opens up the possibility of appreciation, the third element of love in David Richo's model. Appreciation means that I accept whatever joys or challenges life brings me with a willingness to seek out the opportunities they may offer me for living in a way that is more fully connected to my Self. As change and loss inevitably impact me, embracing the spirit of appreciation focuses my awareness on how to engage these challenges in a manner that leads to a fuller, more authentic life. By doing so, gratitude can become my constant companion. By willingly embracing every change as it unfolds, I gradually become more closely aligned with the ground of reality, God.

The alternatives to appreciation leave us stuck in a soul-deadening emptiness. They include indifference, complaint, and blaming. Indifference to suffering, my own or someone else's, gives rise to disconnection. When I am indifferent to the pain of others, my capacity for love is diminished and the flow of life energy within me is deadened. The indifference may help me feel safer at the ego level, but the price is greater rigidity and a false and empty life. If I am indifferent to my own pain, the outcome is similar. I will become disconnected from myself and unmotivated to pursue what needs to be done to find healing or opportunity revealed by the pain.

Spiritual traditions often recommend detachment as an important spiritual practice. Depending on what you detach from, this can be either good or bad advice. If you are detaching from ego identity and the drive to control, then it is one of the most important choices you can make. If instead you are trying to detach from those things that make you uncomfortable, bring pleasure, or elicit strong emotions, then your spirituality is just a masquerade for a life-denying form of egocentricity. Any attempt to become whole that does not appreciate our embodied, human reality is a delusion and guaranteed failure.

Complaint is another alternative to appreciation—one which only adds more suffering atop the suffering being complained about. When I look at my pain, it is natural to wish that it weren't there. Beyond this, complaining is a waste of mental energy that deprives me of bringing to bear all of the resources potentially available to me to embrace whatever opportunities for insight or growth the pain may offer. If my pain is due to the actions of another, it is appropriate and important that I let the other know that what he or she has done has hurt me, and that I then ask for whatever change I feel I need for the relationship to feel safe again. However, continuing to complain to that person or others, or even just to myself in my internal dialogues, disengages me from taking hold of my life in a constructive, liberating response to the challenge presented by the hurtful experience. Continued complaint and the resentment it engenders are a powerful psychic poison. Complaint can easily take on a life of its own and drive the ego into an empty darkness devoid of light, beauty, or connection.

Blame is the third destructive alternative to appreciation. One of the ego's first reactions to pain is trying to figure out who or what to blame. At one level this can be constructive: if a relationship or internal process is toxic and causing unnecessary suffering, discerning the cause of the suffering and taking the required steps to protect oneself is simply good self-care. Once I have done what I can to take care of myself, the more energy I put into blaming others or myself for my situation, the more judgmental and egocentric I become. Where blame and judgment are concerned, it is always important to remember that no one can ever know the internal state of another person. It may be obvious that what a person did was wrong and hurtful, but the mixture of needs and motives that drove the behavior is not ours to know. We cannot even know with any certainty the ultimate sources of our own feelings and behaviors. Instead of blame, compassion and sincere curiosity are by far the most effective way to transcend and transform whatever the hurt may have been.

How will we ever embrace the opportunities that change opens for us if we do not appreciate them?

Affection

Affection is the fourth of the five elements of love in Richo's model. The other four elements—attention, acceptance, appreciation, and allowing—are largely cognitive. They are things you do or attitudes you take because you decide to. Affection is a more spontaneous, emotional response. It can be described as the feeling of warmth and tenderheartedness toward another that gives rise to the urge to be with and physically connect with the other. It is something I can allow or even enhance, but I can't make it happen in the same way that I can choose to pay attention to or accept another person. It is affection that gives love its vitality and creates a meaningful bond. If you are in a relationship with a kind person who offers you all the elements of love but without the feeling of affection, you may well be grateful for the support and lack of drama, but you will still feel empty and hungry for the intimacy and connection that only an emotional bond can give.

When affection is a central part of the relationship, you are drawn to the other and long to be with him or her. This person matters not in an abstract theoretical way, but at a gut or heart level. You have a strong desire to be in his or her presence. At the same time, affection without the other four elements of love will not last or will rapidly degrade into obsession and possessiveness. When supported by these other elements of love, however, affection will deepen and enhance the ability to practice all of the elements.

Affection makes all of the aspects of love natural and spontaneous. Usually, a person who doesn't feel affection for another but practices the other four elements of love toward him or her will ultimately come to feel affection as well.

Many people, especially those who have experienced very little affection in their early, formative years, have a hard time feeling affection for themselves. Some live in a miasma of shame and self-loathing. Some compensate by trying to earn affection through pleasing others or trying to prove their worth through accomplishments. Still others try to fill the emptiness through narcissistic grandiosity. It is hard to be gentle, kind, and warm toward yourself when you did not experience it in your early childhood, but it is possible. Practicing the other four aspects of love toward yourself can awaken the beginnings of genuine affection. However, the most powerful way to experience and internalize genuine affection is to accept an ongoing relationship with the Self, wherein truth and love are freely given in a way that exactly fits the ego's needs and capacity to accept.

Affection for oneself is as essential to healing and transformation as it is to building a meaningful relationship. If I do not feel a sense of warmth and caring for myself, I will not have the committed motivation I need to stay engaged in the healing process and face the darkness and conflicts I must deal with. Moreover, if I do not have affection for myself it is unlikely that I will take seriously that my essential nature is good and beautiful and a gift to the world. Why should I bother trying to open myself to something that I doubt exists anyway?

Allowing

The central theme of the ego is control. Its natural function is to defend against external or internal threats or to create models of reality so that it can understand and manipulate its world. In doing so, the ego is attempting to control a potentially dangerous or chaotic world so that itself, its family, and its tribe might survive and flourish. When this impulse to control is in the service of truth and love, the individual and society will function at an optimum level. When the drive to control takes precedence, the ego loses touch with reality. It begins to give more weight to its models and intellectual constructs than to what actually is. The less it invests in compassion and empathy, the more readily it will perceive others as alien and threatening. This gives rise to defensive barriers and aggression.

Allowing is that part of love that purposefully works to keep the impulse toward control in right balance. Where other people are concerned, this means that on the one hand I make clear that hurtful behavior is unacceptable and that I will do whatever I must to protect myself or those for whom I am responsible; on the other hand, I will not intrude on others people's space any more than necessary. I will respect their autonomy and not seek to impose my agenda. If I feel I have a better way, I will offer it respectfully and then accept whatever decision they decide to make. In an intimate relationship this means no nagging, demanding, cajoling, or attempting to manipulate. Instead of striving to fit the other into my mold of the ideal partner, I put my energy into appreciating who he or she truly is, and then decide if I can live with it or not. A spirit of allowing is essential for a genuinely intimate relationship. It permits the possibility of knowing the reality of another person in a way that goes beyond projections and idealizations.

The spirit of allowing brings a similar grace to the world at large, whether in nature or society. When I suppress my impulse for control in favor of paying attention to and appreciating what lies before me, my relationship to that reality will be deeper, subtler, and less disruptive. As a society we are slowly learning that when we consider altering our environment through constructions projects, it ought to be preceded and moderated by careful environmental studies, so that nature is allowed to flourish and maintain its natural balance. In dealing with other cultures we have learned that attempts to impose our ideals on others, however well motivated, doesn't work unless doing so is welcomed by the other cultures and grounded in a clear understanding of their values and traditions.

Allowing is also important as we seek to come to terms with our own internal lives. Our relationship with ourselves is in many ways similar to our relationships with other people. If we wish to develop an intimate knowledge of our inner life and facilitate important changes, we must be clear about what we want, set limits regarding what we can tolerate, and not seek to impose a preconceived agenda on the evolution of our own psyche. If what I want is to become some image or ideal, then I will almost certainly be in resistance to what is most authentic within me. That which is most deeply real about me will inevitably be much more than any image I can create, and at its core my deepest reality is a flowing process that can never be contained by an ego-created or socially mandated model.

If what I want is to become my authentic Self, then it can only happen through letting go of control and allowing this Self to emerge. As this happens, distorted or polarized elements within my psyche will make their presence known. Once control is lifted, out-of-balance energies that have been kept somewhat at bay will become more forcefully present. In turn some control may have to be asserted in order to maintain adequate stability to function in day-to-day life. Fear, anger, grief, shame, resentment, jealousy, and all the other major painful emotions, as well as the destructive, traumatic histories that drive them, could potentially be disabling and require a certain amount of ego control for a person to function socially. But if I want to move beyond control and toward resolution, I must bring all of the aspects of love, including allowing, to bear in facing these painful emotions. In order to bring these energies into balance, they must be allowed to have the opportunity to express themselves. Ideally, this can be done internally with the support and guidance of the Self.

Through allowing all the parts of myself to make themselves known, I can begin to offer them the attention they need, as well as acceptance, appreciation, and even affection. When I do so they will naturally come into balance. Genuine healing will not happen when allowing is absent. A controlling ego creates a sterile internal environment within which new and authentic life and the unexpected potentials of the Self cannot flourish.

Choosing love is the only path to truth or reality, whether it is the reality of creation, the reality of an external other, or the reality of my own internal life and authentic self. The five elements of love—attention, acceptance, appreciation, affection, and allowing—are meant to be the foundation of our lives, beginning with the mother-infant bond and, as the ego develops, continuing as the central theme of the ego's approach to all realities. The choice to love is a choice that must be made over and over again. Just as in meditation we have to continually draw our mind back to its focus of attention such as the breath, in life we have to continually reclaim our commitment to love.

Recommitting to love over and over again is the way to the truth that will set us free—free from the constrictions of prejudice, rigid belief systems, and culturally conditioned assumptions; free from the drama, burden, and loneliness of control-driven dysfunctional relationships; free of unnecessary personal suffering; and finally, free to actually experience the answers to the fundamental questions of existence: "Who am I?" and "Why am I here?" When the ego embraces all of the facets of love, the authentic Self will begin to flow with greater strength and clarity. This flow is the answer that goes beyond what words can describe. Who I am and why are revealed experientially, with every life experience deepening my insight, broadening my wisdom, and increasing my capacity for love in a never-ending expansive spiral.

CHAPTER NINE

Doing Internal Work

Choosing love in the situations life throws at us is difficult, and learning to love ourselves can be even harder. We need a teacher who will show us how to love by loving us, and who will give us the guidance we need to follow his or her example. The Self is this teacher.

The Self and other internal parts of the psyche communicate with the ego in ways that go far beyond the limits of language. This communication involves not just the analytical, verbal mind, but the body, senses, and emotions as well. This multifaceted communication has great power and the capacity to elicit significant change. Verbal communication can give understanding, which is helpful and motivating, but it cannot begin to approach the impact of the dramatic experiences generated by the Self as described in chapter one. Jungians call this experiential process active imagination. Another common name for it is internal work.

Although internal work is not ego controlled, it is a conscious, intentional activity, unlike dreaming or hallucinating. It is not merely an act of observation, as is found in certain forms of meditation in which the individual simply contemplates certain objects, scenes, or sounds. Nor is it daydreaming, by which I mean the enjoyment of a scene that one purposefully generates or allows to flow with the intention of filling time or feeling good. Finally, internal work does not use imagery to foster egocentric goals such as revenge or control fantasies, or as a way to program oneself to become wealthier or more popular, or to reach other specific ego-determined goals.

Internal work is thoroughly experiential. It impacts the intellect, emotions, and senses simultaneously. I much prefer internal work to any other therapeutic modality I have ever used or studied. The power of its stories, images, and metaphors is often so overwhelming that it shocks the ego out of old egocentric patterns.

Additionally, internal work is a kind of altered state in which typical defenses are lowered. Most ordinary fears and concerns will seem more distant than usual. In internal work a person is more open to truth and not as inclined to resist uncomfortable material as he or she normally would be. What is ordinarily filtered from awareness is made more accessible. Emotions especially are sharper and deeper.

When people are focused inwardly through internal work, their openness to imagery and metaphoric thinking increases. The Self and the internal world in general tend to communicate more by metaphor than by words. Metaphor (i.e., the use of an image or experience to make a point) is richer, more powerful, and more effective than putting the same message in words. In fact, it is often impossible to fully express the experience in words. Internal world experiences engage a person not only intellectually, but also emotionally and physically. They can be transforming in a way that verbal descriptions can never be.

Being in an altered state is almost always necessary for internal metaphors to have their most powerful impact. When an individual is in normal left-brain consciousness, the power of metaphor is limited. The typical left-brain reaction is to analyze the metaphor. This reaction is based on the assumption that cognitive understanding is the key element in embracing the gift that metaphor brings. However, the insights and motivation for change derived from internal work go beyond logic. They are not illogical, but they are far beyond anything that logic or reason could attain on its own. When a person is in a right-brain, altered state of consciousness, she can experience and be in the metaphor. This allows the ego to truly live the inner life instead of merely knowing about it.

Allowing oneself to be immersed in an internally generated metaphoric experience is so much more powerful than merely knowing about or understanding an issue. It is comparable to the difference between being in the Grand Canyon and reading about it or looking at pictures. That said, the intellectual interpretation of internal work does have value. It can cause a change in thinking that will help the ego accept and willingly participate in the growth and changes that the internal work has encouraged. Many find it very helpful after a session of internal work to write down a record of the experience and their understanding of its meaning. Even though this record will inevitably fall short of its full significance, it will nevertheless increase the ego's ability to integrate the experience and actively commit itself to the opportunities the internal work has made available.

The internal world generates potent symbols effortlessly. If the ego will embrace them, these symbols can be so powerful that they effect the transformation they symbolize. I frequently encourage my clients to find and wear—or otherwise keep near to their person—jewelry or artifacts that reflect their inner symbols. Such items frequently take on a sacramental quality for their owners.

For example, I have a client who experiences her Self as the Goddess in the form of a hovering eagle that possesses clear perception, great power, and a very nurturing attitude toward her babies. I recommended not only that the client experience this eagle/Self internally, but that she also buy herself a necklace or pin that has an eagle on it. She has done this, and she wears it all the time. It is not just a piece of jewelry, but an amulet—a numinous, sacramental object. For her, it is charged with energy, emotions, and perceptions that keep her connected to her deepest reality. Such external symbols can be very powerful.

The artistic expression through graphic art, music or poetry of internal processes can also be quite helpful. Again, it is a way of owning internal material and expressing or claiming it at the ego level as fully as possible. Internal experiences can also be powerful source of creative inspiration.

The Self is concerned first and foremost with a person becoming who he most truly is, with the integrated embrace and expression of one's full human potential. It views and comments on every aspect of a person's life from that perspective, generating the awarenesses and experiences necessary to help a person evolve toward the most authentic life possible. It consistently presents clearer insight and direction and more potent healing experiences than those provided by any other source. In doing so, it may address a very narrow aspect of the person's potential by producing a mundane dream designed to help him figure out how to fix a stereo, or it may present a mystical experience of overwhelming power and beauty. There are no limits to its range of expression. Neither I nor my clients' egos can generate anything that even approximates the quality of internal work when it is allowed to proceed in its own direction.

Even when ego-level beliefs or needs set rather rigid parameters for the internal world's mythopoetic expression, it still uses this space to teach fundamental human truths and to further self-awareness as much as possible. If a person enters the internal world seeking entertainment, it will usually accommodate him, spinning wonderful tales full of sound and fury in which the ego is the principal actor. Yet even these experiences tend to draw the person to deeper levels of self-awareness.

The Self-generated stories, internal scenes, and metaphorical events in which the ego participates tend to be dramatic and beautiful. A single ten-minute internal experience or journey may sometimes preoccupy a person for days afterward. Symbols and metaphors can be interwoven into a fabric of revelations and new perspectives that mere mortal playwrights could not possibly excel.

There is a direct negative correlation between the degree of ego constraint and expectation, and the power and number of constructive insights that can be generated in an internal work experience. The practice I have found most effective is to set a scene that gives maximum flexibility within minimal context. For instance, if a person needs to confront his anger I will set a scene that describes anger as dwelling in a cave, but after that, anger itself determines the journey's direction. Whatever happens tends to be accurate and very moving. Under this circumstance of minimal context and maximum freedom of expression for the internal world, the true autonomy of this world and its denizens becomes obvious.

People frequently wonder whether the experiences and parts of the psyche they encounter in internal work are just products of their imagination or whether they have any preexisting reality of their own. In the case of those diagnosed with dissociative identity disorder, the latter is now the accepted position of most individuals in the helping professions. The matter is not so obvious, however, with persons experiencing less dramatic fragmentation and polarization within their psyches.

Anyone with a good imagination can conjure up numerous entities that have little or no relevance to the real structure of her internal world. However, she will not be able to create and maintain a false internal reality for very long. The true inner structure is far more deeply grounded and powerful than a mere ego fantasy. It will be only a matter of time before this preexisting structure will reassert itself in both internal work and dreams.

Autonomous entities are a common experience in internal work. Sometimes they are nothing more than an ephemeral phenomenon that occurs as part of a teaching metaphor generated by the Self, similar to some characters in dreams. Other times they are highly developed ego states whose existence predates any internal work. These latter are usually the sequelae of significant abuse or contain important psychic energies that the ego has denied or rejected. They can be quite benign or they can be mean spirited and aggressive. Some even consider themselves to be demonic and present themselves accordingly, which can be quite terrifying.

So even though at first glance the Self may seem to be just another ego state or part, it is actually a fundamentally different reality. The Self transcends ego states. Unlike ego states, it does not have a clear definition or sense of boundary. It is never self-protective, nor does it ever attempt to force any agendas. It is the undivided core of the psyche that consistently and continually invites all the rest of the psyche into its state of wholeness and authenticity.

It is natural to wonder how real or significant these internal phenomena are. But usually doubts about the validity of internal work seldom last once a person has met a representation of the Self and been touched by its loving wisdom, or once one has encountered a deeply angry aspect of the psyche and realized how powerful it was, or been shown long-repressed experiences by the Hurt Child who still exists internally, continually influencing the person's life.

When people are trying to deal with self-destructive patterns, it is often very helpful to ask the pattern to personify itself during a session of internal work and then to engage it in an open-ended dialogue through which it may be able to show the ego what is driving it and work out alternative ways of getting its needs met. Sometimes these entities already exist as autonomous subpersonalities before they are engaged by the ego. Other times they are artifacts of the internal work process, but nonetheless a very helpful vehicle for resolving deeply embedded dysfunctional patterns. The degree of autonomy and permanence of inner parts is proportionate to the person's capacity for dissociation and the restrictions and/or abuse she has suffered. Most people have had to deny important parts of themselves, and these parts exist internally at varying levels of consciousness and autonomy.

Internal work is a powerful tool for reintegrating split-off parts. No other intervention can even approach the potency of internal work as a vehicle for encountering and communicating with parts. Internal work engages the ego as much as the ego is willing or able to tolerate. It is the ego that decides whether to enter the internal world and interacts with the major aspects of the psyche, embraces the issues, and makes new decisions. The Self is always ready to offer support and guidance, but the ego must do the work.

Whether using internal work to deal with inner conflicts or to pursue personal growth, it is important to begin with a good connection with the Self. The inner world can be complex and at times dangerous. Having a trustworthy guide who knows and loves you is essential. The ideal would be to have internal support from the Self and external support from a knowledgeable counselor or guide who can help the ego appreciate and cope with what is being experienced internally and then integrate it all into everyday life. With internal and external support the process will be significantly more efficient and effective. Unfortunately, very few counselors are aware of the internal structure of the psyche or understand internal work. Moreover, most people cannot afford to hire a counselor in the first place, especially since internal work is unpredictable and cannot be fit into a limited time frame. This is why I have written the first section of the book for those who want to do this work on their own. If a good connection to the Self is maintained, there will be relatively little risk.

The Self knows which issues need to be faced and the order in which to face them. It knows when the ego is resisting and is able to confront it more effectively and subtly than I have ever been able to do as a therapist. The Self also knows when the ego has had all it can tolerate and can comfort and support the ego as it attempts to integrate what it has already learned. Two groups I would caution from attempting to do this on their own are those with a history of psychosis or those who have experienced significant abuse and are prone to flashbacks.

The reintegration of rejected or dissociated parts of the self is a major part of internal work. Reintegration is a twofold process. First the ego must reclaim all those elements of traumatic personal history that remain unresolved. Unclaimed history will continually limit a person's potential. Unresolved traumas are like open wounds: they fester and drain the energy of the entire psyche, creating a persistent state of malaise. Whenever these wounds are triggered through an encounter with a life experience that resonates with them or when ego defenses happen to be lowered, they can erupt in disabling pain. Healing these wounds makes the various split-off aspects or fragments of the psyche that were generated by this traumatic history more able to be reconnected with each other, the ego, and the Self.

Reintegrating history and split-off parts is an interdependent process. Because the psyche fragments in response to past traumas, the continuing unresolved impact of those traumas will make it nearly impossible for the parts to achieve a stable integration.

The healing of psychological traumas has some parallels to the healing of physical wounds. If the damage is severe enough, it will require outside intervention in order for healing to occur. The healing always takes time in order to be complete, and sometimes a relatively minor insult to the healing wound will reopen it or at least trigger a severe reaction.

In fact, because of the possibility of powerfully disruptive material emerging, internal work for those who have been significantly abused, or for those who suspect they have because they cannot account for significant parts of their childhood, should not be attempted unless there is a strong connection to the Self. (Obviously, if a knowledgeable external support person were available, that would be ideal.) Memories are repressed because they have the power to render the ego dysfunctional. Bringing them back without the support of the Self and/or an informed helper may very well cause considerable emotional turmoil and perhaps even a serious crisis. Connecting with a dissociated ego state or part within a badly abused person could cause the ego to become even more influenced than usual by the pain, early-life decisions, and intense, often negative emotions that have been encapsulated in the part. This is why it is so important that the ego allow itself to be supported and guided by the Self in this endeavor.

The process of reintegrating an inner part is usually lengthy and relatively complex. It begins with recognizing the fact of the part's existence and its right to exist. Even this knowledge is sometimes difficult for a person to accept. Additionally, the ego must be willing to fully share the part's experience. This means accepting the behavioral inclinations, emotions, and physical sensations that are unique to the part, as well as the knowledge and thinking style of the part. I have seen no case where a stable integration was achieved that was not preceded by a time of dialogue and mutual sharing. This gives both parties time to connect with each other at all levels.

Once the part's existence has been accepted, dialogue and negotiation can begin. Healing is always dependent on the ego's willingness to accept and then embrace whatever has been previously rejected. Dialogue is the first step. Frequently in the initial dialogue, both the ego and the part will be antagonistic toward each other. They may have shared a long history of mutual enmity. Initially, bringing the struggle to ego consciousness does not imply that it will be any less intense.

The Self will never take sides in this encounter, but will treat all parties with loving respect, giving each all the space it needs to share its truth and pain. If there is a therapist or counselor, he must emulate the example of the Self. He must not take sides and must make sure that both the ego and the part are given every opportunity to express their thoughts and feelings. Any deviation from this course will alienate one or the other and lead to greater overall rigidity.

If the dialogue is restricted so that one or both parties are unable to freely express everything they think and feel, then the true nature and scope of the issues that separate the ego and the part will not be known. This would be a major roadblock to eventual integration.

The initial response to dialogue will probably be negotiation. With the Self and/or the counselor acting as mediator, the ego and the part begin to decide what they can and cannot tolerate from each other. The beginning of negotiation has little or nothing to do with mutual respect or affection. It is motivated by simple self-interest.

Yet negotiation and dialogue lead the way to deeper healing. Once the ego and part begin to know each other and respect each other's needs, the polarization will diminish and a kind of caring will develop. When this happens, it is time for the ego and the part to begin healing the historical wounds that gave rise to the part.

The psyche would not have split originally unless it were somehow traumatized. As long as that trauma remains unresolved, integration is not much of a possibility. Parts and the ego may become good friends, but without healing the history, they will probably not be able to join their energies and become a transcendent third reality.

For the process to be successful, the ego must be willing to experience the behavioral, affective, sensory, and cognitive realities of the part. If the traumas that gave rise to this part have already been resolved, dialogue and growing mutual awareness and respect will be sufficient ground for fostering integration.

When the connection becomes sufficiently intense and the traumas that underlie the split have been worked through, integration usually occurs spontaneously—although sometimes the Self will foster a metaphoric process that helps to facilitate integration. The outcome of integration is a new personal reality that transcends both the part and the ego. This new reality is more balanced, open, and fluid than the previous, fragmented self. The psyche may temporarily lose some of the highly specialized gifts of the split-off part. (These parts will sometimes exhibit a singular focus of energy that in some ways parallels the phenomenon of the autistic savant.) What it receives in return is increased vitality, a broadening of perspective, and new options that neither the ego nor the part ever had before.

If the historical issues embodied in the Hurt Child are not worked through, no amount of work with any other part of the psyche will bring wholeness. The best that can be hoped for is an absence of internal conflict between parts and the ego. Although the individual may feel more comfortable if there is less conflict between the ego and other parts of the psyche, the healing will still be incomplete. The person will continue to be controlled by old fears, automatic responses, and distorted early-life decisions. These patterns can only be healed through resolving history, and this is usually best accomplished through working with the Hurt Child.

When the work with the Hurt Child is done well, other aspects of the psyche are much more readily brought into harmony. A pattern of historical traumas may create many split-off parts, and these continue to be energized until these traumas are resolved. Afterward, the parts are much more flexible and willing to move toward integration.

Usually I prefer to access and work with early-life trauma through the Hurt Child. If this is not possible or feels inadvisable, however, history can be reached through other channels. The most obvious and common is through ego awareness alone. If a person is incapable of internal work (approximately 10 to 20 percent seem to be), then the history that is available for working through is that which is already known or made available in dreams. In this instance, the counselor (or if a counselor is unavailable, the ego) reconstructs the incident or incidents in as great detail as possible. Then, in an open relaxed state, the ego takes the stance of a compassionate observer as the experience is remembered as fully as possible. It is important to be very aware of both emotions and sensations as the experience unfolds. Should a person start to become overwhelmed or lost in the experience, the process needs to be paused so that the ego can once again step back into a compassionate, observant frame of mind. At the completion of the experience, the ego should reach out to the Hurt Child, offering the child nurturance, guidance, permission for expression of emotion, etc. If the ego is not able to do this effectively, the Self or another caring part of the psyche will often offer the Hurt Child the needed nurturance.

When a person notices behaviors, thoughts, feelings, or sensations that are inappropriate in her contemporary context, they are usually either the result of inappropriate assumptions or messages from family or culture, or of dissociated aspects of some unresolved psychological wound. If internal work is an option, the Self will usually clarify the source of the problem and its resolution. If internal work is not an option, a technique I call directed association could be a useful alternative.

Directed association begins with deep relaxation, just as if a person were going to do internal work. Deep relaxation reduces dissociative barriers, as well as most other defense mechanisms. Once deeply relaxed, the person focuses her full attention on the symptom. If the symptom is not currently manifesting, then she must try to remember when it was last experienced. Then she must use the memory as a way to reclaim the symptom.

When the symptom is clearly present, it is important that the person focus her full attention on it. If the symptom is a feeling, it should be given as intense an expression as possible. If the symptom is a sensation, the person should try to be aware of nothing else so that the sensation can be fully present in consciousness. If the symptom is a behavior, then the behavior should be repeated over and over as intensely as possible within the limits of the individual's environment. If the symptom is a thought, the person should say the thought aloud over and over.

Through intensification of the symptom, other components of the original experience—behavior, affect, sensation, and knowledge—may well begin to emerge (Braun 1988). Eventually, a critical mass of awareness will develop, and the source of the symptom will break through. Knowing the source of the symptoms does not automatically imply resolution. The person must experience and express all four elements of the original trauma. Additionally, she must receive appropriate nurturance and support either from herself, the Self, a counselor, or a trusted friend. The entire process may occur within a single session, or it may require several sessions. It may even take a year or more of returning to the trauma or group of traumas several times over, at ever deepening levels, before it is fully owned and released. A reliable guideline is that it is impossible to let go of or transcend anything that has not been fully embraced and expressed.

It is usually not sufficient merely to know what happened to oneself and feel the related feelings. In most cases of severe abuse, some external expression is essential for healing, serving several important functions. When a historical wound is spoken of or even lived out in the presence of a trusted helper, it violates the abuser's demand for secrecy. This action helps the client begin to break free of the abuser's psychological power over her. Moreover, most abuse victims feel that they have been shamed or flawed by the attack. Therefore sharing the experience with someone who unconditionally accepts them will help erode the shame and move them toward self-acceptance. The Self can fulfill this need for a caring witness, but if possible it would be very helpful to have an external support person as well.

Besides utilizing the image of the Hurt Child, a person can also ask the Self to take the ego to those times where healing is needed. It is usually very cooperative in this matter. Another alternative channel to historical material is through a split-off part. Each split-off aspect of the psyche has its own collection of memories and historical traumas that create and define it. Simply asking to be taken to the life experiences that gave rise to the part is usually sufficient for the part to reveal them to the ego if there is a trusting, respectful relationship between the ego and the part. An exception to this occurs in highly dissociative individuals who spontaneously generate parts that are not precipitated by trauma, but are designed to serve more contemporary needs.

A common concern with internal work regressions regards the validity of the experiences uncovered. It is well known that people's memories are frequently inaccurate. Added to that is the problem that many of these "memories" are repressed experiences of which the client had no conscious awareness at all. How then can a person be certain that it is not merely confabulation?

The answer is that one usually cannot know. When I have found people, such as an older brother or an uncle or aunt, who are reliable witnesses, they generally validate the material that comes forward through the regression work with the Hurt Child. Nevertheless, such witnesses are an infrequent opportunity. My best judgment is that ultimately it does not matter how accurate the memories are. The likelihood is very high that what is being shown to the client is either precisely what happened, or similar enough that it can at least facilitate resolution of the pain and early-life decisions precipitated by the original abuse. After all, what one must live with is not objective reality, but one's perception of reality. It is the perceptions of the external world held within the unconscious that need to be responded to and resolved. In internal work I believe that people are experiencing an accurate flow of their perceptions of their life experiences. In my opinion, that is sufficient.

For most people, internal work needs to begin with a relaxation procedure. Some individuals, such as Carl Jung, can enter the internal world merely by changing the focus of their attention. Most, however, need to go through a specific process to switch focus from external to internal realities. Any technique that gets a client comfortable, relatively free of tension, and mildly dissociated (i.e., beyond the usual ego boundaries and preoccupations) is sufficient for beginning an internal journey. In chapter thirteen I will describe two different simple relaxation techniques and the overall process for entering the internal world.

Following a session of internal work, it is important that the ego take some time to integrate the experience. If a friend or counselor is available, talking it through can be a way of owning and more fully appreciating the significance of the experience. If such a person is not available, then writing about it can serve the same purpose. If this is not done, there is a risk that the ego will miss or ignore important themes or even discount the entire experience because of how deeply it may challenge the ego's worldview.

A session with a client, Angela, exemplifies many of these internal work themes such as how the Self can be a catalyst for resolving early life trauma, as it invites the ego to learn to move in unison with itself and through that connect with ultimate reality.

Angela began the session by reporting that she had experienced an extraordinary and very rewarding weekend with her mother and brother. Throughout her childhood the mother and brother had been aligned against her and her father, now deceased. Their anger at her had remained steadfast through the years and contributed significantly to her continued feeling of painful abandonment, with its attendant fears and diminished self-esteem. Through her internal work she had steadily grown in awareness of her genuine value and of the importance of claiming and defending it. She had also been shown clearly for the first time in previous sessions the exact nature of her family pathology. She had accepted this truth and grieved the loss of what should have been and never was. As the Self, manifesting as the Great Mother, guided her through this awakening, it was abundantly clear that neither she nor I were the source of the insights or perceptual shifts that led to her radically altered perspective.

That weekend, for the first time, she had effectively confronted her brother about his inappropriate anger toward her. His wife seconded the confrontation and the brother apologized, something he had never done before. Later that day she and her mother, who is an accomplished vocalist, sang together, and they were able to harmonize effortlessly. Another first. She remains realistic about the unlikelihood of genuine intimacy with either mother or brother, but is very grateful for the changes in herself that have opened the door to at least a positive relationship.

Her inner work during this session began with an eager welcome from the Great Mother, Inner Wisdom, and an attentive masculine part. Entering her internal space gave her a warm, rich, loving feeling of being welcomed home. As she walked across the meadow to an ocean beach, the Great Mother told Angela she had waited long enough, and that despite her fear, she was now ready. She was told that her fear was no detriment and that, being a therapist herself, it would help her have empathy for her own clients as they approached moments of significant transformation in their own journeys.

At this point she began to cry. In response to her thought, "What do we do next?" the Great Mother smiled and told her, "This next one is a big leap!" All then walked into the ocean. The Great Mother urged her to feel the rhythm of the ocean in her body. She then did feel it, and when she felt it she was aware that she could trust it completely. This fundamental rhythm felt completely trustworthy. The rhythm was ongoing and unceasing. It was to be from now on her structure and foundation. She realized that whatever way she constructed her life in the future, it must harmonize with this basic internal rhythm.

Angela commented, "Being one with the ocean is a new feeling, even though it is my metaphor for who I am." The Great Mother then told her not to work so hard thinking and planning. She said, "Just swim with me." The masculine aspect was doing somersaults in the water all around her, inviting her to play.

After a while Angela said she felt a need to stop. She was afraid she might not know what to do next or might even drift off course. Could she be sure she would not get lost as she let go in the ocean? Great Mother's answer was clear. The very ocean that she knew represented herself was also the "allness of God." Angela went on to say, "I get to reconsider a lot of years of believing heaven was somehow on the other side of this life."

The Great Mother added, "You are ready now to receive the joys and depth of love you never felt were possible."

Angela then said, "The fulfillment of my dreams is within this lifetime."

Angela also noted that the balance of masculine and feminine felt so real with Great Mother swimming on one side and her masculine wisdom figure on the other. The Great Mother added that as they swam through the water there was a point in each stroke in which they would be momentarily off-balance; it was necessary in order for there to be movement. She wanted Angela to be fully aware of this. Angela then saw a giant manta ray flying underwater.

A short time later Angela reflected, "I used to fear there wouldn't be enough mountains to climb. I love challenge and exploring." At that the Great Mother showed her the ocean's expanse and told her she could explore as far and wide as she wished. The Great Mother assured her that the depth would use her to encourage others on their own journeys, something Angela longed for.

They then began to swim in the depths of the ocean, but it was different from what Angela had expected. She reported, "However far down we go there is light, and we are made of light. There isn't that much difference between Great Mother, wisdom, and myself. At times it feels we are all one.

"It is both awesome and like a playful game—extremely challenging, but easy. While there may seem to be no sense of direction, the energy to explore and the sense of what to explore will come from Great Mother and Wisdom. I have freedom to swim all directions. As below, so above."

To this the Great Mother added, "You will be powerful. There is no denying the power of the ocean. It is time now to let go of naiveté, (i.e. her inclination to view life through rose-colored glasses) and become the warrior goddess you were meant to be. There are people who are counting on you."

Four angels then partitioned off an area of the water. The sun focused its rays into the center of the partitioned area. Great Mother told her to stand in the light. She hesitated, for she knew that every bit of her familiar old patterns (fears, doubts, scripts, roles, etc.) would go if she accepted the invitation. Great Mother asked, "Isn't this what you have wanted?" Great Mother was firm, but alternately soft and embracing. Promising her, "We will sing," Great Mother encouraged her to embrace the offer.

Angela accepted, and when she opened herself to the light, she was arrayed in radiant bridal attire. She said, "It reminds me I am his [God's] bride, and I've known that."

"It's not that others aren't," Great Mother explained. "Others have not been able to receive it, just as you have not."

Angela responded, "I am going to claim my rightful place as a beloved, cherished one. I realize it is okay."

Great Mother handed her a beautiful bouquet.

The angels moved back, and the space became larger with each step she took. Also with each step, she felt an increase in joy, glory, love, and confidence. The flow of the ocean reminded her that she need not worry about getting stuck. It felt right to keep on walking. From the center she sensed many smiling faces and other angel-like beings. Even though the ocean was boundless, she knew that the marking of the space was very important.

Her masculine aspect took her arm, saying that he would be a stand-in for the groom. He kissed her and she felt the bond between love and joy. She then told me, "The marriage is between God as love and all I have connected with love to a joy that I can own, feel and be."

After she opened her eyes and returned her attention to my office, Angela said, "Like Mary kept this and pondered it in her heart, I am to do the same and not share this journey for a good while."

I too have pondered her journey and appropriated much of it for myself. I knew that I had been in the presence of something holy and quietly offered my own prayer of thanks.

* * *

One of the hallmarks of internal work (a.k.a. active imagination) is its unpredictable nature. Angela had not understood her family pathology until it was shown to her by the deeper intelligence of the Self in the form of a Great Mother figure. The insights and guidance she and most of my clients are given go far beyond anything either I or they can anticipate. Angela's psyche was expressing an original, autonomous intelligence. Neither she nor I could predict what it would generate, but I believe what the Self offers is always more profound and effective than anything either Angela or I could generate in a typical talk therapy session.

Since internal work is dependent on imagination, it is always possible for the ego to control it and generate experiences that fit the ego's expectations or sense of self. This is usually fairly obvious, and when I intuit this is happening, I then de-emphasize internal work and rely more on dream work or experiential methods such as body work, spontaneous writing, or affect-bridging techniques in which presenting emotions are used as a point of mindful focus with the hope that they will lead to an expansion of awareness.

I know that the deepest, best work, however, arises out of a separate intelligence, the Self, that has its own intentions and timing. Because of this I am careful to avoid suggesting a specific treatment plan. Trying to direct a session toward a particular goal, whether it be one set by the client's ego or the therapist, could block the emergence of a much more profound insight regarding what is most appropriate to face and how to work through it. When I am in a session with a client I assume that there are at least four autonomous intelligent entities present: my ego, the client's ego, my Self / Inner Wisdom, and the client's Self / Inner Wisdom. Of the four, the client's Inner Wisdom is by far the most knowledgeable and should always be given the primary authority in the client's healing and transformational process.

In the internal work described above, Angela's Self took the form of three figures: a masculine wisdom figure, a Great Mother figure, and a positive contrasexual element. These three, plus a Divine Child that expresses the person's original innocence and authentic nature, and a wounded or Hurt Child that continues to bear the burden of unresolved early life traumas, are the five most common autonomous entities encountered by clients. In other sessions Angela and I spent considerable time working with both child aspects, but especially the Hurt Child.

The warmth with which Angela was welcomed into her inner world is significant. Most emotionally wounded people are very unsure of their own worth. Even when others are loving or kind to them, they can easily discount it. Typically, they think, *They are just being nice*, or *They are acting lovingly because they believe they should*, or *If they really knew me they would not like me*. An eager, warm embrace from within is an effective counterbalance to those beliefs and will erode them over time.

When it is clear that you are genuinely liked and not just dutifully "loved," especially by an intelligent entity that knows you from the inside out, it is a source of deep comfort and healing. Angela also noted that she felt welcomed home. Finding one's true home within oneself is an essential part of embracing an authentic life. To the extent that a person believes that one's home is outside of oneself, the external world becomes a principal point of reference for knowing who you are. When you know that your true home is within yourself, the drive to live from that inner truth supersedes the need to conform or please others.

Great Mother told Angela that fear is no detriment to the journey and nothing to be ashamed of. Fear is a natural response to the uncertainties that accompany impending change and should be accepted gently even as the process unfolds. Over and over, clients are taught by the Self in these journeys to accept and cease struggling with their emotions. Emotions are often the gateway to deeper self-awareness. Even when that doesn't appear to be the case, there is nothing to be gained by struggling with one's feelings. Gentle acceptance of them gives the ego greater flexibility and energy, which can be very helpful in the healing process.

Angela was invited into the most important lesson and gift life has to offer. Through the experience of being one with the ocean and letting herself truly flow with its rhythms, she came to realize that the ocean was God and she was immersed in divine presence. She understood with every part of herself, body, mind, and spirit, that this divine rhythm or flow was the only valid foundation for her life. The message was very clear. Her foundation was not hard and firm, like concrete or stone, but fluid, always in motion and vastly deep. The response she was encouraged to have to this new understanding was simply to swim and play in the ocean. This was not a time for thinking and planning, but a time for letting go and embracing the experience. Connecting and joining is far more essential. Standing back and analyzing robs her of the precious intimacy of knowing God directly through this metaphor. Angela now knew beyond any doubt that heaven or intimate union with God, with its attendant joy and feeling of love, does not have to wait until after death. Knowing this was life altering for her, as it is for most everyone who is given a moment of cosmic consciousness.

The next lessons the Great Mother had for Angela were that the embrace of God involves a balance of masculine and feminine energies, and that progress toward wholeness requires imbalance (as in the swimming experience) as well as balance. These are significant insights. A common theme in internal work is that of the masculine and feminine working together. Another central theme is the necessity of imbalance or even suffering for progress or growth to happen. Once clients understand this, they can be more accepting of their own pain as well as the pain of the world. Instead of resisting it, they can use their pain or lack of balance as a means for more fully embracing life. The problem of suffering and personal distortion or imbalance is not just a philosophical or theological issue. Suffering must be faced and sufficiently resolved for any individual to fully engage life and surrender to God, enabling him or her to fly just as the manta ray does in the ocean.

Angela felt one with Great Mother and Wisdom because they are all composed of the same light. When the ego lets go of its need for control and genuinely appreciates that the stories it uses to define itself are just stories—stories it does not have to take seriously—it becomes a vessel through which the Self, the authentic core of the person, can flow with minimal distortion. In this way ego and Self can merge.

When a clear, strong connection is established with the Self, it is no longer necessary for the ego to develop a life plan and then organize resources in order to achieve whatever goals may be implicit in the plan. In fact, this approach is counterproductive. As the Great Mother showed Angela, the energy to explore and the sense of what to explore will come from the Self. Aligning one's life with what is deepest and most authentic within oneself is always a better plan than seeking to manifest a life that merely echoes externally imposed values or ego-driven ideals. Establishing a clear connection with the Self is the ego's primary task. Anything that takes priority over this is a distraction and will inevitably lead to a diminished life.

As Great Mother told Angela, "You will be powerful." An authentic life is a powerful catalyst for change both for the person living it and for anyone touched by such a life. Deeply genuine people challenge the lies and distortions of the culture just by the way they live. They also evoke in others a longing to know and live their own truth. Their presence is a promise and model of what a well-lived life can be. A person through whom the light of the Self shines is seductive in the best sense of the word.

Part of the power of the authentic person—i.e., one who is transparent to the Self—is that he or she does not hesitate to see reality exactly as it is. There is no need for rose-colored glasses, as Great Mother told Angela. When you are connected to the Self you have an intimate sense of God's presence in yourself and in all of creation. This makes it possible to appreciate however much ugliness exists on the surface; the depth out of which all things emerge is pure love, which draws all things back into itself.

CHAPTER TEN

An Overview of the Journey

Although everyone's path to healing and ultimate awakening is unique, there are enough similarities between people that I think the story of a person who represents a relatively typical client will be relevant to most readers. Linda's story is actually an amalgam of several clients. The struggles and experiences I describe for her occur repeatedly in the people I have worked with. Although the process, as I describe it, is necessarily based on my observations as a therapist and described from that point of view, this is not meant to imply that a counselor is necessary for this kind of process to unfold. It is possible for a committed individual, working closely with the Self, to accomplish the same thing.

Linda was depressed, occasionally suicidal, and overwhelmed by a life that seemed to be continually thrown off-balance by catastrophes, disappointments, and tidal waves of painful emotions. She was weary and hopeless. I could feel the weight of it as she shared with me her years of pain and unsuccessful struggle.

What probably kept her going through these awful years was her way of not knowing the truth of her life. As harrowing as her story may have been, her truth was worse: her childhood had been poisoned by abuse, rejection, and control. Her adult life was an unconsciously driven replay of the same drama. Sometimes she saw the parallels, but it made no difference.

In the beginning of our work together, her life didn't make sense and felt out of control, but she had persuaded herself that it was her fault and found some solace in that. The solution then was obvious: become even more rigid. She was determined to control herself and her world as much as possible. She tried not to think about painful things and learned to act as if she were okay. It allowed her to survive, but not much else. Life was a dull, heavy effort except for those periods when it was excruciating.

As therapy unfolded, it became steadily clearer that her solutions were leading her down a path of living death. Linda had become numb, incapable of intimacy, scared of the future, and unable to face her own history. Ignorant of her roots, she had no idea who she was. Linda was a lost soul.

Her malaise pervaded her entire being. Body, mind, and spirit all showed the effects of her wounding. She suffered from colitis, debilitating headaches, severe PMS, and frequent insomnia. If her stream of consciousness could have been tracked, 90 percent of her thoughts would have been dominated by worry or shame; either she would be overcome by these emotions or reacting to them. In both cases her attention would be absorbed by the inner struggle, and her awareness and capacity for concentrated focus in the external world would be compromised. She knew she was functioning far below her potential and had been reminded of this many times in her life.

Despite all this, Linda was a good-hearted person who tried to be honest and live by the Golden Rule. Beyond that, however, she didn't have much of a spiritual life. Any sense of connectedness, whether to herself, other people, nature, or God, was weak—nature gave her the most; church felt more like a duty than a celebration. Often the readings or sermons fed her shame, although that may have been the last thing the pastor intended. Linda wasn't able to find meaning in much of anything. She wondered if God existed. If he did, did he care?

Acknowledging her emptiness and facing the fact that her solutions didn't seem to do much good, Linda sought help. In doing so she took her first tentative steps on the path to awakening. Initially, all Linda wanted was an easing of the pain and a happier, more meaningful life. She would have never thought of herself as a seeker of enlightenment. Her goals were much more modest.

Nonetheless, each step of the healing process involved the embrace of experiences, practices, and assumptions that when carried to their logical conclusion led to profound personal transformation and ultimately awakening. Like most of the people I know who are seriously committed to a spiritual path, Linda began the journey through her healing process.

The first thing I did with Linda, once I heard her story, was to reflect on her attempts to control her life and how they didn't seem to bring much satisfaction. She readily understood my point but couldn't conceive of any alternative. Whenever she had attempted to trust or "let go" in the past, it had usually led to more pain, not less.

This time, instead of letting go to another person or God, I encouraged her to simply pay attention to "what is"—i.e., to let go to reality. Instead of fending off her feelings, thoughts, and experiences, I invited her to be with them as a reverent observer of their flow through her life. This was very difficult at first, and even now it is still hard for her at times, but she was willing to try.

As she sat with her experiences, I asked her to hold in the back of her mind the mantra, "I want the truth. I accept its cost." Gradually, her self-awareness began to grow and her perceptions of the external world became somewhat clearer. She also found that by taking a respectful, observant stance toward her own emotions, she could more readily keep her balance when the emotional storms hit. By maintaining the observer position, at least a part of her consciousness could stay above the turmoil.

We frequently practiced this during our sessions. I would encourage her to walk into and let flow whatever emotions or experiences were presenting.

When she seemed well connected with the process, I would ask her to please put into words what she was experiencing. This gave her concrete experience in being a participant observer of the flow of her own life.

Taking this state of mind is a simple, natural capacity. All it demands is willingness and a little practice. There are some groups who develop this state of consciousness (often called mindfulness) to a very high level. I have found, however, that its ordinary expression is adequate for healing and spiritual awakening.

There are many positive consequences for this kind of purposeful attention. Linda found that when she resisted her pain, she would often be stuck with it at a rather high level of intensity; when she took the observer stance toward her pain, she found that the pain had a natural ebb and flow. If she could remain patient and observant, the pain would usually somewhat subside of its own accord. This didn't mean that any significant healing had been accomplished. But, at least, what had been a dramatic, heartbreaking struggle was now a much more manageable, albeit painful, process.

As Linda grew more adept at this observer state of mind, I encouraged her to practice being more observant as a lifestyle. She found that there was both more beauty and pain in the world than she had previously noticed. She also began to see how she was more of a contributor to her external-world dramas and disasters than she had previously assumed. This realization did not yet lead to any significant changes, and in fact was a bit discouraging.

In my estimation, the greatest benefit of the participant-observer or mindfulness approach to the inner life is that it puts the ego in a passive, receptive state that allows room for more profound healing energies to flow. As Linda would attend to her grief, anger, shame, or whatever, after a little while we would notice other feelings, bodily sensations, images, memories, etc., emerging. By focusing on them with the same attentive awareness, additional material would emerge until sometimes it would trigger a shift in awareness or emotion that would, at least partially, resolve the initial presenting pain. Clearly there was an intelligent hand moving the flow of internal material toward resolution. When we would use internal work, this intelligence frequently presented itself as a light-filled feminine presence that responded to Linda like a wise, caring spirit mother.

Neither Linda nor I made this process happen, but by letting go of control we gave it room to act. There were other times when the flow would stop. I would then ask the spirit mother to take her to the origin of the conflict being explored. Usually she would be shown a wounded child. We would then work through whatever trauma or need was being presented by the child.

As Linda continued to benefit from these extraordinary internal interventions, she felt gratitude for the internal support and guidance that were the source of her healing. She noted that she didn't feel as alone anymore and that it felt very good to sense something within her that she could believe in.

These experiences began to make clear to Linda that reality, as she knew it at the conscious level, left a lot out and was often based on false assumptions. Nearly every session challenged one assumption or another about how things are or should be. She saw that her jealousy and insecurity with her present boyfriend was rooted in a grade-school relationship with a little boy who liked her but couldn't admit it and made her life hell instead. She was shown her father, whom she believed to be powerful and cruel. He was in fact pathetic, acting out his self-hatred upon her. She saw images of her potential that were more wonderful than she had dared to hope, and she saw an image of her ego that showed it to be grotesque, clumsy, and ignorant. Even though many of these awarenesses were unpleasant and hard to take, they carried such felt authority that she knew they were true.

Once she began to attend seriously to her inner and outer life and was forced to face the enormous amount of illusion and distortion that clouded her connection to reality, her image of reality began to crumble. Old certitudes about herself and the world started giving way to ambiguity and uncertainty. Once driven by insecurity and the continuing impact of childhood victimization, she had constructed a universe of absolutes and polarities. Like so many, she had sought refuge from a chaotic, dangerous world by clinging to whatever beliefs or certainties might offer her some stability. Being a committed believer was especially important if these beliefs allowed her to become identified with a group to whom she could turn for support.

Besides dividing the world into right and wrong beliefs, her social world had been itself divided along the lines of good people and bad people. This inclination to see life through the lens of right/wrong, good/categories arose from a kind of combat mentality triggered by her abusive childhood. Like most people under attack, she had begun thinking in terms of "us versus them." The mean others were completely bad, while I and those I trusted were innocent, good, and righteous. Both of these patterns of right/wrong beliefs and good/bad people had become self-sustaining and in many ways self-fulfilling. Like all of us, she had tended to notice whatever confirmed her assumptions and ignored or distorted the rest. The spontaneous emergence of her deep truth changed all of that.

The more she saw of her history, the clearer it became that what she thought was her nature was an amalgam of parental messages, regressive, childlike reactive patterns, and automatic behavioral responses, all colored by fear and shame and covered over with various guises of sanity. Linda was very concerned about appearing normal, which was a major challenge, given the complicated, distorted ego she had to deal with.

Linda's most important saving grace was that she was honest. She respected the truth and genuinely wanted to know her own. Despite all of her wounds and distortions, she knew that her only real hope lay in submitting to reality. The importance of this commitment may seem self-evident, but I seriously doubt that more than a small minority of the general population is seriously concerned about personal truth. Most probably know that they would stand to lose a great deal of what they believe are necessary bulwarks for their lives if they dared look at themselves or their world in any depth. This, more than any other factor, condemns them to live in illusion and consequently in lives of limited personal meaning.

Linda was fortunate in a backhanded sort of way. The intensity of her pain and the felt meaninglessness of her life were too great to ignore. She had to face it. Taking the journey into authenticity or wholeness was an offer she couldn't refuse. Although she may have had much farther to go than most of her compatriots, she had chosen to walk the path that they more or less ignored.

In her efforts to be a good and normal person, Linda had identified what she considered to be bad or abnormal aspects of herself. These she tried very hard to control or stifle, never very successfully or for very long. Eventually she came to see that her best self wasn't a program that she could purposefully impose. Yet this concept took time to digest. All her life she had tried to be one thing or another. It seemed to be such an obvious solution. Finding out that the whole effort was wrongheaded was a revolutionary shift in perspective. No longer could she approach her inner life with a predetermined agenda. Instead of attempting to conform herself to a right way of thinking, feeling, or behaving, she learned to put her energy into listening to all aspects of herself. With the support and guidance of her Inner Wisdom, she built a growing rapport with her inner selves. As polarization decreased, her energy and self-awareness increased.

Eventually Linda learned that the less invested she was in any particular worldview, self-image, or the polarities that might arise from either, the more alive she became. With this her perceptive capabilities and intuition improved markedly. Linda was now embarked on a life course that steadily led her to ever increasing transparency and flexibility. She began to feel more integrated, connected, and real.

She readily trusted the nurturing Wisdom that had guided her transformation, even though its own nature remained an elusive mystery to her. Like so many others who have encountered this same healing depth within themselves, she began to notice reflections of it within other people and in the world in general. As that happened, she could not help but live in a spirit of gratitude and compassion.

At this point Linda is solidly committed to her journey. She is still a bit odd and socially inept. Nameless fears still invade her consciousness and occasionally limit her life. This may be as much healing as she is likely to achieve. Recently she was bemoaning her fate to her Wisdom. Why couldn't she have learned these things early in life? How hard the remaining scars sometimes made her life! Wisdom showed her a black butterfly and told her, "You have black wings. Now fly!" Her wings had been formed from the darkness of her life, but they had their own beauty, and with them she could fly quite well.

Whether Linda's healing continues or not, there has been no slowing down in the pace of her growth. Several sessions back she was given a stunning vision. The world looked like a child's drawing populated with stick figures. They moved stiffly in an unreal environment. She knew immediately that this was the world of illusion in which most people lived and which she had worked so hard to escape. The scenario's lack of depth and perspective, as well as the absence of fluidity or flow in the figures' movement, spoke for itself. Beyond this world was a domain of nothingness. The keepers of the nothingness had a spectral quality. They were far from benign and mostly laughed at the fools who took their childish world of illusion so very seriously. In the nothingness Linda felt void and sad. The nothingness mocked her life of effort. She saw with uncompromised clarity the pointlessness of her years of trying hard. Sincerity and good intentions made little difference. A life dominated by ego, well intentioned or not, was child's play and unreal. With my encouragement Linda stayed in the nothingness and felt herself being stripped of whatever illusions she was still holding onto. Finally, when she felt completely empty and unsure of anything, the emptiness parted a little. Light broke through and she began to feel herself being filled up. This time, that which filled her felt profoundly real, although mysterious and indescribable.

Her experiences with the light have continued and grown in intensity. There are ecstatic moments that lead to a sense of connection with the transcendent, which she knows to be her source of life. She is also experiencing times of unitive consciousness in which she merges with aspects of external reality. Some of these experiences are quite intense and highly meaningful to her. Before they began occurring with any intensity in her external world, they were happening in her meditations. It seemed obvious to me that her internal world was preparing for what was about to come. In a sense internal and external realities began to merge. The reality she came to experience beyond the ego's imposed map was deeply integrated and meaningful. It was truly the opposite of nothingness.

There is nothing unusual about Linda's experience. Most of my clients who stay with their process end up in a similar place. In fact, Linda is not an actual individual client. She is an amalgam of many and serves as a kind of standard model. Most of the people I work with go through a roughly parallel transformative course and emerge quite spontaneously and naturally as mystics. It seems to be the ordinary outcome that awaits those who are willing to face their lives in depth.

This leaves open the question of my own professional identity and purpose. From the outset I needed to be informed regarding the identification and proper treatment of psychopathology. However, given the immense value of mindfulness and meditation as a way of healing, my principal work is more akin to that of a meditation teacher and spiritual guide. There are only two significant parts of my work that are based on Western psychotherapeutic research. The first is the working through of unresolved trauma, for which I have found contemporary research in PTSD to be very helpful. The other is the guidance I have received from research in dissociative disorders on how to work with dissociated aspects of the psyche. Besides these two exceptions, my work most closely resembles aspects of Buddhism, Taoism, and the Christian mystical tradition.

From the *Tao Te Ching* I have found much that reflects and supports the natural flow of internal healing when therapist and client allow its free expression. This text teaches that human governance (e.g., psychotherapy directed by the ego of either therapist or client), with its inclination to control and its insensitivity to the profound importance of allowing internal and external harmony to emerge, is the way of destruction.

> Men are born soft and supple; dead, they are stiff and hard.
> Plants are born tender and pliant; dead, they are brittle and dry.
>
> Thus whoever is stiff and inflexible is a disciple of death.
> Whoever is soft and yielding is a disciple of life.
>
> The hard and stiff will be broken.
> The soft and supple will prevail (Mitchell, 76).

The Tao and its internal reflection, the Self, are the source of life and meaning. The Tao/Self is like water. Though seemingly soft and weak, it overcomes the hard and strong. It seeks low and hidden places and gathers to itself unwanted waste. What is typically unwanted and rejected by the ego is where the greatest life will be found. By venturing into the domain of cast-off psychic elements in a spirit of noncontentious openness, the ego draws near to the source of life.

Nothing in the world is as soft and yielding as water. Yet for dissolving the hard and inflexible, nothing can surpass it.

The soft overcomes the hard; the gentle overcomes the rigid. Everyone knows this is true, but few can put it into practice.

Therefore the Master remains serene in the midst of sorrow. Evil cannot enter his heart. Because he has given up helping, he is people's greatest help.

True words seem paradoxical (Mitchell, 78).

Over and over the *Tao Te Ching* describes and celebrates the flexible, nonattached, grounded, humble ego that I have found to be an important prerequisite for significant healing. From this state, right/wrong and good/bad polarities can be transcended so that the unity and goodness that is the foundation of all things might be embraced.

The Tao doesn't take sides; it gives birth to both good and evil. The Master doesn't take sides; she welcomes both saints and sinners.

The Tao is like a bellows: it is empty yet infinitely capable. The more you use it, the more it produces; the more you talk of it, the less you understand.

Hold on to the center (Mitchell, 5).

An additional gift from the *Tao Te Ching* is that it gives ascendancy to the feminine principal.

In the beginning was the Tao.
All things issue from it;
all things return to it.

To find the origin,
trace back the manifestations.
When you recognize the children
and find the mother,
you will be free of sorrow (Mitchell, 52).

Understanding the mother, the feminine, makes it possible to understand ourselves. It is only by honoring the feminine that women and men both are able to even begin the journey. Those characteristics typically considered feminine, such as compassion, tenderness, empathy, a strong desire to nurture and protect life, and the capacity for quiet receptivity, are essential elements of an ego that would hope to be open to the promptings of the depth.

Insights I have drawn from Buddhism have also been a great support to me in my work. Foremost among them is the teaching of "no self." My experience with individuals who possess multiple ego states, as well as the obvious importance of releasing rigid egocentric stances in anyone who seeks significant healing, has made me very aware that a defined sense of self is an imaginary construct usually created as an adaptation to the pain of life. This illusion of an ego-self is embedded in the greater illusion of that ego's sense of the world or its world map. The ego-illusion and the world-illusion mutually support and reinforce each other. An ego caught up in this mind trap is closed, grasping, and dominated by a need to control.

Beyond this fictional ego and its attendant world lies an entirely different reality that is expansive, life giving, able to see all things in their natural oneness and beauty, and eager to help the illusion-bound ego grow toward its own true depth and power.

I have observed over the years that the essence of psychopathology (aside from those disorders that are primarily biogenetic) lies in the ego's drive to control. In Buddhism this is called "grasping at self." Lama Thondup says that it is "the root of all sickness, mental and physical" (1996, 76).

Again, Western psychology is barely even aware of the problem, although twelve-step programs do emphasize the importance of surrender.

The single most important antidote to the egocentric ego's world of illusion is reality, or truth. I emphasize this with all of my clients many times over. Western psychology does acknowledge the existence and significance of defense mechanisms, which are basically automatic, unconscious forms of self-delusion. What it lacks are effective tools for uncovering personal reality. This is not surprising, since meditation is the tool of choice for uncovering personal truth, and until very recently Western psychology had no real place for meditation.

An additional problem for Western psychotherapy and spiritual practice is that, objectively speaking, there is no such thing as a fixed self or ego. Yet many Western personality theories are grounded in the delusion of a fixed ego. The phenomenon of individuals with multiple, shifting ego states is such a powerful challenge to these theories that many psychologists feel compelled to deny the existence of this phenomenon. With such a significant delusion at the core of their understanding, Western therapists or spiritual directors operating out of the assumption that the ego is a fixed reality and the central organizing force within the psyche will be less than optimally effective, to say the least.

In my own life as well as my clients' lives, healing and spiritual growth are intertwined realities. With the exception of self-identified "Christian" therapists and a relatively small group of transpersonal therapists, in Western psychotherapy, spiritual and psychological realities are kept quite separate. In fact, many consider it unethical to mix them. Buddhism makes no such assumption. The internal life simply is what it is. Any attempt to separate it into distinct categories is a major error that feeds the process of self-delusion. Besides, if spiritual realities are not honored, then the ego, rather than the Self, becomes the source of healing and the organizing principle of the psyche. This is a major error that will eventually lead to more unnecessary suffering.

Western psychology pays scant attention to the significance of the spiritual insight shared by Buddhists and many other mystical traditions, which recognize all of reality is an interconnected oneness. Because of this impoverishment, Western psychotherapy clients are deprived of a major source of truth, hope, healing, and joy. My experience has been that the essence of meaning is the experience of connection. There is no experience of connection more impactful or subjectively real than a mystical or unitive experience. These experiences can alter the course of a person's therapeutic process.

After such an experience, the client is typically certain that life is beautiful and good and that she is deeply loved. Anger at God for not having answered her prayers or not protecting her as a child tends to dissipate. For some, these experiences are interspersed throughout their therapy. Most, however, experience them only after the ego has given up a large portion of its need to control. Whenever these experiences come, they are wonderful gifts and hold the promise of a wholly different lifestyle and perspective if the person remains committed to the process. I would hate to think about doing therapy without the extensive use of meditation and the occasional inbreak of mystical experiences that it allows.

A final, fundamental similarity between what I have found to be most helpful in therapy and the Buddhist tradition is the central importance of meditation. The combination of mindfulness meditation and internal work is immeasurably more effective for opening the reality and healing of the inner world to the ego than any other therapeutic practice I have ever seen demonstrated. Both practices are barely a generation old in the West and considered to be dubious by most authorities. Yet In Buddhism they have been practiced and refined for millennia and are held in very high regard.

Many years ago I rejected Christianity as "the" path for my own life. At the same time, over the years since, the relevance of certain aspects of Christianity to the healing process has become increasingly clear. Jesus is still the best example I can imagine of an enlightened spirit. I appreciate his priorities, his antiauthoritarianism, his willingness to live and teach outside of the system, and his courage. His special concern for women, as well as the weak and needy, resonates strongly with me. Apparently he was an earthy man with strong emotions and deep friendships. His internal relationship with the Father through prayer and meditation was a deeply rooted foundation for his life, a foundation I strive to emulate in my own life and the lives of my clients. He was aggressive and even combative at times, but always in the service of truth or the most wounded members of society. Whenever I want to sort out whether a client and I are on the right path, I reflect on my understanding of the kind of man Jesus was—my version of, "What would Jesus do?"

Many teachings and practices of Christianity are still very relevant to my work and life, though my understanding of them probably would not pass muster with a conservative or orthodox observer. Yet still I feel the dour doctrine of original sin contains far more truth than poetry. It may be based on myth and the fear of an irrational, avenging God, but its principal message is painfully true: most of us are born into a distorted world that inevitably corrupts our initial goodness and leaves us lost in a daze of illusion and egocentricity. As such, our connection to the divine within is distorted or nonexistent. Although we contribute to the problem with our life choices, the process is well underway long before we have any say in the matter.

The doctrine of grace is a healing counterpoint to original sin and just as relevant. Grace is the action of an internal, compassionate healing energy (i.e., Spirit) upon an individual's psyche, in which the impact of internal wounds, whatever their source, is undone. Grace exists. I don't have to believe in it. I've seen its impact on the inner lives of my clients time and again.

162

The only control the ego has over the flow of healing and love from the depth (i.e., Self, Spirit, or God within) is that it can refuse the gift. The ego cannot cause Grace to flow through good works. Ego-driven good works, whether they are virtuous deeds or aesthetical practices, are usually just another manifestation of egocentric control. Nor can various spiritual rites and practices earn grace. At best, these and virtuous living serve to open the ego so that it might be receptive to internal healing guidance and loving embrace when grace does emerge.

In fact, I have known many very sincere people who were doing their best to live emotionally healthy, loving lives, but who were largely shut off from this inner life and thus blocked from ready access to their own depth. Their suffering, disconnection, and sense of meaninglessness persisted despite their goodwill and hard work. Genuine healing and growth are a gift. To receive the gift we must return to the source and adapt ourselves to its flow. It will always be there, but it may express itself in ways other than we might expect or want.

Another aspect of Christian teaching and practice, its mystical tradition, reflects many types of experiences that I have observed occurring spontaneously in my clients' internal work. Foremost among these is the experience of being embraced by the light. It can happen anytime in an individual's therapy but is more frequent as the healing aspect of the process reaches completion. There is little or no explicit content, but there are feelings of being loved, welcomed, and transformed from within. Occasionally the light will communicate insights or respond to inquiries, but these instances are the exception. It is a tender and at times almost passionate merging whose closest external analog would be the mother-infant bond or love-making. Those who have experienced this know that the light longs for them as much as they do for it.

Other common experiences in internal work that are also noted in Christian mysticism include the dissolution of ego boundaries and the direct perception of the fundamental unity of all reality. These experiences deeply touch people and greatly intensify their sense of connection to nature and others. As with experiences of the light, feelings of compassion and love are deeply stirred and tend to stay with an individual long after a session involving such an experience. Another hallmark of these experiences is that they are quite dramatic and beautiful.

Surprisingly, these unitive experiences and experiences of the light are not at all unusual, even though they may sound rather exotic. In Christianity and the Eastern traditions, the common assumption has been that they mainly happen to monks, nuns, and saints. Apparently, this is simply not so. Many who seriously seeks to connect with their inner life will be blessed with these gifts.

Many Americans first become aware of the possibility of these experiences either spontaneously or with the help of psychedelics. Aside from the obvious problem of bad trips, however, there was another significant drawback to the latter approach: both drug-induced and spontaneous ecstasies tended to isolate these experiences from the overall transformative process. Without this context, they could be used by the ego simply to develop another layer of egocentricity and self-definition. For example, after a few such experiences, some very wounded people have considered themselves enlightened and no longer in need of the hard personal work they so obviously require. Paradoxically, then, these experiences can sometimes be an effective roadblock to the achievement of wholeness and truth, when misunderstood or misused.

Another parallel to Christian mysticism I have frequently encountered is what has been called "the dark night of the soul." As ordinarily described, the "dark night" is a time of emotional flatness, during which ecstatic or mystical experiences are absent and the world of ordinary experience seems meaningless. Obviously, some "dark night" experiences are little more than major depressive episodes. Others, however, involve much more than unbalanced neurochemistry.

The process of liberation can itself trigger a dark night experience. All liberation involves loss—loss of old patterns, beliefs, hopes, relationships, etc. The greater the liberation, the greater the loss. The liberation that accompanies the emergence of unitive consciousness is pervasive, and for some it can be devastating. When a person finally "gets" at a deep emotional level that his personal dramas, which he thought to be so important, are meaningless; that his beloved attachments are little more than hindrances to a fuller vision of the greater good; and that his own ego-self is nothing but a figment of his imagination, he is at risk of being overwhelmed by grief and a deep sense of futility. Under the circumstances it is hard not to conclude that much of one's life has been a colossal waste. Accepting this is a prerequisite for fully claiming the unitive path.

For some these awarenesses dawn slowly and build by almost imperceptible increments. They are spared the "dark night" experience. Others grow gradually until they hit a break-over point, at which time the dark night experience hits suddenly and hard; often this is triggered by an external loss or an internal journey and does not let up for weeks or months afterward. In the aftermath of this experience, relationships will be altered or lost, as will professional commitments. The transformation process can be the trigger for a very painful series of losses, but what is gained far surpasses any cost it entails.

CHAPTER ELEVEN

Living in Communion with the Self

Over decades of helping clients connect with the Self, I have noticed many qualities expressed by the Self that appear to be universal. Jung noticed the same thing, which is why he called the level of the psyche at which the Self exists the "collective unconscious." The verbatim transcripts between clients and the Self in the first chapters demonstrate most of these qualities.

I have observed from the very beginning, for instance, that the Self is always kind and sometimes very loving. It is unfailingly patient and never judgmental. Even when helping a person deal with clearly self-destructive inclinations, the emphasis is always on healing the wounds or finding better ways to meet the needs driving the unhealthy behaviors. When helping the ego-self cope with aggressive or destructive parts of the psyche, the Self never chooses sides, but will continually encourage all parts of the psyche to be open to dialogue, mutual respect, and eventual integration.

I still continue to be amazed at the extraordinary power of the experiences generated by the Self. Hopefully those that I have described can give a sense of their beauty and impact. I have never seen or heard of any other psychotherapeutic interventions that are even remotely comparable. The Self knows the person's needs, conflicts, history, and potential far better than the ego or any external observer such as I could ever hope to know. Time and again I have found that my own insights or conclusions about a client, even at their best, were never as precise or profound as those offered by the Self.

The obvious underlying intention of the Self, in every person I have ever worked with, is to liberate the person from whatever restricts him or her from being fully alive, real, and connected to both the Self and creation. Although respectful of the ego's story about who or what it is, the Self consistently encourages people to drop their assumptions and self-definitions in favor of simply experiencing who they are as they connect with life.

I realized early on that the best thing I could do for my clients would be to emulate the attitude, perspective, and values I saw demonstrated by the Self. I felt gratitude and awe as I observed how the Self interacted with clients. Its values reflected what I had been aspiring to all of my life. I now know in retrospect that to seek to emulate the Self was the best decision I ever made, both professionally and personally. Living in communion with the Self and striving to share it with clients and others who are open to knowing it is now the essence of my life.

Making this connection the foundation of your life is a multifaceted process. It requires developing the right attitude (a radical commitment to truth and love); intentionally allowing that attitude to pervade your life by living it as best as you can in the ordinary, everyday actions of your life (i.e., living mindfully); practicing mindfulness meditation as a way of strengthening your capacity for living a focused, aware, nonjudgmental life; and using active imagination for directly engaging the Self and working with it in meeting and integrating disowned parts and painful personal history.

The first step is to be in a receptive state of mind, which will allow for the possibility of a growing connection with the Self. Developing a vital connection with the Self requires the same thing of the ego as would be necessary to build any important relationship. First and foremost you must be with the other in the present moment. A real relationship cannot be built on memories, fantasies, or assumptions. It requires openness to knowing who the other really is by paying attention to your direct experience of him or her without judgment or preconceptions. The present is the only time and place where you can actually engage the Self. Learning to live in the present with clear awareness is the essential starting point for living in communion with the Self and thus living an authentic life.

Anyone who sincerely wants to fulfill his or her potential must connect with the Self. The Self is both the source of everything that is most valuable within a person and the wisdom that can show that person the way to releasing this potential. Through the Self a sense of intimate connection with creation and others comes to life. It offers the possibility of the direct experience of reality, both internal and external. By participating in the consciousness of the Self, the ego is able to know goodness and beauty through merging with what is being experienced. In that experience, the ego's search for meaning is answered in a way that transcends words and logic.

Two of the most fundamental realities the Self will reveal are a person's own internal needs and his or her conflicts, so that they might be met or resolved with its help. A third reality that it both protects and helps to set free is the person's own unique combination of talents and sensitivities. Since its very nature is love, the Self also helps the ego create altruistic bonds by energizing compassion and empathy. In this way it is the source of a life-giving moral perspective and a generosity of spirit that seeks no reward beyond the joy inherent in giving.

It is natural to wonder how in tune one is with the Self. There are several criteria I look at as a way of discerning how receptive I am at the ego level to the energy of the Self. The first is to evaluate how freely I express the five basic elements of love (attention, acceptance, appreciation, affection, and allowing) toward myself and in my relationships. The more they are being spontaneously and effortlessly expressed, the more I can be assured that I am in resonance with the Self. Secondly, I must ask myself if there are any difficult truths or painful realities that I am avoiding or would rather not know. If I find that I am pushing away any part of reality, either internal or external, then I am creating a barrier to awareness and an ego wall or rigidity that reduces my ability to allow the energy of the Self to flow readily through me.

When the flow is strong, conversely, I feel a passion for life and am easily able to creatively make the most of the changes and demands that life manifests. This flexibility is accompanied by childlike curiosity and a trust in the ultimate goodness of creation. The only fear that remains is the instinctual fear that arises when a real threat to life or safety is perceived.

In writing about his experience of those who are closely in tune with the Self, Dr. Richard Schwartz, the founder of internal family systems therapy, has developed an eight-part set of criteria for discerning how well a person is connected to the Self. He calls it the eight Cs. They are calmness, curiosity, clarity, compassion, confidence, creativity, courage, and connectedness (34–48).

When I notice that I fall short of the qualities indicative of a life grounded in the Self, it is easy to judge myself as failing in my primary life task. This, however, is an egocentric distortion. Communion with the Self does not come about through effort or control. Diminished connection with the Self is usually not a failure of will or evidence of not trying hard enough. It merely points to blockages within the psyche or unhealed wounds in need of attention. The proper response is self-compassion and a willingness to ask for the Self's help in discerning and healing whatever is standing in the way.

Everyone's fundamental purpose is to align with the Self and embrace the fullness of life that it offers. The offer is gentle and patient and will never be forced upon anyone. I believe that if the offer is not accepted in this lifetime, it will either happen after death or perhaps in lifetimes yet to unfold. The gift of the Self is a living birthright, available to anyone who is willing to do the work and pay the price that will inevitably be required.

The decision to begin the process must start with this twofold commitment: "I will seek my truth, no matter what it may cost, and I will do the best I can to be the most loving person I am capable of being." This commitment is essential, because without it there would be no common ground between the ego and the Self. The Self is our reality and therefore our truth. The avoidance of truth is a way saying no to the Self; sometimes it may be necessary to be deceptive in the outer world for the sake of the greater good, but self-deception only serves to increase the ego's entrapment in illusion and thus creates another barrier to the Self. As for love, it is the essence of the Self. It is somewhat self-contradictory to seek the gifts of the Self if at the same time I am setting a limit on how much like the Self I am willing to become. With this twofold commitment to truth and love in place, the process of aligning with the Self can begin in earnest.

A common mistake that people who seek healing or growth continually make is the assumption that if they wish to change, they should decide what they want to be and then use self-control to become that. There are some areas in life where this is useful and successful, at least to a point. The work of Jeffrey Schwartz in helping people reverse the impact of OCD is a good example. It is based on a systematic program of determined effort that has proven to be highly effective in rewiring the brain, as determined by before-and-after brain scans. It is of note that a significant part of Schwartz's technique involves establishing a strong link with the Self. Alcoholics Anonymous is also famous for its aphorism, "Fake it till you make it," which is certainly preferable to simply giving in to self-destructive behavior. Like Schwartz, AA also strongly encourages its members to connect with and rely on a higher power, which is the same reality that I call the Self. For most people most of the time, however, effortful self-control either doesn't work, or if it does work, it leaves them more disconnected from the Self and trapped in ego than ever.

Willpower is a limited energy. Just as you can only exercise for so long or concentrate for so long, you can only force yourself to resist old patterns for so long; then willpower runs out and the patterns return, usually with a vengeance. This is hardly news, since everyone has experienced it many times over. On those rare occasions when we do succeed, the temptation is very strong to assume that constructive change is the product of ego effort and that trying harder is the key to a successful life. If this assumption becomes embedded, the values and perspective of the Self are never realized. Instead control and its inevitable consequences of disconnection, judgment, and seeking fulfillment through the acquisition of wealth and/or power become the ascendant value system.

In the far more common instances in which willpower fails, the ego's connection with the Self can still be negatively affected. The usual reaction to the failure of willpower is shame and even self-loathing. This tends to make the ego more rigid and drives it to seek out ways to numb the emotional pain by putting even more energy than usual into self-distraction through various substances or intensely engaging behaviors. As this unfolds, the prospect of turning within to connect with the Self is pretty much precluded.

There is an alternative, however. Instead of seeking change and growth through control, much more can be achieved through the opening of awareness. This will allow change to emerge naturally and spontaneously, guided by the wisdom of the Self. Once I am able to see with clarity what my real needs and options are, I will naturally tend to want that which best fulfills those needs. Achieving this kind of clarity does not happen automatically. It requires a breadth of awareness that is usually not spontaneously available to the ego. Most of us only have limited awareness of the needs, internal conflicts, and disowned potentials that motivate and drive our behaviors. We may think we know why we make the choices we do, but there is usually much more to the story than the ego might think.

Achieving clear personal insight requires first that I genuinely want to know my truth and then that I do my best to be a compassionate, non-judgmental observer of my own life, just as the Self is. Instead of responding to life automatically, without self-awareness, it is important to take the time to be attentive to what is happening beneath the surface of myself. This cannot happen if I take a harsh or judgmental stance toward myself, as such an attitude will cause me to shut down and push away from my inner life, just as an external person would if I were treating that person in a harsh or judgmental way. Nor can it happen if I am simply not paying attention to my life, but rather letting myself be caught up in distractions, fantasies, or interminable internal conversations. This latter brain chatter fills my head with irrelevant and usually repetitive thoughts and themes that are nothing more than a mental noise that distracts me from the world of real experience.

Once I become used to paying attention to my life as a kind, curious observer, I will slowly notice more and more about myself that had previously been hidden. As this happens, my choices will naturally be more in tune with who I truly am. Change will then arise as the inevitable outcome of being better aligned with my nature. Very little willpower will be necessary. No longer will I need to be frozen in the rigidity of a life driven by a felt need for self-control. I can relax into the flow of my own potential, which is uncovered and unleashed through the expanded awareness that comes from paying loving attention to myself.

This is not a theory. This is my own personal experience and that of my clients as well. Some few embrace this perspective easily. The rest of us have to work at it, but anyone willing to try can achieve it. Living in harmony with the Self means learning to live spontaneously, without clinging to anything, without being driven by any desire to control others, free of any confining assumptions about who or what I am, and delighting in the immediate experience of reality, uncluttered by the distortions that arise from taking my mental models too seriously. This is the epitome of a life well lived, and it begins by paying attention.

The word for the systematic practice of paying attention to my life as a compassionate, curious observer is *mindfulness*, which describes both a way of life and a type of meditation. One of the essential features of mindfulness is that it keeps us focused on our present-moment experience instead of past or future concerns. Developing the skill to stay focused on present experience is what keeps anyone connected to reality. This is particularly true when the reality is as nonaggressive and subtle as that of the Self.

There are many simple mindful habits that can be very helpful for anyone who wishes to live a connected life that allows the Self and the ego to merge in a harmonious flow. The foundation of these habits is the realization that love is not just for people; it is for all of life. The spirit of love embodied in the five *As*—attention, acceptance, appreciation, affection, and allowing—can permeate all of our life experiences. When we allow love to be our fundamental source of motivation, our immediate response to the world around us is to embrace it. Sadly, the most common response of the majority of people is to push away or ignore most of their experiences and live in their heads, disconnected from the present moment and the actual place or reality in which they find themselves. Sometimes this is driven by significant internal pain. Ways to resolve this pain will be explored later in the book. More often than not, however, a disconnected life is the result of bad mental habits that developed because the person didn't know any better. This can be changed by willingly committing to love as your primary value and systematically doing all of the small practices that are part of loving your life.

A simple starting place is to allow yourself the quiet satisfaction of noticing what you are doing, especially as regards to simple things. For instance, the sensations involved in washing your hands can be interesting and quite pleasing. Sweeping the floor, doing the dishes, folding clothes, and all the other mundane tasks we so easily ignore all contain their own simple delights if we pay attention and let ourselves enjoy them. Just as when you are in love with somebody, being with the other and aware of that person's presence is a delight even if you are not doing anything special, so it is if you allow yourself to be in love with life. This is not a difficult attitude to achieve. It already exists within you at the level of the Self and will flow fairly easily if allowed. Generally, it is enough simply to be willing to approach your life from this perspective and act accordingly.

Childlike curiosity with its natural sense of wonder is another way we express our love for life. As we grow older and busier, this can dim, but it doesn't necessarily have to. The desire to know about the world around us never completely goes away. Tuning into it only requires that we let go for a moment of whatever is preoccupying or distracting us and pay attention without judgment to whatever experience is in front of us. What you will notice, probably rather quickly, is that both great and small things will tickle a sense of wonder when you really see them.

Being mindful and being grateful go hand in hand. Gratitude naturally flows whenever we feel wonder or stop to notice and appreciate beauty. It is also part of appreciating all the other delights life brings us when we pay attention to them. Pleasures of all kinds, moments of affection, intimacy, and connection, or being moved by drama, art, and music all enrich our lives, and gratitude is the sauce that helps us savor these gifts. Brother David Steindl-Rast, a Benedictine monk, teaches that gratitude is at the heart of a happy life. That certainly is my experience. If you are in love with life, you can't help but be grateful, and if you intentionally nurture a spirit of gratitude as a central aspect of how you approach life, you will find more and more every day in which to delight. Brother Steindl-Rast recommends a little exercise he calls, "stop, look, go." He suggests that during the day you frequently pause, pay close attention to whatever you're experiencing, and notice what about it you appreciate, then say thank-you and go on about your day. This makes being mindful a pleasure and something you will really want to do.

Pleasure is also a major path for living in the here and now. Many spiritual paths recommend asceticism and self-denial as a way of connecting with the Self. I strongly recommend the opposite, and I am in good company here. When the disciples of John the Baptist asked Jesus why he didn't espouse their spirituality of self-denial in the desert, he told them that there would be plenty of time for sorrow and loss in life, but when the bridegroom is with you, it is time for celebration. Jesus gladly shared in wedding parties and banquets. He clearly endorsed pleasure.

Clinging to pleasure, just as clinging to anything—including possessions, status, or even pain—is what disconnects us from life and the Self. It is the clinging that locks a person into ego. Pleasure in itself is liberating. Everyone knows that powerful experiences of sexual bonding can dissolve ego boundaries and trigger moments of ecstasy. Delicious food is one of the most powerful things I know of for focusing my attention in the here and now. Beautiful music does the same thing. They take me out of my head and into my body and my senses, which makes me far more receptive to the Self than the smug satisfaction I might feel for having made a successful effort at self-control. Just as pleasure helps us be awake and alive, being awake and alive is pleasurable, and this is just as it should be.

Another way of living mindfully is to do my best to "go with the flow" as internal and external events impinge upon my life. Allowing is the fifth element of love. In an interpersonal relationship it means that you do not seek to control the other, but learn to appreciate him or her for exactly who he or she is, warts and all. The same holds true for my relationship with internal and external reality. If I wish to connect with life and live in a way that is open and receptive to the Self, I must set aside my initial inclination to push away or resist whatever it is that I find threatening unless it is an immediate threat to life or limb. Instead I need to give challenging experiences my full attention, be in acceptance of the fact that everything is changing and that change always brings the risk of conflict and loss, and then seek to appreciate how it fits within the greater scheme of things. Having done this, if I decide that it is best to try to control or alter the course of events, I will do so with clear awareness and remain in tune with the Self as I embrace its creativity in order to make the most of the situation. Living in a state of resistance to those things I would prefer didn't exist or happen makes me rigid and stuck in ego.

Resistance to "going with the flow" is particularly evident when one is suffering from "I don't wanna" syndrome. There are a variety of things in my life that I either need to do or should do, but find myself resisting. Procrastination, not wanting to exercise, or having to force myself to do yucky chores like cleaning the chicken coop are all good examples of this attitude. The essence of mindful living, however, is that the ego embraces life with a full-hearted spirit of "Yes!" My yes to life and my yes to the Deep Self are intimately connected; one cannot exist without the other. Reluctantly dragging my heels as I engage the tasks or responsibilities of everyday life diminishes my connection to what is spontaneous, free, and vital within myself. It makes my existence feel heavy and hard, like walking through mud. Instead of a liberating yes to life, I am stuck with a spirit of grudging compliance, wishing I could be someplace else. This is a deadening attitude. The more it impinges on my life, the emptier life feels.

Two areas in my own life where the "I don't wanna" attitude was recently quite strong involve exercise and cleaning the chicken coop. It is surprising to me how much difference resolving these has made in the degree of openness and connection I feel to the world around me and to my inner life as well. When I was a child, I had a fairly severe case of polio that left me with limited physical strength and endurance for the rest of my life. In reading about "post-polio" care I learned that many experts believed that persons with post-polio should not engage in significant exercise, as it might overstress and damage the limited remaining nerves that survived the polio, causing further deterioration in strength and endurance. This gave me all the permission I needed to become a dedicated couch potato, since I didn't like to exercise to begin with.

Recently, however, a physical therapist and my doctor told me that I needed more exercise and that a judicious regimen would do no harm. My Self made clear when I was meditating that it also agreed and pointed out that if I wanted to live a life grounded in love, I must love myself. Regarding my body, this meant that I must deal with it as a loving mother would her infant, willingly and gently, doing whatever is necessary for it to thrive. Caring for a baby can be hard and inconvenient at times for the mother, but nonetheless she does it willingly and with an open heart.

By using this as a template and allowing the Self to be my fitness coach, guiding me in what to do and the pace at which to do it, I have experienced a radical shift in my attitude toward exercise and how I feel about my body. Part of what helped me make this change and come to the point where I almost enjoy exercising is that I was able to understand and feel compassion for my reluctance and then gently broaden my perspective. Instead of trying to force myself to do something I didn't want to do, I was shown by the Self how exercise was a way of expressing more fully something that was profoundly important to me: living a life grounded in love.

My chicken-coop enlightenment took a similar path. Being a rather fastidious sort who doesn't like to get his hands dirty, scooping up chicken poop was near the bottom of my to-do list. Once again my Self asked me to look at this attitude through the eyes of love, which is genuinely my deepest value. Up to this point I had considered chicken-coop cleaning to be my partner Karen's chore, just as mowing the lawn and taking out the garbage were mine. One day as a spontaneous act of kindness I did it for her, which she very much appreciated. I saw how she felt loved through this gesture. I also became aware of how it had to be so much more comfortable for the chickens to have a fresh, clean place to roost. My creativity then kicked in, and I started to figure out how to make the task as easy and unmessy as possible. I can now honestly say that I actually don't mind doing it and feel much more in tune with love and the Self every time I do it. It is a kind of poop-centered spiritual exercise.

Yet there are some aversive experiences that are so powerful that they could be said to possess the ego. No matter how much a person might wish to remain open, receptive, and focused in the present, the hurt, grief, fear, or rage triggered by these experiences overwhelm the ego and trap it in a disconnected mind-set so focused on past or current suffering that the ability to think or feel anything other than pain and its antecedents is greatly diminished. Events such as the death of a child, betrayal by a trusted friend, severe trauma that triggers PTSD and/or moral injury, relentless oppression, or the experience of severe mental illness, intractable pain, or life-threatening disease can all make it nearly impossible to do anything other than feel their oppressive burden. Medical or pharmaceutical interventions can help with some of these things and should be considered. Such interventions, however, are generally limited in their impact, and even when they are very helpful, most people do not want to be dependent on medications or other such interventions as a long-term solution.

Counselors are growing more and more sophisticated in helping people work through PTSD and moral injury. Internal work can be a very powerful resource to help resolve PTSD, moral injury, and severe loss. Nevertheless, for many there is no realistic hope for release from these profound sources of suffering. Despite this, it is still possible to at least seek and find solace in the midst of the pain. No suffering can eradicate our need for love, even though it may diminish our awareness of the need. A trusted friend who has no agenda other than to be with the one who is suffering with an open heart can keep the flow of love open and in that provide some sense of meaning. Pure compassion is also available from the Self if the sufferer is able and willing to reach inside. Allowing love to flow is a very effective way of staying open to the Self, even if your pain is so intense that it blocks your ability to be fully present to your life.

Although some become more rigid in the face of profound suffering, most are shattered by it. Their sense of self and how the world should be is no longer viable, leaving them adrift and more vulnerable than ever. This can be a time either for despair or for setting aside ego—as it no longer functions effectively—and opening more than ever before to the Self and its welcoming love. This is a hard but not unusual way to awaken. It is possible to say yes to the Self and thus to life even when your heart is breaking and you would not wish your fate on your worst enemy.

Eckhart Tolle has summed up the essence of living mindfully quite beautifully:

> When you say "Yes" to what is,
> You become aligned with the
> Power and intelligence of Life itself.

> Only then can you become an
> Agent for positive change in the world.

The quality of a person's orientation to either the past or the future will strongly determine how effectively he or she can say yes to life.

Reflecting on the past, for example, is an important part of self-awareness. Who I have been and the choices I have made are strong indicators of who I am likely to become if I am not actively choosing a different path. Our memories can be a source of solace and a reminder of things to be grateful for, both then and now. Remembering times when I was in tune with the Self in moments of loving kindness, generosity, or intimate union with others or nature will naturally increase my openness to more such experiences in the present. In these ways the past can be a valuable resource for helping enrich my present life experience. The past becomes a problem, however, when it detracts from my ability to be fully present to my immediate life experience. The present is when I am alive and real. It is the only time I can know the actual truth about myself. While memories may reflect aspects of who I was, they are frozen in time and cannot begin to offer the rich possibilities for new experiences and evolving self-awareness that the present moment brings.

Much of the time when we find ourselves lost in the past, it is driven by regret or remorse. Being caught up in regret or longing for what might have been creates a mind-set that diminishes flexibility because it causes me to cling to what cannot be and thus distracts me from the possibilities that life holds for me in the present moment. Remorse can be useful only to the extent that it motivates me to make better choices in the present. However, living in remorse for mistakes that were made in the past clouds the psyche with an aura of self-judgment, which makes it hard to appreciate that I am so much more than my worst choices. Learning to set aside self-judgment and coming to know myself through the eyes of compassionate awareness, especially as I live my life in the present moment, opens the way to profound self-knowledge and freedom.

Meanwhile fantasies about the future may alert me to important insights about my aspirations and fears. Imagining my future can even be a way of mentally preparing for encounters in which I risk being more loving or genuine than I have been in the past, but it is only in the present that I can make the necessary choices to allow a positive future to unfold. More importantly, it is only in the present experience of myself that I will come to know who I truly am beyond who I have been in the past or can imagine myself to be in the future. Paying close attention to my contemporary experience and my internal response to it opens the way this more profound self-knowledge. And, as mentioned earlier, the present is also the only time I can actually connect with the Self, which embodies the essence of what is most authentic within me. Living with this level of awareness in the present creates a solid foundation for making the best choices possible regarding the future I actually want. On the other hand, the fearful anticipation of threatening possible futures is probably even more destructive than being caught up in remorse and regret. As burdensome as self-judgment can be, fear is even more limiting.

Some fear is a valuable and necessary part of life. Listening to my fears can be an important part of self-care. Healthy fear is a strong motivator for lovingly supporting and protecting myself. Noticing my fears can also heighten awareness of my actual priorities, in contrast with my idealized priorities. This is an important part of truly knowing myself. Beyond this, however, fear is probably the most pervasive cause of disconnection from life in the present as well as from my own internal life. Whenever I am not using my fear as a catalyst for increased self-love or self-knowledge, it will diminish both.

The anticipation of danger triggers three potential reactions: fight, flight, or freeze. All three serve to narrow awareness, focusing attention primarily on the threat. They increase the distinction between self and other and greatly intensify the ego's inclination to control and manipulate. The openness, receptivity, and capacity for empathy that are essential for a meaningful life grounded in the Self are significantly diminished when fear is strong.

Once I have looked at my fears and done whatever I reasonably can to protect myself from realistic potential dangers, any further focus on future threats is self-destructive. The best alternative is to live mindfully, giving my full attention to the present moment and beginning to reap the benefits described above. This can be hard to do because we are so accustomed to living in the past or future, driven by remorse, regret, or fear. Changing this mind-set may require considerable practice. This is why mindfulness meditation is such an important tool. Mindfulness meditation is a systematic way of learning to live in the present with a mind that is capable of maintaining focused awareness, uncluttered by excessive thought and other distractions. It is not meant primarily to be a means to help a person feel better, although this can often happen. Mindfulness meditation's main purpose is rather to help a person become better at feeling.

Touching the energy within the psyche that is pure compassion, the Self, is not hard. As internal family systems theory teaches, all anyone needs to do is ask the parts of oneself standing in the way to please step back so that the Self may come forward. Generally, its presence will then be felt by the ego, which in turn can choose to allow the Self's wisdom and compassion to be expressed externally. Learning to live in such a way that this becomes a lifestyle rather than a fleeting encounter is a much greater challenge. It requires of the ego two fundamental tasks: the ego must be both willing to practice present-moment living and then to participate in the hard work of internal healing. Developing basic skills in mindfulness is the best way I know to accomplish practicing present-moment living, while internal healing is best achieved through internal work or what Jung called active imagination, many examples of which were provided in the previous chapters and which I will describe more fully in chapter thirteen.

Holding firm to a commitment to truth and love and living as mindfully as possible on an everyday basis is the ultimate foundation for an ego that chooses to live in resonance with the Self. This takes a certain steadiness of mind, capacity for focus, and receptive openness, which can all be learned and strengthened through practice. Strengthening the mind with mindfulness meditation has several parallels to strengthening the body through exercise. The more you do it, the better you get at it. When exercising, as you get stronger physically, you can go longer and do more. Also, and perhaps more importantly, your growing strength and endurance affects everything you do. All through the day you have more energy, more stamina, more physical resilience, and you're more in tune with your body. So it is with the relationship between mindfulness meditation and mindful living. All of the elements of living mindfully, as described previously, are more spontaneous and powerful to the degree that the mind is capable of maintaining an undistracted, nonjudgmental, receptive focus on immediate experience. This is precisely what mindfulness meditation trains the mind to do.

In their excellent book, *Mindfulness, An Eight-Week Plan for Finding Peace in a Frantic World*, Mark Williams and Danny Penman outline "the seven characteristics of 'doing' and 'being' modes of mind" (37). The "doing" mode of mind is the typical ego-level instrumental approach to life. It is necessary and helpful, but only if it is in service of the Self. The receptive "being" mode of mind that mindfulness opens for us is how the Self approaches life and reality. The following is a brief summary of their insights regarding these characteristics.

The first characteristic is "automatic pilot vs. conscious choice." For the sake of efficient functioning, most of what we do is automatic and habitual. This propensity of the doing mind to create automatic programs can be very helpful, but it can also get out of hand. If too much of our life becomes automated, we are in danger of becoming modern zombies, minimally conscious and stuck in ever deepening ruts, far from the lucidity and creativity of the Deep Self. The being mode or mindfulness is what awakens us and makes conscious living a real option. By taking the time to pause and be more fully aware of the choices we are making or not making, we give ourselves the opportunity to listen to the wisdom of the Self and decide whether the way we are living is truly in accord with our deepest values.

The second characteristic of the doing vs. being mode is "analyzing vs. sensing." The principal skill of the ego or doing mind is analysis. We are continually thinking about things, trying to figure out how best to be safe, how to manage our relationships, or how to make life easier. Technology and civilization itself are the fruits of this process. The benefits are so obvious that many, especially in Western cultures, consider it the only valid way to approach life. The cost of living mostly in the analytical mind of the ego is that it leads to a disconnected existence that mistakes its models for reality and after a while finds existence to be insipid and empty. In contrast, the being mind of the Self is closely connected to the senses. It encourages us to directly experience our internal and external realities. By being attentive to what we hear, see, feel, etc., we are plugged back into life and become aware of how intimately we are a part of everything around us. This leads to expanded creativity, as perception is no longer limited by the rigidity of our models. It also opens up a felt sense of meaning that transcends the ego's beliefs and dogmas, as well as greater vitality and a passion for life—all of which are reflections of the Self.

The third characteristic is "striving vs. accepting." In the doing mode the ego is inclined to struggle with difficult situations. It feels driven to resist, ignore, or try to fix those aspects of life it considers to be problematic. Approaching the same issues from a mindful or being-oriented perspective opens up an entirely different range of options. A mindful orientation begins with paying attention to what is happening with curiosity and without judgment. This is very different from the ego's doing-oriented inclination to categorize what is happening as bad or wrong, based on its models of how things should be, and then to seek to force reality to conform to its intentions. The mindful approach allows for a much clearer assessment of problematic situations. It sees the connections between things rather than just the conflicts. It appreciates complexity. It can discern what lies beneath the surface and make grounded choices about how and when to respond. This stands in contrast to ego-driven doing reactivity, which primarily notices only the surfaces of things and then responds impulsively. The mindful being response is invariably more aware, creative, and intentional.

The fourth characteristic is "seeing thoughts as solid and real vs. treating them as actual events." Thoughts are such wonderful tools for helping us understand and plan our lives that it is easy to forget that they are not reality, but only point toward it. Mindfulness helps us observe our thoughts and in doing so helps us be aware of both their value and limitations. It also facilitates a more immediate connection with internal and external experience. This protects us from confusing our thoughts with what actually exists or is happening.

The fifth characteristic of the doing vs. being modes of mind is "avoidance vs. approaching." It is natural for the doing mind to steer us toward what we want and away from what we would consider to be painful or threatening. This is one of its primary tasks. Although often helpful in dealing with the external world, this inclination of the mind can be counterproductive, especially when applied to our internal lives, where avoidance only makes matters worse. The mindful way of being encourages us to move toward perceived threats with a sincere desire to understand them. Approaching emotional pain or inner conflicts with curiosity and compassion opens the door to deeper self-awareness and eventual resolution.

The sixth characteristic is "mental time travel vs. remaining in the present moment." We have a strong inclination to "re-live past events and re-feel their pain, and we pre-live future disasters and so pre-feel their impact" (Williams & Penman p 42). Ego can get so caught up in memories and fears that they feel real in the present moment. Mindfulness frees the ego by enabling it to step back from reliving or pre-living and realize that these are just memories or anticipations and not real, present experiences. By returning attention to present experience, fear and pain are displaced by the aliveness and satisfaction that comes from being in one's senses and connected to real life.

The seventh and final characteristic in Williams and Penman's model of the doing vs. being orientations is "depleting vs. nourishing activities." Often there is so much to do in our lives that the doing inclination is the only thing we are aware of. Raising a family, working full time, taking care of social obligations, and caring for those we feel responsible for can leave a person depleted. It doesn't matter that these are all good and important things to be doing. If all of the doing is not balanced by taking time to reflect on your life and notice how well your own needs are being met, you will lose touch with the Self, and life will feel progressively more sterile, despite all the good you may be doing. Intentionally entering a mindful being space on a regular (ideally, daily) basis will serve both you and those you love. It will broaden your awareness and show you what you need to do to love yourself even as you are striving to lovingly care for others. This will allow you to be with them with a full heart, rather than with an exhausted, frustrated spirit. By helping you step back from the all the immediate demands of daily life, intentionally entering a mindful space will give you an expanded perspective that will open up creative possibilities for yourself and those you care for that the busy doing mind would never see.

Mindfulness meditation is an invaluable resource for learning the skills of mindful living. Even when meditation is a struggle, it has important lessons to teach us. The first of these stems from the fact that nearly everyone will have a hard time maintaining focused awareness, even for brief periods of time, as they begin to practice meditation. Some of us will still not be very good at this even after meditating regularly for months or even years. That certainly is the case with myself. Most days, if I can go a minute or two just focused on my breathing or my mantra, without getting caught up in internal self-talk or absorbed in a distraction, I feel I have done pretty well.

When I notice that I have lost my focus and become distracted, I congratulate myself for noticing instead of berating myself for losing focus. If I am gentle and good humored with myself, and patiently return my attention to my breathing and/or mantra, then the meditation continues to be a positive, ego-releasing experience that I enjoy and can look forward to. As soon as I become judgmental and begin to feel like a failure, I am likely to try to find reasons stop the practice, and the practice itself will increasingly become an egocentric struggle focused on self-control. Dealing gently with myself over and over again as I succumb to distraction is in itself an important skill to bring to everyday life.

All of the elements of living mindfully can be thought of as mental states that can be learned and enhanced with practice. Paying attention to the simple things of life, experiencing curiosity and wonder, feeling appreciation and gratitude, fully savoring pleasure, going with the flow, accepting and giving love, and staying in the present moment in the face of fear and regret are all fundamental, necessary skills for a life that is open and transparent to the Self. Just as we are certain to be caught up in distractions while meditating, we are going to fail in our efforts to become adept at these skills. How we handle the failure is the key to how much we will grow in learning to live mindfully. If every time we catch ourselves falling short of how we would hope to be, we gently and without judgment return our attention to whichever of the mindful skills we are practicing, just as we have been doing in meditation, then we can continue on without any internal drama. This will help us peacefully and steadily live in ever deeper resonance with the Self. In this way distraction in meditation can be a very helpful teacher.

Self-talk is probably the principal distracter most people have to deal with when they meditate. In everyday life, self-talk is a large part of ego consciousness. According to Ferris Jabr in the January/February 2014 edition of *Scientific American Mind*, "It occupies about one quarter of conscious experience…We depend on inner speech to solve problems, read and write, motivate ourselves, plan for the future and learn from past mistakes." It is also how we maintain the story of "I," the internal narrative that maintains the sense of the ego-self as a distinct, real entity. Jabr quotes the neuroscientist Jill Bolte Taylor, who noted that when a stroke blocked her capacity for inner speech, "Those little voices, that brain chatter that customarily kept me abreast of myself in relation to the world outside of me, were delightfully silent. And in their absence, my memories of the past and dreams of the future evaporated." Jabr observed, as do many contemporary neuroscientists and scholars, that "the fascinating possibility implicit in such experiences is that our sense of self is an elaborate illusion—a very convenient fiction maintained by our incessantly chatty mind. When our mind shuts up we disappear." As Jabr quotes Taylor, "Jill Bolte Taylor died that day. I did not have her memories, her likes or dislikes, her education, anger, her love, her relationships. Now I don't take Jill Bolte Taylor half so seriously as before."

In the practice of mindfulness meditation we learn to disengage from our self-talk and simply observe it. This can be very revealing as we notice the stories and ruminations out of which we construct the ego-self. In order to let go of something, it is necessary to know what it is in the first place. Releasing the ego's illusion of self by learning to step back from self-talk gives the Deep Self a chance to be expressed more fully. As my attachment to self-talk and the ego's story loosens, the Self then has a chance to get a word in edgewise.

More often than not, I will receive creative, very constructive flashes of insight during meditation. They are precious gifts. I have included many of them in this book. In themselves they are not distractions, but evidence of the Self breaking through. However, if my ego then runs with the insight, analyzing its significance or figuring out how to phrase it and include it in my writing, it does become a distraction and takes me out of the observer stance. The way I usually handle it is to assure myself that I will remember it and write it down as soon as the meditation is finished. This works well for me.

Sometimes in meditation a strong emotion or preoccupation will forcefully present itself, and I will find it very hard not to get sucked in. Usually this intrusion is something I have been struggling with in everyday life, although I may have not been fully aware of it until I quieted my mind in meditation. When this happens, it is actually a gift. I am being reminded that I am out of balance and that something important needs my attention. Promising myself that I will deal with it after the meditation is completed is usually enough for it to quiet down. If it doesn't, then simply naming it as "hurt," "grief," "guilt," "pain," "hunger," etc., is usually enough to help me step back into the observer mode once again. This also works in everyday life. When I find myself preoccupied by some internal process that is demanding my attention, if I sincerely promise myself that I will work on it as soon as possible, its power is generally significantly reduced. If it persists or if there is nothing I can do about it, relaxing myself and simply naming it will help me take the familiar observer stance.

The principal value of mindfulness meditation is that you learn to be in the present moment without judgment and with compassion, thus laying the foundation for an ego that can be deeply connected to the Self in everyday life. Beyond this, however, there are many other important benefits, such as stress reduction, improved physical health, reduced emotional lability, and enhanced self-awareness. By practicing over and over again curious, compassionate nonjudgment toward the mental contents that arise during meditation, I have been able to make this attitude a part of my life. This is one of the most useful benefits I have derived from meditation. As a result I have become much more gentle and accepting in dealing with aspects of myself that are off balance or have been a source of discomfort or shame in my life. These include such things as my quite intense anger— rooted in childhood abandonment issues—social awkwardness, and an inclination to be overweight. Learning through meditation how to fully acknowledge these proclivities without judgment and with a sense of compassion for myself has been a great relief for me. Instead of struggling with them and feeling ashamed of myself, I have learned to treat them tenderly like the wounds that they are, and to welcome the loving care and guidance the Self can offer when I remain in an open state of mind.

CHAPTER TWELVE
Mindfulness Meditation

Living mindfully, with a spontaneous, open connection to the Self, does not happen easily in contemporary Western culture. I suspect that in pretechnological times, when we lived a simpler, more intimate tribal life and were more in tune with our senses and natural environment, awareness of the Self was much more overt and commonplace. Today few people even suspect that such a thing exists. Most of those who do live such disconnected, distracted lives that their access to its profound, subtle, internal presence is severely constrained. Intentionally choosing to live mindfully, as described in the previous chapter, can help, but in most cases it is not enough.

What should come naturally has been forgotten and now must be relearned. Our unnatural lifestyle has caused us to forget who and what we are and how to live in tune with it. Our situation is akin to that of someone who has been bedridden for so long that he has forgotten how to walk. Without purposefully practicing walking, the skill will not return, even though it is a natural part of who he is. The practice of mindfulness meditation is like that. It is a method of intentionally practicing a way of being that will enable us to be connected and aware internally and externally both during meditation and as a part of everyday life.

There are two basic forms of mindfulness meditation. One focuses on releasing the contents of consciousness, while the other focuses on intentionally engaging them. Both are ways of helping the ego merge with the Self. The releasing form of meditation takes the vertical, left-brain perspective of Logos. It stands above or outside of immediate experience as an unmoved, nonjudging observer. In doing so it aligns with the still, quiet, ever aware quality of the Self. In a guided meditation designed to facilitate this Logos perspective, Josephine Sellers beautifully describes the Self and its significance in a meditation which can be found on YouTube as "45 min Transpersonal Meditation HQ with Narration":

This is the Divine moment of Self
that is not identified by your body,
that is not confined by your feelings,
that is not repressed by your thoughts.

Dynamic in its stillness

Thunderous in its silence

Brilliant in its darkness

Complete in its emptiness

The moment of Self that does not expect and yet is ready.
The free will of Self that is present and available.

That is the moment of self that connects you to the whole of creation.

Be aware that your body may be tired and calling for you,
That those feelings may be trying to get you caught up in some cycle,
That your thoughts may be trying to engage you.

Let all that go.

They are but a distraction from the moment Self…from the moment- to-moment experience of your soul.

Give yourself permission to be still…silent…empty.
And in this peaceful space acknowledge your power, your strength, your
love, your intuition.

This is the Divine Moment of Self.

This is the moment that you have always been searching for.
And yet, this is the moment where you have always been.

And in this moment that falls into the next
Present in yourself,
Present in your shared divinity,
Present in your co-creation with the universe.

Acknowledge where you are—connected to and a part of the universe.

And now prepare to take your next step that is your destiny and invite the
divine consciousness of the universe to connect with the consciousness of
your mind.

The engaging form of mindfulness meditation, on the other hand, is an expression of the horizontal, right-brain perspective of Eros. It lets boundaries dissolve and intentionally embraces internal and external experience. This engaging type of mindfulness allows the ego to connect without the distortions imposed by the ego's strong inclination to separate its world into me and not-me. This practice of open receptivity aligns the ego with the expansive, unbounded nature of the Self, through which the underlying unity out of which everything has emerged (Jung's Unus Mundus) can be known.

In the releasing type of meditation, awareness is directed toward something simple and repetitive, usually the breath, but it could also be a mantra, a sound, or something visual, such as a flame. When mental contents such as thoughts, feelings, images, memories, etc., emerge, they are noticed with curiosity and without judgment. Then they are released, and attention is returned to the original focus. It is as if the person meditating is sitting beside the stream of consciousness as various things float by. He notices each, but does not judge them and does nothing to impede their passage. The original point of focus, such as the breath, keeps him anchored beside the stream. When he gets caught up with content as it floats by and finds himself in the water, returning to the original focus helps him let it go and places him back beside the stream.

Another type of this releasing form of meditation is called the disidentification exercise. Dr. Roberto Assagioli, a transpersonal psychiatrist, developed it. The following description of it is taken from his book *Psychosynthesis* (118). The disidentification exercise makes clear that the essence of who I am, my consciousness or awareness, is not any of the specific things I can be aware of. It is a reality that transcends any definitions and has no limits. Doing this exercise or the more traditional, releasing form of mindfulness meditation allows the ego to become one with simple, pure consciousness, and in doing so it becomes open to the Self and ultimate reality:

> *I put my body in a relaxed and comfortable position with closed eyes. This done, I affirm: "I have a body, but I am not my body. My body may find itself in different conditions of health or sickness; it may be rested or tired, but that has nothing to do with myself, my real 'I.' My body is my precious instrument of experience and of action in the outer world, but it is only an instrument. I treat it well. I seek to keep it in good health, but it is not myself. I have a body, but I am not my body.*
>
> *"I have emotions, but I am not my emotions. These emotions are countless, contradictory, changing, and yet I know that I always remain I, myself, in times of hope or of despair, in joy or in pain,*

in a state of irritation or of calm. Since I can observe, understand, and judge my emotions, and then increasingly dominate, direct, and utilize them, it is evident that they are not myself. I have emotions, but I am not my emotions.

"I have desires, but I am not my desires, aroused by drives, physical and emotional, and by outer influences. Desires too are changeable and contradictory, with alternations of attraction and repulsion. I have desires, but they are not myself.

"I have an intellect, but I am not my intellect. It is more or less developed and active; it is undisciplined but teachable; it is an organ of knowledge in regard to the outer world as well as the inner; but it is not myself. I have an intellect, but I am not my intellect."

After this disidentification of the "I" from its contents of consciousness (sensations, emotions, desires, and thoughts), I recognize and affirm that I am a centre of pure self-consciousness. I am a centre of Will, capable of mastering, directing, and using all my psychological processes and my physical body.

When one has practiced the exercise for some time, it can be modified by a swift, dynamic use of the first three stages of dis identification, leading to a deeper consideration of the fourth stage of self-identification, coupled with an inner dialogue along the following lines:

"What am I then? What remains after discarding from my self-identity the physical, emotional, and mental contents of my personality, of my ego? It is the essence of myself—a center of pure self-consciousness and self-realization. It is the permanent factor in the ever varying flow of my personal life. It is what gives me the sense of being, of permanence, of inner security. I recognize and I affirm myself as a center of pure self-consciousness. I realize that

this center not only has a static self-awareness but also a dynamic
power: it is capable of observing, mastering, directing, and using
all the psychological processes and the physical body. I am a cen-
ter of awareness and of power" (Assagioli 1971. 118).

This disidentification exercise can be found on my website, www.
deanschlecht.com.

As the exercise makes clear, whatever a person can define or observe is
not that which is observing it. What this implies is that the self I can describe and generally feel identified with is not the essence of who I am. It is
merely a limited expression of the unlimited possibilities of the Deep Self.

The regular practice of disidentification will significantly change a person's
perspective. The Josephine Sellers meditation is an excellent example of a
disidentification meditation.

The principal gift of disidentification and releasing mindfulness meditation is that they free the ego from being identified with the contents of
consciousness. As Jill Bolte Taylor noticed when a stroke quieted the language centers of her brain, she was able to be in simple, open awareness
without her thoughts defining and limiting her. When a person ceases to
be immersed in a struggle with the contents of consciousness, the ego's
awareness expands. The self-imposed limitations imposed by the story of
"I" or beliefs about whom or what I can be fade away. In their place arises
a quiet receptivity into which the Self will readily flow.

In the second embracing form of mindfulness meditation, awareness is purposefully focused on the contents of consciousness. It is a way of choosing to
be as conscious as possible of whatever the ego is experiencing. The intention
is to create an undiluted, fully aware connection between the ego and internal
or external reality. This is not the same as when the ego gets caught up and
swept away by an experience or drama. Rather, it is similar to the difference

between a skier who skillfully skies down the mountain and a hapless hiker who gets caught up in an avalanche and is swept down the mountain. One is dominated by the experience, and the other is exhilarated by embracing the experience. As in the first form of mindfulness meditation, in this form the ego sets aside its self-talk, presumptions, and preoccupations. In their place it gives its full attention to its experience, losing its artificially imposed ego boundaries and limitations, and thus gaining more autonomy and awareness than ever. There is a quality of flow and intimate connection that arises from this perspective. In these moments ego and Self become one.

A mindfulness meditation can be as brief as thirty seconds or last for hours. My favorite and very brief releasing form of meditation is simply a matter of paying attention to my breathing and intentionally letting it become slow, deep, and regular. This has a way of clearing my mind. As my preoccupations fade from awareness and I settle into simply being for a few moments, I feel refreshed, grounded, and more creative. This brief meditative pause gives me a quick taste of all the benefits that come from resting in a being state of mind. These include taking me out of automatic pilot, grounding me in my senses, helping me let go of striving and be more accepting, releasing my inclination toward avoidance and becoming more welcoming toward my experiences, reconnecting me with the present, and leaving me feeling spiritually nourished. If the slow, deep breathing is sustained for a couple of minutes, it will trigger physiological changes, such as a reduction in stress hormones and activation of the parasympathetic nervous system. This can be very healing physically as well as psychologically.

Another very brief form of meditative experience also involves breathing. In this case no effort is made to slow or deepen breathing. Instead, you simply pause whatever you are doing and notice your breathing. Then, as you inhale, let yourself slightly smile. As you exhale let yourself feel grounded in your body, senses and the present moment. Doing this, even for a minute, can significantly change your perspective by opening you to the gentle, uncaused joy and connection to immediate reality that is the constant experience of the Self. This practice not only feels good, it brings you back home to who you most truly are.

Alan Watts, a well-known spiritual teacher and writer was once asked why he meditated. His answer was, "Because it is fun." The two very brief meditative exercises I just described are genuinely fun to do. Although there is obviously a benefit to disciplining your life so that time is set aside for meditation, personally I would rather approach meditation as a delight I am looking forward to rather than a duty I must somehow fit into my schedule. These two exercises don't demand any alteration of your schedule and feel so good that you will want to do them often throughout the day. You will find yourself drawn to them much as you would be drawn to a glass of cool, clear water when you are hot and thirsty. Once the delight of being in that state of mind becomes evident, it is likely that you will then look forward to an opportunity to meditate for even longer periods of time. A guided experience of these two meditations can be found at my website, www.deanschleht.com.

As usually practiced by most Westerners, the releasing form of mindfulness meditation begins by sitting comfortably in a chair with feet flat on the floor and the back straight as if a string were attached to the crown of the head, pulling one erect. This triggers a state of physical alertness. Eyes may be open with the gaze lowered and unfocused, or closed. Attention is then placed on the breath (or other point of focus, if preferred). No effort is made to alter the pace of the breath; it is simply observed and experienced as fully as possible.

When mental or sensory stimuli divert attention, they are noticed with mild curiosity but no judgment, and then allowed to pass on with attention being returned to the breath once again. It is to be expected that even experienced meditators will be caught up in these distracting stimuli. This is just part of the process and, as discussed earlier, can be a source of useful information to be looked at after the meditation is finished. Once the person has noticed that he or she has been caught up in a distraction, all that is required is that he or she let it go and gently return attention to the breath. It may be necessary to do this over and over again. Personally, sometimes it seems as though that is all that I have done during a meditation. It is very important to keep returning to the breath without being critical of oneself for not getting it right. Critical judgment is the most destructive of all distractions and can turn a meditation into an egocentric exercise of self-control rather than a releasing experience of expanded awareness. One technique I have found to be very helpful when distractions are particularly persistent is to count my exhalations. When I reach ten exhalations, I start over again at one and simply continue this for the duration of the meditation period.

The website Sounds True offers five guided meditations by Jon Kabat-Zinn called "Mindfulness for Beginners." They are an excellent introduction to meditation.

There are a variety of ways to practice the embracing form of mindfulness meditation. A very simple, brief version begins with placing a raisin on the tongue. Notice first its texture and subtle flavor. Be aware of how its presence triggers a flow of saliva. Then bite into it and appreciate the burst of flavor it releases. Notice also the soft internal texture of the raisin. Very slowly chew the raisin and take maximum pleasure in all the flavor this releases. Stay with the experience until the raisin is nearly gone. Finally, notice how long the aftertaste lingers after the last pieces of the raisin have been swallowed. By being immersed in the feel and taste of the raisin, the ego is naturally focused on the present and for the moment unconcerned about its story of "I," status, or dramas that may have been preoccupying it. Intentionally embracing the gustatory pleasure a single raisin can bring is an effective form of mindfulness that opens the ego to the deeper pleasure of a quieted, receptive mind.

Although this example of the embracing form of mindfulness meditation utilized two of the five senses, the same approach can be used with any experience the ego is capable of having. Besides the five senses, the ego can apply the same quality of intentional awareness to the interior feelings of the body, such as muscles, bones, heartbeat, etc., or to any mental contents, such as thoughts, feelings, memories, or images that may arise when the mind is open and relaxed. The same mindful awareness can also be directed toward observing how these mental contents arise into awareness, stay, and then pass on, and also toward what it is like when there are moments devoid of any contents. Another potential area of focus can be our relationships and the variety of feelings they stir. Dr. Dan Siegel has developed a guided mindfulness meditation he calls the Wheel of Awareness, in which he leads the listener through an extensive overview of the multiple possibilities for this kind of mindfulness meditation. I highly recommend it. It can be easily found on You Tube under his name.

Practicing this form of mindfulness meditation can be as simple as slowly and intentionally eating a raisin. It helps to begin by sitting erect with feet flat on the floor, as in the releasing form of mindfulness meditation, and then to briefly pay attention to the breath as a way of switching out of normal, busy ego consciousness into a more aware and attentive state. Following this, either use a systematic process of reviewing the whole range of experience, as in Dr. Siegel's guided meditation, or focus on whatever experiences naturally present themselves as they emerge.

Mark Williams and Danny Penman's book, *Mindfulness, an Eight-Week Plan for Finding Peace in a Frantic World*, is also an excellent, pragmatic introduction to mindfulness meditation and mindful living. It is integrated with a website that offers a series of guided meditations to be used over an eight-week period of time. The book is based on a well-researched program developed by Jon Kabat-Zinn called mindfulness-based cognitive therapy. Although the brief descriptions I have offered are adequate to begin a practice of mindfulness meditation, Williams and Penman's book and the guided meditations that accompany it offer a much more comprehensive and effective introduction.

CHAPTER THIRTEEN

Entering the Inner World

Connecting with the Self through living mindfully is a subtle, spontaneous process. The best way to know that this connection is actually happening is by observing how willingly you give love to yourself and others and how much your life reflects the qualities of the Self as outlined by Richard Schwartz: calmness, curiosity, clarity, compassion, confidence, creativity, courage, and connectedness.

Internal work, as described earlier in this book, offers another very powerful way to be with the Self. It is neither subtle nor spontaneous. It is a form of meditation, but very unlike mindfulness meditation. Instead of focusing on breathing and either letting go of or embracing immediate experience, internal work takes the ego into an alternate reality where the Self and all the other elements of the psyche can be met and engaged face-to-face. What was subtle or hidden becomes overt and powerful. Internal work opens up extraordinary, unforgettable, life-changing experiences. Those described earlier in this book reflect a potential we all share, if we are willing to engage in the process.

For most people internal work is initiated by a structured procedure that enables the ego to become dissociated from external reality and concerns and helps turn its full attention inward through the use of vivid imagination. There are some for whom a structured procedure is unnecessary. Those who have considerable experience with internal work, for instance, may be able to enter their internal world simply by taking a few deep breaths, relaxing, and turning attention inward. An exceptional few, like Carl Jung, experience the internal world opening up to them without going through any kind of preparatory exercise. In working with his own clients, Jung suggested that they simply focus on whatever image may be arising in their awareness or may have presented in a dream. When the image begins to take on a life of its own and function autonomously, a connection with the internal world will have been made.

In the beginning, most people respond best when someone else directs the process. After you have gone through it a few times, however, it is fairly easy to do for yourself. I have prepared a guided introduction to internal work, written out in the following paragraphs, and uploaded it to my website (www.deanschlecht.com). It is the first audio file and is entitled *Journey to the Self.*

Before you engage in this, I would strongly encourage you to review the chapter on "Doing Internal Work" so that you will be familiar with what to expect and potential pitfalls.

To begin internal work, recline or lie down and allow yourself to be fully supported. Then let your arms and legs go limp so that they feel like heavy, dead weights, as if all the energy has been shut off at your hips and shoulders. Turning your attention to the muscles in your abdomen and chest, notice the tension you are carrying there. Intentionally relax these muscles to the best of your ability. Use breathing to help deepen the relaxation. As you inhale imagine that you are drawing tension out of the muscles, and as you exhale imagine that you are expelling the tension from your body. Do the same with the muscles between your shoulders and in the back of your neck. Notice the tension there and then intentionally release your neck muscles, allowing your head to rest comfortably and your shoulders to drop. Once again use breathing to deepen the relaxation. As you inhale draw the residual tension together, like into a ball, and as you exhale send it away from you. After you have relaxed your torso, relax the muscles of your face. Begin by relaxing your jaws, cheeks, and the area around your mouth. Then also relax the areas around your eyes, across your forehead, and over your scalp.

After you have become fully relaxed, imagine that you are at the top of a beautiful, safe stairway with ten steps leading down. Slowly descend the steps, counting each one: ten, nine, eight, and so on. After reaching step number one, imagine that you are stepping into a mountain meadow. Feel the firmness of the ground under your feet. Touch the grass and notice how soft and cool it is. Notice as well the rich green color of the grass and how it contrasts with the colors of the wildflowers—white, yellow, crimson, blue, and many other shades. There is a gentle breeze in the meadow. You can see how it sways the flowers and ripples the grass. Feel how cool it is on the skin, and enjoy the rich earth scent of the meadow and the rich pine scent of the nearby woods that it brings to you.

This meadow is a safe, protected place where you will be able to meet the Self and all of the facets of your psyche in need of acceptance, healing, and integration. As a first step, you will see that there is an extraordinary tree in the middle of the meadow. This is your tree of life, a tree that symbolizes your nature. Go over to it and get acquainted with it in whatever way you can. Don't try to figure it out; just experience it as fully as you can, and notice whatever feelings or associations it evokes in you. After you have done this, go around to the far side of the tree, and you will see there a gift prepared for you by the Self. Open the gift, hold it, and allow it to impact you as fully as possible.

You will then notice a path that leads from the tree toward the woods. Take this path, bringing your gift with you. As the path enters the woods, feel the coolness of the shade and the pine-needle carpet underfoot. Stay on the path as it winds around brush and past trees, taking you deeper and deeper. In a little while you will see that the path leads into a clearing filled with light. As you enter the clearing, there is a presence waiting for you. It is the Self. Go to it. Open your heart and allow it to show you or give you whatever it has for you. Stay with this presence as long as you wish.

When the experience feels complete, simply open your eyes and return your attention to external reality. It is very helpful to take time to write about the experience—how it felt and what it meant to you. As you write, insights will tend to flow, and the significance of the experience will become clearer and sink in more deeply.

Unlike mindfulness meditation, which is best practiced daily, internal work presents experiences that usually take time to digest and integrate. After a powerful experience it may be a few days before a person is ready for the next encounter. Once the ego meets the Self internally, the direction the process will take is unpredictable. If the ego is seeking guidance or support about specific issues, the Self may or may not respond. If it does not respond, it is usually because the ego isn't prepared to understand or appreciate the proper course of action. Generally it is best if the ego sets aside its agendas and trusts that the Self knows where growth is most needed and what insights the ego is capable of integrating at this point in its development. It is very important to remember that the greatest gift of the Self is not in the experiences it generates and the insights it offers, but in the nonjudgmental, loving relationship it offers the ego. This is the foundation of the bond between ego and Self, which can ultimately evolve to the point that the ego is continually open and transparent to the Self.

Beyond the Self, the inner world is generally populated with multiple forgotten or rejected aspects of the psyche that must be reclaimed if the ego wants to be fully transparent to the Self. Unintegrated parts of the psyche continually impact the ego, whether it is aware of them or not. They generate painful emotions even in the absence of any external stimuli. When there are external challenges, they can drive the ego to respond inappropriately, either overreacting or underreacting. They can be a source of compulsive inclinations and harsh, judgmental diatribes. If they are highly developed, they can be heard as actual voices, force the ego to do things it doesn't want to do, and even, in the most extreme cases, take over the body.

It seems to be normal for people to have internal ego states that exhibit varying levels of autonomy and self-awareness. The spectrum goes from fully functioning, highly autonomous ego states, as experienced by persons diagnosed with Dissociative Identity Disorder, to the commonplace experience of thoughts, feelings, or urges that feel alien to how the ego believes itself to be. The presence of unintegrated parts is a trigger causing the ego to become stuck in a struggle for control and thus more rigid and less able to let go into open receptivity to the Self. Any who wish to live at their fullest potential must be willing to acknowledge, encounter, and ultimately integrate all of these parts.

A common impulse upon meeting parts that threaten the ego is to try to suppress or get rid of them altogether. This is understandable and consistent with the ego's natural inclination to control and dominate its environment, whether it be internal or external. Doing so, however, only makes matters worse. The parts will tend to become more alienated and aggressive, and the ego will become more defined, rigid, and reactive. Once the ego accepts that subjugation will not work, integration becomes the only viable alternative. Successful integration is dependent on the ego accepting a set of fundamental assumptions that it will use as a guide in working with these parts:

- With a few rare exceptions (see the chapter on introjects), all of the entities encountered in the inner world are aspects of the same psyche and were originally created to serve some kind of positive purpose.

- At its core, every part not only has a constructive reason for being, but is also an expression of love.

- Even though it might be destructive for the ego to act on the impulses generated by these parts, it is critically important that the ego not categorize the parts as wrong or bad.

- There are legitimate needs that underlie the ways these parts are made, how they feel, and the behaviors they are inclined toward.

- Discerning these needs and finding ways to meet them appropriately is one of the ego's major tasks.

- This is accomplished by building a respectful, nonjudgmental relationship with the part, in which the part feels safe and welcome in disclosing its perspective and history.

- This process will be most efficient and effective when the ego allows the Self to direct it.

- The Self knows better than the ego or any external helper what parts are in need of attention and how best to respond to them.

As the Self introduces the ego to parts, the ego will notice that they are of various ages and can be of either sex. Parts are created for a variety of reasons. Some may contain potentials or talents that the ego has rejected. A common example is a feminine part in men who, because of a patriarchal or overmasculinized family or culture, denies its softer, nurturing inclinations. Other, self-critical parts, might represent a desire to excel that is distorted by society's assumption of what that means and by the idea that success is achieved through negative reinforcement and berating oneself for falling short.

Parts may also be created to contain powerful needs or emotions that would be dangerous to admit or express in the external world, such as anger over previous abuse or unjust cultural norms, or sexual desires that might cause the person to be harshly judged or ostracized. These parts will often present in dramatic and frequently threatening forms, such as dragons, tornados, wild animals, or grotesque human entities. These presentations symbolize how these natural human energies have been distorted by their repression.

The most common trigger for parts is childhood trauma, which includes physical and sexual abuse, as well as significant attachment deficits in which the very young child's needs for nurturance were not met. The pain occasioned by these traumatic experiences can be so great that the parts had to be split away from the ego's awareness either totally or partially in order for the person to function in the world. This splitting is the source of the wounded inner-child phenomenon. Depending on the severity of the abuse and the individual's innate potential for dissociation, there may be multiple hurt children within an individual's psyche, or just one that may present at different ages, depending on the issue being worked on.

Parts may also develop whose task is to further shield the ego from the pain in the wounded child when an event in contemporary life or an inner process such as a flashback or a nightmare threatens to break down the dissociative barrier between the ego and the wounded child. Richard Schwartz, PhD, who developed internal family systems therapy, calls these parts "managers" and "firefighters." On his website Selfleadership.org he describes them as follows:

> When a person has been hurt, humiliated, frightened, or shamed in the past, he or she will have parts that carry the emotions, memories, and sensations from these experiences. Managers often want to keep these feelings out of consciousness and consequently try to keep vulnerable, needy parts locked in their closets. These incarcerated parts are known as exiles [Schwartz's term for the wounded child/children].

The third and final group of parts jumps into action whenever one of the exiles is upset to the point that it may flood the person with its extreme feelings or make the person vulnerable to being hurt again. When that is the case this third group tries to douse the inner flames of feeling as quickly as possible, which earns them the name firefighters. They tend to be highly impulsive and strive to find stimulation that will override or dissociate from the exile's feelings. Binging on drugs, alcohol, food, sex, or work are common firefighter activities.

Work with the inner child can vary widely from person to person, as is probably evident from the transcripts of various clients' experiences I described earlier in the book. What is consistent is that the ego must develop a compassionate attitude toward the child and reclaim its traumas in such a way that nothing of consequence is left out. Also, limiting early-life decisions made in response to trauma must be brought to awareness, reconsidered, and released.

Just because a person remembers what happened doesn't necessarily mean that important aspects of the experience are not still dissociated. Sensations, emotions, and thoughts and decisions that arose in response to the trauma may remain hidden and have a continuing impact on the ego even though what happened is clearly remembered. The Self is by far the best guide for knowing what needs to be done and how best to proceed. It is usually advisable to wait for the Self to decide when it is appropriate to begin working with the wounded child and which issues should be dealt with first.

One thing to be careful about in reclaiming old traumas is the possibility of getting flooded by the experience and becoming retraumatized. This is not helpful and only exacerbates the wound. It is important that the ego remain in the observer mode as the child shares its experience. As the experience unfolds, the ego should be close enough that it can feel the sensations and emotions involved, but not so close that they overwhelm it. After the experience is concluded the ego should spend time with the child in a safe internal place, such as the meadow or a place from the child's life that felt secure, and give the child whatever support and nurturance the child needs. It should also encourage the child to talk about any attitudes, beliefs, or decisions the child may have developed in response to the experience.

The best way to begin work with the wounded child is to use the same relaxation and guided imagery process that was used to go to the mountain meadow and meet the Self. Once you are in the meadow and in the presence of the Self, ask the Self to bring the child forward so that you might get acquainted. If the Self believes that you are ready, it will bring the child to you. If not, it will decline and help you understand why. If an explicit presence of the Self is not available to consult with, then go to the meadow and simply invite the child that most needs your help to come out of the woods and join you. Then do your best to welcome it with an open heart. Make sure that a strong, loving bond has been established between you and the child before you ask the child to take you back to wherever it needs your help.

Working with parts other than wounded children follows a somewhat similar pattern. Sometimes the Self or a dream will draw your attention to a part, which you can then work with internally. Other times the part will intrude on your life in such a way that you cannot ignore it and are forced to deal with it. Voices in your head, especially critical or demeaning ones; strong, unbalanced emotional reactivity; or self-destructive compulsive behaviors are all indications of parts that need to be worked with. If possible, try to approach the part with compassion and kindness. If you cannot sincerely do that, at least be respectful. Also make sure that the Self mediates your encounter with the part. This will assure both you and the part that each will be kept safe. Additionally, the presence of the Self is an implicit reminder that the ultimate agenda is truth and love.

In your dialogue with the part, put most of your energy into seeking to understand the wants and needs of the part and how you might help meet these in a way that is not harmful to you or the psyche as a whole. Although how to do this may all become clarified in your first meeting with the part, it may also take many meetings before sufficient rapport and empathy is established for productive changes to take place. The ultimate goal is a merging of the ego and the part. This should never be forced and should not be seen as a way of "killing off" the part. It is rather a choice by both parties to expand their consciousness in a way that includes the other and results in a newly emergent ego that transcends the limitations of either of its antecedents. As with everything else internal, the Self is the most reliable guide and catalyst for these changes.

The ultimate goal of working with parts is the dissolution of inner divisions and a corresponding relaxation and expansion of the ego's sense of itself. As this unfolds, ego and Self become more intimately connected. Learning to work as a team with the Self throughout the process of inner healing also facilitates a sense of shared values and purpose that help lay the foundation for the final major step in personal evolution. This final step is the unshakable realization that the Self and I are one and that there is nothing I want more than to let it be the driving force in my life.

A current client is awakening to this fundamental insight. In her internal work three sessions ago, she reported the following:

> *The Divine Mother motions for me to join her. We are walking arm in arm beside the ocean. I feel joyful and I feel her peace, stability, love, compassion, and wisdom. I know she is who I really am. I ask her, "Will you help me more and more to embody all I know you are? It is truly a miracle to have your presence so real and available and without any criticism. I ask you to heal what I call depression and give me the courage to do what it takes to come into that healing."*

The Divine Mother tells me, "We want you to be a channel for heal-
ing. Leave off all the trying and struggling. Be in awareness more
than ever. Being an observer can keep you out of some of the lows
of depression. Do not entertain judgment. Be with us in the ob-
server mode. Touch your left shoulder very often to remind yourself
where you are physically and to help you remember to be aware of
my presence."

Divine Mother then continued, "More than ever own the power of
love. Get body, mind, and spirit aligned so we can stream much
more power and light through you. So many are sad and hungry
and almost dying for love. Much light is needed in this communi-
ty. You must not let anything get in the way of being the presence
of love that you are."

As the internal work began in her next session, she said that the Divine
Mother told her more:

"There is so much more that is becoming easier and easier for you
to do and be. Primarily, stay aware of your soul connection with
me and all beings. There is no division at the soul level, just a one-
ness with all."

The client then said that she was relaxing more and feeling a
deeper letting go. Divine Mother told her to rest and enjoy their
loving union. She went on to tell her, "Live with your present body
into what your mind knows so that your whole being is permeat-
ed with love, power, peace, and perfection. All that God is, we are.

"Now that you have cut the umbilical cord to your mother [the
client's mother was very judgmental and rejecting], you have re-
alized that your birth was beautiful and planned by us. You get to

see that you are a blessing to the world." She then noticed that the place where the umbilical cord had been cut was healing.

In the following session the Divine Mother hugged her and drew her close, speaking to her:

"Look deep into my eyes. What do you see?"

She replied, "I see everything I could imagine that is true, deep, loving, and honest. There is no pretense, just total openness. She is able to transform everything into the no-thingness. I see power, gentleness, humor, laughter, and perception—more than I ever dreamed was possible."

Divine Mother then said, "I am real, a mirror showing you who you really are. There is no need for you to plan how to be with me. Learn more and more how to live with me as your soul. Make it your primary choice. You don't have to create the perfection you want."

This profound encounter and merger with the Self that this client is experiencing is a gift that is available to everyone. Deciding to do whatever it takes to accept the gift is the most important decision anyone can ever make.

Choosing love and truth as your highest values, living mindfully with the help of mindfulness meditation, and doing the internal work necessary to heal the wounds that restrict the ego's flexibility and perspective all work together to make possible a truly full, authentic life. Nothing matters more than this!

SECTION TWO

The Counseling Connection

CHAPTER FOURTEEN

For the Client

If what you have read so far resonates with you and you are ready to take this path toward a more authentic, fuller life, you may begin immediately by following these four simple guidelines:

1) Make a clear internal commitment to ground everything you do in truth and love. This is probably an intention that you already live by. The only change here is that you make it an even more explicit foundation for your life than ever before. Don't worry about the details or specifics. Just do your best and trust that as time goes on you will become more and more aware of how to be most loving and appropriately honest with yourself and others.

2) Using the descriptions of the elements of mindful living in the chapter *Living in Communion with the Self,* make a list of those aspects of mindfulness that you are already doing or feel that you could do readily. As in the commitment to truth and love, what I am suggesting is not so much that you make a radical change in your life as that you be more explicit and purposeful in how you live out the qualities that you already value. Once you have identified those mindful ways of being that are most familiar to you, intentionally practice them with greater awareness than you have in the past. Slowly add other elements when you feel ready to do so. Also, if you are not already systematically practicing gratitude, do so using Brother Steindl-Rast's stop-look-go method. As you go through your day, pause for a moment, notice what you can appreciate about your immediate experience, savor it, and then go on about your business.

3) If mindfulness meditation is not already a part of your daily routine, make it so. This is not a difficult or time-consuming practice. Find a time in your day when you can regularly work in at least ten minutes of privacy and quiet. Follow the guidelines I offered in chapter nine, or even better, utilize a guided mindfulness meditation available on line. YouTube offers a wide selection.

4) Utilizing internal work (active imagination), begin to develop an explicit relationship with the Self within your inner world. Unlike the previous three recommendations, this last suggestion is probably a departure from anything you've ever done or even thought about. Nevertheless, most people intuit the existence of a deep, spiritual essence within themselves and have experienced its encouragement and guidance in subtle and sometimes explicit ways. The value of internal work is that it can greatly intensify this relationship and release its full potential. My website (www.deanschlecht.com) has an audio file entitled *Journey to the Self* that will facilitate this connection. There are also several other audio files that will help deepen your internal work and guide the healing process.

Also look for a knowledgeable, loving person who can be a reliable support and companion as you take this journey. Human beings learn new skills best when someone kind and patient is available who understands the process involved and is willing to share his or her expertise. While it is possible to learn how to use a new computer or smartphone by using the manual or help menu, it is far easier if a competent teacher is available. This is even more important when the task is as consequential as radical personal transformation.

Unfortunately, there aren't very many people who understand or appreciate the nuances of the internal world or the power and significance of the Self. Even among those who have some theoretical understanding, not all have actually engaged in the process themselves. They may still be a helpful resource, but far less so than one who is actively committed to his or her own journey—i.e., "walking the talk." If such a person cannot be found, it is no reason to give up. It is likely that your journey will be harder and take longer than would otherwise be the case, but if you are willing and committed, the Self will show you the way.

In Western culture there are two professional fields that could potentially be a resource for someone seeking this kind of guidance: psychotherapy and spiritual direction. Those who have diagnosable mental health issues such as depression, anxiety, compulsive or significant self-destructive inclinations, PTSD, or a history of abuse would be best served by a companion who is also a psychotherapist. Others might do equally well with either a spiritual director or a psychotherapist.

If you are interested in finding a spiritual director or teacher who can support your journey, there are several caveats to keep in mind. A doctrinaire teacher who is bound by a set of dogmas or a literal approach to the Bible will be inclined to try to impose rigid assumptions that will inevitably block or distort the flow of your inner truth. Such a guide will also be inclined to take a judgmental stance toward aspects of your inner life that, in fact, may be out of balance or even antisocial, but nonetheless are parts of yourself that need to be treated with respect and loving care if healing and integration are ever to happen. A constructive spiritual director must be more open and moreover humble. Anyone who presumes that he or she knows what is right or true for you is probably on an ego trip and is likely to do more harm than good, no matter how sincere or well intentioned the person may be. A constructive support person will give primary authority to your Self and encourage you to ground all of your significant decisions in that internal relationship.

Compared to most psychotherapists, there are some advantages to choosing to work with a spiritual director. Most spiritual directors explicitly seek to base their relationships with their clients in love. This is fundamentally important.

Learning to live a life grounded in love and truth requires that the guide or teacher be a living example of such a life, especially as he or she relates to the client.

Although most psychotherapists are good and loving people, their training usually does not overtly endorse love as the foundation of a healing relationship. Empathy, compassion, and rapport are emphasized, but so much emphasis is given in their training to maintaining therapeutic boundaries that most end up offering a caring but detached kind of relationship that falls short of Richo's model of life-giving love.

Another advantage to working with a spiritual director is that by definition they acknowledge the existence of an internal spiritual dimension (the domain of the Self) that transcends ego and is our ultimate source of purpose and meaning. There are schools of psychotherapy that also do this, but they are a small minority. These would include Jungian-oriented therapists, transpersonal therapists, practitioners of a type of therapy known as psychosynthesis, and practitioners of internal family systems therapy.

A third advantage to working with spiritual directors is that they are more likely than psychotherapists to accommodate the fact that the inner journey is a process of profound, cumulative transformation that may take years to unfold. Psychotherapists are often constrained by economics and training, forcing them to give priority to brief interventions focused on specific problem areas. There are many who would prefer to develop an in-depth, long-term relationship with their clients, but do not feel free to do so either because their agencies do not permit it or insurance companies will not pay for it. Therapists in private practice are most likely to offer long-term support for clients who can afford it, or pro bono for at least some who can't. Financial considerations tend to be less of a concern for spiritual directors. What insurance will or will not pay for doesn't matter to them since they are not covered by insurance to begin with. Most also would never decline to work with someone simply because that person couldn't afford to pay for their help.

One of the principal benefits of having a loving, spiritually grounded support person on the journey is that this person can offer the ego an approximation of the kind of relationship the Self is inviting the ego to accept. For many, being in a relationship with someone in the outer world who exemplifies the generosity, attention, acceptance, appreciation, affection, and noncontrolling stance of the Self makes the possibility of such a relationship real and helps them be more receptive to its internal presence. Those who have never known such generous kindness will be inclined to discount its internal presence as not really possible, or "just my imagination."

Another important related benefit is that you have someone in your life with whom you can speak your truth, knowing that you will truly be heard and not judged. A spiritual director who can offer this must have good listening skills and be down to earth enough not to be shocked by your history or thoughts or become critical of you when you admit to them. Spiritual directors like this do exist, but you may have to try a few before you find one who matches these criteria and is a good fit for you personally.

At the same time, if the fundamental characteristics of a constructive companion (loving, humble, spiritually oriented, open to a long-term relationship, and available despite financial limitations) on the journey are in place, psychotherapists can also offer some unique gifts. Their education and experience will help them be more comfortable and effective in dealing with mental health symptoms. This is a significant issue because most people do have some issues in this regard, as do a substantial percentage of those who feel drawn to profound personal transformation; those who are comfortable with their lives are understandably somewhat less motivated to undertake a process of potential radical change.

Many psychotherapists have had overt training in listening skills, and some have become quite adept at this. These skills are fundamental for creating the sense of a safe, nurturing bond that makes facing hard truths and inner conflicts tolerable. Some therapists have also had training and experience in working with parts or ego states and are aware of the Self and how central it is to both healing and personal transformation. As noted above, this would include some of those who identify themselves as Jungians, DID therapists, transpersonal therapists, or practitioners of psychosynthesis or family systems therapy.

Helping a person cope with autonomous internal ego states can be an insurmountable challenge for untrained therapists and many spiritual directors. Of particular concern is the tendency of some spiritual directors to consider ego states a form of possession and seek in one way or another to banish or exorcise them from the psyche. Therapists untrained in dealing with clients' internal realities may have their own version of banishing parts of the psyche with medications or tactics designed to help the ego ignore the parts.

Finding the right spiritual director or therapist may be difficult, but it is well worth the effort. Waiting to begin your journey until you find such a person, however, is not a good idea. Such guides are relatively rare, and it may take years to find one, if you ever do. This is no reason to settle for a life that falls short of your best potential. You have within you all that you need. If you must travel the journey alone, it is no reason not to begin immediately.

CHAPTER FIFTEEN

For the Counselor

If you are a counselor and you wish to give your clients the best support you can in the kind of transformational journey described by this book, begin by exploring that journey for yourself. There is no substitute for your own experience. As discussed in the previous chapter, finding a guide or mentor would be ideal, but if none is available, do it on your own. This is not the same as supervision. The guidance I am recommending is for you, not for how you are serving your clients. It is for your own transformation.

Your first task is the same as everyone else's. Live a vibrant, fully authentic life, grounded in truth and love and as transparent as possible to the Self. If you are enacting such a life, then who you are becomes the most important gift you have to offer. The approach to counseling I am encouraging is radically different from the brief problem-centered or solution-oriented cognitive therapies that are currently in vogue. While these approaches are unquestionably helpful and having expertise in them should be a part of every counselor's toolbox, in the context of this approach, resolution of the typical issues that counseling focuses on—grief, PTSD, inner conflicts, painful emotions, addictions, etc.—is not the ultimate purpose of the relationship. From the perspective I am offering, these issues are simply part of a deeper and broader agenda that transcends anything skillful techniques can accomplish. Wise counsel and kind support can be invaluable in helping people learn how to "do" their lives differently; however, helping them learn how to "be" at the deepest level cannot be adequately communicated in words. It is best shared by being lived.

A person transparent to the Self has a numinous, ineffable quality. Such a person possesses a kind of divine spark or creative vitality that invites and evokes the impulse for self-transcendence. This person also possesses an indefinable uniqueness that stands out but defies categorization. When a person's Self is the dominant presenting energy, judgment, fear, and any sense of boundaries or otherness falls away. In their place is a feeling of receptivity, quiet, patience, clarity, understanding, and welcome.

For clients to experience a counselor (or anyone) in this state of mind generates a powerful sense of presence that draws them toward a similar openness to the Self within their own psyche. The qualities that are the hallmark of such a counselor transcend the normal self-imposed limitations of the ego's usual preoccupations with identity and status. Openness to the Self erases these concerns and in their place is a very real, unpretentious person who does not fit into structured categories. This is not to say that only awakened or enlightened persons can do this work. What I am saying is you must have sufficient connection with your own Self so that when you are in a counseling session, your ego is able to step back enough to allow the Self to be strongly present. Practicing living mindfully and engaging explicitly with the Self in internal work are important catalysts for helping this to happen. If your connection with the Self is strong, quieting yourself at the beginning of a session and inviting the Self to come forward should be enough to initiate an hour of awakened presence, the best and most healing gift you could ever give anyone. Do it often enough, and it might even become a lifestyle.

Developing some skill in living mindfully is very important here. Clients long to be known and heard and can sense when you are truly present. If you are, their defenses diminish and their truth becomes more accessible. This same quality of presence is an essential part of being open to the Self. In order to successfully make a space for the Self, the ego must be in the present moment, clear and undistracted. When the counselor's ego is in this state, compassion and intuitive insight are significantly expanded.

A secondary benefit of embracing the same disciplines, practices, and commitment to personal truth recommended for clients in this book is the insight they give you on how such a life style feels and how difficult it can sometimes be. If clients know that you are sincerely engaged in the same process and can personally appreciate its costs and challenges, they are far more likely to take your guidance seriously and face their own demons when they know you have done the same.

As important as counseling skills, expertise, techniques, or methodologies might be, their healing impact is proportionate to the depth of the counselor's connection to the Self. Unless the Self vitalizes them, they are soulless and will have limited impact. Who the counselor is and the bond this generates with the client is far more important than anything the counselor does. The most potent catalyst for personal transformation is the bond that naturally flows when the counselor's Self embraces the client's wounded ego and evokes the client's Self.

A counseling session from this perspective typically has two parts: check-in and discussion of client concerns, and then internal work. The first part is largely educational and mindfulness oriented. During this part of the session it is important that as the counselor you see yourself simply as someone with useful information to offer, but not in a one-up position vis-à-vis the client. Make careful use of reflective listening skills in order to truly understand and connect with the client. Make sure you hear the client and clearly understand his or her dilemma before you offer any guidance. Earn the right to teach by listening in depth. Never give unasked-for advice. Do not be afraid of being transparent or of self-disclosure. If you have resolved struggles that parallel the client's, sharing what you have gone through can be very helpful. Even though the client's path to resolution may be different from your own, your experience can help instill hope if offered in a humble, sensitive fashion.

Present what you have to offer very gently. Offer your truth as you know it. *Do not try to persuade anybody of anything.* Give your truth as an act of loving kindness, as a gift that might be accepted or rejected in whole or in part, and be okay with that. Always know that you could be wrong or at least wrong for this person at this time. Do not get caught in the "expert" role or any role. Remember that you are just a person who might have something to offer both through the quality of your presence and caring, and through the truth of your insights.

Just as it is important to give up trying to persuade anybody of anything, it is even more important to *give up all attempts to enhance or defend your identity or image.* Remember, your sense of self or status is just an illusion or story. When you direct energy toward "control," whether through persuasion or through protection of identity, you disconnect from the other. Your ability to sense and flow with the inner life of the other is muted and distorted. Additionally, the drive to control locks you into ego and blocks access to the Self. Attempts to control the process will deprive your clients of what they most need from you and will deprive you of the precious opportunity to experience healing energy flowing through you.

The fundamental premise of internal work is that there is a deep, healing wisdom at the core of the client's psyche, which is the Self. It is an incredibly powerful, transformative gift. For that gift to be received, the client's ego must learn to let go of control and be in a receptive state. The counselor cannot effectively support this if he is himself caught up in a control-oriented frame of mind. As we all know, we teach far more by how we are than by what we say.

A deeper issue is also at stake here. The world of internal work is an experiential domain that transforms the ego through powerful metaphors and intuitive knowing. A counselor who tries to negotiate this world using ego-level, control-oriented tools of analysis and logic will diminish the experience and frequently miss the point altogether.

The effective counselor will trust the experience and give nurturing support to the ego as she encourages it to fully engage with the experience and remain open to the flow of awareness coming from the client's Self. Helping the client at this level demands that the counselor be dependent on her own wise Self, because the analytical, thinking mind of the ego is designed to manifest control. It is not a helpful resource for enhancing intuitive flow whether within oneself or for the sake of helping another. It will, in fact, tend to block the flow.

The best way to facilitate another's inner process is to forgo all elements of control. This includes, as previously mentioned, the need to persuade or any desire to protect or enhance your own identity or role. Yet it is also important to set aside any inclination to interpret for clients their own experience unless invited to do so, and then only tentatively and after having drawn out of the clients as much of their own awareness as possible.

By releasing the need to control, you will sense your own intuitive wisdom with much greater clarity. The counseling process then becomes like a dance, but one without predictable form or moves. As long as you stay in a noncontrolling, receptive frame of mind, without judgment and grounded in a heartfelt love, you will know what to say and when to say it.

Finally, treatment plans and ego-determined goals are not conducive to internal work. It has been my consistent experience that what emerges spontaneously from the wisdom of a client's Self is far more relevant and powerful than any therapeutic direction I might have chosen to take.

This is not to say that the counselor's education and skill development are not important. As mentioned earlier in this book, there are a wide variety of schools of thought and training programs available to help counselors who wish to improve their skills in a way that is consistent with the philosophy presented here.

For example, motivational interviewing, with its emphasis on the development of attentive, respectful listening skills and rapport building, is the most powerful methodology for creating a loving bond that I am aware of. Every counselor should at least attend an introductory workshop. *Motivational Interviewing: Preparing People for Change*, by Miller and Rollnick, is the basic text for Motivational Interviewing, and I strongly suggest it as a part of your professional library.

Acceptance and commitment therapy (ACT), developed by Stephen Hayes, PhD, is also a powerful, effective application of mindfulness to the practice of counseling. *The Happiness Trap* by Russ Harris, MD, is a very accessible introduction to ACT that both clients and therapists should find compelling. *ACT Made Simple* is a more technical, practical manual for therapists, also by Russ Harris. Steven Hayes and others periodically offer weekend workshops around the country that are well worth attending.

Three other schools of psychotherapy offer an approach to the psyche that is similar to what I have described in this book. Ego-state therapy, developed by John and Helen Watkins, is based, as is my work, on their experience of DID clients, and then applied to the general population of less fragmented individuals. Psychosynthesis, developed by Roberto Assagioli, and internal family systems therapy, developed by Richard Schwartz, PhD, both emphasize the centrality of the Self (Assagioli calls it the Higher Self) and both take a constructive approach to working with internal parts. Training in any of these three systems would be a good introduction to internal work. All three would technically be considered forms of psychodynamic psychotherapy. When the Self is made an integral part of the therapy, actually, the best description would be "transpersonal psychodynamic psychotherapy."

John Davis in his article "We Keep Asking Ourselves, what is transpersonal counseling?" in the journal *Guidance and Counseling* offers the following description of transpersonal psychology.

> Transpersonal psychology stands at the interface of psychology and spirituality. It is the field of psychology which integrates psychological concepts, theories, and methods with the subject matter and practices of the spiritual disciplines. Its interests include spiritual experiences, mystical states of consciousness, mindfulness and meditative practices, shamanic states, ritual, the overlap of spiritual experiences with disturbed states such as psychosis and depression, and the transpersonal dimensions of interpersonal relationships, service, and encounters with the natural world.

> The core concept in Transpersonal Psychology is non-duality, the recognition that each part (e.g., each person) is fundamentally and ultimately a part of the whole (the cosmos). As obvious as this might sound, it has radical implications for psychological systems founded on the premises of mechanism, atomism, reductionism, and separateness. From this insight come two other central insights: the intrinsic health and basic goodness of the whole and each of its parts, and the validity of self-transcendence from the conditional and conditioned personality to a sense of identity which is deeper, broader, and more unified with the whole. (Davis 2000, 3-8)

Of all the theorists and scholars who have contributed to our appreciation of the structure and function of the psyche, Carl Jung is preeminent. Foremost among his contributions is his appreciation of the Self, its connection to achieving wholeness, which he called individuation, and how the Self also connects us to the ground of being that he called Unus Mundus. His description of the two fundamental types of autonomous psychic entities, which he called archetypes and complexes, opened the way to a radically new, powerful form of psychotherapy. Moreover, his development of active imagination as a vehicle for self-exploration, as well as multiple other important insights, such as the centrality of the Divine Child and the relationship between Eros and Logos, has been an invaluable contribution to my own work. I am convinced that the essential features of his psychospiritual perspective will not only continue to transform psychotherapy but have already significantly affected our culture in general and will continue to be a part of its transformation. In chapters one and twenty three you will find a more in-depth exploration of this assertion and Jung's theories.

It must be reasserted, however, that the counselor's quality of presence and the therapeutic bond it facilitates are by far the most important elements of a healing counseling relationship.

CHAPTER SIXTEEN

The Therapeutic Bond

As in most other areas, Freud and Jung had dramatically different approaches to their understanding of the nature of the relationship that should exist between client and therapist. Based on his personal experience as well as his experience as a therapist, Jung was convinced that we all share extraordinary internal resources of great profundity and wisdom. He believed that the central role of the therapist is to function as a catalyst for the emergence of the client's own deepest competencies and then help the client appreciate their importance and relevance. Jung believed that the contemporary zeitgeist and Freud's approach in particular were corrupted by what he called the spirit of the times. Jung contrasted this with the spirit of the depths, with which he identified.

The spirit of the times is the spirit of scientific materialism, which accepts as real only those things that can be known through logic and analysis. It celebrates control and the role of experts when dealing with psychic realities. The spirit of the depths, which Jung espoused, believes that knowledge should be grounded in experience, especially internal experience, and that there is far more to personal reality than logic can comprehend. Unfortunately, Freud's perspective, aligned as it was with the spirit of the times, came to dominate Western thought in the twentieth century. Rather than respecting his clients' own resources and insights, he took the position of a "scientific expert" who would guide patients toward an understanding of themselves that conformed to his preconceived model.

When Freud decided that most of the childhood sexual trauma related by his clients could not be true, he had to radically change the nature of his work with clients. Instead of seeing his role as one who supported them as they worked through their traumas and the debilitating consequences of these traumas, he decided to develop a therapy that focused on the analysis and interpretation of resistance and transference. By doing so, he hoped clients could recognize how their perceptions of the other were distorted by their own projections and thus come to a more balanced appreciation of their own irrational strivings and assumptions. The means for achieving this was to foster an emotionally disconnected therapeutic relationship. The therapist was to function as an empty space into which the clients could place their fantasies and conflicts. The hope was that ultimately the client would see that these fantasies and conflicts were all about himself and had nothing to do with the analyst who was scrupulously disconnected and nondisclosing. Freud described the proper therapeutic relationship as one that was emotionally cold, akin to that of a surgeon toward someone he was operating upon.

After being considered the most sophisticated form of psychotherapy throughout most of the twentieth century, psychoanalysis is now largely discredited. Few people are being trained as analysts and fewer yet are seeking analysis. There is little scientific evidence that it has done any good at all. Ironically, however, the Freudian model of the detached, disconnected therapist has become for many psychotherapists a presumptive standard of practice, as evidenced by the extraordinary emphasis on boundaries in contemporary literature and graduate-level training.

> Boundary issues mostly refer to the therapist's self-disclosure, touch, exchange of gifts, bartering and fees, length and location of sessions, and contact outside of the office (Guthiel and Gabbard 1993). Boundary-crossing psychotherapy is an elusive term and refers to any deviation from traditional analytic and risk management practices, i.e., the strict, 'only in the office,' emotionally distant forms of therapy (Zur 2004, 27).

Multiple research studies have demonstrated conclusively that the most important factor contributing to a client's healing is the quality of the therapeutic alliance. Progress in therapy is directly proportional to the level of trust, safety, acceptance, and compassion the client feels with the therapist. In other words, clients who are secure in their therapists' wisdom and feel supported by their therapists' unconditional love for them have a foundation for overcoming even the most grievous psychological wounds. This kind of bond is not well served by therapists who feel constrained to follow much of the common wisdom about boundaries.

Regarding self-disclosure, the healing relationship is a deeply human relationship that is diminished by unnecessarily rigid assumptions rooted in the Freudian ideal of the therapist as disconnected authority. A bond of trust is dependent on knowing the other. It is not only acceptable but advisable that the therapist self-disclose at least in matters relevant to the client's needs and struggles. A therapist who is transparent and emotionally present will be experienced as far safer and more welcoming than one who is not.

The therapeutic a taboo on touching is in part driven by the Freudian, analytic approach to therapy, but also out of a concern to protect clients from sexual misuse. There is legitimacy to this latter concern. Nevertheless, avoiding all touch because it might possibly sexualize the counseling relationship is an unnecessary overreaction. Touch can have a powerful bonding impact when needed or invited by the client. Holding a person's hand or giving a hug can make an enormous difference to a client, as it would with anyone, especially when the person is in distress or needing affirmation.

If the giving of gifts to one another either by the therapist or the client distorts the relationship by creating inappropriate expectations or sense of obligation, then accepting or giving such gifts would be an obvious mistake. Yet, the giving of gifts is an ancient form of connection. When done in support of the therapeutic process, they can be very meaningful and significantly enhance the alliance between client and therapist.

The issue of bartering and fees is a very important one, but not in the way that is typically understood by those who frame it in terms of boundary concerns. The exploitation of clients for financial gain is obviously simply wrong. Such exploitation is more of a moral than a boundary issue. It is also wrong, however, to envision the counseling relationship as merely a professional service like plumbing or accounting that is available only to the extent that a person can afford it. Making the therapeutic relationship totally dependent on fees makes it obvious that for the therapist the relationship is a monetary issue and not a matter of the heart. Discontinuing therapy over money when a person is in the midst of significant work is simply cruel. Declining a client's offer to barter for sessions could be felt as a rejection and a discount of the client's gifts. If a poor client is not comfortable with pro bono care and wants to give something other than money in return, this should be honored as a gesture of respect unless it complicates the therapeutic relationship.

The boundary concern about length and location of sessions seems to me to be largely misguided. As I see it, thinking that the flow of a person's inner process can or must be contained only to a defined time or only in a specific place is naive. A genuine therapeutic relationship, like any relationship, has a quality of spontaneity and flow that must be honored if the therapist is to be truly in tune with the client. Flexibility in regard to length and frequency of sessions and openness to phone contact to help with crises between sessions is more efficient in the long run and greatly enhances the therapeutic alliance. In my experience, only a very small minority of clients have inappropriately taken advantage of this flexibility.

Obviously, some limits are necessary in all of these areas. The two determining factors should be the welfare of the client and appropriate self-care for the therapist. Both of these are subjective realities unique to the individuals involved and may change over time. They cannot be predetermined by a rigid set of rules, especially those grounded in the discredited frame of reference of Freudian psychoanalysis.

One theme that inevitably arises when the issue of boundaries is discussed is how clear boundaries protect clients from exploitation, both sexual and otherwise, and therapists from legal jeopardy. Although I am not aware of any research that can clearly demonstrate that clients are at any greater risk from engaged therapists than they are from disconnected ones, it is at least plausible that the possibility of exploitation, intentional or otherwise, increases with the intensity of the bond between client and therapist. As a general rule, the more powerful the tool, the greater its potential for either good or harm. However, exploitation has more to do with the therapist's lack of self-awareness and intentions than it does with whether there are rigid or flexible boundaries in the relationship. Above all else, the therapist must be dedicated to the welfare of the client as his highest value. Any behavior that misuses the client would be abhorrent to any sincere clinician.

Often, however, the beginning of the exploitation was never intended and happened out of the therapist's awareness. For this reason, all therapists, and especially those who have a flexible approach to boundaries, have a duty to engage in whatever practices are necessary to develop as much self-awareness as possible, so that they can catch themselves if they are beginning to lose their balance. They must also accept regular, in-depth supervision so that an outside, objective observer can test their sense of the therapeutic relationship. Just because poorly maintained aircraft often crash and burn is no reason to give up flying. The remarkable power of a strong therapeutic alliance makes the risk well worth it, as long as proper maintenance is provided.

Bill Miller, the founder of motivational interviewing, has made a clear and explicit case for embracing love as the foundation of an effective healing relationship. His article "Rediscovering Fire" (2000) is an excellent summary of the research supporting this premise and its implications. Connection, respect, and affection are transformative in any human context. The more wounded the individual, the deeper the need for these primary elements of nurturance and bonding. Donald Winnicott has also recommended that the therapist create a "holding environment" that emotionally resembles the connection between the "good enough" mother and infant. This is also the basis for David Richo's model of love, which I have referred to extensively in the earlier parts of this book. The love that heals is not an abstract concept and cannot be communicated except through an emotionally connected, flexible, intimate relationship. At the core of many clients' wounding is a significant disruption in this early maternal bond that must be resolved if healing is to be given a real opportunity.

Despite the fact that the therapeutic relationship has a reparenting quality at its core, it is also a relationship unlike any other. It is unique in its purpose—the psychospiritual healing and potentially radical transformation of the client. It is also unique in the high degree of self-disclosure and vulnerability required of the client in order to achieve the healing potential of the relationship. Because of this, the therapist must take extraordinary care to ensure that the client's safety is fully protected. Seen from this perspective, the issue of boundaries is a serious matter even when the psychoanalytic rationale is discounted and there is no danger of client exploitation.

Many things that therapists say and do can legitimately cause a client to feel unsafe and interfere with or undercut the healing process. Insensitivity, attempts to control, lack of transparency on the part of the therapist, or a pattern of the therapist of putting his own needs or wants ahead of the client's all undercut the client's sense of safety. Many boundary considerations around issues such as confidentiality, dual relationships, financial entanglement, and involvement in the personal life of the therapist are areas that have a high potential for making clients feel unsafe or insecure in the therapeutic relationship, and must be taken seriously.

Sometimes it is obvious when a particular boundary violation would diminish the client's sense of security in the therapeutic relationship. Other times there are occasions when the welfare and safety of the client would indicate that a boundary should probably be set aside, such as when confidentiality must be relinquished if a client becomes a danger to self or others. No rule should be absolute, but disregarding common practices that have been designed to protect client safety should be done very carefully. The potential for benefit must significantly outweigh the potential for harm. Conversely, if a therapist refused to violate a boundary because it was the commonly accepted rule or for fear of judgment, even though the benefit to the client would be very significant and the potential for harm small, that would also diminish the healing potential of the relationship. Client safety and welfare must always remain the primary guiding principles in making these judgments. At times these judgment calls are so difficult that the therapist would be well served by maintaining a support group of fellow professionals to help think through the most challenging cases.

Clearly, the two issues of therapeutic boundaries and therapeutic bonding are interrelated, and both are important. Nevertheless, they arise from two different perspectives, driven by distinct value systems reflecting right- and left-brain approaches to reality in general. A counselor who is principally concerned about bonding reflects a right-brain, receptive approach to reality. One who is primarily focused on boundaries is reflecting a left-brain, instrumental approach.

Arthur Deikman, MD, a transpersonal psychiatrist, developed a clear outline of these two distinctive ways of knowing and being. In his model, instrumental consciousness, grounded in the left brain, uses analytical thinking and models rather than direct experience as its principal means of knowing. It focuses on boundaries, difference, forms, and distinction. In instrumental consciousness the experience of the self is as a discrete object, more isolated than not, acting upon rather than as a part of the rest of reality. A counselor invested in this frame of reference would be inclined to follow Freud's model of the therapist as an emotionally uninvolved, detached expert. Boundaries and technique would be his natural focus of attention.

When the therapist approaches her task as a professional or expert endeavor expressed primarily through the judicious application of the right techniques at the right time, the therapeutic encounter becomes an exercise in left-brain dominant, instrumental thinking constrained by all the deficits outlined by McGilchrist and Deikman summarized in Chapter Twenty Two, *Cognitive Neuroscience and Counseling.*

In contrast, a genuinely transformative therapeutic relationship is grounded in a right brain receptive frame of mind focused on bonding with a strong sense of emotional connection and mutual respect. In this context the therapist does not assume any kind of superior role other than having helpful information to offer if the client is interested or requests it. The therapist's best gifts are a loving connection and a belief in the client's own resources for healing, even if the client is unaware of their existence.

Any discussion of the therapeutic relationship needs to be grounded in an appreciation of the intimate connection between relationships, the brain and nervous system, and the psyche or mind, which arises out of the interaction between the two. According to Daniel Siegel, the founder of the field of study known as interpersonal neurobiology, these three intimately interrelated systems give rise to who we are. He makes the point that our embodied brain and nervous system are profoundly influenced by the important relationships in which our lives are embedded. This influence affects not just the content of what we think or feel, but has a concrete impact on the structure and function of the brain itself. Among other things, aversive life experiences, especially insecure attachment in the first years of life, can alter the way the amygdala functions, leaving a person prone to anxiety and panic disorders, reducing the size of the hippocampus and thus impairing memory functions, and reducing the level of connectivity between the medial prefrontal lobes and the emotional brain, which can give rise to poorly modulated, impulsive behavior.

Because of the brain's plasticity, constructive relationships can be an important part of a systematic regimen that supports neuroplasticity and stimulates brain development, possibly undoing damage even after decades of being stuck in maladaptive patterns. We are not just the product of our brains: our brains and relationships mold each other, and together they enable the self-awareness that can, in turn, further shape the evolution of both our relationships and our brains.

A relationship that is powerful enough to actually help reverse old damage and facilitate new brain development must be shaped by a particular set of qualities—similar to those of a healthy, loving parent—on the part of the one who wishes to be a healing influence. This must be matched by a receptive and proactive state of mind on the part of the one seeking healing. Dr. Siegel has summarized a significant body of research, highlighting seven specific activities that support the brain's neuroplasticity, i.e., the ability to make structural, organic changes in response to life experiences. These include aerobic exercise; good sleep; good nutrition (including plenty of omega-3); novelty; the paying of close and careful attention to our experience without distraction; taking time to pay attention to inner sensations, images, feelings and thoughts; and finally, nurturing deep, loving relationships.

A person is most likely to embrace the above-listed regimen when encouraged and supported by someone who is trusted and respected. Moreover, it has been demonstrated (Siegel 2012, 21–22) that patterns of insecure attachment can change in a positive direction even well into adulthood, when the person has a chance to experience a life-giving, loving relationship. Such a relationship can inspire the brain to rewire in a way that undoes the neural patterns set in place by the deficits in early parenting. What this means is that the right kind of relationship can facilitate changes in another person at the most profound levels, both psychologically and organically. This potential to rewire the brain in a more integrated, life-affirming manner is what lies at the heart of truly transformative psychotherapy. This is what the therapeutic bond is ultimately about.

This insight has important implications for appreciating the significance of the therapeutic relationship. Recent research into neuroplasticity (how the brain is altered by experience) makes it very clear that the quality of our relationships actually causes continual alterations in the structure and function of the brain. Together relationships and brain structure and function create a dynamic matrix that has the potential to give rise to an ever evolving psyche: as my brain and relationships change, I become a different person. Although there are limits to how much change is possible, it is hard to know what these limits are without testing them. The counseling relationship can be a profoundly important contributor to this evolution of a person's psyche.

According to Siegel, mental health is the ability of the psyche to evolve or flow in a way that is flexible, adaptive, coherent, energized, and stable (FACES). When this flow is disturbed, chaos or rigidity or both ensue. Two primary factors can contribute to the disturbance of this flow: inborn neurological dysfunction or significant relational impairments. A central factor for facilitating the flow of mental health is a life-giving relationship. Ideally, this begins with a strong positive bond with the initial caregivers and is sustained by loving relationships throughout life. When this has not happened and the person's life is filled with chaos or rigidity, a reparative relationship can become critically important. A counselor who is able and willing to offer this is giving a gift that far transcends technique. Through the creation of a relationship that allows the client the opportunity to experience a nurturing attachment bond, the counselor is giving the client an opportunity to recreate himself and move back into the flow of healing.

Who of us, if we were in need of therapy, would not prefer to work with someone who was humble, respectful, and genuinely loving? We would, of course, want the person to be knowledgeable, but we would also want the information offered to be grounded in a deep understanding of ourselves and given in a way that respects our intelligence and our readiness to take in new information. We would especially want someone with whom we had a deep sense of rapport and who knew how to help us know ourselves in greater depth and learn to draw on our own best resources. The desire for such an affirming, life-giving companion reflects our deepest psychological needs and goes back to infancy.

In the newborn, the right brain is much more fully developed than the left brain and remains so for at least the first two years of life. This means that our initial experience of life is of a preverbal right-brain world focused on the relationship with the primary caregiver—usually, of course, the mother. According to Allan Schore in *The Science of the Art of Psychotherapy*, this emotionally charged relationship is the source of our felt sense of self (the implicit self as opposed to the explicit self of the conscious ego) and lays the foundation for our capacity for affect regulation and social relations as well as potential psychopathologies. Since this initial attachment process and its consequences are preverbal and usually not remembered, they are not part of the left brain's model of the world and self and thus remain out of the ego's awareness. Because of its primitive, nonlinguistic nature, defects in this early attachment process are not amenable to linguistically based interventions.

Contrary to the assumptions of cognitive behavioral therapy (CBT), this affective domain is not the result of how we think about the world and ourselves, but of the experienced reality of how the world is—the world we knew before we even had language. At a gut or emotional level, we "know" that this initial bonding experience defines the world, and no amount of telling ourselves otherwise will change it. Moreover, our initial attachment experience is so powerful that it appears to have epigenetic consequences that can permanently alter our stress-response potential (Schore 2012 p 347).

The mother-infant relationship is based on right-brain to right-brain communication and mirroring. Mother and infant respond automatically to each other's voices, tones, inflections (prosody), touch, gestures, and visual cues, with special attention being given to the mother's face. A positive, affirming bond causes the infant to "know" that the world is a fundamentally safe, welcoming place in which he is a valued participant. This right-brain "knowing" is the person's foundation and is more emotionally relevant and powerful than any consequent cognitive philosophies or beliefs.

If the infant experienced abuse or neglect, on the other hand, the long-term negative consequences have the same quality of "knowing" and are impervious to cognitive or left-brain beliefs and messages. This fundamental insecurity and affect dysregulation, combined with inborn vulnerabilities and temperamental dispositions, gives rise to all manner of Axis I and II psychopathologies. Schore quotes Leckman and March: "A scientific consensus is emerging that the origins of adult [psychiatric] disease are often found among developmental and biological disruptions occurring during the early years of life" (Schore 2012, 16).

Left-brain-focused interventions and techniques of any kind cannot penetrate the right-brain, unconscious, affective knowing of those who were significantly wounded in the first years of life. This does not mean that these wounds are beyond the reach of psychotherapy, but that the nature of psychotherapy as usually practiced must be reconsidered. What is required to undo deep early wounds is a reprisal of the broken mother-infant relationship, in which the client is able to finally experience the loving nurturance necessary to develop a positive sense of self and develop the capacity for appropriate affect regulation.

This corrective reprisal of the mother-infant relationship can arise through spontaneous, unconscious right-brain-to-right-brain communication between client and therapist or counselor. Healing, mother-like acceptance and affection, is communicated through visual facial cues, intonation, body signals, gestures, and even touch, just as it is between mother and infant. This unspoken dialogue of the heart, initiated by a truly empathic, warm, and genuine therapist, will inevitably engage the primitive, unconscious longing rooted in the right brain of the wounded client. Although technique has value and can be an important part of the process with clients who bear deep early wounds, it is always secondary to the quality of the relationship itself and how that is communicated nonverbally and unconsciously. As Alan Schore puts it, "more so than the cognitive mechanisms of interpretation and insight, relational-affective processes between patient and therapist are at the core of the change mechanism" (Schore 2012, 6).

The social-relational right brain is not only dominant in infancy, but should be dominant throughout life and definitely in psychotherapeutic or counseling relationships. When the right brain is constructively engaged in therapy, deep changes happen: "Recent research in brain imaging, molecular biology, and neurogenetics has shown that psychotherapy changes brain function and structure. Such studies have shown that psychotherapy affects regional cerebral blood flow, neurotransmitter metabolism, gene expression, and persistent modifications in synaptic plasticity" (Schore 2012, 10).

The discovery of mirror neurons has important implications for understanding how therapeutic relationships can have a powerful impact. Although there is still some debate among neuroscientists regarding the significance of mirror neuron research, many consider these findings to be quite important. Mirror neurons have been found in various parts of the brain. They all involve imitation and create a sense of connection between the observer and the one being observed. Those located near the center are implicated in tool use and language development. Those located in the right hemisphere appear to be a key part of how we are able to process and experience the emotions of others. These neurons become especially active when we observe others' faces, which are the most emotionally expressive parts of our bodies. They will impel us to match the other's expression and mood so that we will feel what the other is feeling. Persons with mirror neuron deficits, such as those on the autistic spectrum, have a hard time sensing the emotions of others and may therefore be impaired in their capacity for empathy.

This automatic, unconscious drive to imitate the other and feel what the other is feeling, generated by our mirror neurons, has two significant implications in any relationship. First, if I am willing to pay attention to another person, especially that person's face, gestures, and tone, I will begin to have feelings similar to what that person is experiencing. Then I can know from sensing my own emotions what the other person is likely to be feeling. This is at the heart of genuine rapport, in which one person is actually resonating through the action of mirror neurons the inner emotional life of another. Out of this both empathy and morality emerge as spontaneous, biologically grounded human imperatives.

If counselors wish to give their best, they must allow themselves to be impacted by their clients' emotions and inner lives and thus enter some very dark places with deeply wounded people. It is not enough to be merely an observer or teacher or even kindly guide. You must walk beside your clients and feel the harsh texture of their pain with them if you ever hope to truly appreciate their situation or earn their fragile trust. This is hard and costly.

Of course, some conflicts and problems can be resolved through a solution-oriented therapy that relies on analysis, insight, and a bit of personal support and encouragement. We have all given this kind of counsel and done some real good in the process. We have also received it from time to time and been grateful for the gift. There is another level of need, however, for which this is starkly inadequate. A spirit twisted and broken by devastating and intimate cruelties, such as those known in far too many families and elsewhere, needs a heartfelt connection with someone who is able and willing to tolerate and empathically connect with the grief and distress of a deeply wounded soul.

As we all know from our own lives, some painful stories can only be safely told within the confines of a loving, authentic relationship. Such a relationship becomes possible when the listener allows himself or herself to be emotionally impacted by the pain the other is disclosing. Without emotional resonance, there is no relationship in any significant sense of the term. The depth of a person's healing has always seemed to me to be more or less proportionate to the depth of relationship that person has with the therapist. Emotional attunement and nonjudgmental respect create the bond and safe environment necessary for a traumatized person to dare to hope for a life unburdened of its weight of darkness and pain. When the therapist is willing and able to allow in the emotions and existential questions occasioned by significant trauma and abuse, the client will be given the best chance possible to face the horrors of her life and the maelstrom of emotions and questions that are their immediate and unavoidable consequence. Offering this as best I can to my clients and keeping my balance at the same time has proven to be a significant challenge.

The anguish and terrible knowledge of the dark side of the human condition that these stories inevitably convey are burdensome to know and struggle with. My emotional equilibrium and my desire to maintain a trusting, optimistic view of life are severely challenged by helping bear the weight of my clients' darkness. Yet it can't be otherwise. Some degree of vicarious traumatization is necessary and inevitable.

The Adam and Eve myth tells us that we were cast out of paradise because we dared to taste of the tree of the knowledge of good and evil. I believe that the felt knowledge of our clients' wounding is precisely what this story is about. This is powerful and dangerous knowledge. If I let myself really know how depraved and mean spirited life can be for my clients, then my world no longer feels as safe or as good as it had seemed before I tasted this bitter fruit. Those who do not or will not face the terrible darkness that can be a part of the human condition can have the comfort of easily believing that a benign force is in charge of everything and that whatever happens happens for a reason, and all is well in the end. I still want to believe this, but the truth of it is not self-evident. The confrontation with life's cruelty, over and over, day after day in my office by men and women about whom I care deeply is sobering. I don't even have the comfort of being able to honestly tell my clients or myself that all will be well after the therapy is concluded. No one ever heals altogether from severe, prolonged trauma. Therapy always hits a point where it becomes clear that certain affective, relational, and cognitive limitations must simply be accepted and worked around.

Although dealing with trauma effectively can lead to depth of character and a compassionate heart, there are other better ways to get there, such as growing up in a home where the early attachment bond with your mother is deep and trustworthy, where your parents celebrate your individuality and do all they can to promote the emergence of your authentic self, where you have no doubt you are loved deeply, and where depth of character is modeled by your parents and compassion is celebrated by your culture.

It's hard for me to reconcile my desire to believe in a compassionate father/mother God who has everything under control when I spend so much time with people who have known no such thing in their lives, and instead present such immediate, constant, and varied examples of lives deeply compromised by the out-of-control behavior of those who were entrusted with their welfare. For me, this philosophical/spiritual consequence is one of my most significant vicarious responses to my clients' pain. It has forced me to dig very deep in order to build a viable spiritual foundation for my life.

The next most impactful aspect of my clients' suffering is the ongoing struggle with attachment disorders and enmeshment problems that are endemic in dysfunctional and abusive families. Most of the wounded people I know began their lives immersed in abandonment pain flowing out of insecure attachment to their mothers and proceeded to grow up faced with innumerable boundary violations and every kind of enmeshment.

This is personally difficult for me at two levels. First it keeps before my mind facets of my own life that I would just as soon not have to think about. However, over the years my own healing has unfolded and genuine forgiveness of my parents has begun to flourish. The second level of difficulty flowing out of the clients' abandonment-enmeshment dyad is the manner in which it constantly intrudes into the therapy arena. Clients have been conditioned to anticipate and invite interactions that energize either end of the polarity, especially with people with whom they have an intimate bond, such as their therapist or counselor. All too often I catch myself accepting the invitation either because my own unresolved wounds are being activated by the clients' material, or because I simply miss what is going on between us until my inclination to abandon or become enmeshed with the client becomes so obvious that I can no longer not see it. When I become thrown off balance by becoming caught up in the process of abandoning or becoming enmeshed with a client, some of the worst patterns out of my own history are activated with significant ramifications for the therapeutic process as well as my everyday life. Both client and I suffer.

When the wounding is deep, only love can bring genuine healing. I think it would help a lot if the graduate seminar on techniques in counseling included a section on how to love your clients in a deep, heartfelt fashion. In addition to Bill Miller's essay "Rediscovering Fire" and David Richo's book *Daring to Trust*, such a course would include Eric Fromm's classic, *The Art of Loving*. As he points out, love consists of four distinct but interrelated attributes: care, knowledge, respect, and responsibility.

Fromm's four attributes of love clearly describe a healing therapeutic relationship. I must genuinely care about the welfare of the client. How well he or she is doing must matter significantly to me.

I must also seek to truly know who this person is who is inviting me to help her find the Self that she doesn't yet know. It takes an enormous amount of awareness and sensitivity to begin to know the wounded self and the full complexity of its story. It takes even more to begin to sense the underlying authentic Self and help it emerge out of the ruins.

It goes without saying that I must be able to hold this distorted, often regressed, and nearly always angry ego with infinite respect—the kind of respect in which the divine within me bows before the divine within the other. If I don't, I can be assured that I will almost certainly do more harm than good.

Finally, I must be responsible to the relationship with all of its myriad implicit and explicit needs, demands, and wants, which can be akin to walking through a minefield. If I do not execute my responsibilities to the relationship well, both client and I will be hurt, perhaps deeply. I am not talking about getting into trouble with an ethics board or getting sued. What I am alluding to is that if I deeply interact with people in a way that is not loving at its core, I will slowly lose my soul. I will become dehumanized and lose connection with the very energies that give life meaning. Choosing to offer oneself as a healer is a glorious and dangerous thing. You will either grow significantly, or it can harden your heart, which to my mind is the greatest tragedy that can befall anyone. Of all of the facets of vicarious traumatization, this is the worst.

The violation of love in the therapeutic relationship will inevitably be expressed as some form of abandonment or enmeshment. Moreover, abandonment and enmeshment lie at the heart of the pain in the lives of most traumatized clients. It also constitutes the most fundamental dynamic that must be kept in balance throughout the therapeutic process. All therapists will err in both directions occasionally. Those with a personal history of pain around these two issues will have the added pressure of repetition compulsion pushing them to lose their balance. Most therapists will be more inclined to lose balance toward one end of the polarity or the other due to factors of temperament and personal history.

When I stop and think about it too deeply, doing in-depth therapy with those who most need it can feel almost overwhelmingly difficult. On the one hand, you must be emotionally attuned and responsive if there is going to be even a chance of the client taking the risk of baring her soul. Letting myself sense the hurt, grief, terror, hopelessness, and shame of this devastated, lost soul sitting before me is painful and tiring. I am not the kind of person who enjoys horror movies. On the other hand, when I do open myself to that other's story, I then find myself walking a tightrope. I must be careful not to inappropriately connect and thus exacerbate the client's enmeshment wounds or at the very least disempower the therapy. But I must also be equally careful not to abandon the client and activate what is usually the most fundamental and destructive wound of all.

Years ago, as I became aware of the power and centrality of the abandonment-enmeshment dyad, I saw it principally as something caregivers did to children. Then it dawned on me that this is what constitutes the essence of bad therapy. All those incompetent therapists out there are basically people losing their balance either toward the abandonment or the enmeshment side of the polarity. Finally, as I appreciated more fully the specifics of abandonment and enmeshment, I saw that I was one of the incompetent therapists, at least some of the time, as are we all.

Children who suffer from enmeshment are not allowed or helped to find their own voice or live out their own best potential. They have a connection with their parents, but the cost of that connection is that they sacrifice themselves to serve the needs of the parents. Something comparable happens when therapists become enmeshed with their clients. The therapist inclined toward enmeshment is typically kind and compassionate and is willing to go the extra mile to help—just the kind of therapist any one of us would like if we needed therapy. In itself it is an ideal stance for anyone engaged in in-depth psychotherapy. Since the therapist's intentions are so pure and openhearted, it's difficult to see how this could be harmful, which only makes it all the more dangerous for both parties, as a traumatized client's truth is nearly always complex and subtle. The unfolding of that truth is usually going to be hampered by ingrained secretiveness, distrust of others—especially authority figures—shame, and the client's fear of her own dark aspects, some of which can be quite awful. The enmeshed or overinvolved therapist blocks the full evolution of that truth by unwittingly imposing his own usually well-intentioned agenda.

The enmeshed therapist usually violates the therapeutic relationship in one or more of several fairly predictable patterns. Like the enmeshed parent, he may allow to develop a reciprocal dependency in which he needs the client's attention and support as much as the client needs his. Although very affirming to the client over the short term, it is the same kind of false empowerment through role reversal that robs children of their childhood and a chance to mature appropriately, and will do the same to the client. Another form of inappropriate therapeutic dependency is pathological bonding. "You and me against the world," is one expression of it. Getting caught up in the reenactment of the client's trauma bond with an abuser is another.

Just as a healthy parent recognizes that she has a special role in the life of her child that demands certain kinds of interactions and disallows others, so must a healthy therapist. Wounded, suffering people need someone who is confident in her skills and competent to understand their real needs. They prefer a therapist who has known significant wounding herself and is willing to admit it, but they do not want or need a "me too" relationship in which their stories become the occasion for more of the therapist's own story. Our personal stories can come close to the client's but can never be the same. Too much attention to them will invite role reversal, but even when that does not happen, they will block perception of the uniqueness of the client's own truth, which, of course, is part of what happened to them in their original wounding.

Like a healthy parent, the effective therapist must be able to tolerate the sometimes overwhelming needs and feelings of the client without becoming defensively disconnected or detached. This can be very difficult. Some stories are heartbreaking, and some are terrifying, evoking horror and shock. Yet the therapist must stay in balance as a solid point of reference while the client struggles with the intense feelings triggered by these remembrances. Not only must the therapist be able to tolerate the stories, but she must also be able to tolerate the client's intense, painful emotions and not withdraw or be overcome herself.

When the therapist engages the client in a spirit of loving respect, care must be taken that this does not degenerate into idealization of the client, which is merely another facet of enmeshment. In this phenomenon once again the client's reality is discounted and healing is thwarted. It is easy to fall into a good/bad dichotomous worldview when people speak of the atrocities done to them: the perpetrators are bad and the victims are good. Comforting as this model may be, it is seldom true. Perpetrators are usually complex people driven by their own pain and may have had a much more convoluted relationship with the client than a good/bad model can entail. Additionally, the client will almost inevitably have been so distorted and compromised by his suffering that he may well have made choices about which he feels great shame or guilt, some of which may be appropriate; by idealizing the client the therapist implicitly makes some of the most important things the client must explore, his own shame and guilt, off limits. Again, enmeshment deprives the client of his own truth.

Related to the inclination to idealize the client is the inclination to take a position of excessive advocacy or responsibility for the client's life. A kind therapist may be so touched by the very real unmet needs of the client that she may be tempted to make the client's life a personal project. Drawing the line here can be very difficult. After all, a person without minimal food, shelter, and safety in her life is not going to be ready to do in-depth therapy. Nonetheless, when a therapist becomes a primary source of support for clients outside of the therapy context, it greatly increases the complexity of the relationship, making a challenging situation even more so.

A final destructive expression of therapeutic enmeshment has to do with how the recollection of the traumatic event or events is handled. For healing to happen, the story must be told and felt, sometimes many times over. The therapist must be willing and able to truly hear it without judgment and with empathy. She must not, however, become overly fascinated by it or let herself too fully identify with the client as the story unfolds. This will make the story part of her agenda and again rob the client of her own unique reality, diminishing the possibility of achieving resolution. It is the power and drama of the trauma that must be diminished through the telling of the story, not intensified. Then the trauma can be placed in the broader context of the person's whole life history, which is the essence of healing.

At the opposite end of the spectrum, another way of doing bad therapy is to give in to the abandonment side of the dichotomy by taking an avoidant or detached stance toward the therapeutic relationship.

This is a stance that is implicit in the conventional wisdom about boundaries. There are innumerable ways to be avoidant, many of which are considered highly appropriate and "professional." Yet they are in fact the cruelest things a therapist can do to a client, and they echo the awful potential for damage arising from early-life maternal abandonment.

At its most fundamental level, the therapeutic abandonment of the traumatized client begins with the refusal to establish a caring bond. Following this is the denial of the validity of the client's story or the denial of the phenomenon of PTSD as either real or significant. A variation on this theme of abandonment is the unwillingness to discuss traumatic history unless corroborating evidence can be offered, "proving" that it really happened. Another way of detaching from the client is to fail to explore the trauma story, guaranteeing that it will remain unresolved. Pushing the client to recover quickly and/or minimizing the impact of the trauma may please a managed care company, but it is just another form of abandonment. Victims are usually already predisposed to minimize their traumas, but "slower is faster in the long run" is an important axiom to hold onto in the working-through process.

Even therapists who are open to the subjective truth of their clients' stories and willingly engage in the working-through process will sometimes find themselves slipping into an avoidant, abandoning posture. The awful content of the stories and the myriad ways in which clients can be difficult can evoke in therapists and counselors dread, disgust, loathing, numbing, shame, horror, and any number of psychophysiologic reactions, such as nightmares, anxiety states, depression, insomnia, and other somatoform problems. Not surprisingly, therapists dealing with this tend to be relieved when their clients cancel and will themselves cancel sessions for any plausible excuse. Often they will detach by taking a hostile, blaming, judgmental, or disdainful stance toward the client. Eventually they may abandon the client altogether by referring the client elsewhere, overmedicating the client, or declaring the client "well enough" and prematurely terminating therapy.

As bad as the damage done by enmeshment may be, the harm done by abandonment is even worse. We who seek to truly love our clients must never assume that our good intention is enough. We will always be prone to losing our grip on genuine love and falling into enmeshment or abandonment. It is foolish and dangerous for us and our clients to try to walk this difficult path without our own support community.

CHAPTER SEVENTEEN
Dream Work

*The dream shows the inner truth and reality of the patient as it really is: **not** as I conjecture it to be and **not** as he or she would like it to be, but as it is.*
—C. G. Jung

In *The Red Book* Jung stated,

> The spirit of the depths even taught me to consider my action and my decision as dependent on dreams. Dreams pave the way for life, and they determine you without you understanding their language. One would like to learn this language, but who can teach and learn it? Scholarliness alone is not enough; there is knowledge of the heart that gives deeper insight. The knowledge of the heart is in no book and is not to be found in the mouth of any teacher, but grows out of you like the green seed from the dark earth. Scholarliness belongs to the spirit of this time, but this spirit in no way grasps the dream, since the soul is everywhere that scholarly knowledge is not (233).

This perspective is the essence to my approach to dreams.

Dreams serve many vital functions and are a profoundly important aspect of the psyche. In a summary of recent research in the March 2011 *New Scientist*, Emma Young enumerates three important functions dreams serve as uncovered by contemporary neuroscientists. She says, "We now know that this particular form of consciousness is crucial to making us who we are. Dreams help us consolidate our memories, make sense of our myriad experiences, and keep our emotions in check." Researchers have found that dreams can be a way to rehearse both friendly (in non-REM dreams) and aversive encounters (in REM dreams.) They can strengthen negative emotional memories even as they diminish the emotional impact of these memories. This helps us remember and learn from threatening events and thus enhances survival and/or quality of life. (Unfortunately, in PTSD dreams the ability to diminish the emotional impact of a remembered event has become disabled, and the dreams only increase pathology.)

In 2009 the PBS program *NOVA*, "What are Dreams? Inside the Sleeping Brain," offered a more extensive summary of dream research, Some of the most important conclusions it drew from an overview of the work of multiple contemporary researchers are as follows:

- Dreams can be divided into two fundamental types, REM and non-REM dreams. Dreams during non-REM sleep feel more like regular thinking, but with more imagery than most people use during waking consciousness. They tend to be more positive, and when dealing with external others more conciliatory than REM dreams, which can often be confrontational.

- Many dreams are a form of purposeful, conscious thinking that is radically different from the logical, linear thinking that we ordinarily engage in during our waking hours. They utilize intuitive and visual modes of thought that help us see issues from a different point of view than normal waking awareness and offer solutions that are truly outside the box. They give us insights that we might never else have.

- They can be a crucial tool to help us learn from our experience by consolidating memories. They also prepare us for the future by integrating new learnings with old ones and then running simulations in which we can experience this newly integrated perspective.

- Immediately following REM sleep, subjects experienced a 40 percent increase in creativity.

- Dreams often bring to awareness important internal dynamics that were unknown to us before the dream.

- Often it is as though the dreaming self is working through the night in order to prepare us for the coming day, either through increasing awareness or helping us practice an important skill.

- Nightmares, especially in children, can be indispensable rehearsals to aid in survival. For most of human history children had to be hyperalert to the danger of predators (monsters), or the human race would not have survived. Nightmares helped to maintain that awareness. As we mature, nightmares can become rehearsals preparing us to face stressful life events.

- Dreams are a new adventure every time. We don't know whether they will be fun or scary, but they will often be poignant.

Many dreams are produced by a distinct form of intelligence that expresses itself through stories that make extensive use of image and metaphor. As Ian McGilchrist points out (188), dreaming is predominantly a right-brain process, as demonstrated by EEG and PET scans. Just as our ego-self is largely grounded in the analytical and verbal left brain, the right brain has its own consciousness, intelligence, and capacity for choice. In fact, the right brain has a much broader range of awareness and connection to physical, emotional, and external realities than the left brain. Instead of language it uses image, metaphor, and art to express itself. In doing so it generates strong affective and kinesthetic responses that can have a significant transformative impact. Dreams are a primary way through which the wisdom and intelligence inherent in the right brain are given expression. The evidence for this is well documented by Harry F. Hunt in his book *The Multiplicity of Dreams: Memory, Imagination, and Consciousness.*

According to Hunt, there are four basic kinds of significant dreams. These are found in all cultures. Anthropologists report that tribal peoples categorize them as personal dreams, medical-somatic dreams, prophetic dreams, and big dreams, which are archetypal or spiritual in nature.

Hunt teaches that all dreams are grounded in remembered personal material, most of which is of minor importance. However, some memory dreams are very powerful and important. Examples of this include the dreams associated with posttraumatic stress disorder (PTSD) and dreams in which repressed material emerges.

Although about 80 percent of dreams are relatively meaningless reorganizations of memory fragments, right-brain consciousness is very active in the remaining 20 percent. It will transform a mundane, realistic dream into something much more than the simple reorganization of memory. In Hunt's summary of contemporary dream research, these special dreams fall into roughly the same categories as the four categories of dreams reported by primitive peoples.

The first type includes dreams that tell complex stories and often include various types of word play, such as puns and assonance. Frequently these dreams are in reference to unresolved history and emotional conflicts.

The second category reflects a sensitivity to physical health and physiological processes. Dreams will sometimes bring to a person's attention health related issues of which the ego is completely unaware or minimizing. Dreaming about a broken heart might be about personal rejection, but it could also be an indicator of cardiovascular problems.

The third type of dream makes extensive use of visual metaphor and sometimes evolves into archetypal dreaming. Archetypal dreams present "major existential life themes" with a strong sense of "felt meaning and portent" (Hunt 1989, 129.) This sense of meaning and portent is directly within the dream rather than in the "aha" following conscious analysis, which is often the case with other kinds of dreams.

The fourth dream type in Hunt's model includes those dreams that focus on external world concerns and problems, such as dreams of impending disaster or dreams that present intuitive solutions to vexing problems. Any dream that emphasizes one of these types will usually include elements of one or more of the others as well.

Meaningful dream interpretation depends on the realization that dreams are designed for varying purposes. For instance, a scientist might have a type-four dream that offers an intuitive solution to a particular laboratory problem. If he or his therapist insisted on working through the dream under the assumption that all dreams are references to early life history, the real value of the dream would be lost. Similarly, if a somatic dream that was trying to draw an individual's attention to an impending heart problem was interpreted through Jungian amplification as the expression of an ancient archetypal myth, the client would be both misled and left at serious risk.

If a counselor is willing to accept that there are several fundamentally different kinds of dreams, his approach will be much more flexible. Some dreams are quite transparent and easily understood. They need no interpretation, but merely acceptance by the ego. Other dreams, although relatively easy to understand, benefit from being reinforced and amplified so that the ego can receive their full impact. Still others are relatively meaningless to the ego, but upon working through are found to be profound metaphorical comments on internal conflicts and their historical antecedents. These dreams are best approached through some form of associative processing.

Although Carl Jung did not have the benefit of contemporary studies regarding right- and left-brain function, recent dream research, or Hunt's categorization of dream types, most of his insights regarding dream work remain as valid as ever and are only reinforced by more recent scholarship. Jung's approach to dreams can be boiled down to nine basic principles:

1) Dreams can have both objective and subjective relevance. Dream characters may refer to external others or to oneself or both, although most dream characters seem to refer to the self.

2) Dreams include all personally relevant reality, external and internal, and especially reflect the full span of unconscious internal realities. They give the ego an opportunity to ground itself in a far broader and more grounded perspective than normal ego consciousness can achieve on its own.

3) Dreams and active imagination are the primary windows through which the ego can encounter fundamental archetypal resources and experiences. These refer to the great dreams Hunt describes as well as dreams in which we meet inner teachers or wisdom figures, Great Mother figures, the Divine Child, shadow elements, and contrasexual aspects.

4) As Freud proposed, Jung agreed that dreams do reveal repressed aspects of the psyche, such as shadow elements and unresolved trauma, but he made the point that this is only a small part of what dreams offer.

5) Jung taught that dream symbols should not be interpreted outside of the context of the full dream or the client's life, as in using a dream

symbol dictionary in order to "understand" the dream. There should be no preconceptions when approaching a dream symbol or its amplification.

6) Sometimes, albeit rarely, dreams confirm an ego behavior or belief. Usually, they compensate for a limiting ego assumption or lack of awareness.

7) Dreams connect us to an ancient inner wisdom that emerges from the depth of the psyche and is attuned to our instincts and deepest needs.

8) The nocturnal consciousness known in dreams is just as important as the diurnal consciousness of our waking ego. In fact, dream consciousness is more fundamental and connected to reality than normal, analytical waking thought.

9) Jung believed that the counselor should strip the dream of its details and just present the essence of it to the client. This can be very helpful to clients because simplifying the message makes it easier for the ego to comprehend and integrate. Nevertheless, this simplification needs to be balanced by an immersion of the ego within the metaphoric content of the dream through the use of active imagination / internal work as a way of embracing the dream. The perspective of James Hillman, a prominent contemporary Jungian, is instructive here. He taught that it is more important for the ego to allow itself to be impacted as fully as possible by the dream experience than to try to fit the dream contents into the ego's preexisting model of reality. Dreams experienced with this frame of mind have a transformative potential that exceeds what the ego can understand or facilitate.

The dream work methodology I have developed and will now describe in the remainder of this chapter is designed to enhance the ego's connection to the dream without any preconceived assumption regarding the type of the dream. As the ego more and more fully allows itself to be impacted by the dream metaphors and/or narrative, the type of dream and its particular purpose will become evident.

The first decision a counselor needs to make regarding dream work is whether or not to use it in a particular session. I have developed a hierarchy of options for therapy that offers me what I feel to be the most effective therapeutic outcome. If the internal work / active imagination is flowing well, I will usually continue to make it the principal focus of therapy. By "flowing well" I mean that there is a clear, purposeful direction to the process. However, if there has been a major trauma in the external world or a dream that seems to be very important, I will give that precedence.

When the internal work is not flowing well, I will focus on dream work as my next option. If the client does not recall any dreams, I will use a specific guided internal journey (such as anger's cave or fear's abyss) to help open up new material.

Some people, such as myself, struggle with doing internal work. We experience limited imagery or spontaneity in the process. In this instance, dream work is invaluable if the counselor wants to do more than mere ego-level therapy, as dreams are even freer of ego control than most internal work. They also provide client and therapist with established symbols and scenarios that can be reclaimed and embraced through their use in consequent internal work. This is a great help to those of us who have trouble accessing internally generated symbols without the help of a preceding dream. The dream provides images, scenarios, feelings, and other reactions that can be worked with in the same style as internal work. My most powerful personal therapy sessions always occur when we have done in-depth dream work.

Additionally, people who are resistant to internal work, thinking it silly or strange, are much more likely to think that their dreams are relevant and worthy of attention. This is especially so if they have had a nightmare, a repetitive dream, or a dream that feels important. They will tend to be open to dream work, whereas meeting and dialoguing with an inner part may seem bizarre.

There is a world of difference between the dream work that I teach and the dream work typically done in therapy. Dream work is as different from ordinary dream analysis as internal work is from conventional psychotherapy. As with internal work, the principal difference centers on the issue of authority.

Most attempts to use dreams as a resource for healing are derailed because the therapist operates under the assumption that he is "the one who knows." The therapist assumes that the client needs to learn from him the meaning or significance of the dream experience. This assumption greatly reduces the potential impact of the dream, and it makes little difference whether the therapist is right or wrong about the interpretation.

I know of very few resources for dream work that approach dreams in any way other than as something to be interpreted with the help of an expert. This is the case no matter what school is represented, with the exception of certain facets of Jungian and Gestalt therapy. Even those dream therapies that rely on the client's own intelligence and intuition in order to discern the meaning of the dream still often miss much of the dream's gift because they are largely left-brain, analytical exercises detached from the impact of the dream's transformative metaphors.

In Gestalt therapy, the approach to dreams is much more experiential than intellectual. This is a considerable advance over the more traditional modes. Yet Gestalt also falls short because there is too much therapist control. The therapist decides how to attack the dream and which dream figures to dialogue with. He also frequently structures the dialogue, and most Gestalt therapists assume that all dream figures are reflections of the dreamer. This is not true, and such an assumption will frequently distort the dream's message. Furthermore, Gestalt work with dreams, like Gestalt work in general, is psychodramatic work that is usually done without trance, which I perceive as a flaw. When dream work is done without trance, there is frequently too much egocentric distortion for the full impact and meaning of the dream to come through.

Neither the counselor nor the client at ego level can fully know most significant dreams. I have some very intelligent, well-read clients whose interpretations of their own dreams sound quite plausible. Yet compared to dream work, these interpretations are usually inaccurate and/or incomplete. They may be close, but they will often miss important elements or significant nuances. Almost invariably they will miss most of the power in the dream. It is simply not possible to fully appreciate most dreams with the intellect alone.

Most dream symbols and processes are subjective expressions of realities within the client's internal world. I want to underscore that these are personal symbols. There is no code or dictionary of symbols that will ever make possible an objective science of dream interpretation. Dreams are subjective statements, usually presented for the sake of the client's healing. One striking and very rare exception is when an antagonistic, split-off part generates a dream as a way of attacking the ego.

For example, one client dreamed that life was hopeless and that she was worthless. The dream was powerful and the message was clear and convincing. This was exactly the intention of the dream. In the dream work, we sought out the source of the message. It turned out to be a split-off anger that was trying to weaken and control the ego. The dream was useful, but it was not useful based on the simple assumption that everything in a dream is true. There was certainly a truth behind it, which was that a part of the person was very angry and attacking the individual, but the dream message itself was not true.

Dreams can either reflect internal world processes or comment on external world realities that are relevant to the internal world. Health, personal safety, and intimate relationships are frequently the focus of dream content; all of these are central to the pursuit of wholeness.

For instance, whether I am in an unhealthy, manipulative relationship or a genuine, loving relationship is exceedingly important to the internal world. The people of the opposite sex in my dreams are not necessarily representations of my own contrasexual element. The woman in the dream may well be the woman I am engaged to. When I see her turn into a vampire who is drinking my lifeblood, it may be a warning about the relationship. Additionally, it may be that she reflects a negative contrasexual element within myself, but this need not necessarily be the case. Likewise, if I dream that the wheels are falling off my car, it could be saying that my spiritual journey is stagnating. It might also mean that my car is in dangerous condition and I need to take care of it.

Many therapists who work with dreams try to teach people how to modify their dream experience so it will not be so overwhelming, terrifying, or difficult. This is a way of distorting the dream by manipulating it according to what the client or therapist thinks is right and good. The impact of the dream is thereby diminished and its message possibly lost.

On rare occasions, some people seem capable of generating self-serving dreams. These dreams seem to be dominated by an egocentric need to reinforce chosen positions. The ego can generate dreams just like any other part of the psyche. Such an ego must have a very strong need to validate its position. Although a therapist may strongly suspect that a dream is egocentric, it may be very difficult to discern this with any certainty.

All of this being said, the fact remains that most dreams reported in counseling are extremely accurate and very useful.

Repetitive dreams, especially, point to issues of significant consequence. If a person has a repetitive dream, it should be placed near the top of the counseling agenda. Also, if a client presents a crystal-clear dream, remembered in detail, and such dream recall is unusual for him, this is a signal that significant attention should be given to that dream.

I myself once had a dream that was the grounding dream of my life. It was crystal clear and remains so to this very day. It was unlike any of my other dream experiences. That dream was screaming to be paid attention to, and I have benefited considerably from attending to it.

Dreams tend to reflect every function of the psyche—internal issues, resolving history, denied aspects trying to have a voice, inner conflicts between parts or between parts and the ego, ownership of instinctual energies, and protecting oneself from external-world threats of various kinds. Everything the psyche does, dreams reflect. Dreams are part of being fully human and reflect the whole gamut of human experience.

Although the vast majority of dream symbols are subjective, there are some universal patterns to be found in dreams. Jung called these patterns archetypes. Archetypes can be either figures or processes. Inner Wisdom, which often appears in the form of the wise old man, is a universal archetype that I purposefully seek to connect with in internal work. The Great Mother and the Divine Child are similar archetypes.

Moreover, the process of moving through death to life—the death of ego-centricity in order to live out of the Self—is an archetypal process and the core theme of this book. Wherever there are human beings, this process is acknowledged and ritualized.

Other symbols seem to have universal archetypal meanings as well. For instance, water is a fairly universal symbol for entering one's depth or internal world. In different ways, crystals, gold, circles, and squares all seem to represent the Self. For women, horses seem to symbolize masculine energy and sometimes healing. Volcanoes almost always point to anger. There are probably somewhere between twenty and thirty figures, processes, or symbols that consistently present in dreams and internal work. However, there is no reason why the counselor or client should be particularly adept at interpreting them. Their meaning will be self-evident within the course of the dream work. Dreams should be embraced and experienced rather than merely interpreted by either the counselor or the client. Interpreting a dream reduces the dream experience to an analytical process. What could be a transforming encounter is turned into a verbal exercise in analysis or erudition.

There are many false assumptions among counselors regarding dreams and dream work. The first, from Freud, is that the unconscious uses symbols in order to hide unbearable truths. Actually, the unconscious designs its symbols in order to offer the ego the maximum opportunity to encounter internal realities. The symbols are carefully chosen to impact the ego in every way possible in order to facilitate maximal change. They are not designed to hide anything.

A second false assumption is that all dream figures represent internal realities. Although most dream figures do represent internal realities, some are externally referenced.

Another false assumption is that dreams simply replay whatever was done during the day. As many as 80 percent of all dreams may well be just this, but the other 20 percent are far more (Hunt 1988).

A final assumption is that clients dream in ways designed to please the counselor. This is possible but not always the case. If pleasing the counselor or having the right kind of experience is very important to the ego, it can precipitate an egocentrically determined dream that will present exactly what it believes is expected. Because dreams are an attempt by the internal world to communicate with the ego, the ego's beliefs and milieu will always have some influence on dream content. The less rigid the system out of which the counselor works, the less constrained will be the dream processes of his clients.

It is only partly true that special therapeutic expertise is necessary to make full use of clients' dreams. The ability to analyze the content of dreams in terms of archetypes, myths, etc., is of minor relevance to dream work. Knowing how to work with the flow of the dream and how to bring the client into an effective connection with the dream is extremely valuable. The counselor does have a place, but as catalyst, not analyst—not as one who knows, but as one who stands with the dreamer, supporting and encouraging the dreamer as he embraces the dream and the transforming impact of the dream's symbols. This is very different from merely understanding the dream.

The point of dream work is to achieve some kind of potential change. That is why people come to counselors, and that is why people look at dreams. However, dream analysis per se, even at its very best, results only in a change in understanding and rarely leads to any kind of long-term change in lifestyle or personality. Analysis and understanding are minor aspects of dream work, analysis being only a logical dilution of the dream's full gift. By itself, it will always be deficient and frequently in error. A great piece of art can only be known in the full sense through intimate, focused experience; an erudite essay about the artwork is no substitute.

Effective dream work depends on the counselor's attitude toward the client and his capacity for facilitating the most powerful possible unfolding of the dream experience. What is necessary is that the therapist believes in the client's intelligence. More importantly, he must believe in the presence of a deep intelligence and healing drive within the client that are designing the dreams for the purpose of furthering the client's wholeness. A therapist who is able to work effectively with dreams is humble and has an abiding respect for the wisdom that will unfold as the client consciously encounters the dream.

Both the therapist and the client can only truly know a dream through its experience. A good parallel would be the difference between being told about someone and trying to know that person on the basis of that data, as opposed to living with the individual. Effective dream work is living with and in the dream experience.

Remembering and recounting the original dream is not sufficient in most instances to help a person really be in the midst of the dream. Although a person may remember a dream quite clearly, memory itself is still a step removed from the actual dream experience. An individual may have visited Paris and may remember it well enough to describe it clearly to a friend, but that is not the same as walking around the Eiffel Tower or sitting in a Parisian sidewalk cafe. This is the difference between dream work and traditional dream analysis.

The first step in doing dream work is recounting the dream. The client must tell the counselor the dream in as much detail as possible and, using the data the client has provided, the counselor must slowly take the client back through the dream experience. Most of the time it is important to take extensive notes of the dream as the client recounts it, so that the sequence and symbols are in the proper order.

Taking the client into the dream experience begins in the same way as taking the client into active imagination: with a deep relaxation exercise. The intent is to dissociate the ego from external phenomena and concerns and to open the ego so that its defense mechanisms will be less likely to get in the way of the flow of the experience. Once the client is deeply re-laxed, he is taken to the opening scene of the dream.

Reexperiencing the dream with full conscious intentionality is the second step. This process has far greater impact and significance than simply re-calling the dream. The emotional power of the symbols, as well as their ability to actually move or transform the ego, demands that they be thor-oughly and intensely encountered. It is unlikely that just talking about an experience will wrench a person out of her ordinary expectations and in-tentions and demand change. When she is in the midst of an experience, especially one as powerful as a dream can be, then its numinous quality breaks through.

In the reliving of the dream, the therapist continually encourages the client to fully experience the dream with as many senses and as much awareness as possible. For instance, if the dream symbol is a rock, I sug-gest that the client try to lift it. I encourage her to feel the rock's surface, smell it, look at its colors—to actively embrace it with all of her sens-es. As I encourage the client to fully explore the dream symbol, I place special emphasis on experiencing all the emotions precipitated by the dream symbols.

It is also frequently helpful to dialogue with the dream figures. For example, if there is a wolf in the dream, it would be important to experience the wolf in every way that the wolf will allow. I might suggest petting it and looking at it. I would encourage the client to be aware of his feelings as he interacts with the wolf. Additionally, I would suggest that the client ask the wolf who it is and what it wants. Dialogue with dream figures, even inert ones, will usually call forth a response. The response will enable the client to enter more deeply into what that symbol is about. Finally, I might suggest that the client become the wolf and let herself fully experience the wolf's reality. Again, the purpose in this work is not merely to figure out the symbol. Analysis as such will fre-quently foster detachment and diminish the dream's power. The purpose is to be in an intimate relationship with the dream so that it can move one beyond oneself.

Throughout the process, the client should be continually encouraged to be aware of his emotions in response to whatever part of the dream he is exploring. He should also attend to any associations that come to mind or to physical sensations that are precipitated as he encounters the dream object. The associations can involve personal history, external-world issues, or internal-world figures or processes. If this process of connection to emotions and associations is done systematically, the real power of the dream will come through; the client will be moved by the dream. One cannot predict where the associations, emotions, or sensations will take a person, but it will invariably be what the person needs.

This intensification of the dream experience through careful exploration of the symbols should be continued through to the end of the dream. Allow the dream to tell its own story and come to its own conclusion. Whatever manipulation is done to the dream should be done for the sake of re-experiencing the dream, not for making the dream become different.

Once this process is complete, there will be no doubt as to what the dream is about. The impact of a significant dream cannot be contained in words. Nevertheless, it is useful to try to put it into words, so that the analytical part of the mind is honored and can offer its gifts. However, these are almost always secondary.

This is not the end of the dream work. There is a third phase: response. During the response phase, dream processes and outcomes can be altered, but they should not be changed without good reason. To do so would simply be a reflection of an egocentric need on the part of the client and/or the counselor. If the ego alone alters a dream, it will tend to conform the dream to already existing life patterns. The point of most dreams is to foster change. How to respond to a dream is best determined either by one of the dream figures that has an element of wisdom about it or by the client's Self.

The procedure for doing dream work is summarized below.

Dream Work Procedure

1) Have the client recount the dream in as much detail as possible and then guide the client into a meditative state.

2) Guide the client through a reexperiencing of the dream. By focusing on feelings, sensations, behaviors, and cognitive awarenesses triggered by the dream, connect the client as powerfully as possible to the experience.

3) Encourage the client to explore the dream symbols and figures. This may include dialoguing with them.

4) Have the client summarize the dream's teaching.

5) With the client still focused internally, encourage him to respond to the dream, following the suggestions of his Inner Wisdom or Self.

Because most of my clients utilize internal work and have a connection with the Self often in the form of a wisdom figure, it is simple to suggest that they ask it to provide some direction regarding the proper response to the dream. The Self will usually offer some specific directions, which the client then follows within the context of the dream through active imagination. If the changes the client makes within the dream are in tune with the healing the dream was designed to precipitate, they will give the ego a rush of energy and a determination to make parallel changes in the external world. The impact of this internal response to the dream will be like a powerful hypnotic suggestion and will have real potency for altering the client's life.

For example, a female client was working with a dream that pointed out how her willingness to submit to various men who used her in a variety of ways reflected the ways she was used as a child. When the dream work had made the connection powerfully clear to her, we asked her Self what we should do. It said, "Get the hell out of the house [the dream symbol for her oppression by men]. Get out of there." So she did. She left the house, determined never to return. I believe that it is unlikely that she will ever return to that kind of pattern, having left it in the dream. There had been several months of therapy prior that had helped give her the strength to follow through with her commitment. This probably prepared her so that the dream could come with its invitation. But the dream crystallized that particular focus in the therapy in a potent, experiential fashion so that when the Self said, "Do it," she did it with conviction and energy.

In another woman's dream, a positive animus dream figure gave the woman a running commentary on the dream. He explained what was happening, why it was happening, and how she should respond. She was both experiencing the dream and responding to it simultaneously, with the help of expert guidance.

Generally I prefer to keep the two phases separate: first the re-experiencing and embracing of the dream, then the response. However, when a wisdom figure or dream figure assumes direction of the process, I almost always defer to its expertise.

Another way of responding to a dream is to let it continue beyond its original conclusion. This will frequently underscore and reinforce the dream work. Sometimes there will be no need to do anything with the dream beyond embracing what it offers.

A good example of this is a dream from another one of my female clients. The dream had a variety of powerful statements for her. One statement was that a man with whom she was involved was not good for her. He was playing games, and the dream made that abundantly clear. That matter did not need any further elaboration. There was also another male figure, who treated her with the utmost loving, tender respect, in counterpoint to the game player. I encouraged her to go snuggle up to this man, to be embraced by him, to feel his energy and celebrate it. This was no different from what she had already experienced in the dream. I simply encouraged her to go back for more of the same. My belief was that the dream image would be the best possible reinforcement she could have for accepting a nurturing relationship.

In-depth dream work is hard to do without a counselor. Most people need to be in a dissociated state. They also need to be guided and encouraged to fully encounter the dream symbols, which may be threatening or painful. With a counselor serving as a catalyst, it is much easier to embrace the dream.

Usually dream work is best done with recent dreams, but if an old dream feels important and the client has relatively clear data as to what the dream was about, it can be worked with effectively. Sometimes clients will report that they have only a vague sense of a dream, but if they can be encouraged to start talking about the dream, much of it will sometimes return.

Following the dream work, I help the person refocus externally. I take time to make sure that the client is open to the dream. If there are any problems with the dream, we talk them through. Usually there will be no problems, but occasionally the ego will be resistant. If left unresolved, this resistance may undo most of the dream work.

If there is no time or opportunity for in-depth dream work, I will simply suggest to the client that she ask her Self or Inner Wisdom what the dream is about. Most of the time, the wisdom figure will offer a concise explanation. However, even when Wisdom is willing to explain the dream, the person is still deprived of the full impact of the dream. Dreams are designed to precipitate transformation, and that involves the whole of our being—senses, emotions, body, mind, etc.

There are counselors who prescribe rituals or symbolic artifacts to help people embrace their dreams. This can have a powerful impact; however, I prefer that the client make her first response to the dream within the context of dream work. It is much smoother then, and tends to be more powerful because the power of the symbols is being immediately experienced within their original context. Following this, some external expression of the symbols can be helpful, but the first priority is to make the external life changes implicit in the dream. When there has been a response to the dream within the dream work, it will be relatively easy to make a parallel response to life externally. If the opportunity to make this change is not taken soon after the dream work, the energy will dissipate and old patterns will reassert themselves.

One special benefit of dream work done in this style is that during the reexperiencing of the dream, the internal world may modify the dream spontaneously in order to enhance its message or make additional points within the same context. In one instance, several of the client's dream symbols refused to take their original form during the dream work. The dream as reexperienced in the dream work had a very different outcome from the original dream. As we compared the two, we noticed that the original dream was a statement on the individual's destiny should he continue disowning his personal power, while the second version of the dream clearly stated his potential. The contrast between the two was striking and deeply moved the individual.

SECTION THREE

The Broader Context

CHAPTER EIGHTEEN

A Transpersonal Psychodynamic Psychotherapy

The purpose of the psychodynamic psychotherapy that I practice is the achievement of an in-depth restructuring of the psyche. The goal of symptom alleviation fostered by contemporary, brief therapeutic modalities is certainly valuable and in some cases cost effective; however, it does not address deeper internal conflicts, nor can it resolve the impact of significant psychological trauma, especially severe childhood trauma. The effect of brief therapy in these cases will inevitably be limited both in impact and duration. An effective psychodynamic therapy, which addresses these issues, not only offers enduring alleviation of overt symptoms, but also lays the foundation for increased benefits over time—well after the therapy is completed.

> A study in the Journal of American Medical Association compared long-term psychodynamic therapy with various short-term psychotherapies. It reviewed 11 randomized controlled trials and 12 observational studies (included to show the effect of treatment in real world settings). The studies enrolled 1,053 patients diagnosed with personality disorders or hard-to-treat mood or anxiety disorders. The analysis showed that long-term psychodynamic therapy significantly helped patients with complex psychiatric disorders. In fact, patients continued improving after therapy ended (Miller 2010, 1).

In general, psychodynamic therapy focuses on three things:

1) Aversive childhood experiences and disturbed relationships that have an ongoing impact

2) Unconscious and often autonomous psychological forces that influence or control behavior

3) Helping the ego resolve personal history and internal conflicts through enhanced awareness, self-compassion, and insight

The essential key to a successful outcome is the quality of the therapeutic alliance. The therapist must be capable of empathic resonance with the flow of the client's experience and emotions and also foster a strong sense of safety and acceptance in which the client can build a bond of trust.

When performed competently, psychodynamic psychotherapy is at least as effective as any other form of psychotherapy studied. In those instances where clients suffer from significant levels of trauma and dissociation, it is the only therapy that produces lasting results. There is now sufficient research available to make clear that psychodynamic therapy is an evidence-based practice.

I began utilizing a psychodynamic approach to therapy when I initiated therapy with my first DID client in 1978. Unconscious internal conflicts and traumatic history were so obvious and in need of resolution that a psychodynamic approach was unavoidable. As I generalized from this client to others with similar but less severe symptoms, it became obvious that this approach could benefit most of my clients. From this I developed an approach to psychotherapy that is very similar to that of Watkins and Watkins who, like myself, ground their work in their experiences with DID clients (Watkins 1997). My work is also significantly influenced by the work of Carl Jung and theorists in transpersonal psychology.

Watkins and Watkins strongly emphasize the use of hypnosis as the most effective vehicle for accessing ego states, working through conflicts, and resolving trauma. There is no question that this is a highly effective tool when handled appropriately. I made fairly extensive use of hypnosis when I was initially developing my own version of ego-state therapy. However, I eventually found that Jungian active imagination could accomplish the same thing as hypnosis. Additionally, "hypnosis" carries connotations of mind control by the hypnotist, which makes many clients uncomfortable. Active imagination, on the other hand, tends to facilitate a sense of autonomy in clients. It is also a much simpler modality and easier to teach to student therapists. Later in this chapter I will give a more concrete description of how I use active imagination and the distinctions between it and hypnosis.

A recurrent theme for Watkins and Watkins is the need for a briefer form of psychodynamic psychotherapy than the multiyear endeavor of traditional psychoanalysis. They believe that working directly with covert ego states and early-life trauma through hypnosis is more effective and far faster than traditional talk therapy. I have also found this to be the case, except that I use active imagination as my primary tool.

The primary focus of the Watkins' therapy is ego states. They are the main vehicle for accessing unresolved trauma and addressing internal conflicts. This has also been my experience. Carl Jung said that "the complex [his term for ego state] was the 'via regia' to the unconscious, the architect of dreams and of symptoms."… "It is not a very royal road, more like a rough and uncommonly devious footpath" (*CW 8 para.* 210).

Ego states may be highly developed and reflect significant knowledge, behavior, and abilities or competencies, such as "the student" or "the family man," or the more limited and focused "sports fan" part of a person, for instance. These competencies can be organized around a particular age or feeling or life experience, especially if the experience is a traumatic one.

Watkins and Watkins define an ego state as "an organized system of be-havior and experience whose elements are bound together by some com-mon principle, and differentiated from one another by boundaries that are more or less permeable" (Watkins & Watkins 1997, 15). At the most adaptive, constructive end of the ego-state continuum are those state-specific patterns of knowledge, feelings, behavior, and relationship styles that tend to cluster around particular roles or activities. When I am in the role of father, I tend to think and feel in certain predictable ways and even have access to a train of memories that are quite different from the thoughts, feelings, and memories I have when I am in the role of boss. There is not necessarily any conflict between the roles nor any barriers to awareness flowing between one and the other. At the most pathological end of the spectrum are fully autonomous ego states, hidden behind an amnesic barrier, of which the ego is completely unaware although they may significantly influence it.

In my experience and according to Watkins and Watkins, three factors seem to precipitate ego states: the normal differentiation of our lives into various roles as described above; the introjection of significant others ei-ther through identifying with them and becoming like them externally, or creating a part that repeats the introjected other's behavior toward the self; and confrontation with severe adverse childhood experiences that may cause a child to dissociate from the experience, precipitating the for-mation of an ego state focused around that experience. As a general rule, the more defined and isolated from the ego an ego state becomes, the more likely it is to drive self-defeating or self-destructive behaviors and precipitate treatment-resistant mood disorders.

Although some ego states may grow and mature (though not necessar-ily at the same pace as the body or ego itself), others will remain quite young, and their thinking will be caught in the concrete, magical, or fanta-sy-prone processes of a child, rather than in the analytical, rational think-ing of an adult.

Any discussion of autonomous, self-aware ego states inevitably gives rise to the question of how a single human being can have more than one center of consciousness. I believe that the psychiatrist, Roberto Assagioli, a contemporary of Freud and Jung, has the best answer to this question. He made the point, long acknowledged in Eastern thought, that consciousness itself is an indivisible process that has no limits and is not the same as its contents. A simple exercise Assagioli called the disidentification exercise (described in chapter twelve) makes this abundantly clear to anyone who cares to look within himself or herself. Through doing the exercise one realizes that although you can experience your body, thoughts, emotions, or story, you are none of them. Rather, you are the conscious point of awareness that knows them. You, as consciousness, are not the same as those things of which you are consciously aware. Consciousness and its corollary, autonomy, are nothing and thus indivisible. This means that when any part of the psyche becomes sufficiently organized to become self-aware, it is not a new consciousness possessing the psyche; it is simply an aspect of the psyche that is able to share in the self-awareness and autonomy that resides at the depth or apex of the psyche that Jung called the Self and Assagioli called the Higher Self.

People who have experienced overwhelming trauma in childhood and had no access to a nurturing protector to help them work through and release the trauma must dissociate the experience or else be destroyed by it. This dissociation is often said by clients to have been fostered by the Self. Disintegrating the psyche was the only viable option, even though it is directly contrary to the Self's principal drive toward integration and wholeness. Splitting off the Hurt Child as described in Chapter Four allowed the ego to function in the external world without being overwhelmed by the pain that child contained.

There are two inevitable consequences of dissociating the Hurt Child in particular. One is the feeling of nameless terror and/or deadness that emanates from the wounded child and continually reverberates throughout the psyche until that child is found and healed. The other is the emergence of a primal rage which itself becomes an autonomous ego state. This rage generally lashes out at other aspects of the psyche, particularly the ego, and will usually attack external others as well. The client who has to contend with this terror or deadness and the attack of an aggressive, malevolent ego state or states cannot be other than profoundly debilitated. Since this malevolent ego state shares in the consciousness and autonomy of the Self, as do all of the autonomous ego states, it could be said that its existence reflects the "dark side" of the Self that Jung referred to. The Self, at least indirectly, gave birth to it and is the ultimate source of its awareness and autonomy. The Self is also the cause of the terror or deadness, as it was the Self that split off the traumatized child on the basis that the resulting state of ongoing terror was a preferable option to the destruction of the psyche.

Far more people than those specifically diagnosed with DID have autonomous, covert ego states that drive behavior and mood in ways that significantly degrade the individual's quality of life. These states can precipitate personality disorders, be the source of psychotic phenomena, and trigger substance abuse and other overtly self-destructive behaviors. Unless these ego states are uncovered, rapport established, and better integration achieved, clients have very little hope of recovering their true potential and living an authentic, full life. By working with the Self and utilizing active imagination, I have been able to constructively connect with these ego states. Then, by using the same attitude of respect and compassion as I do with DID clients, we (myself, the Self, and the ego) are able to foster reintegration and healing.

Contacting ego states through active imagination is a fairly straightforward, simple matter. As stated earlier, the client is first guided through a relaxation procedure as a way of opening up, letting go of defenses, and turning attention away from the external world and toward internal realities. Then I count the person down a safe ten-step stairway.

This helps enhance the sense of separation from the body and external concerns. It also helps focus attention. At the bottom of the steps I take the client into a beautiful mountain meadow, which I describe in as much sensory detail as possible. This helps the client become fully engaged in an internal frame of reference and open to deeply experiencing internal realities. After establishing a working alliance between the ego and the Self (which will often present in the form a Wisdom or Great Mother figure), I will invite the Self to take the person into whatever experience is most appropriate for today's work. This may turn out to be a transformative, metaphoric experience or an encounter with an ego state that needs attention. I may also request that if the Self deems it appropriate, I would like the ego to invite forward whatever ego state may be driving a particular pathological pattern that the ego is currently struggling with.

When the ego state presents itself, the Self may immediately engage it and the ego in a healing experience. If this does not ensue, then a more paced process will need to begin. In the *Handbook of Dissociation* Watkins and Watkins (441) have outlined six points of inquiry that are important to pursue in order to most effectively work with the presenting ego state: 1) its age and origin, 2) its name, 3) its needs, 4) its function or internal behavior, 5) its degree of permeability, and 6) its gender. Gathering this information is not to be handled in the manner of an intake assessment, but gathered gradually as the relationship with the part grows. All communication with the ego or ego states must be done in the full awareness that other ego states may well be listening in, and any comments that could be construed as derogatory or discounting of them could alienate them and impede the healing process. Just as the therapist must maintain a curious, nonjudging, compassionate attitude toward all aspects of the client's psyche, the ego needs to be encouraged to do so as well. This will facilitate communication between the ego and internal ego states. Enhanced internal communication will lead to less rigid boundaries and foster integration.

Ego-state therapy is an effective form of treatment for complex trauma disorder. The consensus of experts in the treatment of complex trauma disorders, especially DID and its lesser expression, usually identified as "dissociative disorder not otherwise specified" (DDNOS), is that treatment should follow three phases:

Phase 1: Symptom reduction, stabilization, and skills building
Phase 2: Treatment of traumatic memory
Phase 3: Personality (re)integration and (re)habilitation (Van der Hart 2006)

Van der Hart lists distinct sets of phobias that must be faced at each stage of the process. In Phase 1 the phobias needing resolution are those of attachment to the therapist, trauma-related mental actions, and dissociative parts. In Phase 2 the phobias needing resolution are those of unresolved attachment to the perpetrator, attachment of dissociated parts to the therapist, and traumatic memories. In Phase 3 the phobias needing resolution are those of a normal life, healthy risk taking and change, and intimacy. Van der Hart's model accords well with my experience and provides a broad framework for understanding how the therapy process unfolds.

The core to resolving internal fragmentation is the healing of traumatic memories. According to Bessel A. van der Kolk, the leading researcher in the field of traumatic stress, the essence of processing a traumatic experience is "the exposure of traumatized individuals to feared conditions in contexts where the individuals experience social bonding and some degree of personal control" (1996, 547). He recommends using hypnosis to aid in "(1) recovering dissociated or repressed traumatic material; (2) reconnecting missing affect with recalled material; and (3) transforming traumatic memories" (548).

Five themes are important to keep in mind in doing this part of the therapy:

1) There is an appropriate order for the memories to be surfaced. This is not something the therapist can know or intuit. Either the Self will guide the process, or the memory will present spontaneously, or an ego state will emerge that is willing to face the trauma that originated it. The therapist should not make any assumptions about the nature of the client's trauma or the timing of its resolution. This would be much more likely to distort the process rather than facilitate it.

2) Awareness of a repressed trauma is not the same as resolution. Human experience has four aspects, and all must be included in the reclaiming of the trauma. These are the behavioral element, the affective reaction, the somatic dimension, and knowledge or cognitive awareness. If any element is left out in the initial reemergence of the memory, the therapist should help bridge from one to the other until the experience is complete. Once this is done, the memory should be transformed. During the reexperiencing the therapist must make sure that the client remains aware of the therapist's presence and support. Otherwise there is a danger that the process will result in retraumatization without any resolution. At the completion of the abuse scenario, it is very helpful for the part that was hurt to be nurtured by the ego, the Self, or some other part of the psyche that can offer support and protection. During this nurturing time the child should be given permission to express any and all emotions triggered by the abuse. Recent research into memory tells us that whenever a memory is brought to conscious awareness, it can be altered. Working through the memory as described above will give the client a new story about the event. Although the reality of the abuse remains, in the new memory or story there is a kind, supportive person with the child as she suffers the abuse. This kind helper cares for and loves the child afterward and gives her permission to express all of her feelings, including terror and rage. This new story becomes the operative memory and the event then loses it power, becoming simply a part of the individual's narrative history.

3) Occasionally, a traumatic event can be so threatening that the memory will be divided up between many ego states. The memory work may have to be done several times over from the perspective of each part before it is finally resolved.

4) Sometimes complete scenarios can be dealt with in a single session. Other times, even though the experience is contained in a single ego state, the memory will have to be returned to over many sessions before it is completed.

5) In almost every severely dissociated individual I have ever worked with, the deepest wound and the last to emerge was disorganized attachment to the mother in the first months of life. The impact of this wound tends to be more profound and disabling than any of the later traumas. The pain for the infant is primal and beyond words. It usually leads to an all-consuming rage or a hopeless, broken spirit that gives rise to profound feelings of emptiness and deadness. Although the adult ego may not have any memory of the maternal abandonment, the rage or deadness or both will be an inescapable burden that colors every aspect of the person's life. The resolution of this wound demands significant time and attention from the ego. There must be an internal reparenting process established in which the ego systematically supports and nurtures the infant on an almost continuous basis for as long as it takes.

All of the therapy described above is done from a transpersonal frame of reference. The term *transpersonal* means "beyond the mask." It refers to the utilization in ancient Greece of masks by actors. The mask both signified the role that the actor was playing and hid who the actor really was. Likewise, a basic assumption in transpersonal psychology is that at the ego level we are both playing a role or many roles and at the same time hiding even from ourselves our own true nature.

Transpersonal psychology considers the human psyche to be an integrated whole. Any attempts to make a distinction between psychological and spiritual aspects of the psyche are artificial and deleterious. The development of human potential has always been the result of an interplay between what are commonly thought of as psychological processes and what are usually considered to be more spiritual aspects. These would include the search for values, the emergence of wisdom, intuitive awareness, and the longing for transcendence. Transpersonal psychology offers a comprehensive and holistic view of the psyche.

A fundamental assumption in transpersonal psychology is that reality is basically nondual. By this it means that who we know ourselves to be at the ego level is not ultimately separate from or other than our deepest spiritual reality or the external world and all the other people in it. The sense of otherness that seems so real to us is actually an illusion produced by the thinking mind as it seeks to analyze and control itself and its internal and external experiences.

The search for integration that lies at the heart of the therapy I have described is grounded in the appreciation of this nonduality of personal reality. The realization that egos and ego states are nothing more than roles and stories and that the only thing in the psyche that is fundamentally real is consciousness itself is a core theme in transpersonal thought. The understanding that your authentic self is a unique process that is ever unfolding from your own depth, no role or story comparing with it in depth, power, or beauty, is another transpersonal insight that undergirds my work.

Another central transpersonal theme is that the psyche has a depth to it that is compassionate, wise, and capable of leading the psyche toward integration (often with the help of external support for the ego from a counselor). This integration, which depends on the ego letting go of its rigid defenses and story of self, will lead naturally to a sense of oneness with consciousness itself and all of creation—what Jung called *Unus Mundus*.

The process itself is commonly called awakening. Integration and awakening are among the highest achievements of the human spirit and my hope for myself and everyone with whom I work.

CHAPTER NINETEEN

Introjects

It has been my consistent experience with the most deeply wounded of my clients that there are entities in the internal world that are not a part of that person's own nature. They are like parasites—enlivened by the individual's energy, yet distinct and autonomous. These are what I refer to as introjects.

Usually, introjects are energized by the resistance given them by the ego. This process is comparable to the way split-off parts become stronger the more they are fought. For instance, perhaps the abusing father is on the mind of the individual. The individual may find himself saying internally to his father, "I hate you. I want no part of you." That stance will energize the presence of the father, which will usually fight back with a corresponding energy.

An introject begins out of the same process that gives rise to a child's identification with his family and social context. Every child forms some kind of bond with the primary caregivers. It is natural for the child to build an internal image of these people and their messages. If the behavior and messages of the original caregivers are consistent with the child's authentic nature, the benign caregivers tend to fade away as sources of internal authority, and their place is taken by the flow of the child's own internal energies. This happens only if the external presence is in harmony with the natural internal processes of the child.

If the external caregivers are not benign, the child will still create an image and a system of messages in response to the presence of those people.

This time, however, the child will continue to experience a living internal representation of these external others. As the child becomes conscious of the flow of his own true energies, he will find that these representations do not fit or function in harmony with his true self. These representations then continue as distinct entities in their own right.

Introjects will actively subvert the flow of the child's energy, maintaining internally the same subversive attack that is expressed externally by the caregivers. Even after the external people who are the model for the internal image are no longer present, the internal presence remains. It continues actively pursuing its original intention of conforming the child to its authority.

If the messages are not very destructive, they may not have much life. They will be like old tapes—mindless assumptions that keep repeating in the child's head. Frequently, however, in cases of severe abuse, these entities develop a kind of intentionality or consciousness. They do not simply repeat old messages; they purposefully continue the old controlling, abusive patterns in ways that are appropriate to both the present context and past history. In other words, they will both reenact old abuse and respond destructively to contemporary realities. In dreams and even in waking imagery they may attack. Old ridicule, beatings, and molestations may be repeated. Whatever happened then can happen now, and it does not necessarily happen only to a wounded child ego state, but to the ego as well. A person seeking to make fundamental changes will be hindered by these entities if the direction of change is contrary to what they perceive to be in their own interest. Such entities are full-blown introjects.

Well-developed introjects are intelligent entities on the attack. It is not that the attackers are returning—they never left. The abusers do not leave until the person has found genuine healing and is able to let them go. Until that point is reached, the introjects are going to be present in the psyche. Ego intentions have nothing to do with it. The ego can either agree with them or fight them, but they will be present.

A person's relationship to an introject is fundamentally childlike. Even if the ego is adult, the introject was usually embedded by the time the person was very young. Introjects are moreover overpowering authorities, and dealing with them will inevitably trigger a regressive response. To use an external-world example, an individual may be a successful fifty-two-year-old, but if, during a visit with his now-aging mother, she expresses disappointment in him, he may still crumble. Likewise, introjects may also exert this kind of power over an individual.

I believe that this is about as close as humans get to actually being possessed. It is not demonic; it is human possession. But it is exceedingly powerful if the abusers have been powerful in a person's early life.

The way to distinguish an introject from a part of the individual is to look at how the entity presents in the internal world. If it is an introject, it will have the look or feel of the abuser. If it is a facet of the individual, it will look like the person, or at least be different from what the individual had to contend with as a child. Another way to distinguish between the two is to ask the part who it is or where it came from. Of course, if a client tells me, "My father is here trying to rape me again," I assume that we are dealing with an introject.

The introjects that I have been describing up to this point are ego-dystonic: they are present, but the ego struggles with them and would stop them if it could. However, not all introjects are in opposition to the ego. Some people build large systems of introjects because they do not believe that they themselves have any authority of their own. These are ego-syntonic (i.e., ego-compatible) introjects.

If the ego believes that it is incompetent or inadequate, it will look outside itself to find someone or some group of persons to provide what it perceives as lacking in itself. It will then absorb what it finds and use it as the principal internal resource for gathering the strength or insight it needs to make important life decisions.

Ego-syntonic introjects are not quite as dangerous to the psyche as the punitive introjects are; nevertheless, they are poisonous. The ego gives up looking for its own authority in favor of external (which have now become internal) authorities. This precludes the possibility of ever moving beyond the limits of external experience. Such an ego is blocked from fully aligning itself with the Self. It should also be noted that introjects are fundamentally static realities: they may respond to a person's contemporary experience, but it will be through a reapplication of old themes, teachings, and behaviors. They lack the flow and flexibility that an individual's Self has. Because no external authority can ever approach the vitality and rightness of a person's center, such an introject will always draw a person away from his genuine potential. This is my major argument against the guru system. In many instances, a guru will set himself up as the spiritual authority. The seeker is expected to submit unquestioningly to him so that identification with the guru becomes complete (i.e., the guru becomes an introject). The person then has the guru internally available on an ongoing basis as a source of guidance in every life situation.

That introjects exist is an undeniable fact. That they must be eliminated is also absolutely true. There can be no peace or wholeness when the internal world is cluttered with relatively autonomous external influences that are not thoroughly consistent with the individual's own Self. However, removing them is extremely difficult. Attacking them head-on may simply energize them by underscoring their importance. Similarly, aggressively fighting introjects strengthens them to the extent they are resisted.

My usual response to introjects is to encourage the ego to be aware of where these messages and behaviors are rooted. I help the client understand that what he keeps hearing in his head is coming from his mother, father, and/or other significant people in his life. If he names it for what it is, he will be able to evaluate its validity in a more balanced fashion.

Secondly, I encourage the client to begin to build a bond of trust with his Self in the form of Inner Wisdom and the Great Mother, which are his own fundamental energies that nurture and teach him. By doing so, he is starting to build a new ground of authority and action. The weight of psychological influence is pulled away from the introjects, not by aggressively resisting them, but by simply stepping away from them. There is now a life-giving point of reference to which the person can turn for support and guidance that will undercut the power of the introjects. By turning to archetypal healing energies, a new, flexible, flowing ground is found that erodes the authority of the introjects.

As the wounds of the past are healed, the behaviors, feelings, and lifestyle choices that were grounded in the abuse begin to fade. When automatic ways of responding to life end, another level of the introjects' power is diminished. They can no longer make a person feel or behave the way he has before, because the energy of the unresolved history is not there pushing him in that direction. Without unresolved history driving an individual into self-destructive behavior, the introjects' invitation to limit or harm himself will seem strange and inappropriate. When history is not healed, such an invitation will feel overwhelming and irresistible.

As healing flows, appropriate, self-protective anger will also emerge. This anger gives a person a sense of stature and righteous indignation. It enables the ego to quite vigorously say no to the introjects. This is not so much a matter of fighting them as simply slamming the door on them, without any need to explain, defend, or attack. It takes anger to do this— the anger that has gradually been owned in response to working through the abuse.

Yet even at that point when anger has been owned and the door has been closed, the introjects are still present in the psyche. They will take advantage of any regression or trauma that weakens the ego, in an attempt to reestablish their authority. Ultimately, introjects must be eliminated.

Thus the final step in overcoming introjects occurs when the ego becomes strong enough to genuinely forgive them of all the abuse. The key to forgiving is to perceive the abusers with straightforward clarity as the wounded children they inevitably are. When the ego can love these wounded children, despite all the harm done, the introjects will vanish.

There is another way to destroy an introject. It is an emergency tactic, and very risky, because it lays the therapist's authority as a healer on the line. If an introject is extremely aggressive and exceedingly abusive, attacking the client in a way that is profoundly debilitating, it has to be dealt with immediately. In one instance, an introject was repeatedly raping the client internally, which rendered her completely dysfunctional. To simply stop it for the time being was not helpful, because it could resume the attack at any time. Even the thought of its possible attack was debilitating to the client.

If the therapist at this point decides that the introject must be stopped, but fails to do so, the introject wins. However much the client may want to believe in the possibility of healing, it begins to appear that maybe the negative side has the greater power. Perhaps the destroyers are finally going to win. This level of intervention is not something to be taken lightly, but sometimes it must be done anyway.

In this instance, removing the introject is done through direct attack. All the anger energy that the client has available is gathered, and then client and therapist fight back, through ritual and psychodrama, until they have won, however long it takes. (One such experience took more than forty-eight hours.) This undertaking should be done intuitively, guided by the client's Self if that is available, or out of the therapist's Self / Inner Wisdom if the client's is not available. The encounter must be extremely aggressive and persistent, and should only be done when there is no other option.

For all practical purposes, this amounts to an exorcism.

CHAPTER TWENTY

Dissociative Identity Disorder, an Overview

In this chapter on DID I will be addressing history and epidemiology, differential diagnosis, diagnostic tools, basic treatment guidelines and issues, the healing relationship, psychopharmacology, and the broader relevance of the insights drawn from DID therapy to psychotherapy in general.

History and Epidemiology

Dissociative defenses and their relationship to trauma were significant areas of interest in psychological and psychiatric practice and research in the last two decades of the nineteenth century. William James and Morton Prince in the United States and Jung, Breuer, the early Freud, and Pierre Janet all wrote on the topic. Janet, who was influenced by William James's work with multiple-personality disorder, or MPD (the former term for DID), and who in turn was closely followed by William James and Morton Prince, developed a sophisticated psychodynamic psychology at the turn of the century derived from his own extensive study of MPD. It was trauma informed and saw dissociation as a primary driving force in psychopathology. He was the first theorist to use the terms "dissociation" and "subconscious."

Later, in 1914, one year after his break with Freud, Carl Jung published *The Psychogenesis of Mental Disease*. In it he discussed how trauma and dissociation could drive psychosis. Interestingly, Jung believed that his own mother might have suffered from MPD. Jung developed a very effective methodology for working with dissociative patients that featured active imagination and writing. Both his techniques and theories regarding the structure and function of the psyche are foundations for my own work. Active imagination is the most powerful psychotherapeutic tool I have ever encountered.

By 1915, however, a new psychodynamic psychology that discounted trauma and the significance of dissociative defenses was aggressively fostered by Freud and his school. It supplanted the work of Janet and James and marginalized Jung's contributions. Major resistance to the very idea of MPD developed within the professional psychological community. A common consensus developed that if MPD existed at all, it was the rarest of all psychological disorders. Those who took it seriously were considered either to be dupes of attention-seeking clients or participants in a *folie à deux* that was responsible for iatrogenic psychosis.

Decades later in the late 1960s, the women's movement brought to public awareness the astounding prevalence of sexual abuse and incest. At the same time, the PTSD suffered by so many Vietnam War veterans forced the psychiatric community to look seriously at the connection between trauma and psychiatric disability. Beginning in the 1970s, a few American psychiatrists began to consider childhood trauma a contributing factor to mental illness and to reconsider MPD as a viable diagnosis. Their successes sparked the development of a community of psychiatrists who began to focus on the research and treatment of MPD. Ralph Allison was an early leader in this renewed interest.

Throughout the 1980s, research on the impact of psychological trauma and its relationship to dissociative disorders grew rapidly. The journal *Dissociation* was founded in March of 1988, and the number of professional articles related to dissociative disorders peaked in the mid-1990s. Currently, even prominent mainstream medical and psychological journals such as the *American Journal of Psychiatry*, the *Archives of General*

Psychiatry, and the *Psychological Bulletin of the American Psychological Association* are now publishing studies focusing on the impact of psychological trauma and dissociation.

According to Colin Ross, MD, a major researcher and leader in the field of DID, researchers in North America and Europe have determined that about 1 percent of the general population meets the diagnostic criteria for DID. Studies of adult psychiatric inpatients found that at a minimum 5 percent had undiagnosed DID. In my experience, there is a much larger population whose history and symptoms are very similar to my DID clients, but whose level of fragmentation is not as severe as in those with DID. Technically, these persons should be diagnosed with dissociative disorder not otherwise specified (DDNOS). They and DID clients are frequently misdiagnosed, however, as schizophrenic, schizoaffective, or bipolar because of their experience of voices due to internal communication with alternate personalities, which many clinicians consider to be a primary diagnostic indicator for one of these three major psychotic disorders. Since the DDNOS group is at least three to four times larger than the DID population, I would estimate that 15 percent or more of a typical inpatient population is on the severe end of the dissociative spectrum.

A common critique lodged against clinicians who work with DID clients is that it is an iatrogenic condition. According to the 2005 *Guidelines for Treating Dissociative Identity Disorder in Adults,* "no study of any clinical or research population has yet demonstrated that the full clinical syndrome can be produced in this fashion" (83).

Differential Diagnosis

When Eugen Bleuler introduced the term "schizophrenia" in 1911, he described a clearly dissociative pathology, although he considered its origin to be biomedical rather trauma based. He wrote in 1924, "It is not alone in hysteria that one finds an arrangement of different personalities one succeeding the other: through similar mechanisms schizophrenia produces different personalities existing side by side." The term "schizophrenia" here means "split-mind disorder." Later understandings of schizophrenia, while keeping the name, discarded the obvious dissociative implications and considered it to be only a biogenetic disorder.

Most DID therapists use a fairly simple rule of thumb to differentiate between DID and "true" schizophrenia, which most consider to be an organic rather than a trauma-driven disorder. While both exhibit many of the Schneiderian first-rank symptoms (voices, delusions of control, thought withdrawal and insertion) and both respond to antipsychotic medications, most DID clients do not exhibit the negative symptoms of schizophrenia: thought disorders, bizarre delusions, or diminished mental acuity. Clients who acknowledge the first-rank symptoms but demonstrate none of the others are almost certainly DID or DDNOS.

Recently, this distinction between dissociative clients and schizophrenics, while useful, has begun to become blurred. Twin studies have demonstrated that although there is a genetic component to schizophrenia, environmental factors also play a significant role in the development of the disorder, trauma being one of the most significant contributing factors. A 2008 study by Ross and Keyes indicates that there may be a subgroup of schizophrenics who also meet the criteria for a dissociative disorder: "They had more severe trauma histories, more co-morbidity, and higher scores for both positive and negative symptoms." In their article "Positive and Negative Symptoms in dissociative identity disorder and schizophrenia: a comparative analysis," Ellason and Ross

> …investigated the pattern of positive and negative symptoms in patients with DID and compared it with norms in schizophrenia. A total of 108 patients with a clinical diagnosis of DID were administered the Positive and Negative Syndrome Scale. The positive-symptom and general psychopathology scores

were significantly more severe in the dissociative identity group than the norms for schizophrenia, while the negative symptoms were significantly more severe in schizophrenia. Since patients with DID report more positive symptoms of schizophrenia than do schizophrenics, while schizophrenics report more negative symptoms, a primary emphasis on positive symptoms may result in false-positive diagnoses of schizophrenia and false-negative diagnoses of DID." (Ellason and Ross 1995, 236.)

Positive symptoms are the "hot" symptoms of psychosis. They reflect a mind that is out of control generating disordered thinking, bizarre behavior, delusions and hallucinations. Negative symptoms are the "cold" symptoms of psychosis. They may involve low energy, flattened emotions, and a restricted capacity for pleasure, motivation, or socialization. Negative symptoms may also include slowed thinking and restricted speech.

In my opinion, whatever the source of the positive symptoms might be, using standard DID therapeutic techniques for working with voices/alters and trauma history would do no harm and might prove helpful.

Attempts to distinguish between the two disorders are further confused by the ability of DID clients to create alters who mimic external others. A DID client who has been exposed to schizophrenic clients in an inpatient setting might, as a way of adapting to the environment, develop an alter who exhibits all of the characteristics of schizophrenia.

DID clients are also sometimes misdiagnosed as bipolar I due to the presence of depression, poor judgment, impulsivity, manic-like irritability, and psychosis. They are sometimes given the specifier "rapid cycling" because of the different mood presentations that are noted when alters switch. This is actually a misuse of the term "rapid cycling," since the moods described must meet the full DSM criteria for duration.

It is also not unusual for DID clients to be misdiagnosed as schizoaffective since most DID clients suffer from major depressive disorder and their psychoses (e.g., voices) persist whether they are depressed or not.

The most common diagnostic confusion involving DID clients lies in the distinction between DID/DDNOS and Borderline Personality Disorder. (BPD)

A person suffering from BPD feels a profound emptiness inside, a strong sense of disconnection from others, an intense longing to be loved and accepted and an equally intense rage over never having felt that kind of love through a secure attachment with the mother early in life. Their motto is said to be, "I hate you. Don't leave me." Persons with BPD alternately cling to others, or push them away for little or no good reason. Typically they feel unlovable and intense shame for who they perceive themselves to be, although they tend to lack any clear sense of self. Usually, they also struggle with depression, anxiety and substance abuse. All of this appears to be rooted in significant attachment deficits during the first two years of life. (Schore 2012, 330)

Individuals with DID almost always suffer from BPD as well since disorganized attachment in the first years of life is a major contributing factor for DID. The development of DID, however, involves more than just disorganized attachment. The combination of disorganized attachment, significant child abuse and an innate capacity for dissociation are the primary catalysts that give rise to DID. This means that only a subset of those who suffer from BPD will also suffer from DID. (Liotti 2004, 481)

Some authors see DID as no more than a dramatic expression of borderline pathology since the DSM IV-TR criteria for BPD would fit almost every DID client. Others see borderline personality disorder as simply at one end of the dissociative spectrum. A recent 2008 study by Ross found that 59 percent of borderline clients meet the criteria for a dissociative disorder.

Another 2008 study by Sar et al. found that 64 percent of individuals with BPD had an Axis I diagnosis of a dissociative disorder. It would appear that there is a subgroup of BPD clients who do not report significant dissociative experiences, but they are a minority. Additionally, a great majority of persons diagnosed with BPD report significant trauma in their histories. It would thus appear that BPD is not a dissociative disorder, but the two are closely related.

DID clients typically exhibit two layers of symptoms. There is both a surface or obvious set of symptoms and also a more hidden and core set of symptoms. The obvious symptoms include feelings of being possessed, substance abuse, hallucinations, panic attacks, obsessive-compulsive tendencies, suicidality, time loss, sexual dysfunction, somatoform disorders, mood swings, anorexia, phobias, self-mutilation, flashbacks, mania, antisocial acts, and depression. The typical DID client exhibits many of these surface symptoms, which are typically the symptoms initially presented to a therapist. It is only with deeper probing that the core symptoms emerge. Until the core symptoms are addressed, the surface symptoms will not achieve much lasting resolution. There are five core symptoms shared by all DID clients. These include amnesia (or memory problems involving difficulty recalling personal information), identity alteration (switching or a sense of acting like a different person), identity confusion (or an inner struggle about one's sense of self/identity), depersonalization (a sense of disconnection from one's self or feeling like a stranger to one's self), and derealization (a sense of disconnection from familiar people or one's surroundings) (Steinberg 2008).

Diagnostic Tools

Many effective instruments have been developed to diagnose DID and help therapists assess its five core symptoms. Foremost among them are the DES, the DDIS, and the SCID-D. The SCID-D (Structured Clinical Interview for DSM-IV Dissociative Disorders) has been rigorously tested and validated by NIMH, the National Institute for Mental Health. It is also expensive and requires special training for its proper utilization.

The DES 2 (Dissociative Experiences Scale), on the other hand, is free, easy to use, self-administered, and has very good validity and reliability. It can be completed in about ten minutes and scored in about five minutes. It is a highly effective screening tool that can help a therapist determine with some confidence whether a client who is presenting with one or more of the above listed surface symptoms is also suffering from the more hidden, core symptoms of dissociation. Those who have a moderate to high score on the DES 2 would then be candidates for a more in-depth analysis, such as that offered by the SCID-D and the DDIS. The DDIS (Dissociative Disorders Interview Schedule, DSM-IV version) is a very reliable instrument and has frequently been used in peer-reviewed research. It is free and can be used by any seasoned clinician. The structured interview format it offers is both diagnostically helpful and a good foundation for initiating the therapeutic process. Both the DES 2 and the DDIS are available online.

Basic Treatment Guidelines and Issues

The third revision of treatment guidelines for DID was published by the ISSTD (International Society for the Study of Trauma and Dissociation) in 2011. It is based on the consensus of expert clinicians and researchers regarding the most safe and effective care of adult DID clients. Its insights are also applicable to clients who exhibit fundamentally similar but less extensive expressions of dissociation, such as ego-dystonic voice hearers.

Contrary to common assumptions, DID is neither rare nor necessarily dramatic in its presentation. Many clients are reluctant to acknowledge their symptoms, and may only disclose them if asked directly by the clinician. Without the utilization of an appropriate structured diagnostic interview, there is a strong likelihood that clinicians will only treat surface symptoms and miss the more significant core issues.

Multiple factors appear to contribute to dissociative tendencies. Some appear to be biogenetic in origin, such as schizotypal personality traits or high hypnotizability. Recent research has also indicated that disorganized attachment may also be a significant contributing factor. Trauma, in combination with these predisposing factors, leads to dissociation in which behaviors, affect, sensation, and/or cognition are disconnected from one another as a way of protecting the psyche from being overwhelmed by negative stimuli. DID clients have the highest level of childhood trauma of any clinical group.

When a psyche splits off into significant contents or functions, these will typically give rise to ego states that will ordinarily be experienced as voices. An ego state is simply a less elaborated version of the ego that nondissociated persons tend to identify themselves with. Both the ego and ego states are products of imagination or constructs of the psyche. Although voices are the most obvious indicators of these ego states, they can also influence or control behaviors, drive regressive tendencies, or even be sources for nurturance and insight.

How a person responds to these voices or ego states will determine the person's level of psychiatric disability. The capacity to dissociate under stress is much more a skill than a weakness. Although some of the predisposing factors, such as schizotypal traits and disorganized attachment, are clear deficits, others such as high hypnotizability are important skills that give the psyche creative and flexible ways of coping with traumas that might otherwise destroy it. If the voices are thus seen positively as the personification of personal resources and truth, then respectful engagement and integration will naturally follow; these individuals are unlikely to end up as part of a clinical population. If their presence is interpreted negatively, however, it will lead to internal conflict and a wide variety of psychiatric symptoms. Integrative therapeutic techniques that help the client move toward a more positive interpretation of the voice and ego-state phenomenon will lead to integration and the alleviation of all the other psychiatric symptoms.

The focus of DID therapy is to facilitate better-integrated functioning. This arises out of improved coordination and communication between the parts or ego states. No one ego state is the "real" self: the client is the sum of the entire spectrum of personalities and more. Thus it is a mistake to try to get rid of any personalities, including those that are threatening or difficult. They all serve a purpose and have something positive to contribute to the whole.

The ultimate goal of therapy is in fact fusion, or the complete integration of all the personalities. Some clients may be unwilling or unable to achieve this. In this case the best outcome is resolution, in which parts work together cooperatively so that the person can live the most productive life possible. Working on the integration of the psyche begins long before any personalities have fused and continues after "final fusion," when there are no longer any separate personalities.

In general, the more intense and comprehensive the treatment, the more successful the outcomes have been. As might be expected, there is a wide variation between DID clients. As stated in the 2005 *Guidelines for Treating Dissociative Identity Disorder in Adults:*

At one extreme are relatively high functioning and highly motivated patients with relatively few co-morbidities and reasonable social supports who have a relatively rapid and straightforward treatment course. At the other extreme are those who function at the level of disabled, chronically and persistently ill psychiatric patients…

Treatment of DID follows three phases:

1) Safety, stabilization, and symptom reduction,

2) Working directly and in depth with traumatic memories, and

3) Identity integration and rehabilitation (Chu 2005, 88–89).

Most DID clients experience what is often called complex PTSD. They have suffered multiple traumas throughout childhood, involving different developmental periods. They not only suffer from PTSD symptoms but also "have major difficulties with affect regulation, dissociation, and body image, the latter often manifesting itself as eating disorders, self-destructive attacks on the body, and somatization. They may have substantial relational pathologies, including major problems with trust and enmeshment with violent or abusive relationships. They often view the world as dangerous and traumatizing and see themselves as shameful, damaged and responsible for their own traumatization. These patients commonly have significant problems with self-destructiveness" (2005, 90). The betrayal trauma they suffered from their primary caregivers makes it very difficult for them to trust anyone deeply, including their therapists.

The initial phase of therapy for these clients should focus on stabilization, crisis management, and symptom reduction. Only after these are established should traumatic memory work and system integration proceed. Sometimes, however, traumatic memories will present themselves so aggressively that they will have to be worked with even if stage-one goals are not yet met. The SAFER model of John Chu offers clear guidelines for the initial stages of therapy, as well as a good summary of what is involved in middle- and late-stage therapy. I have also found that teaching clients mindfulness skills as elaborated by ACT (Acceptance and Commitment Therapy) has been very beneficial throughout the entire therapeutic process and especially in the initial stages. The *Treatment Guidelines* offer a more extensive discussion of all the phases of treatment.

It is often useful at the outset of therapy to invite the client to develop a system map in which the ages, functions, and interrelationships between the parts can be clarified. Besides being helpful for the therapist, this can help enhance client self-awareness and lay the groundwork for developing a higher level of internal communication.

Negative alters can frequently be a serious challenge. DID clients will almost always have a deep well of anger that is dissociated into potentially violent and often aggressively self-destructive alters. It is not without reason that some DID clients think they are possessed by demonic entities. Any attempt to get rid of these alters will inevitably make matters worse. At their core they embody an essential self-protective capacity that the person as a whole needs to function effectively.

In contrast to the negative alters are the helper personalities and especially the Inner-Self Helper (ISH). Helper personalities can be sources of insight, nurturance, and support for the host and other parts of the system. The ISH—first systematically described by Jung, who called it the Self, and later rediscovered by Ralph Allison—is an extraordinary resource that has manifested in every DID client I have ever worked with. It is not a personality as such. Its purpose is the healing, integration, and spiritual evolution of the client. It knows almost everything that is happening within the system, what issues need to be attended to next, and how best to address them. It can modulate the flow of affect as needed and even control somatic processes. It never imposes its will on any part and will help with the therapy process as an internal co-therapist. Utilizing this resource as a co-therapist will lead to a much more precise and effective therapeutic endeavor. By working with the ISH, the therapist is making clear to the client that her deepest and most reliable authority is within herself, which can be profoundly affirming. The ISH guides, teaches, and transforms parts primarily through powerful, metaphoric transformative experiences.

DID clients tend to live in two worlds, inner and outer, both of which are equally important to them. The outer world is the familiar shared reality in which we all participate. The inner world is a unique, subjective reality expressed through rich, multisensory, metaphoric experiences. When encountered internally, the parts may look very different from one another and vary widely in age, sex, and form. There will tend to be various levels or domains in the inner world, and different parts or groups of parts will have their own places. As Jung discovered, the metaphors embedded in the structures and processes of the inner world are highly meaningful and impact those who experience them at multiple levels.

The traumatic memory work that is at the core of the second phase of therapy is complex and intense. It is much easier if the therapist and the ISH work closely together in this process. Beyond that, it is critical that the therapist pay close attention to the treatment guidelines. All of the issues involved in working through complex PTSD are present, but complicated further by the varied reactions of multiple parts.

There is no way to determine the historical accuracy of the memories clients present unless credible witnesses are available. Nor is it necessary to determine whether the memories are accurate or not: unless the memories are worked through as they are experienced by the client, there will be no healing. Clients are often as inclined to discount their memories as are the purveyors of the "false-memory syndrome" school of thought. My standard response to clients is that we must work through what is presented. Whether it is accurate history or metaphor may never be known with certainty—although after stable integration is achieved, there may be greater clarity about what actually happened.

Some point to recent research regarding the malleability of memory as a way of challenging the validity of traumatic memory work. Whenever a memory is brought to consciousness, it is also available for modification and elaboration. This means that we can never be certain about the historical veracity of any of our memories. This very malleability, however, is an important mechanism for helping to heal traumatic memories.

The healing of a memory requires that all of the elements of the trauma be brought to awareness. This includes behaviors, affect, sensations, and cognitive elements (the BASK model). As the memory is intentionally reengaged, it is important that the observing ego has enough disconnection from the experience that it is not terrified or overwhelmed by it. An abreaction in which the client simply relives the trauma is an exercise in retraumatization and serves no good purpose. Processing the memory without terror is a healing modification of the original experience. An additional healing modification of the memory is to have the sense of a loving, protective presence (either the therapist or an internal resource) throughout the experience. A final modification would be for the ego to comfort and support the wounded child after the experience.

The third phase of therapy, integration and rehabilitation, has its own particular risks. Premature fusion, when pushed by either the therapist or the client, can cause significant stress and destabilize the system, sometimes requiring a return to the themes of phase one. Ideally, fusion either occurs spontaneously or when facilitated by the ISH. It can also be helpful for the therapist to suggest the possibility of fusion when there is clearly no longer any benefit for the part or parts to remain dissociated. However, I would never do anything more than offer a gentle suggestion. The resolution of traumatic history and the emergence of respectful, caring internal communication will usually give rise to fusion sooner or later. The psyche has a natural drive toward wholeness. The therapist's principal goal is to help remove the barriers to its natural unfolding. With continued integration the client will have more psychic energy, more resilience, and more inner peace.

Ultimate fusion can be unstable in the first few months, and the psyche can redissociate quite readily if confronted with a sufficiently powerful stressor. Even after the fusion is stabilized, there is much work left to be done. The trauma history may have to be revisited from a unified perspective. Awareness of all the losses occasioned by the traumas may lead to profound grief. The client will also have to learn to deal with negative life experiences without resorting to dissociative defenses. Reembracing the mindfulness skills learned in phase one is particularly useful here.

The Healing Relationship

As important as the correct methodology may be, the correct relationship is even more significant. For the client to risk facing terrifying memories and extreme levels of shame, hurt, and grief, she must feel safe and protected in the therapeutic relationship. Building such a therapeutic alliance requires what Eric Fromm identified as the four basic components of love: care, accurate knowledge of the other, respect, and responsibility to the relationship. Significant deficits in any of these areas will undermine the process.

Additionally, I have found that transparency and appropriate self-disclosure enhance trust and consequently foster a more healing relationship. DID clients have typically been so badly wounded in their primary relationships that trusting anyone is difficult and may remain tenuous well into the therapy process.

Two commonplace tendencies of therapists can interfere with the process by precipitating resistance on the part of the client and desensitizing the therapist to her own intuitive sensibilities. The first is attempting to persuade the client for or against some particular course of action or point of view. It is one thing to be frank about your concerns and point out what you consider to be likely negative consequences for a particular course of action, and another to try to talk the client into thinking or behaving differently. DID clients are hypersensitive to any attempts at control. They will either become resistant when they sense someone attempting to control them, or they will become superficially compliant without any real change happening.

The second controlling tendency is the inclination of therapists to so identify with their role that they put significant energy into maintaining and defending their professional identity or stance with the client. Even as the client is being encouraged to be open and genuine, she is faced with a therapist trying to play a role rather than being an open, genuine person in his own right. Efforts at persuasion and investment in defending one's own identity diminish awareness both of the client and of the therapist's own deeper wisdom.

Psychopharmacology

Psychotropic medications can be helpful adjuncts to DID therapy. Klonopin can diminish switching between alters and reduce the intensity and frequency of flashbacks. Antipsychotic medications will suppress alters and voices; some say it feels like they are put to sleep, and others say that it is like they are put behind a wall. This effect can be useful if destructive alters need to be contained, but it is only a temporary solution. As one aggressive alter told me, "She can't keep me drugged forever. Eventually, I'll get out and do what I need to do." Since DID clients typically have nightmares, Prazosin can be a valuable support by suppressing norepinephrine and, in so doing, allow the psyche to naturally work through the traumas that the nightmares reflect. Most DID clients also suffer from major depression and may respond to antidepressants. Additionally, they generally report various anxiety disorders and may be helped by anxiolytics. As the therapy progresses and the client achieves fusion, the psychotic phenomena and co-morbid disabilities fade, as does the need for psychotropic medications.

Conclusion

There is a profound shift underway in the world of psychotherapy. Research and clinical experience are demonstrating conclusively that the medical model of psychopathology no longer fits the facts. The assumption that severe and persistent mental illness is wholly or mostly biogenetic in its origin is simply wrong. The insights of Janet, Jung, and James accord far better with clinical reality. Once again the consensus is growing that trauma and subsequent dissociation are significant if not the primary drivers behind psychiatric disability.

As therapists realign their approach to clients in accord with this new information, the possibilities for recovery are increased significantly. DID clients represent the most extreme expression of the impact of trauma and dissociation on the psyche. If they can heal and live full, meaningful lives, then many, many more who have not been wounded as deeply have an even better chance at full recovery. The same methods and sensibilities that have proven effective with DID clients are equally as effective with most of our general client population. Even those whose mental illness appears to have a strong biogenetic component benefit from learning mindfulness techniques, working through trauma, dealing respectfully with voices, and learning how to be receptive to their own inner wisdom.

This new in-depth psychotherapy, grounded in the trauma/dissociation frame of reference, has enormous potential for good. The only real drawback is that it is not a brief therapy—nor, once the working through of trauma has begun, is it a therapy process that can be safely stopped in the middle if funds or insurance run out. I am hopeful that eventually, as the effectiveness of this approach becomes evident, it will be seen as ultimately cost effective by funding agencies, since so many actually recover and no longer need psychiatric or psychotherapeutic services.

CHAPTER TWENTY ONE

What to Do about Voices

Hearing voices that others cannot hear is one of the most puzzling and disturbing aspects of mental illness. The standard psychiatric response has been less than helpful. Current general psychiatric consensus is that voices are a hallucinatory aspect of psychosis. The common assumption is that the voices should be drugged into oblivion, or failing that, ignored and/or resisted by both client and therapist. Any consideration of the idea that the voices might have something important to say is considered naive and destructive, as it is assumed that this would potentially exacerbate an already troubling pathology.

A new perspective grounded in clients' own experience of voices contradicts this professional stance and has led to improved therapeutic outcomes with less dependence on antipsychotic medications than traditional psychiatric practice. A group for voice hearers reported in *Netlink* that was based on a willingness to acknowledge the voices and learn from them "reduced anxiety, depression, and voice hearing, and in the long term three members of the group stopped hearing voices and returned to work" (Coupland 2005, 3).

The traditional reaction of the psychiatric community to voices reflects a cultural assumption that "hearing voices" is a bizarre experience that sets the hearer apart from the community of "normal" people. The hearers themselves usually share this assumption. They often feel a need to hide this experience from others, if possible, and consider themselves to be abnormal and crazy because of it. Due to their shame and the everyday impact of the voices themselves, many who hear voices become socially isolated. At least some of the social isolation noted in mentally ill people is a result of the mentally ill sharing society's judgment of their experience and of not having the means to cope with or respond to the voices. Mentally ill persons often stigmatize themselves as readily as anyone else.

"Hearing voices" is not as uncommon as contemporary people might think. It is not necessarily limited to persons with mental illness or those in the throes of a psychotic episode. Ancient and traditional cultures valued voices. The Old Testament and other ancient literature are full of references to voices and visions that were taken quite seriously. Jesus heard voices, Joan of Arc heard voices, and Gandhi heard voices. Carl Jung heard voices. So did Florence Nightingale and Winston Churchill. Anthony Hopkins still hears voices. This list is long and would be longer still if all who heard voices would be willing to admit it. A large study of 15,000 people living in Baltimore discovered that 2.3 percent regularly heard voices on a frequent basis (Tien 1991, 287-292). The study further stated that 10 percent of respondents acknowledge hearing voices on an occasional basis. Barrett and Etheridge suggest that the life time prevalence may be significantly greater (Barrett & Etheridge 1992, 379-387).

Despite the typical professional assumption among mental health workers that hearing voices is conclusive evidence of psychosis and a probable indicator of severe mental illness, it seems extreme to me to label a phenomenon pathological that 10 percent of the population admit experiencing. My own rule of thumb is that if the other major elements of psychosis, such as delusions, thought disorders, or lack of insight, are absent or understandable, given the content of the voices, the person is not suffering from psychosis or a major mental illness. The voices are more likely a dissociative phenomenon in which the integrative function of the psyche has been disrupted. Usually this happens because the psyche was subjected to an event or series of events whose impact overwhelmed an individual's repertoire of coping strategies.

Most persons struggling with voices that I have known and with whom I have worked fall into this latter group. Their voices are an important resource that have the potential, if handled appropriately, of enriching and deepening the person's life. Therapies that identify them as pathological and attempt to shut them down through drugs or other mechanisms of control offer short-term comfort to the ego in lieu of a long-term potential for significant growth. Most voices, whether benign or antagonistic, reflect unintegrated aspects of the self and thus a potential gift. Some voices are not of the self, but are the introjected presence of significant others who have had a deep, disruptive, and as yet unresolved impact on the person's psyche. Their presence is an ongoing reminder of a hurtful relationship and consequent wounds still in need of healing. As such, these voices are also a gift.

Jamie, a client I once worked with, had been hearing voices most of her life. She was depressed, anxious, and embarrassed because she believed the voices were clear evidence that she was insane. Even though she was successful in school and able to hold down a responsible job, she felt like an imposter with an enormous shameful secret. Her goal in therapy was to get rid of the voices and be normal. Ultimately, she achieved that goal, but the path was unexpected and paradoxical. The "normality" she achieved was far different and richer than what she had imagined.

She had to begin by surrendering her conviction of insanity. Instead of seeing herself as the victim of a major mental illness, she came to see herself as presiding over and responsible for a community of unacknowledged hurts, disowned potentials, and polarized emotions that over the years had evolved into autonomous and highly verbal ego states. As she learned to acknowledge, listen to, and eventually even love them, they became part of her and she became a very different woman. After gathering the voices into herself, Jamie became more self-aware and emotionally stronger than the great majority of people who have never had the experience of voices or never learned to embrace those voices that they did have.

Whether the person hearing the voices fits the criteria for a major mental illness does not make a significant difference in the experience of voices or how best to respond to them. Unless the mentally ill person is decompensated to the point where communication or clear thinking is not possible, working with the voices is one of the most constructive options available. Some observers say that among those with a diagnosable major mental illness, such as schizophrenia, bipolar disorder, severe depression, or dissociative identity disorder, negative voices tend to predominate over benign, while in the rest of the population benign voices tend to predominate. Others claim the proportion of negative to benign voices is approximately the same in all populations. Unlike the patient population, the nonpatient population, (i.e. those who do not feel a need to seek professional help) is not afraid of the voices and less distressed by them (Romme 1993). All populations benefit from taking the voices seriously and responding to them constructively, instead of attempting to resist or deny them.

Persons with severe mental illness and PTSD have a higher incidence of voices than the rest of the population. About 83% percent of those diagnosed with schizophrenia in the US hear voices (Jones 2012, 160). In other cultures far fewer people are diagnosed with schizophrenia because they hear voices. In the study by Jones, 31% percent of those with Bipolar I hear voices (Jones 2012, 103). Everyone with Dissociative Identity Disorder with whom I have worked hears voices as well. Holmes reports that 65 percent of combat veterans with PTSD report hearing voices (Holmes 1995, 1).

This is probably because their mental illness and/or trauma impairs the psyche's ability to integrate and modulate disparate aspects of mental function. Among the clients with whom I have worked, their negative voices are much more aggressive than those of the general population.

These negative voices often express fixed and bizarre delusions that are at the extreme end of the rational/irrational continuum. In their delusions, disordered thinking, and lack of insight, they seem to embody the most dramatic elements of the individual's psychosis. These can have a very severe disabling impact, and often the best short-term solution is an antipsychotic medication that will diminish or silence the voices. Some individuals, however, cannot tolerate these medications and are left with the painful and frustrating choice of a life diminished by voices or a life diminished by medications. Moreover, 30 percent of those who take antipsychotic medications experience relatively little diminishment of the voices. In my estimation, nearly all of the above individuals would benefit from an opportunity to learn how to work with the voices to reduce their impact though enhanced internal communication and awareness.

When I managed a nineteen-bed psychiatric crisis-respite facility, voices were a very real experience for many of our residents. To understand and effectively support the participants in our program, it was important that we appreciated the impact of this phenomenon. These voices were often a dominant factor in determining the quality and direction of the lives of those who experienced them.

One resident, Sadie, lived with a voice that claimed to be her mother. It sounded like her mother and it acted like her mother—sometimes helpful, but usually critical. This voice was so real to Sadie that when her mother died, Sadie didn't believe it because she was certain that she was talking to her mother every day telepathically. It's easy to see how this voice could have a major impact on Sadie's life. Imagine that your mother followed you everywhere you went, observed everything you did, and even knew what you were thinking, then proceeded to tell you exactly what she thought about it all. This was Sadie's dilemma. It was enough to make a person crazy. An internal mother like this is extremely difficult to ignore and impossible to hang up on.

Besides being surprisingly common, voices can also be surprisingly real—as real to the hearer as any external conversation. Brain scans of persons hearing voices demonstrate activation of the speech area of the brain (Goleman 1993) This means that the voices are not an imaginary experience, though it's quite understandable that persons with voices might be confused or uncertain of whether the source of the voice is external or internal. I have noticed that DID populations are much more likely to identify voices as internal phenomena than are schizophrenics who are more inclined to externalize the source of their voices. This is probably because schizophrenics are more prone to delusions and disturbances of thought than are those who suffer from DID.

John as well as others in the psychiatric crisis-respite program I managed readily admitted that they had a hard time discerning whether they were hearing internal or external others saying things to them. This led to socially awkward situations that increased their inclination toward withdrawal. Others, like Vince, whose voices were mean spirited and demeaning, sometimes thought that the comments were made by external others in his environment and would become aggressive in reaction to the perceived provocation. Vince would calm down after he had been assured that the latest insult was internally generated and that there was no need to retaliate by striking out.

Audible voices that sound real to the hearer beg for some kind of explanation. In order to reduce the cognitive dissonance caused by the experience, the psyche will often quickly generate a delusion explaining the source of the voice. This is true especially for non-DID voice hearers with a major mental illness. They will develop beliefs such as: *The TV is talking to me*; or, *The CIA has implanted a chip in my brain through which they are broadcasting instructions to me*; or, *My hand [or some other body part] is talking to me*. Often these "explanations" can interfere with the hearers' willingness or ability to work with the voices.

The common religious response of considering the voices demonic can do great harm. If accepted by the ego, it will very likely increase the hearer's fear of the voice. Moreover, the ego state that generates the voice may buy into this religiously inspired delusion, especially if it is inclined to be antagonistic. A part that self identifies as a demon will act accordingly and thus become much darker and far more difficult to work with.

Although many voices sound just like someone in the room saying something to you, not all voices are experienced in this fashion. Sometimes the voices are experienced as anyone would experience their own thoughts, except that the thought comes from some other source than the ego itself. Whether it is an audible voice or an autonomous thought, the hearer does not make it happen and has no idea what will be said next. Sometimes the voice is actually many voices. They may sound like the conversational buzz heard at a cocktail party, with no reference to the hearer at all. Or they may be having a group discussion about the hearer, usually commenting on the individual's various shortcomings.

At one end of the spectrum, some voices are focused on a single theme and have very little personality structure. At the other end, voices may seem to emanate from a complex personality that has a name and sense of personal history as well a distinct personal reality, such as Zoltan, the emissary from Jupiter, or Princess, the talking unicorn.

Sometimes voices begin in childhood and are lifelong companions. Others begin in adulthood. Trauma is almost always a factor in their origination. The voices that begin later in life are usually easier to resolve.

I know from my own experience as a therapist that the resolution or integration of voices is possible. I also know that it is a very challenging and time-consuming process that requires considerable individual therapy. A different approach has recently been developed in England and the

Netherlands that uses a group process whose goal is not the integration of voices, but helping people learn how to cope with their voices more effectively. An effective approach to voices, whether through group or individual work, is dependent on several fundamental premises.

First, if the voices are so intense that the person cannot function or they are irresistibly commanding self-destructive behaviors, antipsychotic medication may be required before any effective work can be done. Additionally, effective work is usually not possible if the person is going through a severe psychotic decompensation, especially if a delusional system or thought disorder blocks the possibility of forming any kind of therapeutic alliance. If insight is so lacking that the individual doesn't see that there is a problem, or if the person is convinced that there is nothing that can be done about the problem, any attempt at intervention will probably be fruitless. A further exclusionary criterion is the continued use of heroin, amphetamines, etc., or large amounts of alcohol.

Marcia, a longtime resident in the program I managed, had two principal voices, God and the devil. God was largely comforting and made many predictions and promises to her, including one that He was going to punish me for making a decision Marcia didn't like. The promises were seldom kept and the predictions never came true, but Marcia continued to listen carefully to whatever God told her. As might be expected, the devil was often mean and aggressive and would say terrible things to her about herself. She was quite frightened by the devil. But, like God, the devil also supported ego-level desires that, when she acted upon them, she would explain by saying, "The devil made me do it" and sincerely mean it. Although it was not possible to engage Marcia in therapy regarding these voices, I doubt that much would have been achieved, given their delusional supportive structure and their ego-syntonic messages. Accepting that they were just internal aspects of her would have been extremely threatening and costly to the ego.

The acceptance of voices as internal aspects of the self is not an awareness that comes easily for many voice hearers. Nor is it necessary in order to begin working effectively with the voices. What is necessary is a willingness to consider the possibility that there is a better way to deal with the voices than trying to shut them out or control them. Strange as it may seem, voice hearers are more willing to consider this option than most mental health professionals. In fact, the "Hearing Voices" movement in Europe was grounded in voice hearers' own life experiences and what they discovered worked best in helping them learn to live productively with the voices. The first lesson they learned was that trying to shut the voices up was not productive. It seems to be a rule of thumb in the psyche that resistance energizes that which is resisted.

They also learned that agreeing with the voices or doing whatever the voices command is not productive. Voices are frequently wrong in their assertions about the individual or others in the person's life. Their predictions, even when stated with great authority, as in Marcia's case, seldom come true. Worst of all, many of the things they command are patently harmful to the hearer or others. These commands, technically known as "command hallucinations," can feel almost irresistible. Sometimes the commanding voice won't be irresistible but will threaten to punish the hearer if its command isn't followed. One typical punishment is internally caused severe pain, such as headaches.

Another insight that came from seriously listening to voice hearers is that some voices are genuinely benign. Others are both benign and profoundly wise. In my work as a therapist, finding an internal wisdom figure such as this was like finding pure gold, and it served as a powerful asset in the therapeutic process. Making the most of this resource that I and others have called the Self has obviously been the main theme of this book. The ancient belief in angels or an indwelling divine presence is probably well grounded in a healthy inner connection to just such a voice.

A central assumption of the Hearing Voices movement, validated in my own experience as a therapist, is that all of the voices—the good, the bad, and the ugly—must be heard. The key issue is the stance the ego takes in listening to them.

Unthinking surrender to the voices will almost always be destructive and often disastrous. The negative voices are driven by hurt, fear, anger, and shame. The perspective toward life they engender is controlling, rigid, and paranoid. Even if they were not pushing the ego toward acting in accord with their point of view, their way of seeing the self and the world is deeply distorted and limiting. In most instances they tend to be profoundly judgmental of the ego and external others as well. They tend to continually erode what little confidence the ego has with an unremitting shame and guilt-inducing commentary the hearer can't ignore. The hearer who already feels insecure and odd simply because of the voices' existence is further diminished by what they have to say. The behaviors they encourage or command invariably involve either attack or withdrawal. More often than not, the attack is toward oneself.

When the ego acquiesces, the pressure from the voices will often ease temporarily. However, a new marker will have been established. An action the ego would not have considered, before giving in to the voice, is now within the realm of plausible action. Voices that push for profoundly self-destructive or even suicidal behavior do not usually consider themselves at risk for the consequences of such behaviors.

Mark had put up an epic battle against his various negative voices. He refused their commands and argued vociferously and loudly against their demeaning commentaries. Since one of the voices was his mother, this made the struggle all the more poignant and painful. These arguments would be so loud at times that they would disturb the other residents in the shelter where he lived. Mark was clearly a good man fighting for his honor against an intractable foe, but the battle was never won. The more energy Mark put into the battle, the more energized the voices became. Medication and a calm, protective environment have helped reduce the intensity of the struggle, but the struggle goes on. Mark now lives a socially withdrawn, limited life, far removed from his true potential. There is hope, however. Mark will soon be joining a "Coping with Voices" group. Perhaps there he will learn an entirely different way to approach this dilemma.

Benign voices are obviously easier to live with, but they are not necessarily constructive companions. They will often fuel grandiose assumptions that may help compensate for the demeaning commentaries of negative voices but lead to foolish choices and self-destructive behaviors. They may speak with an air of great authority, as if they had special knowledge, which will be very impressive to the ego, but often turn out to be wrong. The accuracy of their knowledge about the person's inner thoughts and needs can persuade the person that they have equal perspicacity on external persons and events. Like an indulgent caregiver, they often try to "help" by helping the person avoid hard truths and giving it permission to engage in self-soothing or self-aggrandizing behaviors that ultimately make matters worse.

The Self as Inner Wisdom is unlike these other helpers. It is deeply loving, but it never sugarcoats reality. It makes clear that it is in the service of the entire psyche. It will not assist in diminishing or removing any voice. Rather, it will help the ego listen to and understand what is driving the voices and show the way to ultimate integration. This extraordinary source of wisdom and healing is far more common than most contemporary people would imagine. Whether this resource is used or not in trying to help a person respond constructively to voices, its perspective is invaluable.

The healing process begins with acceptance and a commitment to truth. This is one of the initial and most powerful gifts that a Coping with Voices group can offer. Here the voice hearer can speak frankly with others who really understand, without fear of stigma or judgment. This alone is a momentous life change: after so many years of struggle, isolation, and shame, it has finally become possible to be known, heard, and respected. Obviously this can happen in individual therapy too, but the group context, if well run, can enhance the experience.

The next step in the healing process involves the dawning realization that no matter how the voices may identify themselves, they are all part of the same psyche, including the ego itself. However primitive, distorted, or alienated they may be, they are part of oneself and at their core a gift—although discerning and integrating the gift may take a great deal of time and energy.

Once this truth is accepted, the hearer is then ready to explore the inner life through the agency of these voices. Resisting the voices is slowly replaced by learning to listen to them in a way that breaks down the divisions and polarization between ego and voices. This listening seeks to understand the perspective and needs of the voices. It neither agrees nor disagrees with the voices' commentaries, but is very interested in why they say what they say and what gives rise to them. It is respectful and nonjudgmental. It truly wants to know. A hearer taking this path may choose not to follow the voices' advice or commands, but will explore as deeply as possible the fundamental intent behind the advice or command. The intent will almost always involve some kind of self-protective strategy.

In a nutshell, a voice hearer committed to this path will neither acquiesce to nor push away the voice. When the gift within the voice is discerned and welcomed by the hearer, integration will flow naturally in its own time.

The general outlines of this process are easy enough to describe; the accomplishment of them may be one of the hardest challenges the voice hearer will ever face. The alternative, however, is well known to the voice hearer, and few would choose it if they knew that there were a genuine, life-affirming way out.

CHAPTER TWENTY TWO

Cognitive Neuroscience and Counseling

Neuroscience has been a significant area of interest to therapists for many years. The hope has been that if we could understand brain processes more clearly, we could make better-informed decisions as to how to facilitate the change process. This hope is now beginning to be fulfilled. Contemporary cognitive neuroscience has much to offer counselors. Just as it is beginning to clarify the biological basis of the various psychiatric disabilities, it is also proving to be a valuable resource for understanding and improving the practice of psychotherapy. The themes I consider to be its most significant are the importance of accessing the emotional or mammalian brain as a resource for personal change, right- and left-brain interrelationships, the neurobiology of attachment and its implications for therapy, the malleability of memories and how the reconsolidation process can be used to resolve trauma memories and other embedded self-destructive patterns, mirror neurons and how they facilitate an empathic therapeutic bond, and the neurological underpinnings and value of hallucinogens as a powerful resource in psychotherapy. I will be exploring all of these in this chapter, beginning with an overview of the importance of the emotional brain.

In the 1960s Paul MacLean developed the concept of the triune brain. He proposed that the human brain recapitulates in its basic structure our evolutionary development. There is some dispute about the correspondence between evolution and the triune structure of the brain, but there is broad agreement that this structure exists and is highly relevant to understanding human behavior. The deepest and most primitive structure is the reptilian complex. It is the source of our basic instinctual drives, such as aggression, dominance, territoriality, and ritual displays. The next level, the paleomammalian complex or limbic system, is what some call the emotional brain. MacLean proposed that it evolved to support the nurturing and bonding impulses necessary for creating a family unit and caring for the young. The third level is the neomammalian complex or the cerebral neocortex. It facilitates the development of language, abstract thought, and the ability to plan and make choices.

Most psychotherapy focuses on neocortical skills, whereas most of the conflicts that give rise to our clients' suffering are driven by the emotional or paleomammalian brain, which does not necessarily have access to these skills. These two brain structures clearly interact, and it is obvious that cognitive restructuring at the neocortical level can change some emotional patterns, as seen in the success of cognitive behavioral therapy. But there are many instances in which no amount of insight or behavioral change will effect long-term change, as every practicing therapist is fully aware. This is because the emotional brain operates very differently from the neocortex. It is engaged by experiences that impact the senses and emotions rather than by verbal explanations and well-thought-out plans. No matter what a person may think about an issue or life circumstance, the emotional brain's response is what triggers the neurotransmitters and hormones that impel our reactions, even though they may contradict our best logic.

If the emotional brain is going to change its responses, it must be addressed within its own frame of reference, i.e., through powerful, deeply felt experiences. Therapists who can help clients access emotionally powerful experiences that balance or undermine their self-destructive patterns will facilitate significant change in what had seemed to be intractable behavior patterns. There are a wide variety of experiential techniques that can be helpful in this regard. Bringing to mind powerful, constructive life experience relevant to the client's conflict; psychodrama; playful interaction with the client; imagery; and especially active imagination or internal work are all ways of connecting with the emotional brain on its own terms.

An even more significant structural reality of the brain is its bicameral nature. Research into the bicameral structure of the human brain has grown significantly over the last three decades. Neuroscientist Jill Bolte Taylor described in her book *My Stroke of Insight* how different her experience of reality was when her left brain was shut down due to a stroke and she came to know herself and reality in general from an unqualified right-brain perspective. She lost language, her sense of sequential time, and her capacity for planning. She lived in a heightened state of awareness and connection that very closely paralleled what has been described as enlightenment. Once she regained her capacity for language, she retained her new capacity for global consciousness, and she states with profound conviction that this ability to see the wholeness of things and feel how everything is connected is the real truth. Although she eventually regained her left-brain function, her life was transformed as she experienced the heightened and integrated awareness of the right brain. Through her right brain she fell into the embrace of the spirit of the depths, and the world came alive for her. She fully experienced the bliss and sense of meaning that arise from being immersed in the direct, interconnected experience of reality.

The research of Ian McGilchrist on right- and left-brain function is one of the most important contributions of neuroscience to psychotherapy that I am aware of. Unfortunately, the healing potential of a holistic, connected, intuitive right-brain approach to therapy, as described by McGilchrist, has been largely discounted. The control-oriented, disconnected, model-building proclivities of the analytical left-brain permeate both our culture and most psychotherapy as it is currently taught and practiced.

The following is a summary of the findings of contemporary research on right- and left-brain processes as outlined by McGilchrist in his book *The Master and His Emissary*:

- "To understand the landscape we need both to go out into the felt, lived world of experience as far as possible, along what one might think of as the horizontal axis [the domain of the right hemisphere], but also to rise above it, on the vertical axis [the way of the frontal lobes and left hemisphere]. To live headlong, at ground level [on the horizontal axis] without being able to pause (stand outside the immediate push of time [on the vertical axis]) and rise (in space) is to be like an animal; yet to float off up into the air is not to live at all—just to be a detached observing eye" (21).

- Distance on the vertical plane can either lead to detachment, which allows us to plan how to best exploit the other, or it can lead to empathy, which allows us to see the other as like ourselves and use that awareness to create a deeper bond (i.e., return to the horizontal plane with more intentionality and energy) (22).

- Brain lateralization is widespread in vertebrates because it conveys significant benefits: "The left hemisphere yields narrow, focused attention, mainly for the purpose of getting and feeding. The right hemisphere yields a broad, vigilant attention, the purpose of which appears to be awareness of signals from the surroundings, especially other creatures, who are potential predators or potential mates, foes or friends; and it is involved in bonding in social animals" (27).

- "The right hemisphere sees things whole and in their context, where the left hemisphere sees things abstracted from context, and broken into parts, from which it then reconstructs a 'whole'" (28).

- "The capacities that help us form bonds with others—empathy, emotional understanding, and so on—which involve a quite different kind of attention paid to the world, are largely right-hemisphere functions" (28).

- Through the right hemisphere, "we *experience* the live, complex, embodied world of individual, always unique beings, forever in flux, a net of interdependencies, forming and reforming wholes, a world with which we are deeply connected. In the other [left brain] we 'experience' our experience in a special way: a re-presented version of it, containing now static, separable, bounded, but essentially fragmented entities, grouped into classes, on which predictions can be based. This kind of attention isolates, fixes, and makes each thing explicit by bringing it under the spotlight of attention. In doing so it renders things inert, mechanical, lifeless. But it also enables us for the first time to know and consequently to learn and to make things. This gives us power" (31).

- The right hemisphere is attentive to simply what is out there and thus very receptive to whatever is new or unique. The left hemisphere can only know within the frame of its own expectations or structures. Consequently, the right brain "outperforms the left whenever prediction is difficult" (40).

- In problem solving the right hemisphere can see multiple options, whereas the left hemisphere tends to focus on the one solution that best fits what it already thinks it knows (41).

- "The left hemisphere takes the local, short-term view, whereas the right hemisphere sees the bigger picture" (43).

- In contrast to the left-brain's proclivity for classification, the right brain's inclination is to identify individuals (51).

- "Because the right hemisphere sees nothing in the abstract, but always appreciates things in their context, it is interested in the personal, by contrast with the left hemisphere, which has more affinity for the abstract or impersonal" (54).

- "The right hemisphere is concerned with living individuals rather than manmade objects. This flows naturally from its interest in whatever it is that exists apart from ourselves, and its capacity for empathy—as well as from its capacity to see the whole...The left hemisphere has an equal affinity for what is mechanical. The left hemisphere's principal concern is utility. It is interested in what it has made and in the world as a resource to be used" (55).

- "Self-awareness, empathy, identification with others, and more generally inter-subjective processes are largely dependent upon... right-hemisphere resources" (57).

- "The right hemisphere has by far the preponderance of emotional understanding. It is the mediator of social behavior. In the absence of the right hemisphere, the left hemisphere is unconcerned about others and their feelings: social intercourse is conducted with a blanket disregard for the feelings, wishes, needs, and expectations of others. Patients with right frontal deficits, but not left frontal deficits, suffer a change of personality whereby they become incapable of empathy" (58).

- "In all forms of emotional perception, regardless of the type of emotion, and in most forms of expression, the right hemisphere is dominant...The one exception to the right hemisphere for the expression of emotion is anger. Anger is robustly connected to left-hemisphere activation" (59).

- "It seems to me a possibility that those emotions which are related to bonding and empathy, whether we call them 'positive' or 'negative,' are preferentially treated by the right hemisphere...By the same token, those to do with competition, rivalry, and individual self-belief, positive or negative, would be preferentially treated by the left hemisphere" (63).

- The right hemisphere also has a closer physiological relationship with the body than does the left (66).

- Contrary to common assumptions, the right hemisphere plays a significant role in language and communication. It uses language not in order to "manipulate ideas or things, but to understand what others mean." Through it "we understand the moral of the story as well as the point of the joke" (70).

- "The right hemisphere specializes in nonverbal communication. It deals with whatever is implicit, where the left hemisphere is tied to more explicit and more conscious processing. Subtle unconscious perceptions that govern our reactions are picked up by the right hemisphere" (71).

- "The right hemisphere is more realistic about how it stands in relation to the world at large, less grandiose, more self-aware, than the left hemisphere. The left hemisphere is ever optimistic, but unrealistic about its shortcomings...Denial is a left-hemisphere specialty: in states of relative right-hemisphere inactivation, in which there is therefore a bias toward the left hemisphere, subjects tend to evaluate themselves optimistically, view pictures more positively, and are more apt to stick to their existing point of view" (85).

- The right hemisphere has a tendency toward melancholy. "This can, in my view, be seen as related not only to being more in touch with what is going on, but more in touch with and concerned for others. The more we are aware of and empathically connected to whatever it is that exists apart from ourselves, the more we are likely to suffer. Sadness and empathy are highly correlated" (85).

- The right hemisphere is the source of moral values. Moral values are not logical constructs based on more fundamental principles: "Such values are linked to the capacity for empathy, not reasoning; and moral judgments are not deliberative, but unconscious and intuitive, deeply bound up with our emotional sensitivity to others. Empathy is intrinsic to morality" (86).

- The right frontal lobe's capacity to inhibit our natural inclination to selfishness means that it is also the area on which we most rely for self-control and the power to resist temptation (86).

- "The self as intrinsically, empathically inseparable from the world in which it stands in relation to others, and the continuous sense of self, are more dependent on the right hemisphere, whereas the objectified self, and the self as an expression of will, is generally more dependent upon the left hemisphere" (87).

- "The right hemisphere [is] that [which] 'connects the individual to emotionally salient experiences and memories underlying self-schemas' and which therefore forms 'the glue holding together the sense of self'"(88).

In summation McGilchrist says, "In reality we are a composite of the two hemispheres...They work together most of the time at the everyday level. But that does not exclude that they may have radically different agendas, and over long periods and large numbers of individuals it becomes apparent that they instantiate a way of being in the world that is in conflict with the other" (91). The world of the left hemisphere is explicit, abstracted, compartmentalized, fragmented, static (though its bits can be reset in motion like a machine), essentially lifeless. From this world we feel detached, but in relation to it we are powerful. (93): I believe the essential difference between the right hemisphere and the left hemisphere is that the right hemisphere pays attention to the Other, whatever it is that exists apart from ourselves, with which it sees itself in profound relation. It is deeply attracted to and given life by, the relationship, the betweenness, that exists with this Other. By contrast the left hemisphere pays attention to the virtual world that it has created, which is self-consistent, but self-contained, ultimately disconnected from the Other, making it powerful, but ultimately only able to operate on, and to know, itself…*The gifts of the left hemisphere have helped us achieve nothing less than civilization itself with all that that means. [Nevertheless] these contributions need to be made in the service of something else, that only the right hemisphere can bring. Alone they are destructive. And right now they may be bringing us close to forfeiting the civilization they helped create* [italics mine]. (93)

The ramifications of this research for psychotherapy are significant and pervasive. A common Western assumption about psychological healing and growth has been that how we think about our world and ourselves is the most important determining factor underlying our psychological health and spiritual life. Many in the counseling profession assume that if a client thinks or believes in the "right" way, she can resolve her emotional conflicts and live a more productive, meaningful life.

We all know there is some truth in this. Cognitive behavioral therapy (CBT) has proven to be a highly effective tool. Sometimes we know in our own lives that the right advice at the right time can be extremely helpful. Most of the brief and solution-focused therapies involve the application of verbal analysis and logical principles to the conundrums facing our clients. They work well up to a point.

We also know, however, that there are multiple other factors that either facilitate the cognitive aspects of therapy or transcend them altogether. The therapist's ability to help a client reconsider a self-limiting point of view is roughly proportionate to the depth of the empathic bond between them. We also know from our own personal experience, as well as that of our clients, that many of our internal conflicts (especially the most disturbing) seem impervious to our own best efforts to think our way out of them.

As McGilchrist points out, a left-brain-dominated approach to internal or external reality is a good vehicle for the kind of understanding that comes from analysis and enhances our capacity for controlling internal and external processes. It does not, however, give us the kind of connection to our impulses and emotions and their root causes that the right brain can afford. Moreover, the range of personal options that the left brain can perceive is constrained by the premises and models it uses to construct its image of the world. The right brain is not dependent on models. It draws its awareness from its sense of immersive connection with reality through direct experience. Consequently, it is aware of a far broader range of options than the left brain can conceive of, and can thus be a much more creative resource for problem solving.

Each hemisphere has its own primary mode of communication. The capacity for conceptual thinking and language, in which the left brain excels, is not the only way for the psyche to express itself. Music, art, ritual, metaphor, and powerful, transformative, internally generated experiences are all ways in which the right brain expresses itself. The impact of these can be far more profound than even the best use of language and analysis can offer.

When I compare an effective, meaningful session of conversational therapy with one in which I used active imagination or dream work (the primary vehicles of right-brain-oriented therapy) to help a person experientially engage the wisdom and depth of the right brain, the difference is striking. A constructive session of conversational therapy may result in the client achieving greater clarity regarding a personal conflict or in helpful insight about potentially constructive changes that the person might want to consider. On the other hand, an experience of active imagination is likely to open up unexpected perspectives on matters of significant consequence. The client and therapist may have both thought that the ego-level concern that the client was presenting was what needed attention. Yet in the active imagination experience it may become very clear, through the guidance of a wisdom figure and/or the unfolding of a dramatic, metaphoric experience, that the ego's left-brain perception of the issue at hand and of what is truly important is far off the mark.

Additionally, the experiences generated by right-brain-oriented therapy (primarily active imagination) are much more than sources of insight and encouragement. They tend to affect the person at multiple levels, involving body, senses, emotions, and cognition. The impact of these experiences often leaves the ego shaken and changed. Rather than encouraging the ego to take a new point of view, as in the case of ordinary, left-brain, conversational therapy, right-brain therapy transforms the ego, impelling the person to spontaneously make the changes implicit in the internal experience. This change can erode in time as the old belief systems and patterns of the ego reassert themselves, but if the ego is willing, it can embrace this impetus. The changes can then become permanent. As McGilchrist puts it, "Imagination, then, is not a neutral projection of images on a screen. We need to be careful of our imagination, since what we imagine is in a sense what we are and who we become" (250).

Most of what we know to be most effective in counseling draws primarily from right-brain skills. Creating rapport, expressing empathy, possessing accurate intuition, being willing to be with the other in a spirit of nurturing openness without a need to control outcomes, and creating a safe space where the client can dare to speak his own truth and tell his darkest secrets all require that the therapist be firmly grounded in the receptive consciousness of the right brain.

Most deeply wounded clients are trying very hard to control their inner and outer lives and failing at both. The best they know to do is to try harder. Eventually that fails, and they become discouraged and often angry. An empathic, warm, genuine, and nonjudgmental counselor can model a different way of being with the client's pain and frustration that in time the client may begin to emulate. The therapist's receptive quality of presence communicates much more than words. The client's ego and left-brain processes may not appreciate what is happening, but the client's right brain will take in the therapist's loving presence and be moved by it.

For the counselor to be authentically present in this fashion, the counselor must be committed to a life grounded primarily in the values and perspective of receptive consciousness. If you live ordinarily out of a controlling or instrumental mentality, it would be very difficult to genuinely move to a truly receptive mode during a counseling session. What usually happens, to those who try, is that underneath their expressions of warmth and empathy lie judgment and a strong drive to persuade the client to make whatever changes the counselor thinks would be in his or her best interest. Most counseling functions at this level.

Despite our best intentions, we are deeply influenced by our culture, which is heavily invested in a left-brain, instrumental, and controlling mentality. Because of this we get in the way of creating the kind of interpersonal environment in which the client's own deepest values, wisdom, and authentic self have an opportunity to emerge and become the true anchor and ultimate resource for healing.

Right-brain awareness and the impact of mirror neurons, as discussed in the chapter "The Therapeutic Bond," can be thwarted by not paying attention to the other. In the counseling context this typically happens because we are distracted by thinking about what we plan to say next, or because we are in reaction to the contents of the client's communication and withdrawing from connection, or because we are strongly invested in a left-brain, controlling mind-set as we strive to control the therapeutic process. All of these diminish sensitivity to right-brain perceptions and connection to one's own emotional state. If you are unaware of how you are feeling, you will obviously be unaware of how those feelings may be reflecting the feelings of the person you are with. When this happens you lose your most effective, powerful tool for understanding and bonding with the other person.

Perhaps the most life-affirming thing we have to offer as either a counselor or a friend flows from our willingness to pay attention to the other and our own feelings as we engage the other. The empathy and connection that arise from this are the foundation that opens up all the other transformative possibilities in the relationship.

Another very important recent discovery in neuroscience is that memories are malleable and subject to transformation every time they are brought to consciousness. Given that PTSD is one of the most common Axis I disorders dealt with by psychotherapists and co-morbid with multiple other diagnoses, this is a critically important insight. Dr. Karim Nader of McGill University in Montreal demonstrated that long-term memories are not permanently set, but that they can be altered when brought to awareness. The following was reported by Greg Miller in the May 2010 *Smithsonian Magazine*, "How Our Brains Make Memories":

> Nader decided to revisit the concept with an experiment. In the winter of 1999, he taught four rats that a high-pitched beep preceded a mild electric shock. That was easy—rodents learn such pairings after being exposed to them just once. Afterward, the

rat freezes in place when it hears the tone. Nader then waited 24 hours, played the tone to reactivate the memory and injected into the rat's brain a drug that prevents neurons from making new proteins.

If memories are consolidated just once, when they are first created, he reasoned, the drug would have no effect on the rat's memory of the tone or on the way it would respond to the tone in the future. But if memories have to be at least partially rebuilt every time they are recalled—down to the synthesizing of fresh neuronal proteins—rats given the drug might later respond as if they had never learned to fear the tone and would ignore it. If so, the study would contradict the standard conception of memory. It was, he admits, a long shot.

"Don't waste your time, this will never work," LeDoux told him.

It worked.

When Nader later tested the rats, they didn't freeze after hearing the tone: it was as if they'd forgotten all about it (Miller 2010).

Alain Brunet, a professor in the department of psychiatry at McGill University in Montreal, has applied Nader's findings to the treatment of PTSD, as described in the same Smithsonian article:

The patients in Brunet's study, published in 2008, had each experienced a traumatic event, such as a car accident, assault or sexual abuse, about a decade earlier. They began a therapy session sitting alone in a nondescript room with a well-worn armchair and a television. Nine patients took a propranolol pill and read or watched TV for an hour as the drug took effect. Ten were given a placebo pill.

Brunet came into the room and made small talk before telling the patient he had a request: he wanted the patient to read a script, based on earlier interviews with the person, describing his or her traumatic experience. The patients, all volunteers, knew that the reading would be part of the experiment. "Some are fine, some start to cry, some need to take a break," Brunet says.

A week later, the PTSD patients listened to the script, this time without taking the drug or a placebo. Compared with the patients who had taken a placebo, those who had taken the propranolol a week earlier were now calmer; they had a smaller uptick in their heart rate and they perspired less.

Brunet has just completed a larger study with nearly 70 PTSD patients. Those who took propranolol once a week for six weeks while reading the script of their traumatic event showed an average 50 percent reduction in standard PTSD symptoms. They had fewer nightmares and flashbacks in their daily lives long after the effects of the drug had worn off. The treatment didn't erase the patients' memory of what had happened to them; rather, it seems to have changed the quality of that memory. "Week after week the emotional tone of the memory seems weaker," Brunet says. "They start to care less about that memory."

Nader says the traumatic memories of PTSD patients may be stored in the brain in much the same way that a memory of a shock-predicting tone is stored in a rat's brain. In both cases, recalling the memory opens it to manipulation. Nader says he's encouraged by the work so far with PTSD patients. "If it's got any chance of helping people, we have to give it a shot," he says. (Miller 2010).

Kevin Hand in a May 2006 *Popular Science* article explained how the process works neurochemically:

1) Trauma triggers the amygdala to release stress hormones, which enhance memory formation in the brain.

2) Memories of the trauma are first stored in the hippocampus. Then a chemical reaction encodes them into neurons in the cerebral cortex, cementing them into long-term storage.

3) When a victim recalls the trauma, the memory transfers back to the hippocampus, where it can trigger the release of more stress hormones.

4) Propranolol blocks the effects of the hormones and softens the victims' perception of the trauma. The brain restores the newly edited memory. (Hand 2006, 37)

Propranolol-assisted therapy for PTSD shows considerable promise. However, the malleability of PTSD memories has been an implicit assumption in all of the various successful psychotherapies for PTSD. The neuroscientific insights offered by Nader and Brunet help to give us a deeper understanding of how and why patients can overcome the debilitating impact of traumatic memory. Whether exposure therapy and other CBT techniques, EMDR, or psychodynamic psychotherapy is used, the goal is the same. The memory (or memories) currently triggering the symptoms of hyperarousal, intrusion, and/or avoidance typical of PTSD must become part of the person's normal autobiographical memory and lose their power to automatically trigger PTSD symptoms.

Reconsolidating a traumatic memory so that it can no longer trigger symptoms involves several steps. First, the entire memory must be reclaimed, including its affective, sensorial, and cognitive aspects. Then it needs to be put into language, which allows the person to begin to gain some perspective and distance from the experience. This in itself will help to facilitate the transformation of the memory from traumatic to narrative.

More importantly, the new memory should include the caring presence of a trusted companion, the psychotherapist, which will have a significant soothing impact.

An additional helpful step in reforming the memory is to use active imagination to help the person view the trauma from a partially detached perspective, so that as the memory reforms, the emotional impact is significantly diminished. Another use of active imagination that has proven to be very helpful is to have the ego or an inner helper comfort and support the traumatized part, usually a wounded child. A final, very helpful use of active imagination is to invite an inner teacher or wisdom figure to help the ego find whatever meaning there might be in the experience or to turn it into a positive resource if possible. The new version of the memory will still contain the awareness of what happened historically, but it will be placed in an entirely new frame that can be constructive and life affirming.

In the July/August 2013 issue of the *Psychotherapy Networker*, Bruce Ecker describes how he uses this memory reconsolidation process as a central theme in his practice of psychotherapy. He calls it "coherence therapy," which he describes as follows:

> The particular usefulness of our Coherence Therapy approach
> is that its steps match those of the reconsolidation process:
> first evoke into direct experience the emotional learnings
> underlying the client's unwanted patterns. Then find a vivid

knowledge or experience that contradicts those learnings. Finally, combine those two into a juxtaposition experience and repeat it several times (Ecker 2013, 7).

Just as the alteration of memory with the help of propranolol has the potential to simplify and expand the treatment of PTSD, consciousness itself can be greatly expanded with a remarkable potential for psychospiritual growth and healing through the appropriate use of psychedelics. A great deal of research was done in this field in the 1960s and early '70s, but was discontinued due to extremely restrictive legislation in reaction to popular media and cultural bias, rather than to a genuine consideration of its true potential. *LSD Psychotherapy*, by Stanislav Grof, MD, is an excellent statement of this early research. The field lay dormant until 1990, when Rick Strassman, MD, began his systematic study of DMT, a chemical cousin to LSD. His findings are summarized in the book *DMT, The Spirit Molecule: A Doctor's Revolutionary Research into the Biology of Near-Death and Mystical Experiences*.

Recently there has been a renewed interest in the potential of psychedelics as catalysts for psychological healing and spiritual growth. Charles Grob, MD, led a research group from 2004 to 2008 at UCLA "examining the safety and efficacy of psilocybin [a close analogue to DMT] as a treatment for advanced-cancer anxiety." In 2010 he reported in the MAPS Bulletin 20 (1) that participants had "psycho-spiritual epiphanies, along with powerful autobiographical insights, that were of significant value in establishing heightened levels of emotional well-being." (28) Additional similar studies have been initiated at Johns Hopkins University, New York University, UCLA, and Imperial College, in the UK. Clearly, we are at the beginning of a new phase of research into the utilization of psychedelics as a significant resource in facilitating psychospiritual growth. Aside from cancer anxiety, psychedelic research is also focusing on obsessive-compulsive disorder, PTSD, and the nature of mystical experience.

In the May/June 2013 issue of *Scientific American Mind*, Erica Rex details her experience as a participant in the Johns Hopkins study. She was a breast cancer survivor who was suffering significant emotional distress in the aftermath of her breast surgery. She was highly depressed, suicidal, and scared. After a single psilocybin session, she reported the following:

> My mood has improved, and my sense of myself as a person occupying a certain space in the universe has altered.

> I have come to realize that the universe consists of more than what readily meets the eye. An abiding sense of the inexplicable vastness of what is real and what is possible has affected my worldview. I no longer define myself by what has happened to my body, or even my emotional life since my cancer diagnosis...

> When talking about my hallucinations with the clinicians and my guides, I found they provided me some profound truths about my life. My tendency to judge myself with a kind of murderous harshness has ebbed. I am now able to feel more compassion both toward myself and toward others. I no longer spend my days worrying about what the future holds and whether I'll have a cancer recurrence or whether I'll die alone (Rex 2013, 66).

Grof describes the action of psychedelics as catalysts and amplifiers of the psyche. The Greek translation for *psychedelic* is "to make clear or manifest the mind." Given the intense mental activity triggered by psychedelics, it would be natural to assume that psychedelics are some kind of mental stimulant, but, in fact, the opposite is true. In the *Proceedings of the National Academy of Sciences USA* "Neural Correlates of the Psychedelic State as Determined by fMRI Studies," by Nutt, Wise and Fielding, the authors state the following:

It has been commonly assumed that psychedelics work by increasing neural activity, however, our results put this into question...We used an advanced and comprehensive fMRI protocol to image the brain effects of psilocybin. These studies offer the most detailed account to date on how the psychedelic state is produced in the brain. The results suggest decreased activity and connectivity in the brain's connector hubs, permitting an unconstrained style of cognition. [These hubs are part of the brain's default-mode network (DMN).]...The brain's default-mode network is "posited to have a role in consciousness and high level constructs, such as the self or 'ego.'"...Indeed, the DMN is known to be activated during self-referencing and other high level functions linked to the self-construct...

These results may have implications beyond explaining how psilocybin works in the brain by implying that the DMN is crucial for the maintenance of cognitive integration and constraint under normal conditions. This finding is consistent with Aldous Huxley's "reducing valve" metaphor and Karl Friston's "free-energy principle," which propose that the mind/brain works to constrain its experience of the world. (Nutt et al. 2012, 2138)

Essentially, this is saying that psilocybin diminishes the ego's (i.e., the explicit self's) ability to limit awareness to the ordinary, everyday interests that are usually its focus of attention. In doing so, a much broader field of awareness is opened to experiences that are felt to be real, if not more real than those available to ordinary awareness. Rather than creating hallucinations, psilocybin and the other psychedelics may be opening the "doors of perception," in Aldous Huxley's words, to realities that are already there but usually blocked from awareness. When these doors of perception are opened, four basic types of phenomena are experienced: 1) empathy and a sense of connection to others and nature, 2) mystical experiences and a sense of intimate union with God, 3) powerful, internally generated psychotherapeutic experiences, and 4) autonomous entities, both helpful and threatening.

There can also be negative, destructive experiences, but they are rare and can be minimized if the mind-set and setting of the subject taking the psychedelic are appropriate. Although there is considerable room for discussion about how real these experiences are or what the nature of their reality is, there can be no debate about the reality of their impact. When psychedelics are taken with the right intention (i.e., seeking enhanced self-knowledge, healing, or spiritual depth) and in the right context (i.e., a safe environment with the support of knowledgeable counselors), their impact is usually transformative and frequently life altering. The experience described above by Erica Rex is the rule, not the exception.

Psychedelics have been shown to have a striking impact on alleviating depression. In Dr. Grob's study of psilocybin for cancer patients, he found that there was sustained improvement on their Beck Depression Inventory six months after they received their psilocybin treatment. In the 2012 Proceedings of the National Academy of Sciences, Dr. David Nutt, a neuropsychopharmacologist, said that his research indicated that psilocybin reduced activity in two brain regions, the medial prefrontal cortex (mPFC) and the anterior and posterior cingulate cortices. The mPFC is known to be hyperactive in depression, "leading to the pessimistic outlook and pathological brooding characteristic of the condition." Diminishing its activity may be part of the reason for psilocybin's antidepressant effect.

Presumably this would also be so for LSD and DMT, the two other major, closely related psychedelics. An atypical psychedelic, ketamine, which has been used as a dissociative anesthetic, is also a highly effective antidepressant when given in small doses. In a replication study by the National Institute of Mental Health reported in *Nature Reviews Neuroscience*, "almost

70 percent of patients who are resistant to treatment with all other forms of antidepressants were found to improve within hours after receiving ketamine. However, its clinical use has been limited because it has to be delivered intravenously under medical supervision and in some cases can cause short-term psychotic symptoms" (Welberg 2010, 666).

As in every field of study, contemporary neuroscience as practiced by most researchers is grounded in a set of basic assumptions that limit and focus its attention and thus the range of insights it can generate regarding the nature of mind or consciousness. One assumption is that the data that is derived from "random samples of subjects, control groups, and statistical modes of data analysis are the only valid means of acquiring new knowledge" (Kelly and Kelly 2007, xxviii). Another assumption is that mind or consciousness is either an illusion or an artifact of the brain, following the laws of classical physics. A third assumption is that observations that supersede or contradict either of the first two simply cannot be so, and nearly any attempt to explain them away is an indication of scientific sophistication. These assumptions are strongly challenged by psychedelic research as well as by clinical experience with expanded states of consciousness and a large body of careful research into extraordinary mental states such as mystical experiences, various paranormal phenomena, and near-death and out-of-body experiences. All of these indicate that consciousness is a reality that lies outside of the physical constraints of the body. Rather than being an artifact of the brain, it appears that the brain is functioning as an instrument that tunes into a field of awareness that transcends the limits of physical reality.

The engendering of expanded consciousness through the use of psychedelics has enormous implications for both psychotherapy and spiritual direction. When ego control is loosened and consciousness is free to engage our full human potential, healing and growth flow from within. The wisdom that guides us comes from our own depth. There is no real distinction between the spiritual and the psychological. The therapist or spiritual guide are important sources of external support, but ultimately only an adjunct to the internal, autonomous, and powerful forces that engage the client when he or she has been opened to their presence.

Psychedelics are not the only way to achieve these states of expanded consciousness. Meditation, fasting, and various other spiritual disciplines can open the same door, but, except for a very small minority, it usually takes a lengthy time of extended practice to get there, and even then it may not be effective. I have found that the technique called active imagination or internal work can open up this domain for most of my clients, but its impact, although significant, is not as powerful or deep as that experienced by those who have taken psychedelics. I am very hopeful that as the new research into the neuroscience and effects of properly monitored psychedelic therapy becomes widely known, along with the proper relationship between right and left brain, it will become the catalyst for a radical transformation of psychotherapy, spirituality, and ultimately the culture.

The ancient Greek aphorism "know thyself" is as important today as ever; however, it is not as simple as it may sound. There are at least four selves we must all know and bring into right balance. First there is the most surface self, or persona. This is the self we put on for the benefit of others in order to fit in, do our jobs, or conform to some ideal. Sometimes we spend so much time and energy in this constructed self that we think that it is who we really are and forget that it is just a role we are playing. The second level of self is what Alan Schore calls the explicit self. This is the self at the level of ego awareness. It is largely dedicated to understanding and controlling both inner and outer reality. It tends to live a step removed from direct experience.

Some of the most important questions for this surface self or ego to ask are, "What do I want and need?" and "What do I most profoundly value?" These questions, if asked earnestly and persistently, will lead to an awareness of what Schore identifies as the third level or implicit self. This is the feeling-centered self that was formed in the first years of life by the relationship with the mother. It is the unconscious driver of the most profound beliefs and emotional/relational patterns of the surface or explicit self. It resides in the right brain and can be known through artistic expression, dreams, spontaneous writing, active imagination, or psychedelics. Using these methods to enter right-brain consciousness as a way of experiencing the implicit self also opens the possibility of engaging the deepest Self of all. The intentional release of control by the explicit self that these methods entail enables the possibility of encountering a self that is far wiser, more authentic, and more grounded than any other part of the psyche. Anyone who wishes to claim all that life can offer must come to know this deepest Self of all.

In their extraordinary book *Irreducible Mind: Toward a Psychology for the 21st Century*, Kelly and Kelly draw a compelling, research-based picture of this deep Self. According to them, and in my own experience with hundreds of clients, this Self is far more knowledgeable, gifted, aware, and capable of controlling the body in extraordinary ways than the ego. It is also the source of psychic competencies. This Self can function independent of the body, as in near-death and other out-of-body experiences, and is capable of maintaining awareness even when neurological systems necessary for brain function are shut down.

As fantastic as these claims may sound, they are strongly validated by the research compiled in *Irreducible Mind*. The self we know ourselves to be at ego level is a highly reduced, filtered expression of the full depth and breadth of consciousness that exists at our core. There is probably an evolutionary advantage for the ego's limited participation in consciousness, likely having to do with the need for maintaining an external focus in order to defend against predators and other threats, or to control resources necessary for survival. This, combined with the left brain's predisposition to cling to models rather than directly experience reality, has probably been a major contributor to the ego's loss of connection to its own deepest internal reality.

My own experience over many decades as a psychotherapist has validated over and over again the reality of this deep Self and its invaluable contributions to the healing process of literally hundreds of clients. One of the first things I do for any client I work with is to help that person connect with the Deep Self through the utilization of active imagination, in which imagination becomes a powerful faculty of perception. Between 80 and 90 percent of clients are able to connect with this deepest aspect of their consciousness, which usually presents as a wisdom or Great Mother figure. The teaching and experiential metaphors these figures generate have a powerful, transformational impact that turns peoples' lives around and can heal even the most horrendous damage inflicted upon their psyches.

I have also observed this deep Self bring about physical healing, accurately share information that could only be known through clairvoyant means, and introduce clients to profound mystical experiences. The point I need to make here is that the Self is real and by far the most important connection anyone who wishes to embrace his or her true potential can make. Contemporary neuroscience, because of its bias toward scientific materialism, has no way of appreciating or utilizing this gift that is by far the most powerful, healing experience anyone can have.

CHAPTER TWENTY THREE

Jung, Regaining the Soul

Anyone who has been paying attention, is aware that mankind is at a critical juncture. Climate change and the growing efforts of the developing world to emulate the consumer practices of Western cultures are rapidly degrading the planet's capacity to support its human population and already provoking significant ecological, climatic, and social instability that is almost certain to increase in the next decades.

In the short term, unless cultures and governments make deep changes away from an acquisitive, greed-oriented approach to life, the world will be wracked with disease, famine, and mounting social unrest. World consciousness must undergo a radical shift, or mankind is doomed to a long period of misery and conflict. If this shift happens within the next decade or two, much of the misery will be avoided, and we will be able to adapt effectively to the changes already underway. If this shift doesn't happen soon, it will probably happen after the worst predictions have come true, and people will see with clarity the horror unleashed by modern and postmodern values and philosophies.

As recorded in *The Red Book (Liber Novus)*, Carl Jung said that he was told that he was called to be the prophet of a new age for mankind. He also wrote in his original notes from which he developed *The Red Book* that this new age would come into its fullness in eight hundred years. "How can I fathom what will happen during the next eight hundred years, up to the time when the One begins his rule? I am speaking only of what is to come." (LN 306 n236)

"The spirit of this time" was how he described the contemporary, unbalanced perspective of our current age, which is leading us toward disaster. Jung was called to be a catalyst for the emergence of the spirit of the depths—the counterpart to the spirit of this time and a necessary balance to its out-of-control, destructive impulses. The ascendancy of this spirit would be the hallmark of the new age. The focus of this chapter is reviewing the psychological and spiritual significance of the spirit of the depths as explored throughout this book.

Describing the spirit of this time, he says, "The spirit of this time would like to hear of use and value." It made him want to think about "reasons and explanations." It is an extroverted, materialistic, rationalistic, and controlling energy. The spirit of the depths showed him a very different way:

> [It] forces me to speak beyond justification, use and meaning…He took away my belief in science, he robbed me of the joy of explaining and ordering things, and he let devotion to the ideals of this time die out in me. He forced me down to the last and simplest things. The spirit of the depths took my understanding and all my knowledge and placed them at the service of the inexplicable and the paradoxical. He robbed me of speech and writing for everything that was not in his service, namely the melting together of sense and nonsense which produces the supreme meaning (Jung 2009, 229).

The dichotomy between the two spirits had long been a driving force within Jung's psyche. From childhood on, Jung had experienced two personalities within himself, which he called Number 1 and Number 2. Number 1 embodied the spirit of this time, and Number 2 the spirit of the depths. Number 1 was drawn to the sciences and Number 2 to the humanities. Number 2 was felt to be most real and considered, Number 1 as someone to be tolerated (Jung 2009, 195).

351

The spirit of this time uses control, acquisition, and disconnected analysis as its principal instruments for responding to experience. It seeks to dominate whatever it encounters and is especially invested in defending against attack. It believes that truth and thus reality are known through the mental models that language constructs. It has a static, mechanistic approach to life that focuses on boundaries and distinctions. The spirit of this time is the domain of the egocentric ego.

The spirit of the depths knows reality through embodied direct experience as mediated by the senses and emotions. It knows that words and mental models are only crude approximations of reality, which is fundamentally a continually evolving, interconnected mystery. The spirit of the depths prefers to express itself through imagery and metaphor, as these afford a more immediate, accurate reflection of what is and engage the recipient experientially rather than merely cognitively. It embraces flow, merging, and empathy instead of control as its fundamental value. Because it does not make a firm distinction between self and other, it is spontaneously inclined to be altruistic, generous, and inclusive in its thinking and behaving. The spirit of the depths is the domain of the Self. It is the image of God within the psyche. It is that profound aspect of ourselves that "knows" beyond the limits of language, contains our true potential, celebrates mystery, expresses itself through love, and is our supreme meaning.

The tension between these two spirits is an ancient one, particularly in Western culture. Each has enjoyed its periods of ascendancy. Pre-Socratic Greek philosophy reflected essential features of the spirit of the depths, while Plato and his successors articulated the philosophical underpinnings of the spirit of the times. Christianity held both in tension. The Catholic Church's bureaucracy and theologians were heavily invested in control and verbal models as their essential preoccupations, but church practice and the mystics celebrated mystery, metaphor, ritual, and unitive consciousness. The Reformation later stripped these elements of the depths away from Christianity and attempted to ground human experience in a disembodied focus on the "Word" as part of its search for certainty. Anything that did not fit its verbal framework was considered superstitious or worse.

The Renaissance expressed the perspective of the depths. The early Renaissance, with its emphasis on seeking knowledge grounded in direct experience rather than authority, on harmony and perspective in art, and on a more balanced understanding of the relationship between the individual and society as well as between male and female, challenged the more authoritarian aspects of the medieval Church. In succeeding centuries the later Renaissance also stood in counterpoint to the rigid, authoritarian, disembodied worldview of the Reformation.

The Enlightenment in the eighteenth century then supplanted the Renaissance as the defining cultural focus. On the one hand, it emphasized reason and tolerance and offered a balanced vision in which analysis and verbal constructs were grounded in the direct experience of reality. On the other hand, its embrace of rationality devolved into the philosophical dead end of the Enlightenment's principal philosopher, Rene Descartes. By totally grounding his reality in the verbal, analytical mode, Descartes was left with a disconnected, lifeless, mechanical, unreal world. This is one of the most salient features of the spirit of the times.

In the nineteenth century, Romanticism reclaimed the depths' awareness of reality as a continually evolving, interconnected phenomenon that can never be truly known except through experience. The Romantics realized that the static, fragmented products of logical analysis only have value when undergirded by the direct apprehension of things that flows from being fully engaged in life. As Ian McGilchrist states, "That we take part in a changing world, and that the world evokes faculties, dimensions, and characteristics in us, just as we bring aspects of the world into existence, is perhaps the most profound perception of Romanticism" (360).

Romanticism in turn gave way to an extreme expression of rationality and control in the perspectives of modernism and postmodernism in the twentieth century. This spirit of the times that Jung was called to rectify now dominates our culture. It is marked by competition, aggression, disconnection, meaninglessness, and alienation. The tension between these two fundamental perspectives that has been played out throughout Western history has now come to a head. The apparent current victory of the spirit of the times is powerfully and obviously degrading the human condition and is not sustainable. In order for there to be a viable future for mankind and a meaningful life for individuals, the spirit of the depths must be given its rightful place as the foundation for how we experience culture, reality, ourselves, and spirituality.

These two approaches to experience are not simply artifacts of culture. They are fundamental to being human and are grounded in the structure of the brain itself. The spirit of this time is principally a product of the left brain, and the spirit of the depths is a product of the right brain. The difference between these two spirits and their significance was clearly described by Jung one hundred years ago. Contemporary neuroscience has validated his insights and offers us an even deeper appreciation of their functions and relationship.

Allan Schore, PhD, one of the preeminent theorists exploring the interrelationship between neurobiology and psychotherapy, has explored in great depth the fundamental significance of right-brain function in psychotherapy. Grounded in neuroscience, his insights are having a transformative impact on how therapy is understood and practiced. Anyone who wishes to understand the latest, best thinking in this area should read his most recent book, *The Science and Art of Psychotherapy.*

In his book *The Master and His Emissary: The Divided Brain and the Making of the Western World*, Ian McGilchrist presents a comprehensive summary of the best contemporary neuroscience research regarding right- and

354

left-brain function and its significance culturally and individually. This is the most important book I have read in the last two decades. He makes clear, in great depth, that the ramifications of our divided consciousness cannot be overstated. It permeates everything human. Our mental and spiritual health, the viability of our culture, and the protection of our environment all depend on an appreciation of the difference between these two "spirits" or elements of the psyche and how to maintain the right balance between them. McGilchrist describes the neuroscience and its cultural implications. In *The Red Book,* Jung describes the process and personal significance of working out that balance within his own psyche. In doing so, he serves as an exemplar for the rest of us.

McGilchrist's analysis of research into right- and left-brain function, summarized in the chapter, "Cognitive Neuroscience and Counseling," clarifies and deepens our understanding of what underlies and drives the spirit of this time and the spirit of the depths. The spirit of this time arises from a culture that has given precedence to left-brain function. The spirit of the depths recognizes that the right brain is our connection to reality and each other.

Keeping the proper balance between right- and left-hemisphere proclivities, between the spirit of the depths and the spirit of this time, is the great challenge of this age. The first step is to identify the distinction and tension between these two fundamental perspectives, which Jung and neuroscience have each done with great clarity. Slowly, this framing of the central problem of our age is coming into focus and being more and more broadly accepted. I look forward to a time in the near future when the cutting-edge work of McGilchrist, Schore, and allied researchers becomes the common wisdom of psychology and psychotherapy. I also believe that Jung's transformative inner journey, outlined in *The Red Book*, will come to be appreciated as a path-breaking venture into reality as mediated by the right hemisphere, and serve as a model for us all.

Not much can be done for those who do not see that there is a problem. Most, however, do, but are confused as to its nature and have little or no idea about its resolution. Many who do see the problem, as it is reflected in environmental destruction and cultural disruption, try to rectify it through external measures with only limited success.

The problem is fundamentally one of internal balance within each of our psyches. Outward reality will inevitably reflect internal reality. Achieving proper internal balance will require that the more direct apprehension of reality given to us by the right hemisphere be given precedence, and that the gifts of the left hemisphere that enable us to analyze, manipulate, and control be used to enhance and serve the right hemisphere's predilection for empathy and connection. When this shift happens, its ramifications will penetrate every facet of human experience.

Jung's discussion of the relationship between Eros and Logos in Appendix B of *The Red Book* (365) offers a clear insight into what constitutes a balanced relationship between right- and left-brain function. The right brain is the domain of Eros, which gives us connection and relationship through emotion, sensing and intuition. It is immersive, vital, chaotic, and ever changing. As Jung put it, "It is not form-giving, but form fulfilling; it is the wine that will be poured into the vessel; it is not the bed and direction of the stream, but the impetuous water flowing in it. Eros is desire, longing, force, exuberance, pleasure, suffering" (365). Logos meanwhile describes the left brain when it is functioning at its best. In Jung's words, "It is an independent principle of form that means understanding, insight, foresight, legislation and wisdom" (365).

Jung makes a distinction between Logos and Nous, or intellect. The purpose of intellect is abstract reasoning and analysis. Logos has a broader perspective and remains connected to the "feeling, presentiment, and sensation" of Eros. When intellect forgets that it is the servant of Logos, it inevitably becomes a destructive force. It must serve Logos just as Logos must fully embrace reality as given to it by Eros: "They are two fundamental psychic powers that form a pair of opposites, each one requiring the other" (365).

The balanced embrace of Logos and Eros, left brain and right brain, must begin with a reevaluation of who or what we think we are. Most people's ego or sense of self is a self-created construct made of a complex, interwoven set of external identifications, fervently believed stories about "who I am," scripts embedded in childhood that are being lived out automatically, and networks of defense mechanisms that protect the ego from emotions and awarenesses that might threaten its stability. Control is the principal focus of this constricted ego. The perspective and strengths of the left hemisphere are its natural home.

A much more life-giving alternative to this constricted ego is an ego that reveres the sense of an internally grounded authentic Self. For those who experience this Deep Self, it is felt to be more real and important than all the ways the external world invites and often demands us to become. An ego committed to this perspective actively seeks internal and external truth knowing that this search, although difficult, will lead to fullness of life. Surrender to reality is the focus of this ego. Its hallmarks are openness, freedom, spontaneity, transparency, and lighthearted good humor. The authentic Self that this ego reaches for is recognized to be an unfolding mystery beyond any comprehensive description or control. It is known through the direct experience that flows from embracing life. Although the Self is the all-inclusive ground of the psyche, the right brain is the path through which it can be directly encountered.

The constricted ego, bound by its own self-definitions, defenses, fears, and conditioning, is a natural outcome of basic Western assumptions about the nature of the psyche, which themselves reflect a left-hemisphere-dominant perception of reality. The constriction of the ego is exacerbated by less than adequate nurturance in childhood and often compounded by abuse. The surrendered ego, on the other hand, reflects a transpersonal vision of personal reality that sees individual consciousness as merely a facet of a unitary, universal consciousness. In Western culture this vision is usually attained only after much hard work and healing.

Although Western psychology offers many varied theories about the nature of ego, Self, and psyche, there are several basic assumptions about ego and its relationship to the psyche that seem to be accepted by most of these theoretical systems. The most fundamental of these assumptions is that a process of identification with the external world, especially with early caregivers, forms the ego. This gives the ego structure and a bond with family and culture that is critical for survival. A second common assumption is that the ego sits atop an inner world of unruly instincts and irrational energies that the ego must contain and organize.

In the Western perspective a healthy ego is one that has achieved clear self-definition (hopefully based on the good use of analytical intelligence) and has learned to exercise sufficient self-control to properly contain the irrational urgings of the unconscious. In the West personal growth and healing is all about the centrality of the ego, the importance of control, and the use of analytical competencies as the principal tool for dealing with oneself as well as the world. In this frame of reference, the ego is regarded as real and as the central organizing force within the psyche.

In my experience and in the understanding of the psyche given to us by Jung and contemporary neuroscience, however, the ego's nature and role is quite different from the standard Western model. Although the development of an ego is a natural, universal process, the form the ego takes is an imaginary fabrication of the psyche. The psyche, in my experience, is a multidimensional field with no ultimate boundaries. The rigid, egocentric ego creates boundaries as a defensive response to what are perceived to be significant internal and external threats.

Within this field of the psyche, consciousness can become intensely focused into a single ego state, or it may be divided into discrete ego states with self-awareness, a sense of personal history, a capacity for choice, and a proclivity for self-identification. The rigidity and tenacity of an individual ego or ego states tends to be proportionate to the degree of unresolved suffering an individual has had to tolerate. Within the psyche there can also be other less well-defined concentrations of mental energy formed from various combinations of elements of unintegrated personal history, strong dysphoric emotions, and unrecognized or disowned instinctual drives or needs. Most therapists experienced in the treatment of DID clients agree that all the ego states, as well all the other less well-defined elements of the psyche, must be integrated into a single, flexible sense of self. This healthy ego no longer feels driven to gird itself with defensive boundaries and no longer needs to continue trying to hold at bay inner or outer realities that would challenge rigid self-definitions.

Ideally, a well-integrated, healthy, strong ego is on the one hand flexible, open, and disinclined to constrain itself by limiting self-definitions or personal myths. On the other hand, it has a highly developed capacity to deflect any attempts to box it in with externally imposed agendas or culturally driven assumptions about who or what it should or must be. This healthy ego knows that it is merely the outer face of an inner depth that goes far beyond anything that words can possibly describe. An ego at its best joyfully admits that ultimately it is impossible to know who or what it is.

The inner space of psyche has unlimited potential for expansion in much the same way as does the outer space of the cosmos. This inner space is constituted of what has been variously called spirit, light, or being, whose essence is oneness, beauty, truth, joy, and compassion. This is the common experience of many I know personally who have probed their inner lives in depth, and it is the universal experience of mystics in every spiritual tradition.

An individual psyche may constellate this space in a variety of ways. It can be transparent to this inner vastness and let light or spirit shine through in a way that enhances and expresses the unique beauty of the person's own inborn potential; or a person may create hidden and/or closed-off places within the inner world that impede the light and spur the ego into a reactive, defensive shell, greatly limiting how much light can flow through and into the world. As the light is diminished, so is joy, meaning, and vitality.

Arthur Deikman, MD, a transpersonal psychiatrist, has developed an extended model of these two basic ways of knowing and being in the world. The first way, centered in the belief that ego is the most important factor in the psyche, is invested in what Deikman calls instrumental consciousness, which, as McGilchrist points out, is the approach to experience taken by the left hemisphere. As Deikman describes it, instrumental consciousness is dedicated to individual survival through the manipulation of experience and reality. It evolved to gain resources needed for survival and to defend against attack. It focuses on boundaries, difference, form, and distinction. Meanwhile the second vision of ego, with its emphasis on transparency to spirit, flexibility, and openness to connection internally and externally, is inclined toward what Deikman calls receptive consciousness. Receptive consciousness (the way of the right brain) is a way of being and knowing that gives priority to empathy, flow, and merging. It allows connection to be experienced and creates altruistic bonds. It is the source of felt meaning and offers the possibility of the direct experience of reality.

The ego-centered or egocentric view of the psyche, with its inevitable identification with instrumental consciousness, can ask the big questions but cannot hear the answers. It leads to meaninglessness, alienation, and fear of dying. In the instrumental context the self is a separate, discrete, isolated object, inclined to act upon or against whatever is perceived as "not me," rather than to acknowledge itself as an integral part of the rest of reality.

From the egocentric, instrumental perspective, the environment is seen simply as something to be possessed and used or fashioned according to one's intentions. Since one sees oneself as an object distinct from the environment, he will be strongly inclined to choose whatever is in his individual best interest without much regard for the impact his choice might have on the rest of reality. Choices are made on the basis of, "What is in it for me?" Service and apparent altruistic behaviors are motivated by the desire for future reward, or for many the fear of punishment delivered by an all-knowing God that is itself a separate, distinct entity like the egocentric ego perceives itself to be—just bigger and more powerful.

A transpersonally oriented ego, with its proclivity toward receptive consciousness, is grounded in the right hemisphere. It knows itself experientially in the present moment in a sensual, nonconceptual fashion. Its intuition of self is diffuse and flowing. Self is felt to be the expression of larger life processes. This expansive sense motivates choices grounded in empathy. Service is generous and beneficent in intent, and no reward beyond the joy of giving is sought, as the self is freed from object goals and enlarged by connection. The principal intention of an ego grounded in receptive consciousness is to take and grow in an expansive fashion. It facilitates allowing and merging.

In receptive consciousness one knows the other by doing his best to "be" that other through nurturing the capacity for empathy as much as possible. This naturally leads to an effort to engage the other through service and love, which opens an intimate connection to the larger context and in varying degrees allows the knower to become the known.

In my perspective, all of the most important things I know come to me out of the space that is beyond control and logic. Even though this knowledge or insight might be expressed in language, it was not arrived at through logical analysis. Over and over again it proves to be true and has led clients, my students, and myself to significant growth and change. This is what some people would call "intuition," but "intuition" is not strong enough a term. The knowing I'm speaking of is bigger, deeper, and more comprehensive than anything logic or analysis can possibly generate. The insights it offers are based on a breadth of experience that my tiny frame of logic couldn't possibly emulate. As I evolve spiritually, this deeper knowing and global consciousness are my primary way of being in and knowing the world. Analysis and logic are simply used to facilitate the ways in which I might choose to live out or utilize the gifts of this deep awareness. As Jung said, "There is a knowledge of the heart that gives deeper insight. The knowledge of the heart is in no book and is not to be found in the mouth of any teacher, but grows out of you like the green seed from the dark earth" (Jung 2009, 233).

This connected, immersive way of being in the world has two immediate consequences. First, it sparks a strong creative urge that drives the knower to seek to be a part of the unfolding of evolution. When reality is directly experienced, it is experienced as energy and flow; it is an evolving process that is going somewhere. From the Big Bang on, it has been generating ever increasing levels of complexity and consciousness. The creative urge that is felt by those who connect deeply with reality allows them to be a part of the emergence of the next step in this ongoing process of creation. The pull of this creative energy, which is simply an expression of the creative energy at large, underlies everything, and its impact on the individual can sometimes be profound.

The creative energy can even feel irresistible. Broken or wounded people whose egos lack coherence or stability are sometimes driven by this creative energy and produce significant works. Certain kinds of mental illness, such as bipolar disorder, seem to loosen up and energize people and put them in touch with this drive, at times resulting in extraordinary fruits. Most who experience this creative flow, however, do so not because their egos are broken, shattered, or dysfunctional, but because they have released the rigidity of their self-story and now appreciate that logic and language and the need to control must be set aside in favor of a much more connected way of knowing and being. When they succeed in doing this, creativity bubbles to the surface powerfully as they intentionally dance in balance with the creative flow of the universe.

As stated above, the first consequence of a connected, immersive life is to be driven by the creative energy of the universe to participate in evolution. The second consequence is expressed at the interpersonal level. A connected life creates a powerful, felt need to embrace and share joy and wonder. The same creative energy that pushes creativity also pushes loving connection. When a person is immersed in unitive knowing, all she really wants is to help make life wonderful for everyone she encounters. She is selfless. Her joy comes from the flow of caring, loving energy to the other. She doesn't do it for herself, but in giving of herself for the other, she participates in the love that is of the essence of being itself.

Being able to live in this space requires that first the person recognizes that it is valuable and that achieving it is worth whatever the cost may be. Second, there must be an unconditional commitment to the truth, however painful or disruptive that truth might be. The truth that is embraced must first be the truth that is known at the level of ordinary logic, language, and awareness. More importantly, however, the primary truth of experience, both internal and external, must be given precedence. It is not enough for a person to recognize that the receptive consciousness of the right hemisphere should be his foundation and to try to live accordingly. Although this is far better than the alternative, it is still likely to be merely another model of reality and "right living" deployed by the instrumental consciousness of the left brain.

What is required is that this way of being possess the individual. The person must allow himself to be transformed by those immediate experiences that have the power to give him a new vision and perspective. These experiences convey far more than words could ever hope to contain. They can be either internal or external. External experiences of communion, love, passion, and connection all support and enhance the person's potential for receptive consciousness. They can be transformative and leave the person grounded in receptive consciousness as his or her fundamental resource. Usually, however, they are not powerful enough to undo the impact of the cultural assumptions of modernism's grasping, greed-driven, controlling ethos. Nor are they usually enough to undo the psychological wounds that drive a person into a fearful, angry, controlling stance toward life. Internal experience is the most powerful resource that can overcome both culture and wounding for those who genuinely want to embrace a life of connection and compassion. In this Jung showed the way.

Jung gave us three major gifts: 1) he identified the problem with unique clarity, which was the tension between the spirit of this time and the spirit of the depths, 2) he also showed us by his experience how to directly engage the spirit of the depths and how powerful it can be, and 3) finally, he showed us what is required to achieve the degree of wholeness necessary to naturally and spontaneously live from the core of oneself. *The Red Book*, which chronicles his internal experiences, has much to teach us. Partly this is because what he experienced has a universal resonance. From it we can learn a great deal about the internal structure and function of the psyche. The essential outlines of everything he taught and wrote from that time on were grounded in these experiences. Of equal importance, he gave us a model of how to initiate the direct experience of the internal world through becoming immersed in the wisdom and ways of the right hemisphere. To me this is a major gift of *The Red Book*. When we decide to take a similar journey inward to this unfamiliar but very powerful realm, his example can guide and support us like no other.

Jung's journey into his depths primarily used active imagination. This and attending to dreams are the natural vehicles for encountering the realities and wisdom of the unconscious. Neither should be thought of as a psychotherapeutic "technique." They are simply our natural means of experiencing internal realities, just as our senses are our natural means of experiencing external reality. The internal world of our unconscious (i.e., all of psychic reality that is not in conscious awareness) can only be truly known through direct experience, which is mediated by the right hemisphere and enabled by active imagination. Words and analytical thinking cannot even begin to uncover it. The kinds of visions, dialogues, and metaphoric experiences Jung recounts in *The Red Book* are not unique to him. Almost anyone who would wish to reclaim his or her soul can use active imagination just as Jung did and encounter the same right-hemisphere-driven quality of experience.

Those who choose to follow Jung's lead will face experiences and demands quite similar to his. In one way or another the egocentric ego will have to release its control and eventually die, just as Jung had to shoot Seigfried, the mythic German/Norse conquering hero encountered in a dream-vision at the beginning of his inner work (241). Disowned parts of the psyche must be engaged and owned. The inner teacher (in Jung's case Elijah and later Philemon) must be met and honored. The ego must recognize that it is not its place to direct or control the process, but to accept that a greater intelligence and deeper wisdom is creating the experiences and controls the flow of the process. The ego must also learn to accept that its gifts of language and analysis are of secondary value when it comes to the deepest issues of life. Metaphor, internal dialogues, encounters with others within, and transformative experiences of all kinds are the means by which the deep makes itself known. Eventually, the ego will be led to a point where it will have to come to accept and surrender to what Jung calls supreme meaning or the God image. The journey's ultimate purpose is to achieve the wholeness necessary to fully accept the embrace of the divine, which arises from within.

Throughout all of this the ego does have an important role to play. It is up to the ego to decide whether to even begin to take this perilous and tumultuous journey. Once the journey starts, the ego must be able and willing to tolerate and trust the powerful, challenging experiences and painful emotions the journey engenders. Even as it relinquishes its fantasy of being the most important or central part of the psyche, the ego must be willing to use its analytical gifts to the fullest extent possible. It must question, think about, and be prepared to deal with the consequences of engaging the deep.

Jung had many charged debates with the figures in his visions. As in Jung's case, the deep encourages the self-protective and analytical inclinations of the ego. As also as with Jung, the deep expects the ego to take what it has been taught back into the world and become an agent of change, which demands a strong but not egocentric ego. One thing the ego must not do is attempt to determine the course of the journey. Only the soul (or Self) has the perspective and wisdom to know what needs to be experienced, how to do so, and when. At the beginning of his inner work Jung became aware that he had lost his soul and cried out for it. The soul responded, and one of its messages was, "Do you still not know that the way to truth stands open only to those without intentions?" (Jung 2009, 236).

As Jung came to realize, the ultimate purpose of the journey is to find God. Jung's title for *The Red Book* is *Liber Novus*, the "New Book." He sees this as the new Scripture, in counterdistinction to the old Scriptures. He begins with four different quotes from Scripture. Three are from Isaiah and one is from John. All of them point to the coming of a savior figure and a new dispensation of salvation.

One of the most important conclusions Jung draws is that the great flaw of Christianity is that it sought only goodness, but not wholeness. By dividing reality into good and bad, we are off balance and paradoxically driven by what we will not own. Salvation flows from the reconciliation of opposites. This is the way of wholeness. God or supreme meaning includes everything, and so must we. In the final vision Philemon and Jung are reverential toward Jesus, but it is clear that some things have to be corrected.

Addressing his soul, Jung wrote, "… your meaning is supreme meaning, and your steps are the steps of a God." (235) Through encountering the soul we come to know the supreme meaning/God as much as it can be known, but ultimately what we know is only an internal reflection that points toward an incomprehensible mystery. Yet this mystery beckons to us and invites our embrace.

Once again neuroscience offers some insight into pathways for responding to this most fundamental invitation. As McGilchrist pointed out, the psyche is designed to function in either a vertical or horizontal mode. Each of these has its own way of finding God. Jung made clear that the attempt to find God through the verbal, analytical mind (a principal tool of the vertical path) obscured supreme meaning through the development of rigid verbal systems and organizations, i.e., theologies and churches. This turned the source of life into a dead, human artifact. Interestingly, the traditional view of God is of one who sits above, omni-everything, the ultimate disconnected observer—an extreme expression of the vertical.

There is, however, a way in which the vertical can be an effective vehicle for encountering the divine. Mindfulness meditation, in which the ego trains itself to be a nonjudgmental observer of the passing of internal and external phenomena, is primarily the activity of the left frontal lobe. Neuroscientific research has demonstrated that this purposeful activation of the left frontal lobe has a quieting effect on the limbic system (the realm of emotions) as well as on the language-producing aspects of the left hemisphere. It offers a way to stand apart from emotional processes, verbal chatter, and internal storytelling. By doing so, a clearer and calmer perception of reality can emerge, albeit from a disengaged observer stance.

With practice, this mindful orientation can lead to two major avenues for awakening. The first is the "releasing" form of mindfulness. By merely noticing without judgment the contents of internal and external experience and letting them pass, a person can achieve a sense of disidentification with any discrete realities, including one's own body, feelings, and thoughts. This can lead to the powerful awareness that at my core I am not anything that can be named or described, but a part of pure consciousness, which has no limits. If God and consciousness are understood to be intertwined or even the same thing, as some mystics teach, then this is clearly a path to encountering God. This experience can be an effective tool for awakening practitioners to the realization that fundamentally they are the expression of a oneness that transcends all divisions. The corollaries to this are significant. By truly knowing through experience that you are not separate from the source and are, in fact, a part of it, you are freed from the search for meaning, fear of death, and the sense of emptiness and alienation that is the hallmark of our times.

Nevertheless, this path to God through pure consciousness, while very meaningful, can still leave practitioners disconnected from their own internal processes and shadow aspects, as well as from the divine that is embodied within physical reality. The passionless, disembodied spirituality that it fosters is the best the left hemisphere has to offer, but it falls far short of being fully alive and truly awakened. A vital, deeply authentic life, in which the divine within has the opportunity to express itself powerfully in the world, can only happen through embracing the path of the right hemisphere.

The second option for awakening is embodied in the "embracing" form of mindfulness meditation. By learning to live in an open, receptive state in which I embrace the contents of experience without grasping or pushing away, I lay the foundation for being intimately connected with my life experiences. This will lead me back into connection with a profound realm of the psyche that can open the way to significant inner awareness, healing, and a vibrant connection with creation.

Many benefit greatly from this ability to face their inner conflicts through the utilization of the receptive, open, observing mind as practiced in this embracing form of mindfulness meditation. This type of mindfulness has given people a way to be with their pain and maintain balance and perspective at the same time. Although this may feel like a brand-new insight to those who are new to this potential, the fact is that it is a pathway to the Self, a profound and universal aspect of the psyche that has been a part of everyone from the earliest dawning of his or her own awareness. Developing this skill of mindfulness is actually a way of aligning with the welcoming, loving stance of the Self.

The Self sees with clarity exactly what is happening to the individual externally and internally. It does not judge, and it is deeply compassionate toward all parties involved in every experience. It knows the psyche of the individual within whom it resides from the inside out. It knows the person's needs, motives, emotional structure, and defenses. Although the ego or egos may be ravaged by horrendous experiences and emotional storms, the Self is not affected but nevertheless, lovingly present. It simply sees clearly what is happening. It understands deeply the impact of the trauma and knows how to undo its damage to the extent that such a thing is possible. This entity is not an ego state in the normal sense of the term. It doesn't define itself. It never seeks to control. It exists to serve. It does not perceive itself as having been created, but simply as always having been present. Seeking to learn the skill of open, receptive, embracing mindfulness is like being in an apprenticeship to the Self—which could eventually lead to a union between ego and Self.

When I teach clients about the value of stepping into this type of mindful awareness and show them how to do it, I am not teaching them a skill that heretofore had been missing within their psyche. In reality, I am simply awakening within the ego the awareness of a competency that has existed within that person all along and is readily accessible. Being in the stance of a nonjudgmental, compassionate, and engaged observer is like tuning a radio to a very important station or signal; the better the client becomes at clearly observing internal and external reality, without judgment and with compassion, the more that ego will resonate with the Self. As the resonance improves, the flow of awareness between ego and Self increases, so that in time the ego simply becomes the recipient or vessel of the Self's presence and energy.

The skill of being able to put oneself in this frame of mind is not something that the ego does. It is rather something the ego allows, by stopping itself from engaging in self-defeating distortions of truth or attempts at control through merging with or fighting against threatening internal energies. The essence of being an effective, mindful observer is making a decision to accept and seek the truth no matter the cost, as well as giving up the drive to control in favor of trusting that there is a reliable, deeper guidance that can and will help the ego make the best of every situation. This giving up of control and letting go into whatever is real or true is a kind of nondoing. Some clients understand this immediately. Others who have invested significant time and energy in their egos' stories and their various defenses may struggle with this invitation to embrace a nondoing or receptive mode of consciousness.

The more a person practices being mindful, the better. This is why regular meditation is so frequently recommended for those who wish to advance along this path. And though it is certainly beneficial, it is not a prerequisite. Most clients understand the concept after one or two sessions and find it very helpful immediately. As soon as they see how helpful taking an open, receptive stance can be, they may only need a little encouragement to make this practice more and more a part of their daily lives. The skill will grow not only through formal meditation, but simply as the natural consequence of taking the stance of a nonjudgmental observer over and over again as they seek to find emotional stability on a day-to-day basis.

The most effective path for developing this observer stance is to give the clients an opportunity to encounter an image that reflects the Self, such as Inner Wisdom, through an internal journey as described earlier in this book. As they experience the nonjudgmental, compassionate, loving embrace that the Self offers, they will know experientially at every level what being in an open, receptive, mindful state is truly like. Having known this pure form of presence from their experience of the Self, their ability to practice it as they engage their own inner life and outer struggles is enhanced significantly. And having made a significant personal connection to the Self, they will more readily feel it move through them and will be more ready to align with it when they seek to move into the receptive openness of fully embracing their own lives.

Shedding control and investment in one's personal story in favor of connecting with the Self results in clarity of perception, inner quiet, some extraordinary internal powers, and a strong capacity for compassion. The extraordinary internal powers that the Self (ISH or Inner Wisdom) possesses first came to my attention through working with DID clients. When the psyche is stretched to the farthest limits of its tolerance by abuse or tragedy, bizarre and dysfunctional patterns will inevitably emerge. Alongside these, however, extraordinary innate potentials that might otherwise be overlooked are brought into bold relief. Of note are the abilities to modulate the flow of emotions, to insert and remove thoughts in the consciousness of the ego, to create dreams designed to trigger important awareness, to interpret accurately the significance of somatoform disorders, and occasionally to discern physical illnesses of which the person may be consciously unaware and even facilitate or enhance healing. As is obvious, these gifts are quite amazing. Even more amazing is the fact that they are universally available and not restricted only to those suffering from DID or allied disorders.

If the ego were aware of these possibilities and also sufficiently committed to truth and the release of control, the Self would give these gifts freely. As powerful as they are, these deep energies will never force themselves upon an ego. They must be invited and welcomed. If they are, not only can they give the above-mentioned gifts, but they can also know the path for healing the psyche. As observers from the beginning, they know the true history of each person. They know what wounds need healing and the right order for that healing to be achieved. They know the ego's defenses and fears and how to work with and through them. If the ego is willing to trust and has adequate external support, if needed, profound transformation will unfold.

The embracing form of mindfulness will lead through the Self to a profound, healing encounter with one's own internal world and the horizontal, engaged domain of the right hemisphere. Those who are awakened to their own true natures, through meditation or other avenues, and thus enlightened have found a great gift, but that is only part of the great human task.

Enlightenment or awakening is simply the clear apprehension of reality, and in this it is also the realization that the Self and not the ego is the real foundation of the psyche. This realization gives the person the ability to be with what is in an open, receptive state of mind. Fully appreciating that the Self is the foundation of the psyche is not something we accomplish. It is simply what is left when we put aside our blinders and just be with what is. Awakening is not a process of learning, but of unlearning. Anyone who genuinely wants to know who he or she truly is and how things really are on an experiential level is a seeker of enlightenment.

The core truth that emerges when reality is directly apprehended is that everything is profoundly interconnected and that separation or "otherness" is merely a useful fiction. Language, science, technology, and the need for self -protection cause us to make mental distinctions or boundaries. These are useful in the same way that a map is a useful guide for negotiating the earth. Just like a map is an artificial overlay that helps us control our geographical progress, our mind's ability to make distinctions and create stories or hypotheses is a useful vehicle for asserting control. An enlightened or awakened person appreciates this mental capacity but understands its artificial nature and is firmly rooted in the fundamental, interrelated unity of all reality.

Unenlightened individuals become so accustomed to viewing reality through the lens of their maps, models, and stories that they mistake them for reality itself. The consequences of this common mistake are quite significant and touch on every aspect of human existence. They include alienation, environmental destruction, a sense of meaninglessness, and almost all psychological dysfunctions that are not primarily the results of neuropsychological deficits.

Enlightened individuals have an entirely different experience of life. For them, the map is clearly recognized to be an artifact. Their attention and connection is focused on the undivided reality that lies underneath. They are much more open to their senses and emotions than most people. They are very aware of the difference between self-awareness and self-identity. Usually, they strive to be fully aware of all of the unfolding complexities and potentials within themselves, but refuse to become trapped by any mental structures or stories that would define or identify themselves. The consequences of this position are extraordinary. If they are committed to continue to engage in the lifelong task of individuation (i.e., becoming their fullest, authentic self) the inevitable conflicts and changes that ensue will be handled with a loving wisdom that constantly frees new potentials.

The consensus of awakened individuals is that life is filled with wonder—never boring, highly meaningful, often touched with bliss—and that their strongest interpersonal energy is love. Having set aside the need to defend their story of "I," which they realize is just a mental construct, their awareness of their full potential is no longer artificially limited. This unleashes significant creativity and opens access to profound internal wisdom. They have enormous faith in reality, which they see as an expression of God, but do not "believe in" doctrines or sacred texts. They always give experience precedence over theories. They never live for an anticipated future reward or outcome, but find meaning and purpose in the immediate experience of life. They no longer argue with reality, but dance with it in an intimate embrace.

This deep awareness of reality that is the epitome of awakening or enlightenment cannot be forced any more than you can make your eyes see or ears hear. If you are wearing blinders or earplugs, you can remove them if you wish, and then the seeing and hearing will happen spontaneously. You allow yourself to see and hear, but you do not make it happen.

Fundamental reality is like the air we breathe. It is all around us and within us. Yet the human condition provides that we cannot freely breathe it in, because the flow is constricted by our egoist illusions, the constructs of our disconnected left hemisphere. Many have had periods of time when they could breathe freely for a while, what Adyashanti calls nonabiding awakening (Adyshanti 2008, 29), but like someone with asthma, the breathing became constricted again and the free connection with reality remained only as a memory. Most people have never breathed freely at all, although some intuit that such a thing might be possible.

The vast majority of people who have had the experience of awakening lose it after a period of time, whether it be hours, days, weeks, or months. The blinders come back on automatically, driven by the ego's need to control. This reversal is triggered by the denial or dissociation of those things that the ego does not want to admit or face. The issue is the same for those who have never awakened but want to. The whole truth of one's own life must be known, felt, and expressed. Moreover, with rare exceptions, truth must be spoken in every circumstance. Indulgence in dishonesty or distortion is an exercise of the ego's need to control and a way of disconnecting from the Self and fundamental reality.

Letting go of all that the ego is hiding from, as well as its proclivity to control the flow of life, is very difficult and something that few people can do by themselves. It is painful and disorienting. Most require that this process be facilitated by a relationship that is grounded in an unconditional commitment to truth, where love flows freely and what has been lost can safely be grieved and released. Whether this relationship be called friendship, psychotherapy, or spiritual direction doesn't matter. What matters is the integrity, passion, and commitment to truth shared by both parties.

Whether such a relationship is available or not, the majority of those who have tasted enlightenment must still do the hard work of dissolving the egocentric ego. Like Jung at the beginning of his process, we must kill our version of Seigfried, the conquering hero who symbolized the egocentric ego. This may happen before or after an initial awakening, but it must be done. Having had an awakening experience may help the process, but it does not excuse one from engaging it. Some who have awakened and can rightly be considered enlightened are convinced that their ego has died and are unaware that internal healing is still needed. You can be enlightened and an off balance, difficult person at the same time.

Claiming and resolving one's full internal reality, rejected aspects of oneself, unresolved history, stories of "I," and rigid belief systems, must happen before awakening can be complete and the God within can rise to a new and full life. This can only take place through allowing oneself to become immersed in the mystery, interconnection, and wisdom of the right hemisphere, in which wholeness rather than mere goodness is sought and given. Whether the seeker begins with the disengaged path of disidentification or simply descends into the depths, seeking the Self in a search for personal authenticity, this engagement must happen for fundamental reality (or "supreme meaning," in Jung's words) to be known deeply and embraced in a stable fashion.

When Jung indicated that he was bringing forth a new dispensation of salvation, he was not exaggerating. This is precisely what *The Red Book* is about. Whoever seeks an undistorted, transparent connection with reality and supreme meaning must be willing to enter unconditionally the domain of the soul and allow himself or herself to be challenged and transformed by the experiences, metaphoric encounters, alien energies, and teachers that spontaneously emerge, just as Jung did. In this new dispensation the distinction between what is spiritual and psychological falls away. Jung's insights from the experiences he described in *The Red Book*, supported by the findings of contemporary neuroscience and enriched by contemporary spiritual teachers such as Adyashanti, Frazier, Tolle and many others give us a clarity we have never had before about what is truly involved if we wish to save our souls.

CHAPTER TWENTY FOUR
Gnosticism Revisited

There are many striking parallels between the psychospiritual teachings of the ancient Gnostics and the implications for life and spirituality that flow from the perspective of this book. Like my own, the Gnostics' insights were based on experience rather than traditional teachings. Moreover, those experiences were largely the result of utilizing active imagination as a means of inner exploration. This is what I have been doing for the last several decades, and it has led to the same basic insights.

Most of the original Gnostics were an expression of early Christianity, with the exception of one group that was derived from the paganism of the time but taught fundamentally the same things. Unlike what later came to be considered Orthodox Christianity, Gnostic Christianity was grounded in internal experience rather than in externally imposed dogmas and rules. These internal experiences led to several fundamental conclusions similar to my own.

The first is that the true Godhead is the fullness out of which everything emerges, yet itself is nothing. It is beyond all definition and description. This unutterable mystery beckons us and can be known in the sense of being experienced by the sincere seeker who is committed to love and truth. Although I have not had this experience personally, I have participated in several sessions with clients who have touched that depth in an active imagination process and were deeply impacted by it. They usually speak of it as an indescribable nothingness that is full of love and feels like their true home.

The second basic conclusion of the Gnostics is that a spark of the original divine light is at the core of every individual's being and longs to return to its source. This divine essence is the authentic Self that resides at the center of every human being. It is the common experience of my clients that such a reality exists within them and that it manifests itself in various forms, drawing them toward itself with profound wisdom and unconditional love. It is basically indistinguishable from the true Godhead, except that it manifests itself through images so that the ego may more readily connect with it. This reality is consistently present whether the person "believes in God" or not.

The Gnostics also took the problem of evil quite seriously. They were very sensitive to how much suffering there was in the world, both natural and manmade, and because of this considered creation to be defective, the work of demigods who had forgotten their source in the true Godhead. The vast majority of my clients sought me out because the suffering in their lives had become unbearable. Like the Gnostics, they knew that evil was real and were desperate to make sense of it. What they learned was that love was deeper and stronger than the evil they had known and would gladly draw them to it, healing the worst of their wounds. In order to fully accept the gift, however, they had to go through a process similar to what the Gnostics described. They had to confront and transcend all of the demiurges and false gods in order to have the freedom to rest ultimately in the embrace of the true God.

The false gods that hold contemporary man in their thrall are materialism, all the various philosophies and dogmatic systems that claim to offer final explanations for reality, and moral imperatives and political movements that assume that the imposition of the right kind of external social structures will initiate a utopian future. As long as any of these external, ego-constructed frames of reference are embraced as an ultimate value (i.e., worshipped as a god), then the ego remains as the dominant force and inner healing cannot proceed, thus assuring that suffering will grow unabated. There are also a myriad of dark internal forces that feel like lesser gods or demiurges that can terrorize or control the ego, making internal work very challenging. Like the external false gods, they must not be surrendered to, but faced and transcended with the help and guidance of the wisdom and love of the Self.

The one way in which my perspective on evil differs from the Gnostics is that I do not believe that the false gods were responsible for creating a flawed world. They and the internal demiurges are rather the inevitable products of a world that simply could not exist if suffering were not an integral part of it. A universe that existed in static perfection might be beautiful in the same way that a statue can be beautiful, but it cannot be a wellspring of life and evolving consciousness. A dynamic universe evolving toward ever higher levels of consciousness will of necessity be full of conflict, pain, and volitional evil. Evolution and destruction are two sides of the same coin. Moreover, volitional evil is the price to be paid for the gift of consciousness. The divine prerogatives of awareness and choice will inevitably be misused until egocentricity itself is shed like the confining cocoon of the transforming butterfly.

The typical life experience of most of my clients has been that they sought to find salvation or healing by trying to conform themselves to what they had been taught were right beliefs and correct behaviors. Whether they were successful in this didn't seem to make much difference: the effort did not lead to healing or a more meaningful life. What they finally learned through their internal work is that these intentional endeavors, no matter how well meant, only affected the surface of the psyche. Until these clients differentiated themselves from external authority and surrendered to the direct experience of the Self, they were stymied. Without the direct experiential knowledge of their Self (gnosis), there was no salvation. With it, they have been transformed. This is precisely what the Gnostics taught. Salvation comes through gnosis, not through an effort to please a judging god with right behavior and right belief.

Because they believed that salvation could not be attained through right behavior, the Gnostics were accused by their orthodox detractors of being antinomian, or people who rejected commonly accepted morality. Although this was not true, it was true that they did not consider rules or morality to be the final determinants of their choices. They claimed a higher level of personal freedom than their contemporaries could understand or tolerate. For the Gnostic and for myself, we are either moving in the direction of fulfilling our destiny by living lives ever more in tune with our authentic Self, or we are living in the thrall of lesser gods and forces who vastly reduce our options and meaningful choices. Externally imposed rules, however well-conceived, can never equal inner guidance in providing accurate direction for anyone seeking to embrace the authentic self. If these rules are relied on in lieu of listening to one's own depths, they will become a sterile prison. There is some comfort in this imprisonment, because it gives the prisoner a false sense of assurance of living righteously and protects him from the challenges of the radical freedom that pursuing one's true destiny always entails. The Gnostic's freedom is not the same as the willful "freedom" of an ego that revels in its ability to do whatever it pleases. This willfulness is merely an expression of shallow impulses that lead nowhere, or that more likely leads to an illusion of choice that is actually driven by powers of which the ego is simply ignorant.

Each person's destiny is a given. Everyone has a fundamental, authentic nature and a deep Self. We are not free to choose who we are. Every choice people makes either aligns them more fully with what is most real within them or leads them away from that toward some form of illusion and disconnection from life and meaning. True freedom resides in learning to make the choices that increase our options for living genuinely and expand our potential for embracing a powerful, effective, and creative life.

The Gnostics also believed that a major contributing factor to achieving gnosis was the healing influence of Lady Wisdom, Sophia. I have come to a similar conclusion. Human consciousness has two principal dynamics, a receptive dimension and an instrumental dimension. The receptive dimension is associated with right-brain function and the instrumental with left-brain. The receptive aspect is universally considered feminine and the instrumental masculine. Giving this feminine aspect of the psyche (Sophia) precedence opens the door to one's depth and authentic self. On the other hand, giving precedence to the masculine, instrumental mind condemns a person to live a detached, unreal life in which models take the place of vital experience and the ego cannot even imagine that there might be a healing authentic self within that could free it from the prison of illusion.

The Gnostics also venerated Jesus, Buddha, and other enlightened teachers who showed us, by their example, what an authentic life could be and through their teachings, how to escape the grasp of the lesser gods and release our illusions. I too see Jesus as a saving figure, not because he appeased a punishing god through his death, as taught in orthodox Christianity, but as one in whom the divine light shone brightly and who made clear to us that not even death can extinguish that light.

It is unfortunate that Gnostic Christianity did not become the mainstream Christian voice. One of its great leaders, Valentinius, was almost elected pope in the second century. If that had happened, I believe that Western culture would be much more highly evolved than it is today. Nevertheless, what is true and real will ultimately gain ascendance because it is always stronger and more deeply rooted than the alternative. I have a strong hope that once again the ancient vision of the Gnostics is coming back to life. There is no questioning its power in the lives of my clients, who are unwittingly retracing this path laid out so long ago. It is also clearly evident that significant elements of the culture at large, as well as some aspects of contemporary psychology and spirituality, are embracing Gnostic sensibilities. Even as out-of-control instrumental consciousness wreaks havoc on our environment and the lives of so many, Sophia's voice is being heard by more and more. She is calling us back to our authentic self and through this to God.

CHAPTER TWENTY FIVE

Returning to the Feminine Ground

A version of this chapter first appeared as an article in the January 2000 issue of the *Journal of Counseling and Values*.

The therapy session I am discussing in this chapter was our eighth since Ron had begun ten weeks earlier. Typically, a session would be equally divided between verbal sharing and active imagination. Most of the dialogue aspect of the therapy would precede the internal work, although there would always be some dialogue following it to help explicate its themes and discuss their personal relevance. These were not guided experiences, nor was any explicit problem or theme proposed as their focus. My part in the process was simply to take him through a relaxation procedure and invite him to turn his attention inward. As the images and awarenesses would begin to flow, Ron would report his experience and I would occasionally interact with him to help clarify or emphasize different aspects of it.

Ron's principal presenting concern when he entered therapy was a life-long pattern of conflicted and sometimes destructive intimate relationships with women. As the therapy evolved, he seemed to come into better balance and made a strong commitment to reinvest himself in his primary relationship. Subsequently, our focus and the internal work moved toward more existential and spiritual concerns. These interests were not couched in traditional religious language, but emerged from the same drive for authenticity and meaning that lies at the core of most spiritual quests. What follows is an account of Ron's active imagination experience that occurred at the point of transition from relationship issues to a focus on spirit, purpose, and meaning.

Ron has a superior intellect and is well versed in philosophy. In his professional life, he is high in the hierarchy of a very aggressive organization. He had focused throughout his life on developing his analytic and assertive competencies. Both served him effectively but left him feeling off balance and in pain at the same time. He is a master of what Arthur Deikman identified as instrumental consciousness, and what Taoism would describe as *yang*, a more masculine, aggressive way of being. His relationship to the other side of consciousness—the open, expansive, empathic, and intuitive dimension that Deikman calls receptive consciousness and Taoism *yin*—was sorely lacking.

That this imbalance should precipitate significant problems with intimate relationships is self-evident. By learning to value and intentionally embrace receptive consciousness, however, he became more aware and empathic in his relationships and made significant changes based on an increased sense of concern for the well-being of others.

In Deikman's model and in the general consensus of the wisdom traditions from which he has drawn, receptive and instrumental consciousness are necessary and complementary to each other. They are not, however, of equal significance. As Deikman points out in *Transpersonal Knowing Exploring the Horizons of Consciousness*, "The Instrumental [analytic] mode can raise the Big Questions—"Who am I? What am I? Why am I?"—but it cannot hear the answers...To the extent that instrumental consciousness rules experience, life can easily seem meaningless. Meaning arises from connection [the domain of receptive consciousness]; instrumental consciousness features separation" (Deikman 2000, 310). Instrumental consciousness is the vehicle of control and dominance and the preferred choice in our culture. Receptive consciousness is the path of surrender, bonding, and service. The consistent teaching of every wisdom tradition has been that purposeful, controlling intention or action (yang) must be grounded in and directed by a connected, empathic, I-thou frame of mind (yin.) Without this grounding, a person will career off track when attempting to navigate important relationships or a meaningful connection to life itself.

Given his philosophical bent, my client was well aware that the themes emerging in his active imagination experiences, including the one featured in this article, were clearly reflective of the perennial philosophy honored in both Eastern and Western mystical traditions and, as such, "spiritual" in nature. As described by Roger Walsh in his 2001 essay "The Perennial Philosophy", the first assumption of the perennial philosophy is that "this physical world we live in and see and touch is not all there is to reality; that underneath it—in fact at its source—is another world, a sacred world, a world of spirit or consciousness or Mind with a capital *M*, or *Geist*, or *Tao*". In consequent sessions Ron had several explicit mystical experiences during the active imagination part of his session in which he felt immersed in that sacred world.

This particular active imagination began with a beacon of turning light suspended in space, which then disappeared. Shortly afterward a sword appeared. It was short, double edged, and brightly polished. The cross-piece was gold. The sword's hilt fit his hand perfectly. It fit so well that the sword felt like an extension of his body. It was as if he and the sword were one. As he held the sword, he said, he felt solid, confident, strong, and well grounded. The blade was very beautiful and very, very sharp. The sword made him impenetrable. With it in hand, his boundaries could not be violated.

Inner light is a relatively universal symbol of immanent divine presence (Underhill 1942, 103). As the opening scenario of his internal work, it struck me as a way of underscoring the spiritual significance of the unfolding imagery. It was clear to the client that the sword was a symbol of masculine energy at its best. It was precious, partly of gold. Being brightly polished, it was very capable of reflecting light, although it was not itself a source of light. This precious, shining masculine energy fit Ron perfectly. He is very masculine and readily celebrates this part of himself. He is, as he puts it, an "alpha male." Intentionally embracing his masculinity made him feel powerful and real—confident, strong, and well grounded. The sword's very sharp double-edged blade impressed both of us as a striking metaphor for a highly developed analytic mind: it cuts to the heart of issues very easily and separates things readily into analytic categories, while its double-edged nature makes it an ideal tool for approaching both sides of a polarity with discernment.

A final gift of the sword was that it made him impenetrable. With the sword in hand he was quite capable of stopping anyone who would threaten his boundaries. The sword allowed him to be precisely who he was, whether others liked it or not, which was consistent with how he experienced himself.

His attention in the active imagination then shifted to a new awareness. Even though the sword remained with him, he was most captured by a pulsating energy flowing through him. In counterpoint to the sword's capacity to divide and define things, this new flow was flexible, open, and alive. It was something to be received rather than purposefully sought after or achieved. Unlike the sword, this new energy invited him to simply receive. As he relaxed into the energy, his body began to feel as though it were a flag waving in the breeze, receptive, yielding, and undefended, at one with the flow rather than controlling or analyzing it.

At this point he found himself on the ground. A tree was growing out of his forehead. He could feel the roots going into his cranium, through his brain and body, and into the ground. The roots were vibrant and alive. The tree had a deep awareness and stillness about it, yet it was also full of energy. Everything seemed to be centered on this tree. The tree was conscious of everything and yet totally silent. In its stillness it was the anchor and source of all the other forces. He felt the tree reaching. It was using every ounce of its energy to reach to the sky and to the sun. As it did, it kept getting stronger and stronger and stronger. As he felt this, he said, "I don't think I've ever felt anything as powerful as the tree.

"Life surrounding this tree comes and goes. Birds, sunsets, and dawns, freezing winters all pass, but the tree remains. The branches reach to the heavens. The roots keep the tree tied to the earth. The roots stretch and pull. The trunk of the tree is so strong."

When I introduce my clients to active imagination, one of the first images I suggest that they request from their depth, the Self, is the "tree of life," which I tell them is a symbol for their true nature. Sometimes the tree that they see reflects back to them how badly life has wounded them. It will be stunted, struck by lightning, or even dead. Usually, however, the tree reflects back to them who they were born to be, their personal potential. As such it helps to underscore a fundamental premise in most schools of transpersonal psychotherapy: that the point of healing and of life itself is not adjustment or comfort, but the emergence of the true Self and an authentic life (Kornfield 1993.) By becoming transparent to the Self, who we are at our core, we become real, whole, and grounded in genuine strength.

The tree grew out of his head. The authentic Self is first and foremost a matter of consciousness. How aware I am, how committed I am to facing whatever is within me, how willing I am to listen to a deeper wisdom than my own analytic mind, how ready I am to live a life that is open and transparent, all determine whether the tree, my Self, will be given expression or not.

When I say "yes" to the tree, that is, when I open myself to the emergence of my Self, several consequences follow. As Ron said, "The roots of the tree move beyond my brain, embrace my body, and connect to the earth." As I become less defined by my ego and more in tune with who I was meant to be, the changes that ensue, having begun in the mind, affect the body in many ways both obvious and subtle. Enthusiasm for life and physical energy are increased. Eyes sparkle. Health usually improves. Passions intensify. In the words of Hildegard of Bingen, a twelfth-century mystic, one who seriously engages in becoming real becomes a "juicy" person. Rich Heffern describes them this way:

> "Juicy people" are folks who are so filled with wonder and curiosity, with lusty appetites and high spirits, that they embrace life, liberty and the pursuit of happiness with a burly grinning bear hug. To be juicy is to be: a fearlessly joyous optimist, a trouble maker tirelessly afflicting the comfortable, a passionate lover of good talk and tasty food, and an anonymous prophet hovering over the cosmological riddle, a frequent violator of the ordinance against indecent exposure of the heart, and a guerrilla in the insurrection against Dream Molesters everywhere (Heffern 1999).

This enthusiastic earthy vitality is the mark of one who is rooted in all of himself—mind, spirit, and body.

The core Self is not agitated, has nothing to prove, and doesn't strive for dominance. It simply is, and as such could be said to be a point of stillness within the psyche. From this still point awareness is undisturbed, penetrating, and clear like the view offered in a calm, clear pool of water.

As Ron said during his active imagination, the tree, the authentic Self, is at the turning point of all the forces within the psyche. It is the point of reference against which all preoccupations, interests, felt needs, and ambitions must be tested in order to see if they will actually enhance life by being in resonance with what is most real within the individual.

Ron felt within the tree one overwhelming drive, to reach for the sky. Every ounce of its energy was given to this embrace of spirit and light. The more the Self embraces, the stronger it becomes. The tree or the authentic Self is by far the most potent, effective, and resilient facet of anyone's psyche. No other aspect of ourselves can withstand as much stress or bear as much fruit. Its strength is constantly growing because it is forever being renewed by the unlimited energy of light and spirit.

Amid all the changes of life, the tree (the Self), remains solid and constant. Even as it reaches to the heavens, it remains rooted in the earth, strong and balanced. When we discussed the tree's meaning, Ron felt that the preceding interpretation matched his experience.

The active imagination then shifted perspective. "I am now looking back and down at the tree. The tree and its world are like a droplet in the midst of blackness. The energy of the droplet world is so solid, so substantial, so strong. The energy of the blackness is hard to describe. It envelops the droplet energy. It wraps itself around so lightly that I can't tell the difference. I now feel it all becoming one. I am nothing but energy. It is so firm and so subtle at the same time. There is no word to describe it. Just 'pure.' It is purity. No contrasts. There is no way to define it."

"This is ultimate reality. The energy here is almost overpowering. If I let myself go to it, I'd never 'be' again."

Claiming the Self inevitably opens consciousness to ultimate reality. The two finally cannot be separated. The insight that Jesus was both human and divine isn't unique to him. Anyone who is willing to take the risk of becoming as real as possible will find himself reaching to spirit and light spontaneously and becoming lost in its embrace. This embrace is soft, subtle, welcoming. In it there is no distinction. Otherness is erased in a return to original oneness.

This active imagination experience is a striking summary statement of the transformational journey as I have seen it unfold in client after client. For most people, both men and women, it begins as it did for Ron, with a willingness to respect and to intentionally use the double-edged sword of analytic consciousness and self-protective boundary setting. This is the task of the masculine aspect of ourselves. It is necessary for survival. Without it we would be lost to superstition and unable to defend ourselves against those who would presume to impose upon us any agenda other than the emergence of our own Self. Useful as it is, however, the masculine, even at its best, can only reflect the light. It is like a warrior who valiantly protects what is pure and innocent. It is like a crucible that separates the dross from the gold, but it is not itself gold, nor does it create it. Its strength makes the journey possible, but the journey itself depends on an entirely different energy.

In this experience, the sword gave way to a flowing receptivity in which Ron was undefended and completely open, like a flag waving in the wind. The strong masculine yang of the sword made it safe to relax and let go into a receptive, feminine, yin mode of being. For both men and women, feminine or receptive energy is the gateway to the transformative journey. The feminine qualities that make it possible to even begin to claim one's Self have been recognized as fundamentally important in almost every great spiritual tradition. These include valuing relationship and connection over autonomy and control, respect for intuition, a sense of comfort with mystery, openness to listening and times of quiet, a sense of connection to the earth, tenderheartedness, and a willingness to nurture children, animals, and the weak and needy. In essence the transformative journey demands a willing acceptance of the primacy of love and connection over power, and of unitive or mystical consciousness as more meaningful and fundamental than the products of reason and technology.

Respecting and actively pursuing a noncontrolling, open, feminine way of being is the only way to make possible the emergence of the Self. Those who seek to live only out of the masculine style are continually trying to create or recreate themselves out of some imposed or preconceived model. Because they are not inclined to quietly listen to their own inner life, they have little respect for intuitive awarenesses. They are not fearless and open enough to make a space for something that comes from their own depth—that is beyond their own understanding and control.

Once the juicy nature of the Self is experienced and lived, it inevitably points beyond itself to a deeper, subtler, and vastly more powerful reality that is itself the epitome of the feminine. As he described in his internal work, Ron's ultimate destination was within an encompassing darkness that enveloped everything and with which everything became one. It was mystery, purity, the source, and the cosmic womb.

To be a bit anthropomorphic about all of this, ultimate reality is a lot closer to being a goddess than a god. Moreover, the way to her temple is in the hands of the priestess. By conforming myself to the feminine, yin way, I will be able to give birth to my Self and thereby to rest in the Source. As in the ancient goddess religions, the masculine principle is always secondary. It is a lover of the goddess, one who lives to serve her agenda.

Although the feminine and masculine constitute one of the principal polarities of the human psyche, they are not equal. Right order will be achieved only when the masculine enthusiastically seeks to dedicate itself to values that are grounded in the feminine.

Ron was deeply impacted by this experience and in subsequent sessions deepened his sense of connection with the Self and the ground of being. Once you have glimpsed ultimate reality, you cannot ever again not know.

ACKNOWLEDGEMENTS

To my clients—this book is the fruit of their suffering. What I have learned and shared in these pages is grounded in the lives of hundreds of clients who have shared their pain, inner worlds, and healing with me. Although many scholars and writers have greatly enriched my perspective, it is my clients' experiences that form the foundation and core of what I have learned. The courage and integrity with which they have faced their fears and demons made this book possible. I hope that it will serve as a worthy tribute to their work and as a source of encouragement to those who are considering beginning their own inner journeys.

To Karen, my life partner—you are both my best friend and my intellectual companion. You have been a constant support and my principal mentor over the years as I have sought to bring this book to completion. It would have been far different without you. Your feedback and editing have greatly enriched what I have written and how I wrote it. I greatly appreciate the time and effort you have put into helping me with this. And I am deeply grateful for the intelligence and facility with language that you have so freely shared with me.

To my friends Mac Fulfer, Deanna Walker, Valerie Cisler, Peggy McGurn, and Emmett Pybus, who took the time to read and critique earlier versions of this book—your feedback has been invaluable to me. Because of you, I have been able to improve the book both radically, by changing its fundamental structure, and stylistically, by being encouraged to find ways to express myself in a clearer, smoother fashion. Thank you for your kind and generous help.

To the scholars and neuroscientists whose insights and research have been an invaluable resource—even though this book is primarily derived from clinical experience, your insights have greatly enriched and clarified what I have experienced clinically. Principal among these scholars are Carl Jung and Ian McGilchrist. Their conclusions and observations resonate strongly with what I have seen and have given me the courage to trust the validity of my clients' processes. They have also been instrumental in helping me appreciate the profound cultural and philosophical significance of how we understand and approach the inner life.

And finally to my daughters, Reanna and Kirstin—through most of the years of your growing up I put significant amounts of time into writing and researching what has become this book. Your patience and support was and is deeply appreciated.

BIBLIOGRAPHY

Adyashanti. 2008. *The End of Your World: uncensored straight talk on the nature of enlightenment*. Boulder, CO: Sounds True.

Allison, R. 1980. *Minds in Many Pieces: The Making of a Very Special Doctor*. New York: Rawson, Wade Publishers Inc.

Arkowitz, H., H.A. Westra, W. Miller, and S. Rollnick. 2008. *Motivational Interviewing in the Treatment of Psychological Problems*. New York, London: The Guilford Press.

Aron, E. 2004. HSP's Meditation and Enlightenment. *The Comfort Zone newsletter*, May 2004.

Assagioli, R. 1976. *Psychosythesis: A Collection of Basic Writtings*. New York: Penguin Books Ltd.

Barrett, T. and J.B. Etheridge. 1992. "Verbal Hallucinations in Normals: People Who Hear Voices." *Applied Cognitive Psychology*. 6, 379-387.

Braun, B. 1986. *The Treatment of Multiple Personality Disorder (Clinical Insights Monograph)*. edited by B. Braun. Washington D.C.: American Psychiatric Press Inc.

Chodron, P. 1997. *When Things Fall Apart: Heart Advice for Difficult Times*. Boston: Shambala.

Chu, J. 1996. "Posttraumatic Responses to Childhood Abuse and Implications for Treatment." *Handbook of Dissociation*. Edited by L. Michelson and W. Ray. New York, London: Plenum Press.

Chu, J. et al. 2011. "Guidelines for Treating Dissociative Identity Disorder in Adults." *Journal of Trauma and Dissociation.* 12: 115-187.

Clarke, J. 1994. *Jung and Eastern Thought: A Dialogue with the Orient.* New York, London: Routledge.

Coupland, H. 2000. "The experience of focused group-work for voice hearers experiencing malevolent voices." *Netlink, The Quarterly Journal for the Network for Psychiatric Nursing Research.* 16: 3-4.

David, D. 1999. "Psychotic Symptoms in Combat-Related Posttraumatic Stress Disorder." *Journal of Clinical Psychiatry.* 60 (1): 29-32.

Davis, J. 2000, "We Keep Asking Ourselves, what is transpersonal counseling?" *Guidance and Counseling.* 15 (3): 3-8.

Deikman, A. 2000. "A Functional Approach to Mysticism." *Journal of Consciousness Studies.* 7: No. 11-12.

Deikman, A. 2000. "Service as a Way of Knowing." *Transpersonal Knowing Exploring the Horizon of Consciousness.* edited by T. Hart, P. Nelson and K Puhakka. New York: State University of New York Press. (303- 318)

Ecker, B. 2013. "Unlocking the Emotional Brain." *Psychotherapy Networker.* July/August 2013 7-17.

Ellason, J.W. and C.A. Ross. 1995. "Positive and negative symptoms in Dissociative Identity Disorder and Schizophrenia: a comparative Analysis." *Journal of Mental and Nervous Disorders* 183 (4): 236-241

Ellenberger, H. 1970. *The Discovery of the Unconscious: The History and Evolution of Dynamic Psychiatry.* New York: Basic Books.

Fadiman, J. and R. Frager. 1994. *Personality and Personal Growth* New York: HarperCollins College Publishers.

Frazier, J. 2012. *The Freedom of Being: At Ease with What Is.* San Francisco, CA/Newburyport, MA: Weiser Books.

Fromm, E. 1956. *The Art of Loving.* New York: HarperCollins Publishers.

Gangaji. 2005. *The Diamond in Your Pocket: Discovering Your True Radiance.* Boulder, CO: Sounds True.

Grob, C. 2010 "Commentary on Harbor-UCLA Psilocybin Study." MAPS Bulletin 20 (1): 28-29.

Grof, S. 2008. *LSD Psychotherapy, exploring the frontiers of the hidden mind.* Saline MI: McNaughton & Gunn.

Hand, K. 2006. "The Spotless Mind." *Popular Science* May 2006: 36-37.

Hayes, S. 2005. *Get Out of Your Mind and Into Your Life: The NewAcceptance and Commitment Therapy (A New Harbinger Self-HelpWorkbook).* Oakland, CA: New Harbinger Publications.

Harris, R. 2009. *ACT Made Simple: An Easy-to-Read Primer on Acceptance and Commitment Therapy.* Oakland, CA: New Harbinger Publications.

Harris, R. 2007. *The Happiness Trap: How to Stop Struggling and Start Living: A Guide to ACT.* Boston: Shambhala.

Heffern, R. 1999. *Daybreak Within: Living in a Sacred World.* Leavenworth KS: Forest of Peace Publishing Inc.

Hillman, J. 1979. *The Dream and the Underworld.* New York: Harper & Row.

Hoeller, S. 1982. *The Gnostic Jung: and the Seven Sermons to the Dead.* Wheaton IL: Quest Books.

Holmes, D. 1995. "The Problem of Auditory Hallucinations in Combat PTSD." *Traumatology* June 1995 Vol. 1 no. 2, 1-7.

Hunt, H. 1989. *The Multiplicity of Dreams: Memory, Imagination and Consciousness.* New Haven, London: Yale University Press abr, F. 2014. "Speak for Yourself." *Scientific American Mind* January/February 2014: 45-51.

Janet, P. 1907. *The Major Symptoms of Hysteria: Fifteen Lectures Given in the Medical School of Harvard University.* New York, London: The Macmillan Company - The Classic Reprint Series.

Jones, S. 2012. *Hearing Voices: The Histories, Causes and Meanings of Auditory Verbal Hallucinations.* Cambridge, New York: Cambridge University Press.

Jung, C. G. 1959. *Aion, Researches into the Phenomenology of the Self.* Princeton: Princeton University Press.

Jung, C. G. 1973. *Experimental Researches.* Princeton: Princeton University Press.

Jung, C. G. 1959. *The Archetypes and the Collective Unconsciousness.* Princeton: Princeton University Press.

Jung, C. G. 1953. *Two Essays on Analytical Psychology.* Princeton: Princeton University Press.

Jung, C. G. 2009. *The Red Book Liber Novus.* edited by S. Shamdasani. New York, London: W.W. Norton and Company.

Kelly, E. and E. W. Kelly. 2007. *Irreducible Mind: Toward a Psychology for the 21st Century.* Lanham MA: Rowan & Littlefield Publishers, Inc.

Kornfield, J. 1993. *A Path With Heart: A Guide Through the Perils and Promises of Spiritual Life.* New York, London: Bantam Books.

Lao-tzu, and S. Mitchell (translator). 1988. *Tao Te Ching.* New York: HarperCollins Publishers, Inc.

Liotti, G. 2004. "Trauma, Dissociation, and Disorganized Attachment: Three Strands of a Single Braid." *Psychotherapy: Theory research, practice, training* 41: 472-486.

MacLean, P. 1990. *The Triune Brain in Evolution: role in paleocerebral functions.* New York: Plenum Press.

McGilchrist, I. 2009. *The Master and his Emissary, The Divided Brain and the Making of the Western World.* New Haven, London: Yale University Press.

McGurn, P. 1998. *The Divine Child Archetype in Jungian Psychological Thought and Practice: A Doctoral Dissertation.* Ann Arbor MI: UMI Dissertation Services.

Michelson, L. and W. Ray 1996. *Handbook of Dissociation: Theoretical, Empirical, and Clinical Perspectives.* New York, London: Plenum Press.

Miller, C. 2010. "Merits of Psychodynamic Therapy." *Harvard Mental Health Letter.* 27 (3): 1-3.

Miller, G. 2010. "How Our Brains Make Memories." *Smithsonian Magazine.* May 2010.

Miller, W. 2000. "Rediscovering Fire: Small Interventions, Large Effects." *Psychology of Addictive Behaviors* 14 (1): 6-18.

Nutt, D., R. Wise, and A. Fielding. 2012. "Neural Correlates of the Psychedelic State as Determined by fMRI Studies." *Proceedings of the National Academy of Science USA.* 109 (6): 2138-2143.

O'Donohue, J. 2000. *Conamara Blues.* UK: Doubleday.

Rex, E. 2013. "Calming a Turbulent Mind." *SA Mind.* May/June 2013.

Richo, D. 2011. *Daring to Trust, Opening Ourselves to Real Love and Intimacy.* Boston, London: Shambala.

Richo, D. 2002. *How to be an Adult in Relationships.* Boston, London: Shambala.

Romme, M. and S. Escher. 1993. *Accepting Voices.* Mind Publications.

Romme, M. 1989. "Hearing Voices." *Schizophrenia Bulletin.* 15 (2): 209-216.

Samuels, A. 1985. *Jung and the Post-Jungians.* Boston, London: Routledge.

Schore, A. 2012. *The Science of the Art of Psychotherapy.* New York: W.W. Norton and Company.

Schwartz, J., and R. Gladding. 2011. *You Are Not Your Brain: The 4-Step Solution for Changing Bad Habits, Ending Unhealthy Thinking, and Taking Control of Your Life.* New York, London: Penguin Group.

Schwartz, R. 2001. *Introduction to the Internal Family Systems Model.* Oak Park, Ill: Trailheads Publications.

Segal, G., M. Williams and J. Teasdale. 2002. *Mindfulness-Based Cognitive Therapy for Depression: A New Approach to Preventing Relapse.* New York: Guilford Press.

Sellers, J. *45 min Transpersonal Meditation HQ with Narration.* YouTube Siegel, D. 2012. *Pocket Guide to Interpersonal Neurobiology: An Integrative Handbook of the Mind.* New York, London: W. W. Norton & Company.

Smith, A. 1998. My Experience of Cosmic Consciousness: An MD's Account. *Journal of Consciousness Studies.* 5 (1): 97-107.

Steinberg, M. 2001. *The Stranger in the Mirror: Dissociation-The Hidden Epidemic.* New York: HarperCollins.

Strassman, R. 2001. *DMT The Spirit Molecule: A Doctor's Revolutionary Research into the Biology of Near-Death and Mystical Experiences.* Rochester: Park Street Press.

Taylor, J.B. 2006. *My Stroke of Insight, A Brain Scientist's Personal Journey.* New York: Viking.

Tien, A. Y. 1991. "Distributions of hallucinations in the population." *Social Psychiatry and Psychiatric Epidemiology.* 26: 287–292.

Thondup, T. 2000. *Boundless Healing: Meditation Exercises to Enlighten the Mind and Heal the Body.* Boston: Shambhala.

Tolle, E. 1999. *The Power of Now: A Guide to Spiritual Enlightenment.* Novato, CA: New World Library.

van der Hart, O., E. Nijenhuis, and K. Steele. 2006 *The Haunted Self: Structural Dissociation and the Treatment of Chronic Traumatization*. New York, London: W. W. Norton & Company.

van der Kolk, B., A. McFarlane, and L. Weisaeth (editors). 1996. *Traumatic Stress: The Effects of Overwhelming Experience on Mind, Body, and Society*. New York, London: The Guilford Press.

Underhill, E. 1911, 1995 *Mysticism: The Development of Humankind's Spiritual Consciousness*. London: Bracken Books.

von Franz, M. 1981. *Puer Aeternus: A Psychological Study of the Adult Struggle with the Paradise of Childhood*. Santa Monica CA: Sigo Press.

Walsh, R. 2001 "The Perennial Philosophy." *Ions Noetic Sciences Review* December 2001.

Watkins, J. and H. Watkins. 1997. *Ego States Theory and Therapy*. New York, London: W. W. Norton and Company.

Welberg, L. 2010. "Psychiatric disorders: Ketamine modifies mood through mTOR." *Nature Reviews Neuroscience* 11: 666-667. (October 2010)

Wilber, K. 1979. *No Boundary, Eastern and Western Approaches to Spiritual Growth*. Boston, London: Shambala.

Zur, O. 2004. "To Cross or Not To Cross: Do Boundaries in Therapy Protect or Harm?." *Psychotherapy Bulletin*. 39 (3), 27-32.

ABOUT THE AUTHOR

At the age of eight Dean had a strong awareness that someday he wanted to be both a Catholic priest and a healer. This was a compelling intuition that shaped the rest of his life. He entered Minor Seminary when he was thirteen and remained in a seminary environment until he was twenty-six, when he was ordained.

He began his professional life as a priest in 1967, but quit to get married in 1973. He then went back to graduate school for two years to study Pastoral Counseling with the goal of becoming a spiritually oriented psychotherapist. In 1975 he began working for a Pastoral Counseling agency and in 1976 was hired as a psychotherapist by a public mental health agency. It was at this agency in 1978 that he began working with his first Multiple Personality Disorder client. His work with her and later with others who also had well developed internal ego states had a significant impact on how he came to understand the internal workings of the psyche.

In 1979 he started a private practice in Oklahoma where he was licensed as an LMFT offering transpersonal counseling as well as workshops and seminars for other therapists. In 1982 he founded and sponsored the Oklahoma City C. G. Jung Study Group. In 1999 he moved to Eugene OR to be with his life partner, Karen.

In 2000 he became the manager of The Royal Avenue Program, a crisis respite program for indigent persons with a psychiatric disability. He also maintained a small private practice during this time. Dean retired from The Royal Avenue Program in 2013 and now devotes his time to his private practice as a Spiritual Director, writing and enjoying the good life.

Dean lives with Karen on a beautiful acreage in the country. He has two daughters, three grandchildren, one dog, and seven chickens.

GLOSSARY

Active Imagination: A method using imagination as a way of encountering and building a relationship with aspects of oneself that reside within the unconscious. Experiences occasioned by active imagination are similar to dreams except that in dreams the ego is usually passive whereas in active imagination the ego is an active participant.

Archetype: The accumulation of human experience over eons has led to the development of universally inherited patterns for categorizing and motivating responses to internal and external experience. These patterns often generate images that interact with the ego.

Borderline Personality Disorder (BPD): A persistent, deeply rooted pattern of dysfunction both in relationships and internally. BPD is rooted in an impaired bond with the mother figure in the first years of life. Because of the deficiency in this bond these individuals feel a deep longing for love and acceptance that they cannot fill and an inner rage that this profound need has never been met. They are prone to depression, anxiety, substance abuse, shame and tumultuous relationships. Typically, they have a very poorly developed sense of self.

Cognitive Behavioral Therapy (CBT): A type of counseling that is focused on specific problems and encourages changes in thought or behavior that are designed to resolve the problem. Special attention is given to challenging self-limiting patterns of thought or assumptions.

Collective Unconscious: The domain of inherited, autonomous psychic structures and predispositions which include both instincts and archetypes and are shared by all human beings. They organize human experience and motivate the ego to respond in particular ways consistent with the archetype's or instinct's nature. Although their influence is often obvious most people are unconscious of their source or nature. The Collective Unconscious differs from the Personal Unconscious in that the former is universal and the latter in unique to each individual.

Complex: Carl Jung's term for ego states or parts. Complexes reside within the personal unconscious. Jung stated that complexes were the "royal road" to the unconscious.

Complex Trauma Disorder: Also known as Complex PTSD, it differs from ordinary PTSD in that it is not caused by a time limited traumatic event. Complex Trauma Disorder is caused by long lasting or repeated traumatic events such as physical or sexual abuse in childhood or living in an abusive relationship. It has a pervasive, destructive impact on self perception, and the capacity to make positive connections with other people. It can also lead to a hopeless, pessimistic approach to life.

Consciousness: The fundamental ground out of which all things emerge. From a transpersonal perspective, consciousness and God are the same thing. Consciousness has three primary constituents: awareness, capacity for choice, and love. As entities become more self-aware, the presence of consciousness becomes more evident. Consciousness is not an emergent that somehow happens when sufficient neural complexity is achieved, but the underlying reality that becomes clearer as greater complexity evolves.

DID: Acronym for Dissociative Identity Disorder. It is a mental disorder in which an individual possesses two or more autonomous ego states which can assume executive control of the body. DID was formerly known as MPD or Multiple Personality Disorder.

Disidentification: An exercise designed to give a person the experience of pure consciousness separated from the many objects of consciousness that occupy most peoples' attention most of the time. These objects of consciousness include such things as body awareness, sensations, feelings, thoughts and imagery. This experience of pure consciousness creates an intimate connection with the deep Self.

Dream Work: The utilization of active imagination as a means of re-experiencing a dream and intentionally engaging its metaphors and figures.

Ego: The familiar self, a left brain expression of consciousness that has an individual sense of self, differentiated from unintegrated aspects of the psyche and from the external world. Ego can choose to relate to internal or external others in either an open, connecting, receptive fashion or in an acquisitive, controlling instrumental manner. Ego is usually grounded in its models of reality instead of direct experience.

Ego State: A part of the psyche that is ... "an organized system of behavior and experience whose elements are bound together by some common principle, and differentiated from one another by boundaries that are more or less permeable." (Watkins and Watkins. 1997. p 15) Individuals can have many or only one ego state. Ego states vary in degrees of self-awareness and autonomy, from almost no self-awareness or autonomy to being very self-aware and fully autonomous.

Egocentric Ego: An ego that is focused on the preservation of its self-identity as its principal goal. The egocentric ego perceives others, either internal or external, principally in terms of how well they support or challenge this self-identity.

Enlightenment: The state of mind of a person whose egoic self merges with the deep Self and who from that point on engages life from the perspective of the deep Self. The realization of this union is not an intellectual understanding, but an actual, ongoing experience. Through this experience the ego sees that who or what it thought itself to be before enlightenment was unreal, a made up fantasy, similar to a thought, and that the deep Self is its true source. The deep Self is an alert awareness that perceives reality "without bias, agenda, self-interest, or discomfort." (Frazier. 2012. p 11)

Eros: Jung's term for right-brain function. Eros is a mental orientation that is receptive and grounded in the body, senses and emotions. "Eros is desire, longing, force, exuberance, pleasure, suffering." (Red Book p 365) It is attuned to relationships and seeks connection. Jung identified it as a feminine style. Its counterpoint is logos.

Iatrogenic: Refers to an illness caused by the treatment offered by a physician. As applied to psychotherapy it means that a psychiatric disorder was caused by the therapy.

Individuation: The term Jung used to describe the related life-long processes of knowing and embracing one's own ever unfolding nature, (i.e. living your full potential) and simultaneously maintaining an ego that is deeply grounded in the Self.

Internal Work: The same as active imagination.

Introject: An internal psychic entity that can function like an autonomous ego state, but is not an actual part of the individual's own psychological structure. A person develops an introject when he or she creates an internal representation of a powerful external other that then continues to relate to that person as had been the case externally. This could be an abuser who continues attacking the person internally in ways similar to the original abuse. A more benign example would be when a person continues to hear the voice of a parent internally.

Left-Brain: The hemisphere of the brain that is connected to reality through the experiences mediated by the right-brain. The left hemisphere thinks in a linear fashion, depending primarily on language and analysis. It creates boundaries, focuses on details and is inclined to judgment.

Logos: Jung's term for left-brain function. Logos is "form giving ... ordering and insistence". (Red Book p 365) It is a mental orientation that is detached, intellectual, focused on language, models and boundaries, assertive and objective. Jung identified it as a masculine style. Its counterpoint is eros.

MPD: Acronym for Multiple Personality Disorder. It is currently called Dissociative Identity Disorder.

Mental Health: The resilience, harmony and vitality that one experiences as the mind moves toward increasing levels of integration. This means banishing Introjects, learning to live in harmony with instincts and archetypes and building relationships with ego states which will ultimately lead to fusing with them.

Mind: A synonym for psyche. It is the totality of the structure and function of a person's own consciousness. It is a process rather than a distinct entity. Three interrelated factors contribute to the unique nature of each person's mind: internal subjective experience, the influence and limitations of the brain&body substrate, and the impact of past and present relationships. The fundamental drive of mind is integration or wholeness.

Mindfulness: A state of mind that is achieved by focusing on the present moment, noticing with compassionate curiosity any sensations, feelings or other mental contents that may emerge.

Moral Injury: A state of mind triggered by involvement in an experience or set of experiences that significantly threaten a person's ability to consider him or herself a good or moral person, such as being required to kill as part of the duties of war. It is marked by sorrow, shame, guilt, regret or alienation.

Parts: See ego states.

Personal Unconscious: The aspect of mind that contains the awareness and ongoing presence of those internal and external experiences which the ego has repressed. Carl Jung observed that the personal unconscious was primarily the domain of complexes (i.e. parts or ego states).

Psyche: See "mind".

Right-Brain: The hemisphere of the brain that has direct contact with reality. It is focused on the present moment. Its experience of reality is within the context of the interconnectedness or unity of things. It is the source of our capacity for empathy and the felt (vs. rationalistic) sense of meaning we find in life.

Self: The deep Self is the core and unifying principal of the psyche. It is the pure expression of consciousness within an individual. It has no form or defining limitations, although it can communicate with the ego through various archetypal metaphors such as Inner Wisdom, Great Mother or Divine Child. The Self is the means through which the individual psyche can connect with universal consciousness or God.

Unconscious: Those aspects of mind of which the ego is unaware either through simple ignorance or because psychic contents have been repressed due to the threat they pose to the ego. Jungians divide the unconscious into the personal and collective unconscious.

Made in the USA
Columbia, SC
01 January 2022